The Enchanting Rose

A Collection of *Rose is Rose* Comics

Created by Pat Brady
By Don Wimmer

Rose is Rose is distributed internationally by United Feature Syndicate, Inc.

The Enchanting Rose copyright © 2007 by United Feature Syndicate, Inc. All rights reserved. Printed in China. No part of this book may be used or reproduced in any manner whatsoever without written permission except in the case of reprints in the context of reviews. For information, write Andrews McMeel Publishing, LLC, an Andrews McMeel Universal company, 4520 Main Street, Kansas City, Missouri 64111.

07 08 09 10 11 WKT 10 9 8 7 6 5 4 3 2 1

ISBN-13: 978-0-7407-6555-1
ISBN-10: 0-7407-6555-8

Library of Congress Control Number: 2006937891

www.andrewsmcmeel.com

─── **ATTENTION: SCHOOLS AND BUSINESSES** ───

Andrews McMeel books are available at quantity discounts with bulk purchase for educational, business, or sales promotional use. For information, please write to: Special Sales Department, Andrews McMeel Publishing, LLC, 4520 Main Street, Kansas City, Missouri 64111.

Other *Rose is Rose* Books

She's a Momma, Not a Movie Star

License to Dream

Rose is Rose 15th Anniversary Collection

The Irresistible Rose is Rose

High-Spirited Rose is Rose

Rose is Rose Right on the Lips

Rose is Rose Running on Alter Ego

Red Carpet Rose

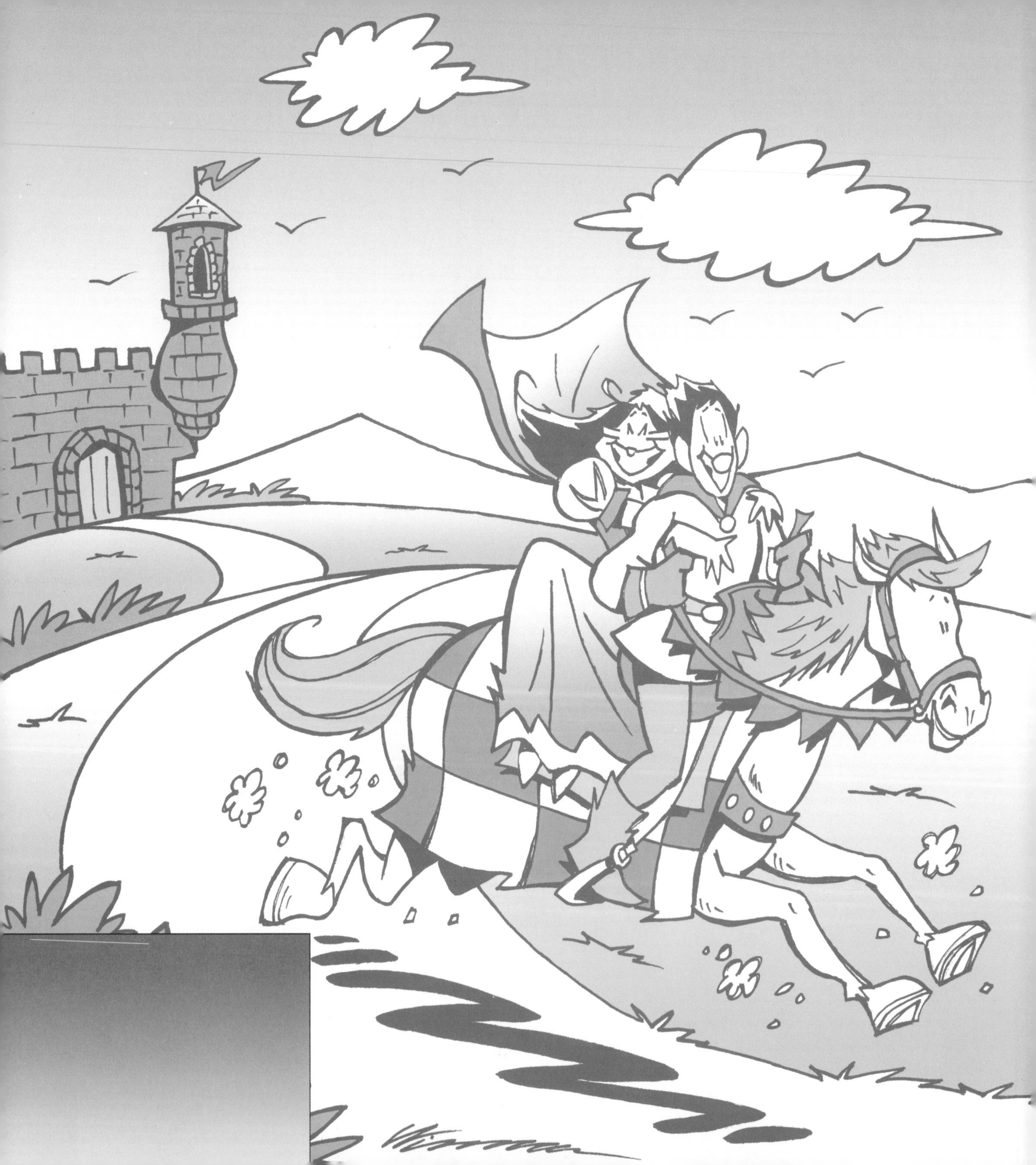

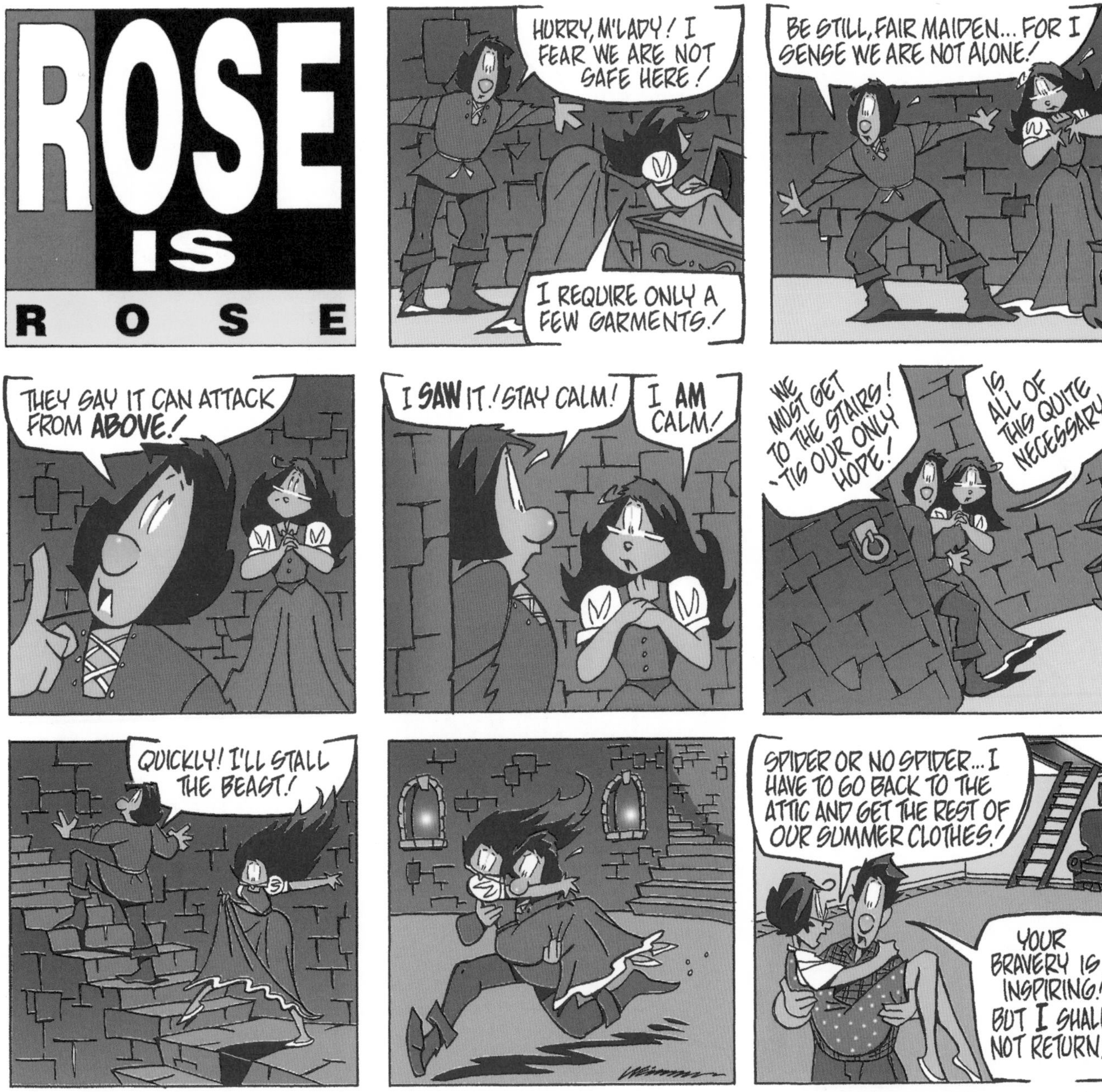
ROSE IS ROSE
HURRY, M'LADY! I FEAR WE ARE NOT SAFE HERE!
I REQUIRE ONLY A FEW GARMENTS!
BE STILL, FAIR MAIDEN... FOR I SENSE WE ARE NOT ALONE!
THEY SAY IT CAN ATTACK FROM ABOVE!
I SAW IT! STAY CALM!
I AM CALM!
WE MUST GET TO THE STAIRS! 'TIS OUR ONLY HOPE!
IS ALL OF THIS QUITE NECESSARY?
QUICKLY! I'LL STALL THE BEAST!
SPIDER OR NO SPIDER... I HAVE TO GO BACK TO THE ATTIC AND GET THE REST OF OUR SUMMER CLOTHES!
YOUR BRAVERY IS INSPIRING! BUT I SHALL NOT RETURN!

FLIP THE PAGE CORNERS FROM FRONT TO BACK AND WATCH BOTH SIDES TOGETHER!

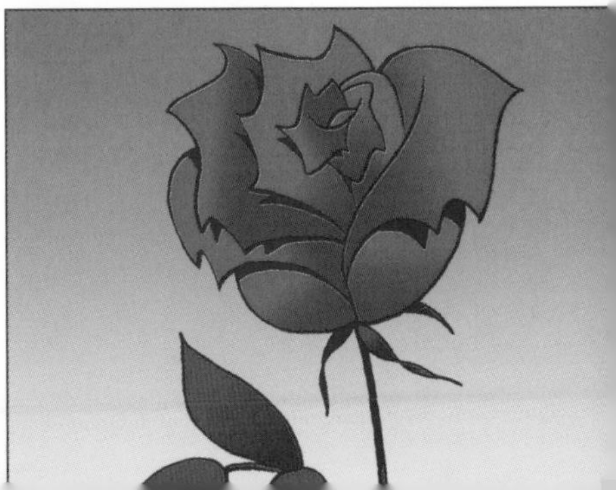

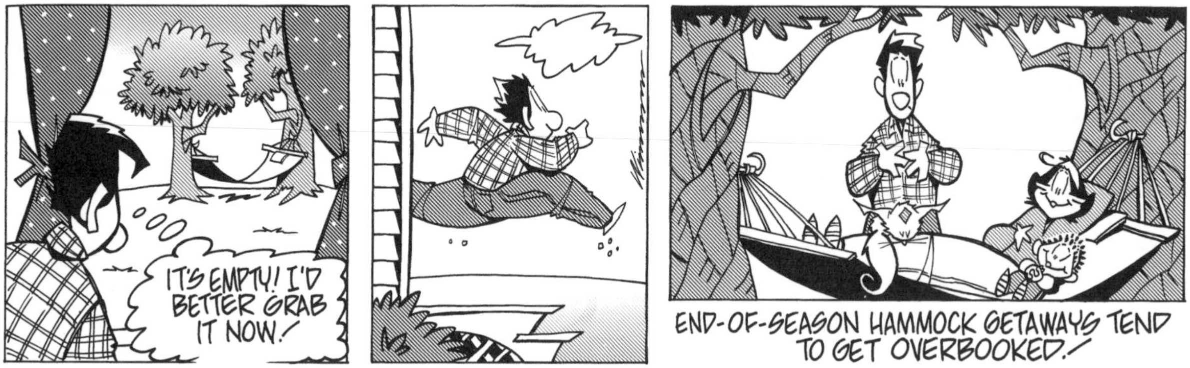
IT'S EMPTY! I'D BETTER GRAB IT NOW!
END-OF-SEASON HAMMOCK GETAWAYS TEND TO GET OVERBOOKED!

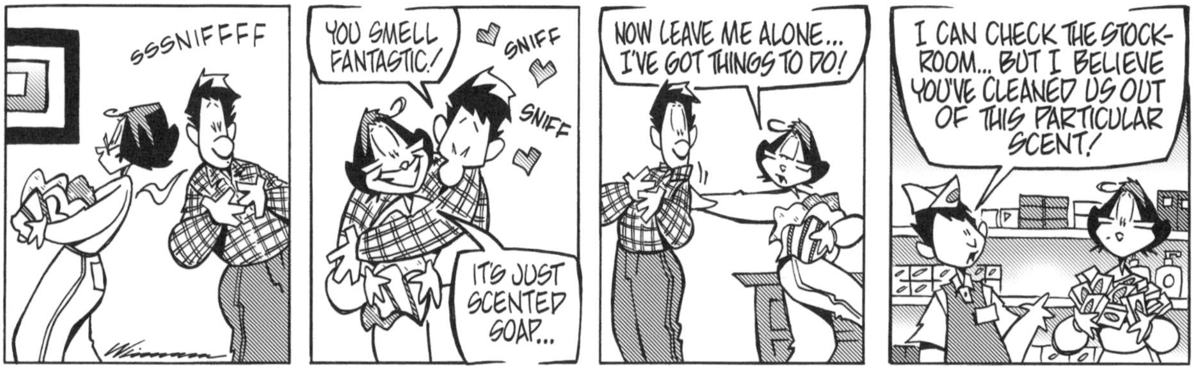
SSSNIFFFF
YOU SMELL FANTASTIC!
SNIFF
SNIFF
IT'S JUST SCENTED SOAP...
NOW LEAVE ME ALONE... I'VE GOT THINGS TO DO!
I CAN CHECK THE STOCK-ROOM... BUT I BELIEVE YOU'VE CLEANED US OUT OF THIS PARTICULAR SCENT!

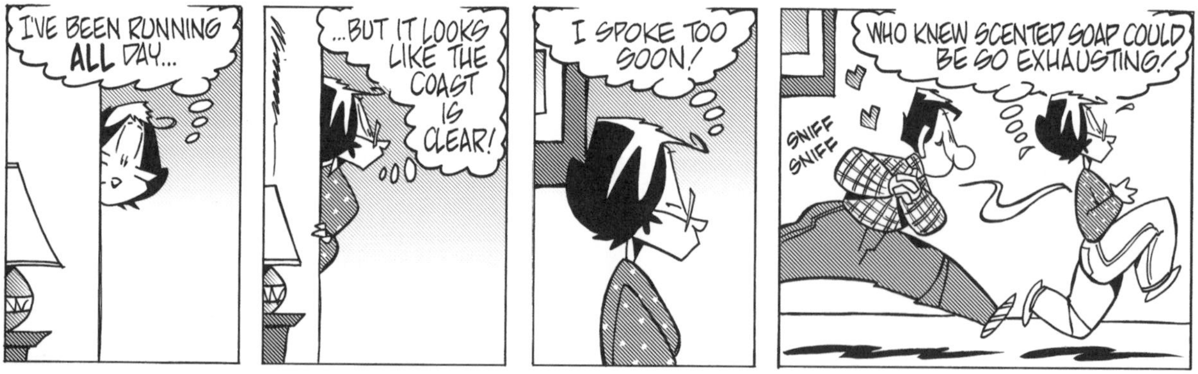
I'VE BEEN RUNNING ALL DAY...
...BUT IT LOOKS LIKE THE COAST IS CLEAR!
I SPOKE TOO SOON!
WHO KNEW SCENTED SOAP COULD BE SO EXHAUSTING!
SNIFF SNIFF

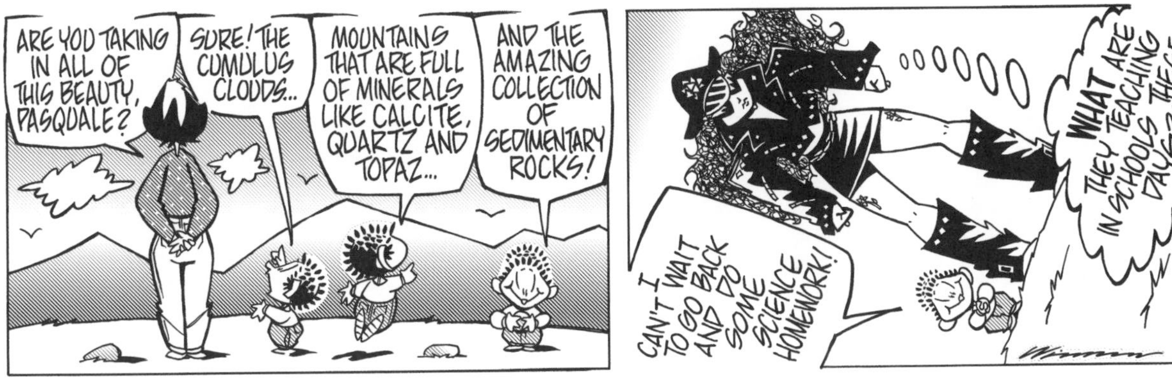
ARE YOU TAKING IN ALL OF THIS BEAUTY, PASQUALE?
SURE! THE CUMULUS CLOUDS...
MOUNTAINS THAT ARE FULL OF MINERALS LIKE CALCITE, QUARTZ AND TOPAZ...
AND THE AMAZING COLLECTION OF SEDIMENTARY ROCKS!
I CAN'T WAIT TO GO BACK AND DO SOME SCIENCE HOMEWORK!
WHAT ARE THEY TEACHING IN SCHOOLS THESE DAYS?!

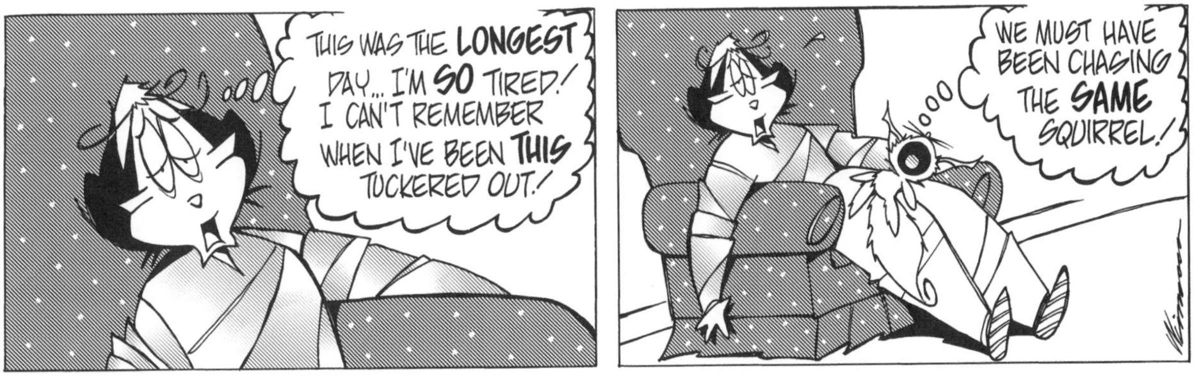
THIS WAS THE LONGEST DAY... I'M SO TIRED! I CAN'T REMEMBER WHEN I'VE BEEN THIS TUCKERED OUT!
WE MUST HAVE BEEN CHASING THE SAME SQUIRREL!

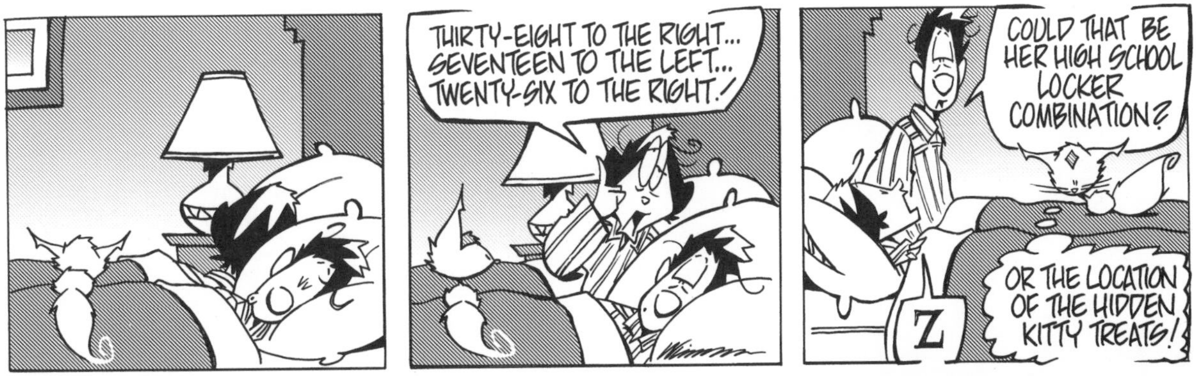
THIRTY-EIGHT TO THE RIGHT... SEVENTEEN TO THE LEFT... TWENTY-SIX TO THE RIGHT!
COULD THAT BE HER HIGH SCHOOL LOCKER COMBINATION?
Z
OR THE LOCATION OF THE HIDDEN KITTY TREATS!

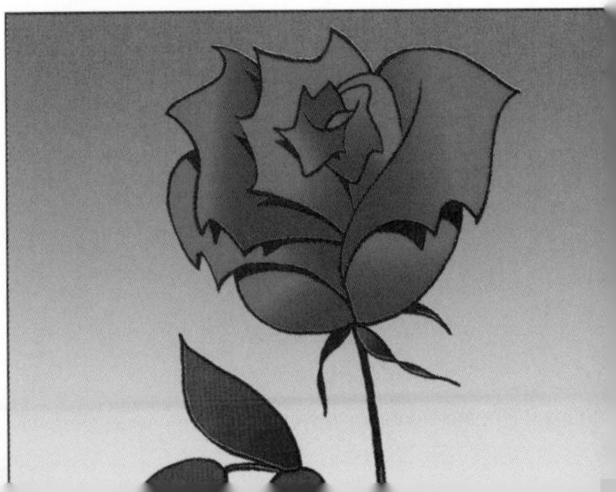

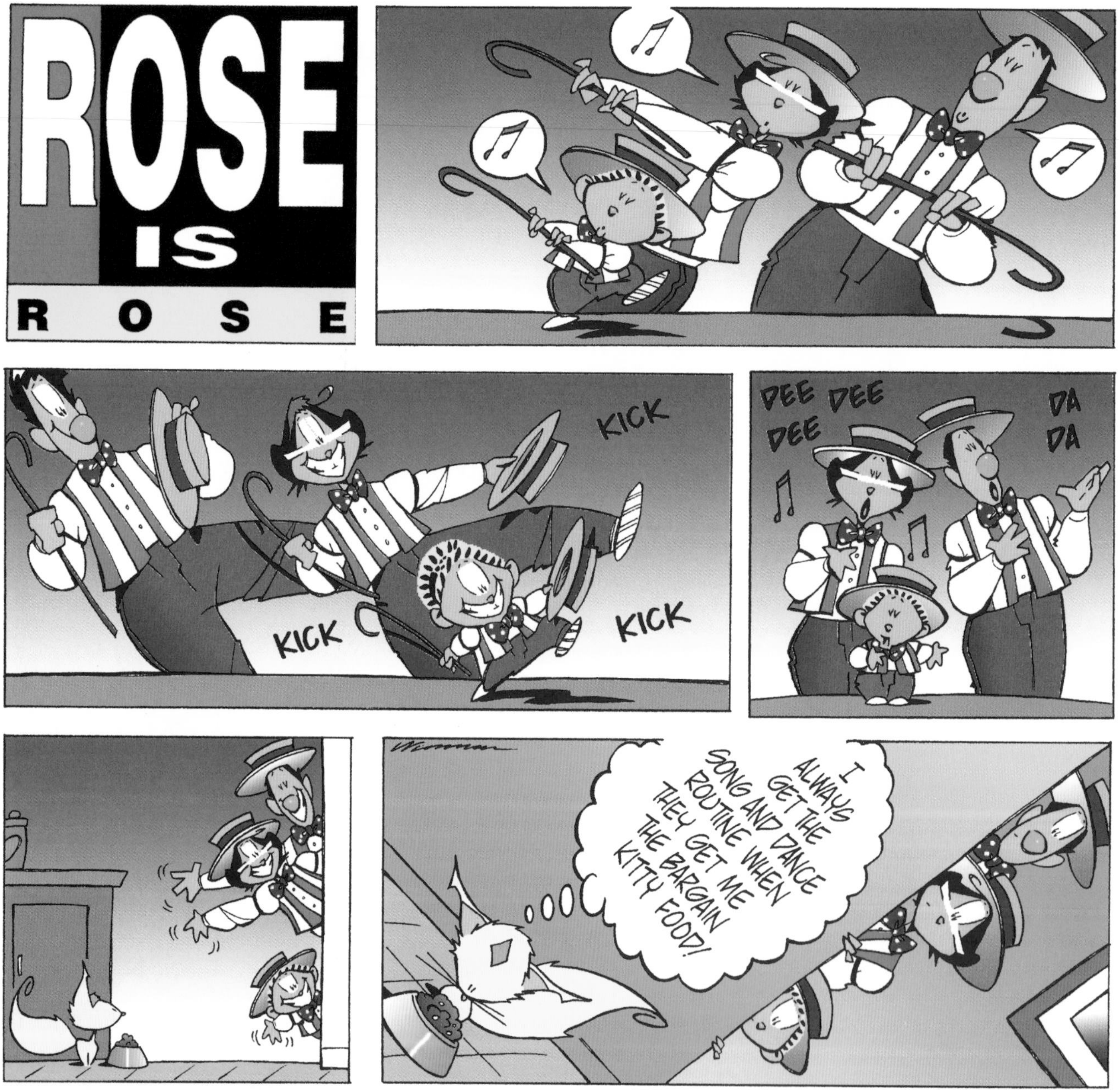
ROSE IS ROSE
KICK
KICK
KICK
DEE DEE
DEE DEE
DA
DA
I ALWAYS GET THE SONG AND DANCE ROUTINE WHEN THEY GET ME THE BARGAIN KITTY FOOD!

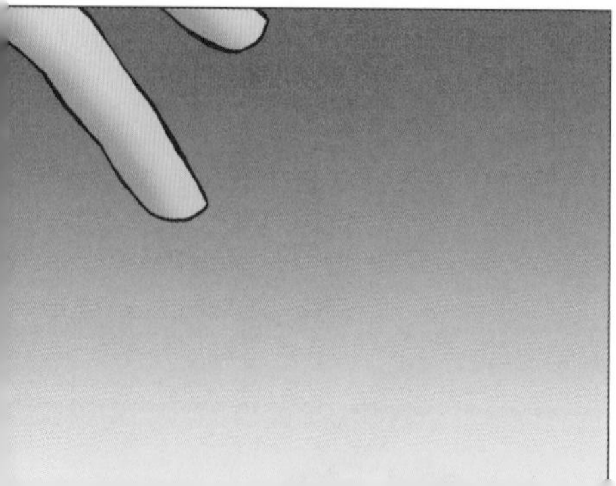

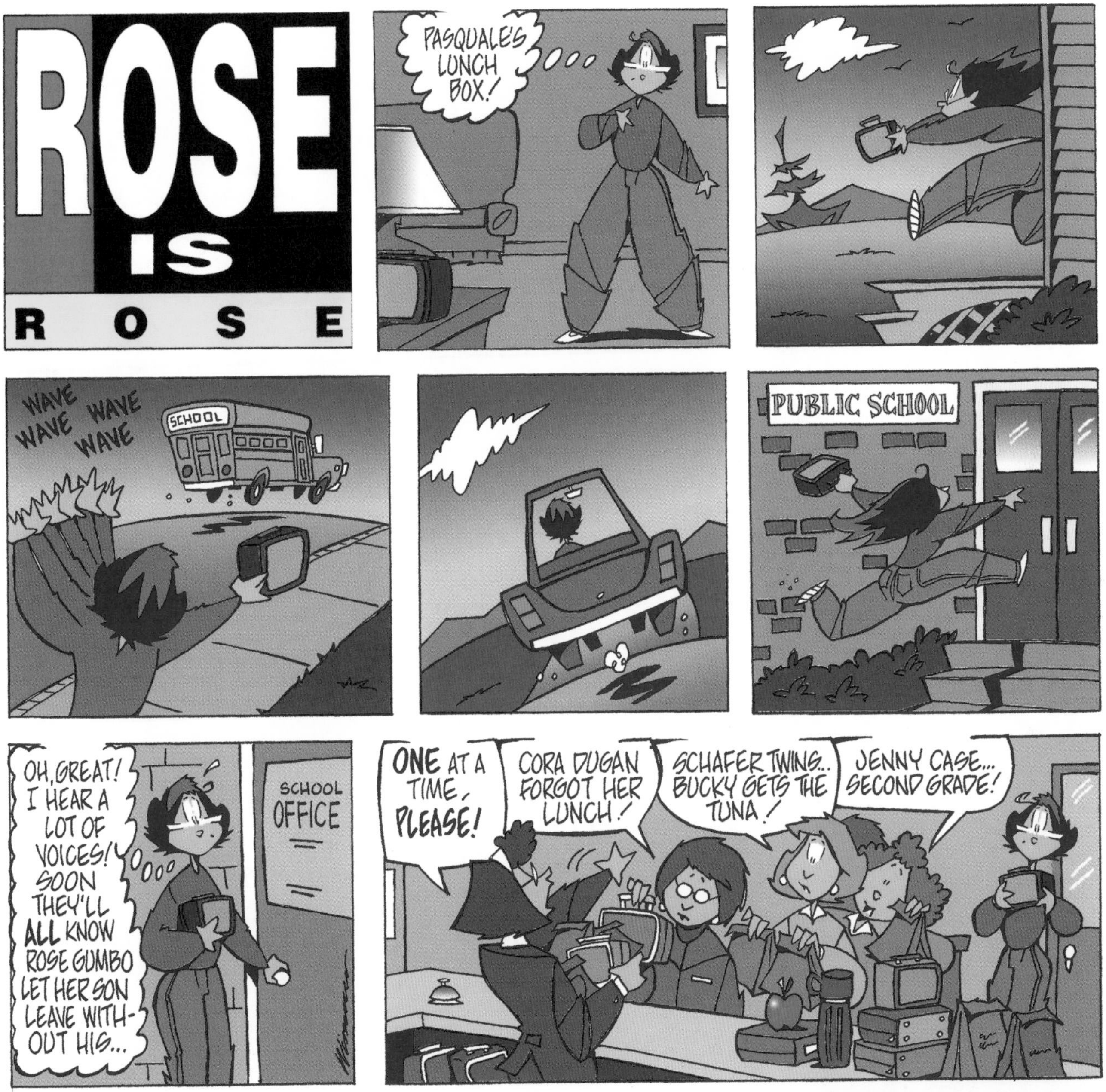
ROSE IS ROSE
PASQUALE'S LUNCH BOX!
WAVE WAVE WAVE WAVE WAVE
SCHOOL
PUBLIC SCHOOL
OH, GREAT! I HEAR A LOT OF VOICES! SOON THEY'LL ALL KNOW ROSE GUMBO LET HER SON LEAVE WITHOUT HIS...
SCHOOL OFFICE
ONE AT A TIME, PLEASE!
CORA DUGAN FORGOT HER LUNCH!
SCHAFER TWINS... BUCKY GETS THE TUNA!
JENNY CASE... SECOND GRADE!

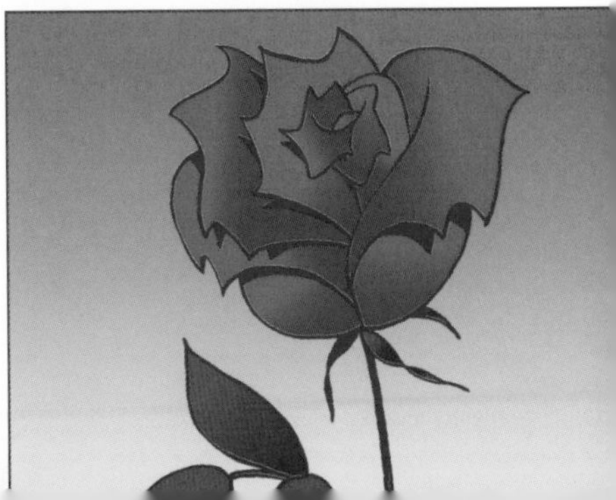

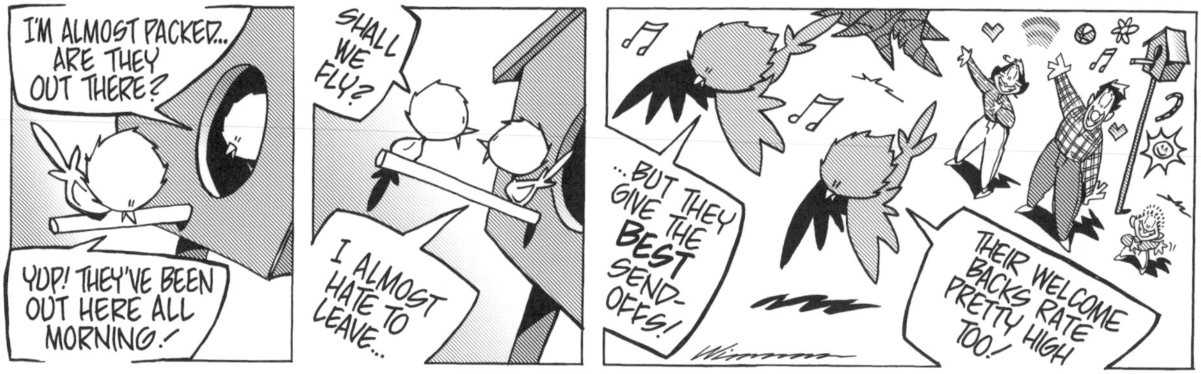
I'M ALMOST PACKED... ARE THEY OUT THERE?
YUP! THEY'VE BEEN OUT HERE ALL MORNING!
SHALL WE FLY?
I ALMOST HATE TO LEAVE...
...BUT THEY GIVE THE BEST SEND-OFFS!
THEIR WELCOME BACKS RATE PRETTY HIGH TOO!

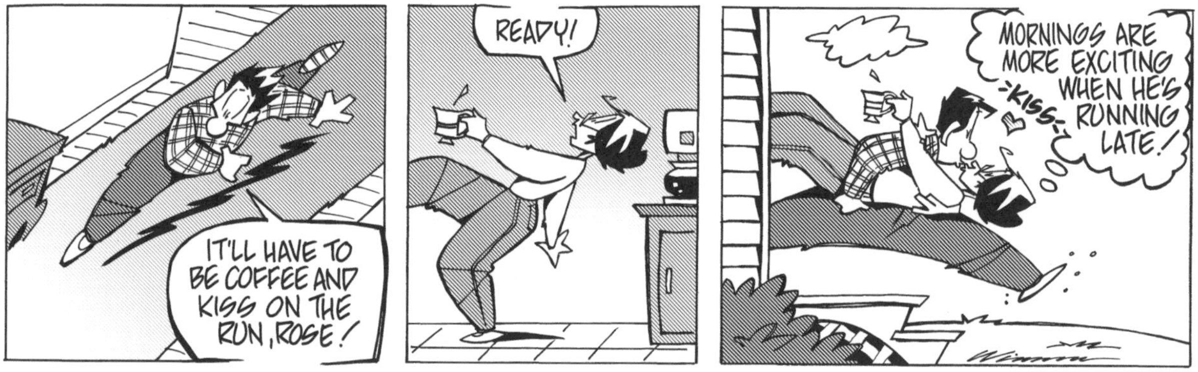
IT'LL HAVE TO BE COFFEE AND KISS ON THE RUN, ROSE!
READY!
KISS
MORNINGS ARE MORE EXCITING WHEN HE'S RUNNING LATE!

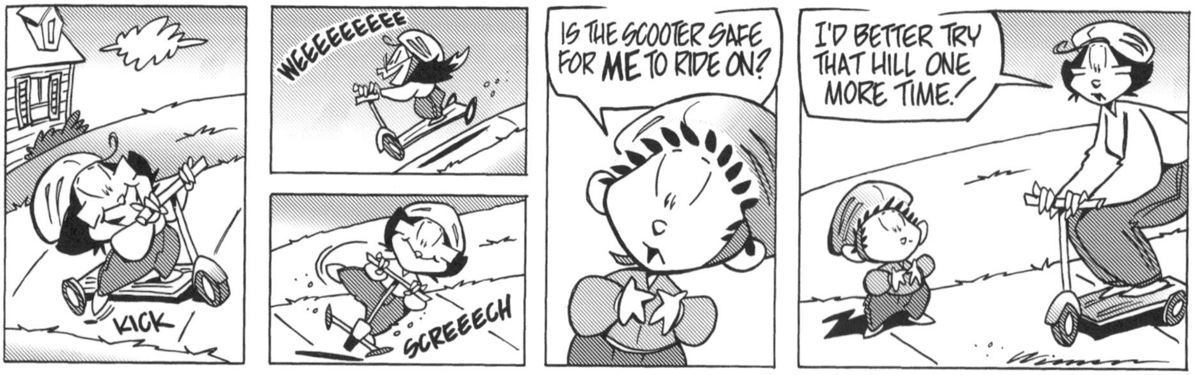
KICK
WEEEEEEEEE
SCREEECH
IS THE SCOOTER SAFE FOR ME TO RIDE ON?
I'D BETTER TRY THAT HILL ONE MORE TIME!

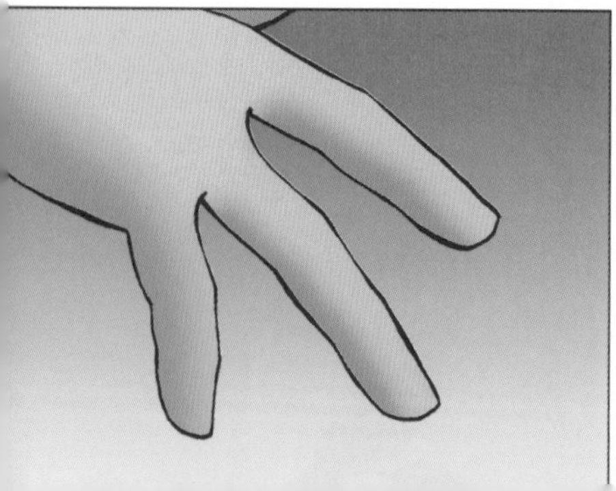

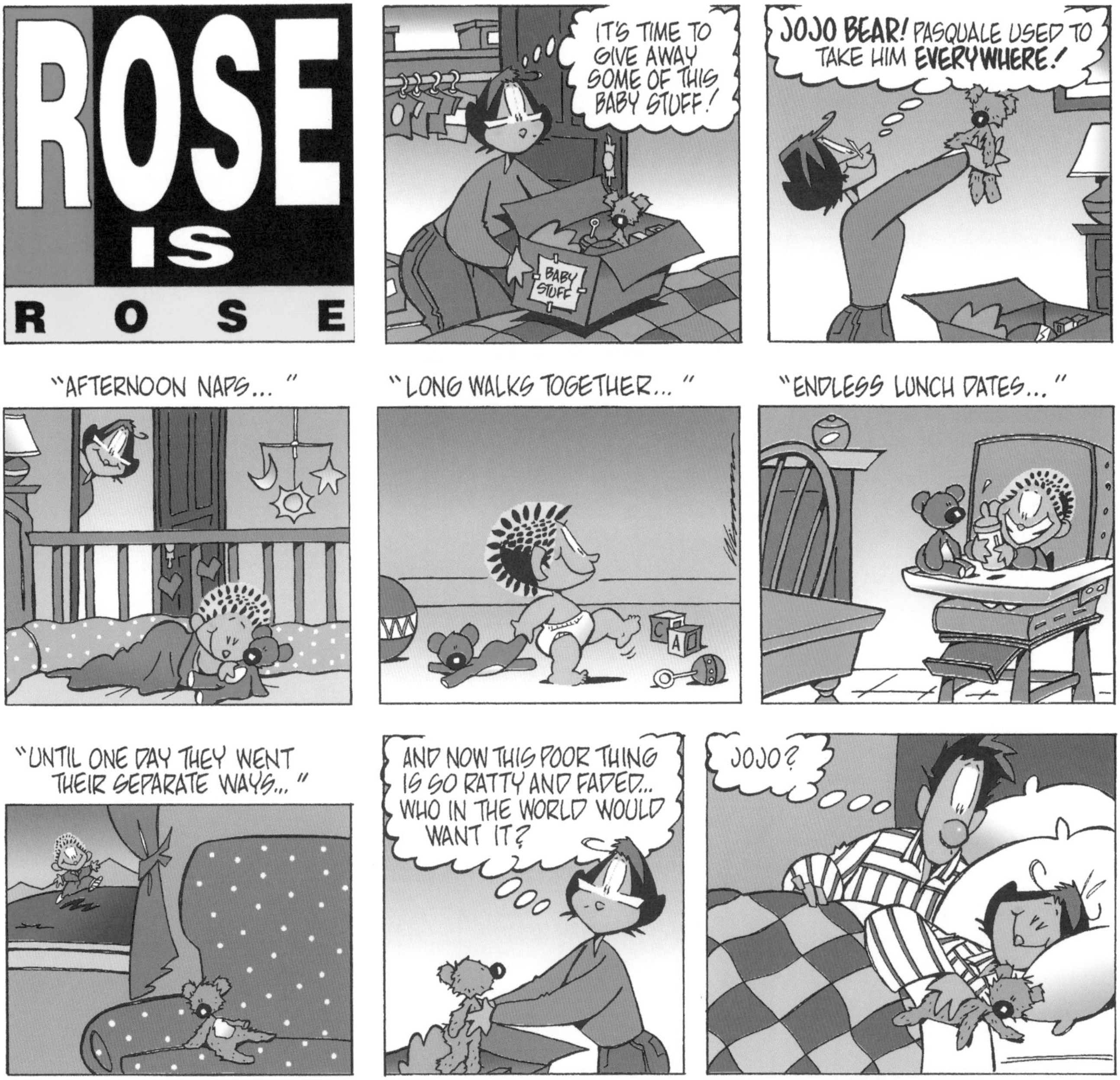
ROSE IS ROSE
IT'S TIME TO GIVE AWAY SOME OF THIS BABY STUFF!
BABY STUFF
JOJO BEAR! PASQUALE USED TO TAKE HIM EVERYWHERE!
"AFTERNOON NAPS..."
"LONG WALKS TOGETHER..."
"ENDLESS LUNCH DATES..."
"UNTIL ONE DAY THEY WENT THEIR SEPARATE WAYS..."
AND NOW THIS POOR THING IS SO RATTY AND FADED... WHO IN THE WORLD WOULD WANT IT?
JOJO?

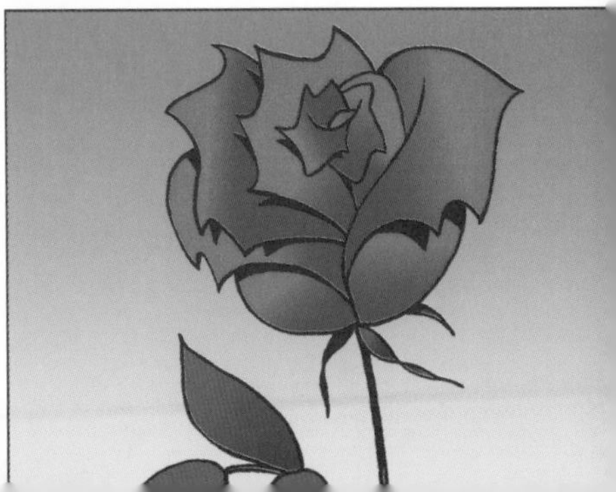

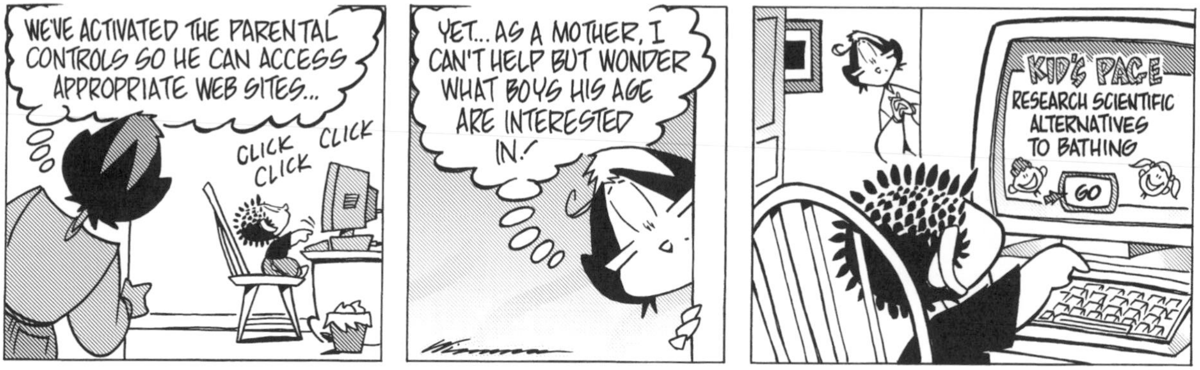
WE'VE ACTIVATED THE PARENTAL CONTROLS SO HE CAN ACCESS APPROPRIATE WEB SITES...
CLICK CLICK CLICK
YET... AS A MOTHER, I CAN'T HELP BUT WONDER WHAT BOYS HIS AGE ARE INTERESTED IN!
KID'S PAGE
RESEARCH SCIENTIFIC ALTERNATIVES TO BATHING
GO

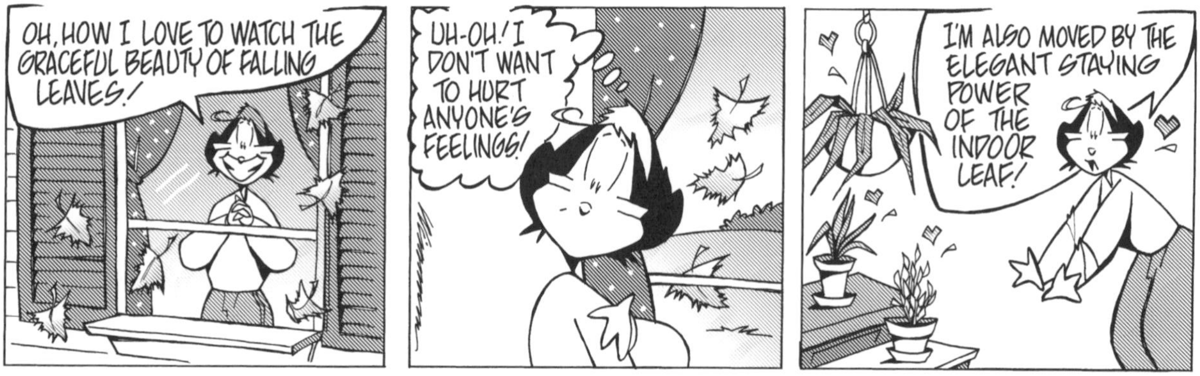
OH, HOW I LOVE TO WATCH THE GRACEFUL BEAUTY OF FALLING LEAVES!
UH-OH! I DON'T WANT TO HURT ANYONE'S FEELINGS!
I'M ALSO MOVED BY THE ELEGANT STAYING POWER OF THE INDOOR LEAF!

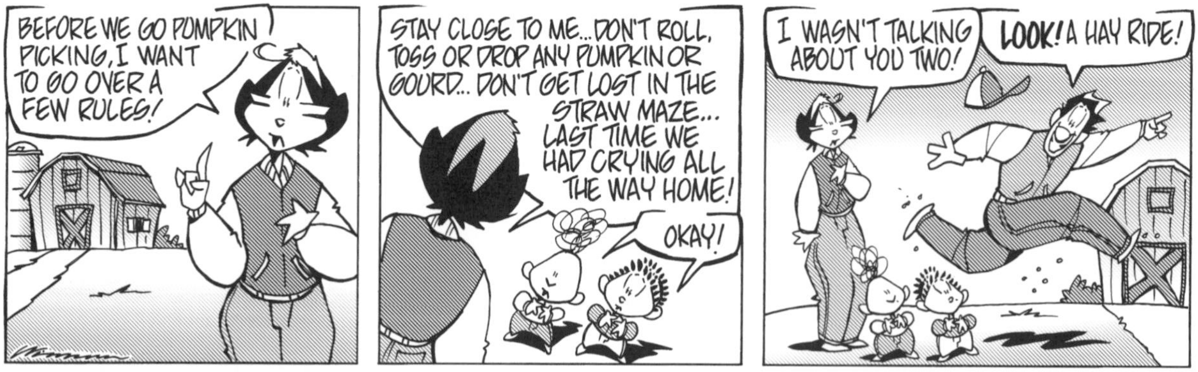
BEFORE WE GO PUMPKIN PICKING, I WANT TO GO OVER A FEW RULES!
STAY CLOSE TO ME... DON'T ROLL, TOSS OR DROP ANY PUMPKIN OR GOURD... DON'T GET LOST IN THE STRAW MAZE... LAST TIME WE HAD CRYING ALL THE WAY HOME!
OKAY!
I WASN'T TALKING ABOUT YOU TWO!
LOOK! A HAY RIDE!

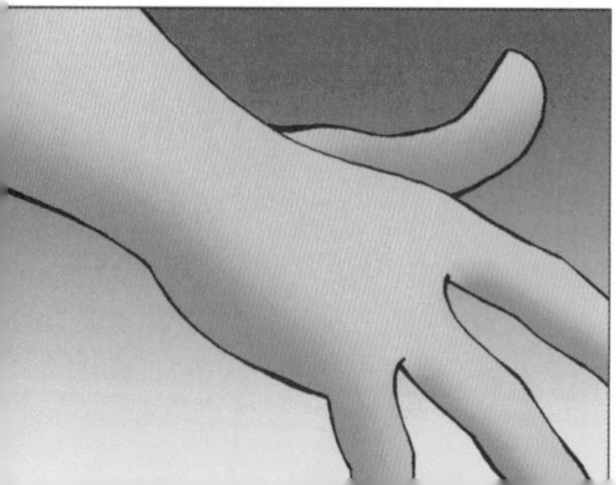

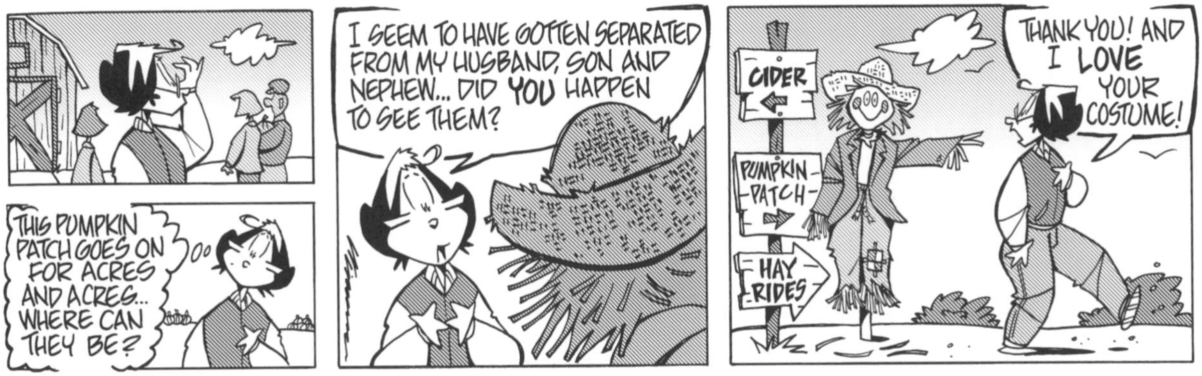
THIS PUMPKIN PATCH GOES ON FOR ACRES AND ACRES... WHERE CAN THEY BE?
I SEEM TO HAVE GOTTEN SEPARATED FROM MY HUSBAND, SON AND NEPHEW... DID YOU HAPPEN TO SEE THEM?
CIDER
PUMPKIN PATCH
HAY RIDES
THANK YOU! AND I LOVE YOUR COSTUME!

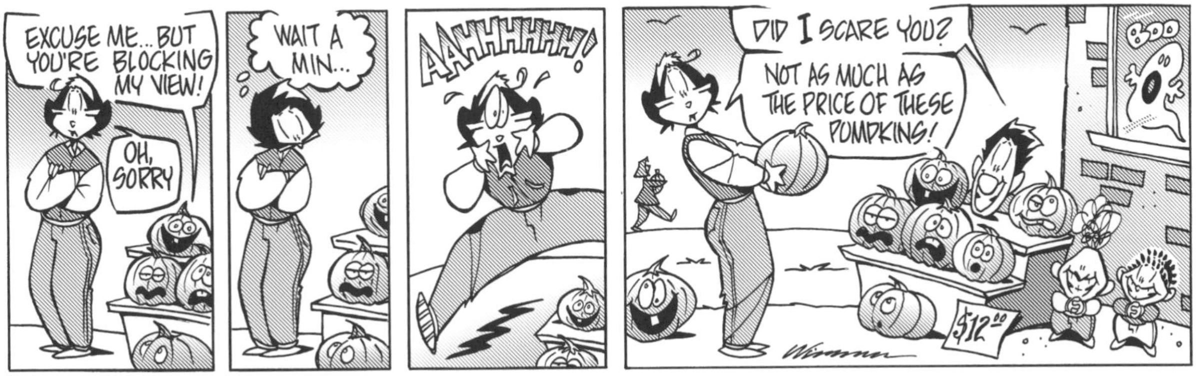
EXCUSE ME... BUT YOU'RE BLOCKING MY VIEW!
OH, SORRY
WAIT A MIN...
AAHHHHHHH!
DID I SCARE YOU?
NOT AS MUCH AS THE PRICE OF THESE PUMPKINS!
BOO
$12.00

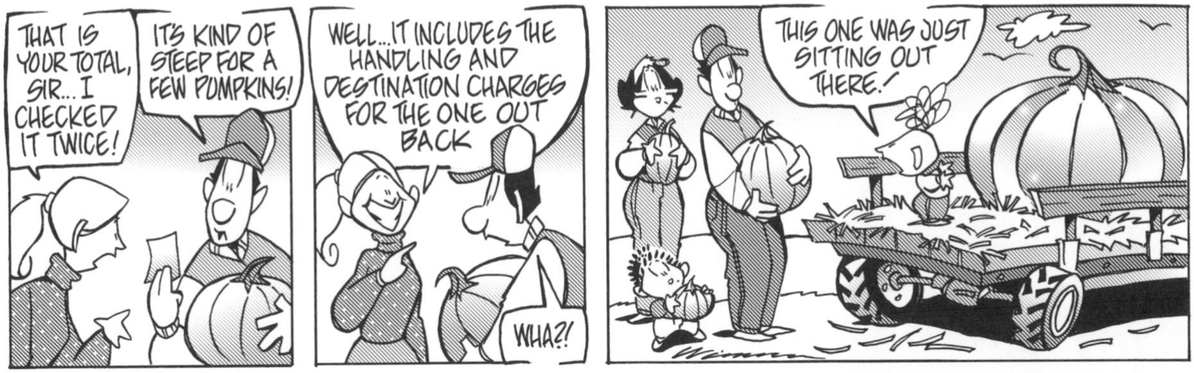
THAT IS YOUR TOTAL, SIR... I CHECKED IT TWICE!
IT'S KIND OF STEEP FOR A FEW PUMPKINS!
WELL... IT INCLUDES THE HANDLING AND DESTINATION CHARGES FOR THE ONE OUT BACK
WHA?!
THIS ONE WAS JUST SITTING OUT THERE.

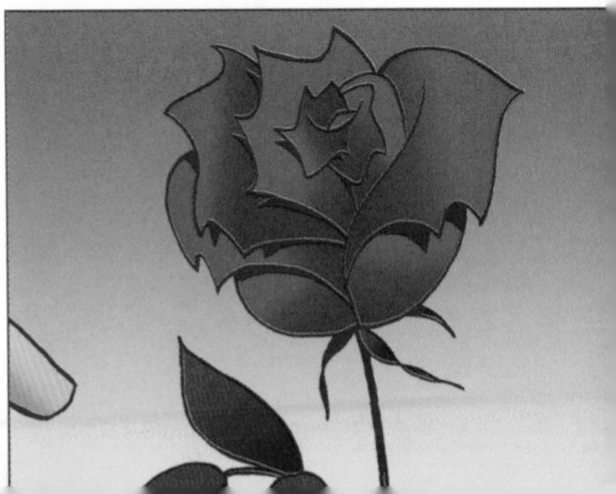

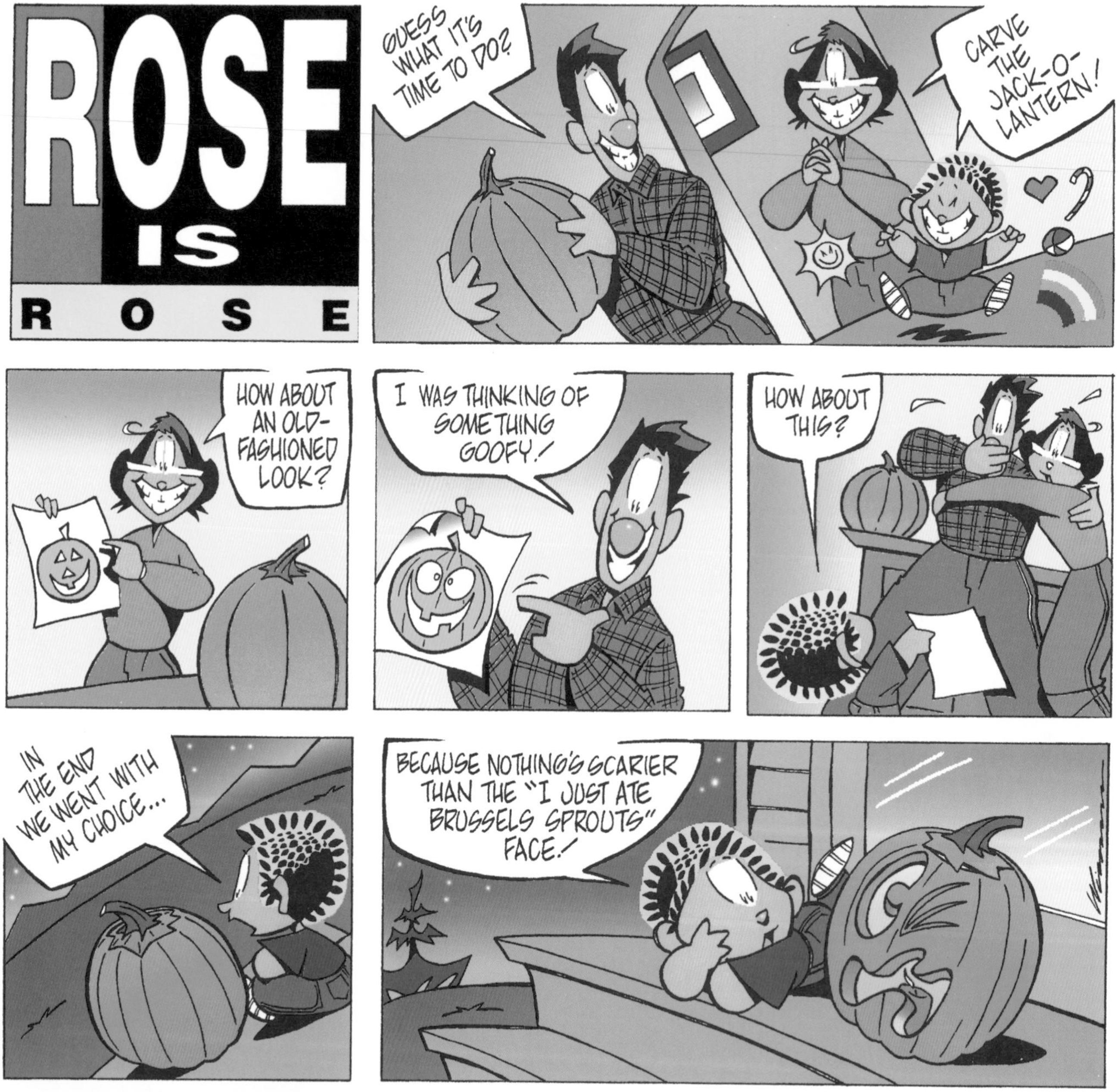
ROSE IS ROSE
GUESS WHAT IT'S TIME TO DO?
CARVE THE JACK-O-LANTERN!
HOW ABOUT AN OLD-FASHIONED LOOK?
I WAS THINKING OF SOMETHING GOOFY!
HOW ABOUT THIS?
IN THE END WE WENT WITH MY CHOICE...
BECAUSE NOTHING'S SCARIER THAN THE "I JUST ATE BRUSSELS SPROUTS" FACE!

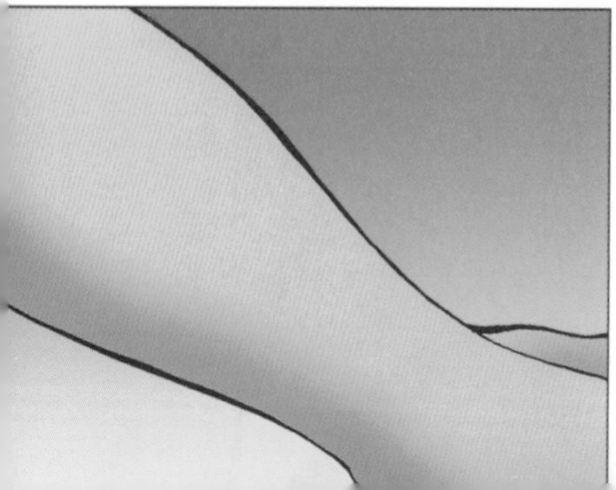

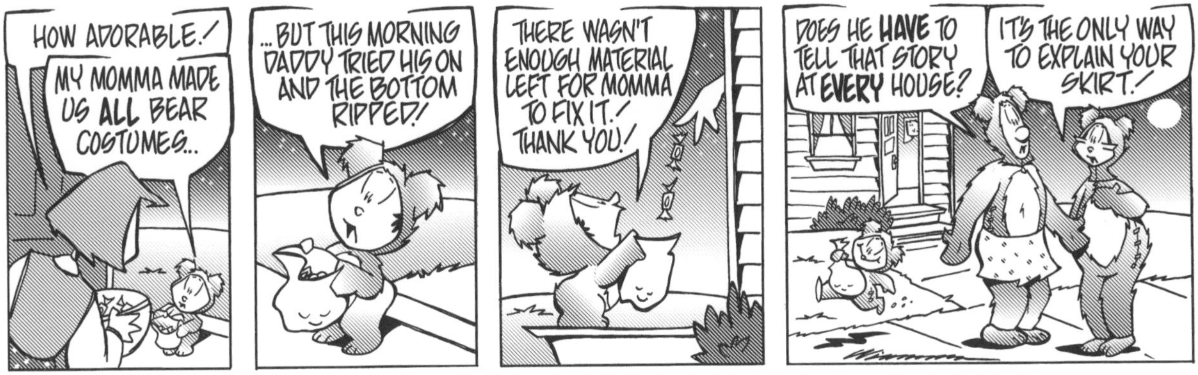
HOW ADORABLE!
MY MOMMA MADE US **ALL** BEAR COSTUMES...
...BUT THIS MORNING DADDY TRIED HIS ON AND THE BOTTOM RIPPED!
THERE WASN'T ENOUGH MATERIAL LEFT FOR MOMMA TO FIX IT! THANK YOU!
DOES HE **HAVE** TO TELL THAT STORY AT **EVERY** HOUSE?
IT'S THE ONLY WAY TO EXPLAIN YOUR SKIRT!

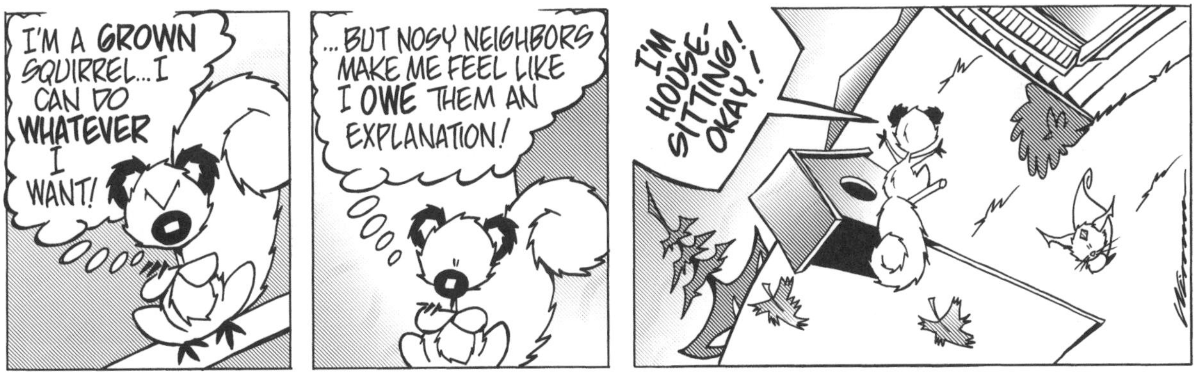
I'M A **GROWN** SQUIRREL...I CAN DO **WHATEVER** I WANT!
...BUT NOSY NEIGHBORS MAKE ME FEEL LIKE I **OWE** THEM AN EXPLANATION!
I'M HOUSE-SITTING! OKAY!

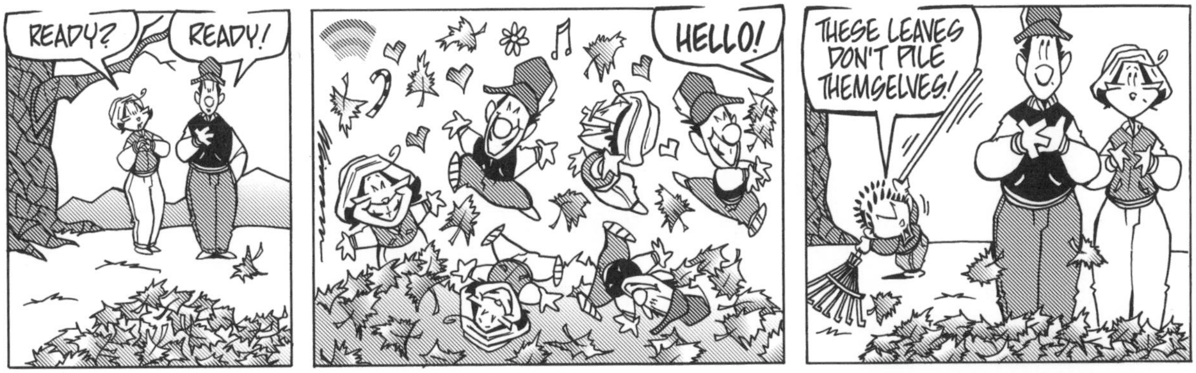
READY?
READY!
HELLO!
THESE LEAVES DON'T PILE THEMSELVES!

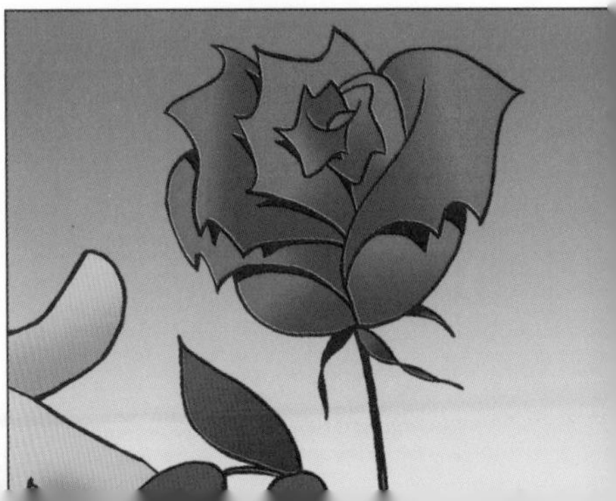

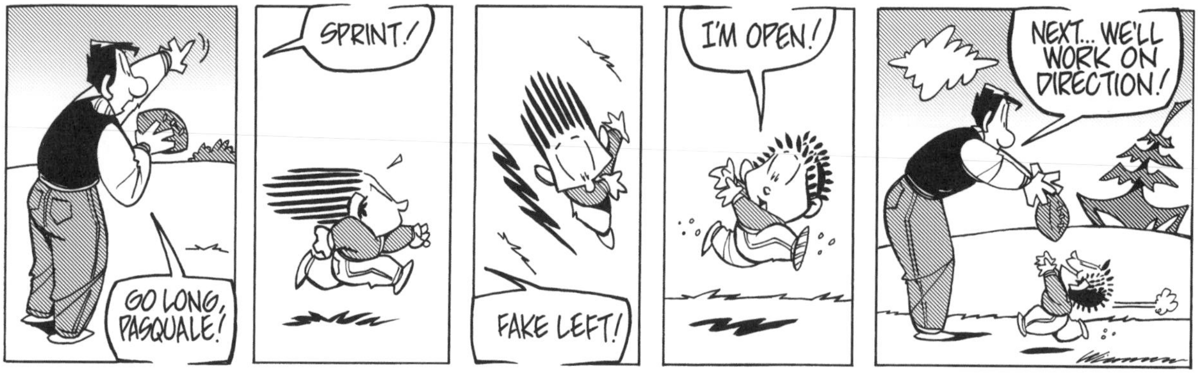
GO LONG, PASQUALE!
SPRINT!
FAKE LEFT!
I'M OPEN!
NEXT... WE'LL WORK ON DIRECTION!

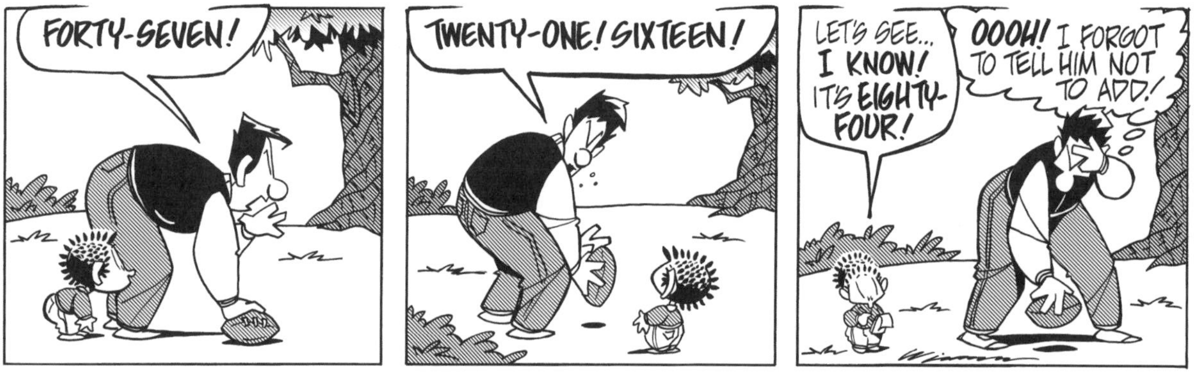
FORTY-SEVEN!
TWENTY-ONE! SIXTEEN!
LET'S SEE... I KNOW! IT'S EIGHTY-FOUR!
OOOH! I FORGOT TO TELL HIM NOT TO ADD!

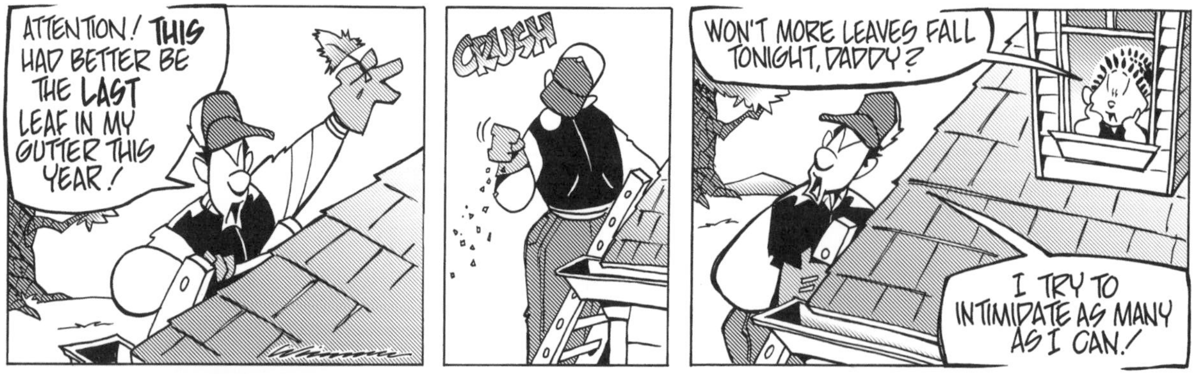
ATTENTION! THIS HAD BETTER BE THE LAST LEAF IN MY GUTTER THIS YEAR!
CRUSH
WON'T MORE LEAVES FALL TONIGHT, DADDY?
I TRY TO INTIMIDATE AS MANY AS I CAN!

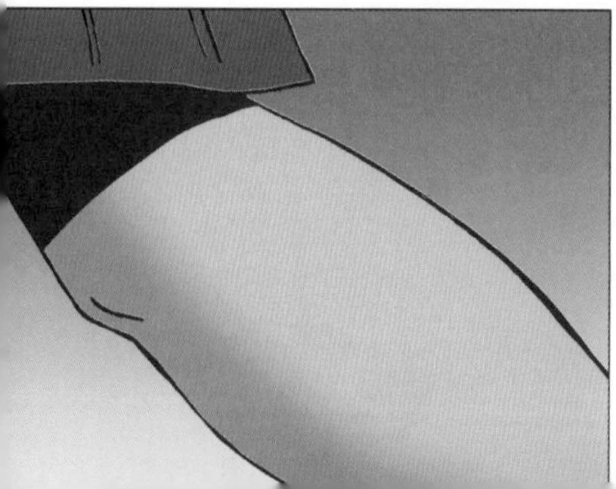

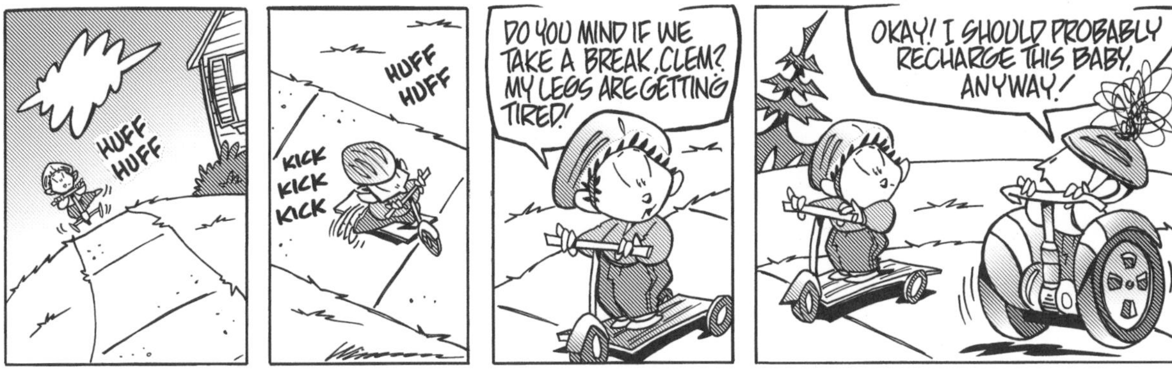
HUFF
HUFF
KICK
KICK
KICK
HUFF
HUFF
DO YOU MIND IF WE TAKE A BREAK, CLEM? MY LEGS ARE GETTING TIRED!
OKAY! I SHOULD PROBABLY RECHARGE THIS BABY, ANYWAY!

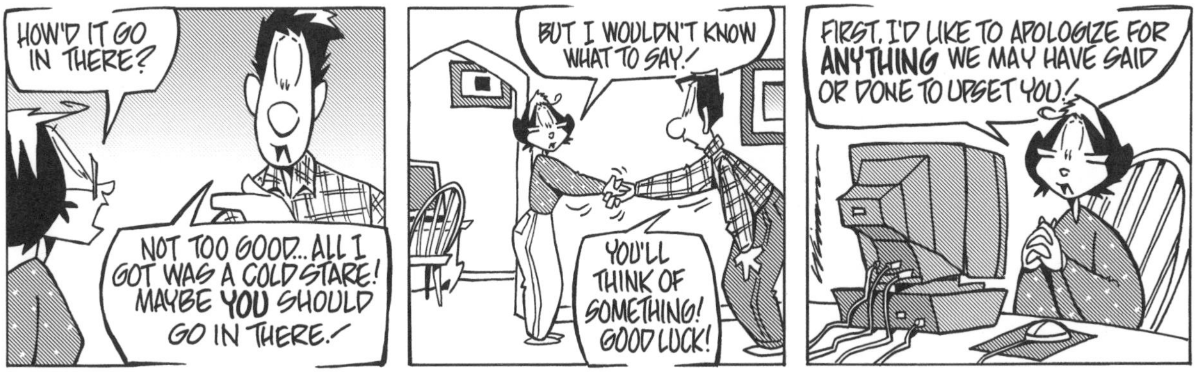
HOW'D IT GO IN THERE?
NOT TOO GOOD... ALL I GOT WAS A COLD STARE! MAYBE **YOU** SHOULD GO IN THERE.
BUT I WOULDN'T KNOW WHAT TO SAY!
YOU'LL THINK OF SOMETHING! GOOD LUCK!
FIRST, I'D LIKE TO APOLOGIZE FOR **ANYTHING** WE MAY HAVE SAID OR DONE TO UPSET YOU!

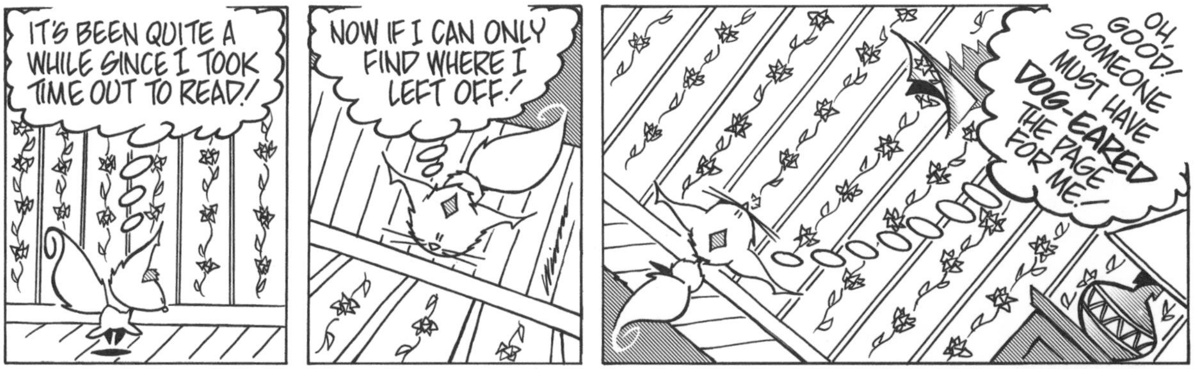
IT'S BEEN QUITE A WHILE SINCE I TOOK TIME OUT TO READ!
NOW IF I CAN ONLY FIND WHERE I LEFT OFF!
OH, GOOD! SOMEONE MUST HAVE **DOG-EARED** THE PAGE FOR ME!

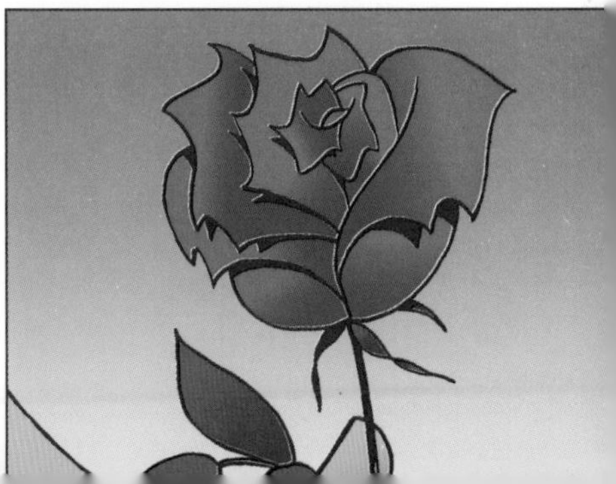

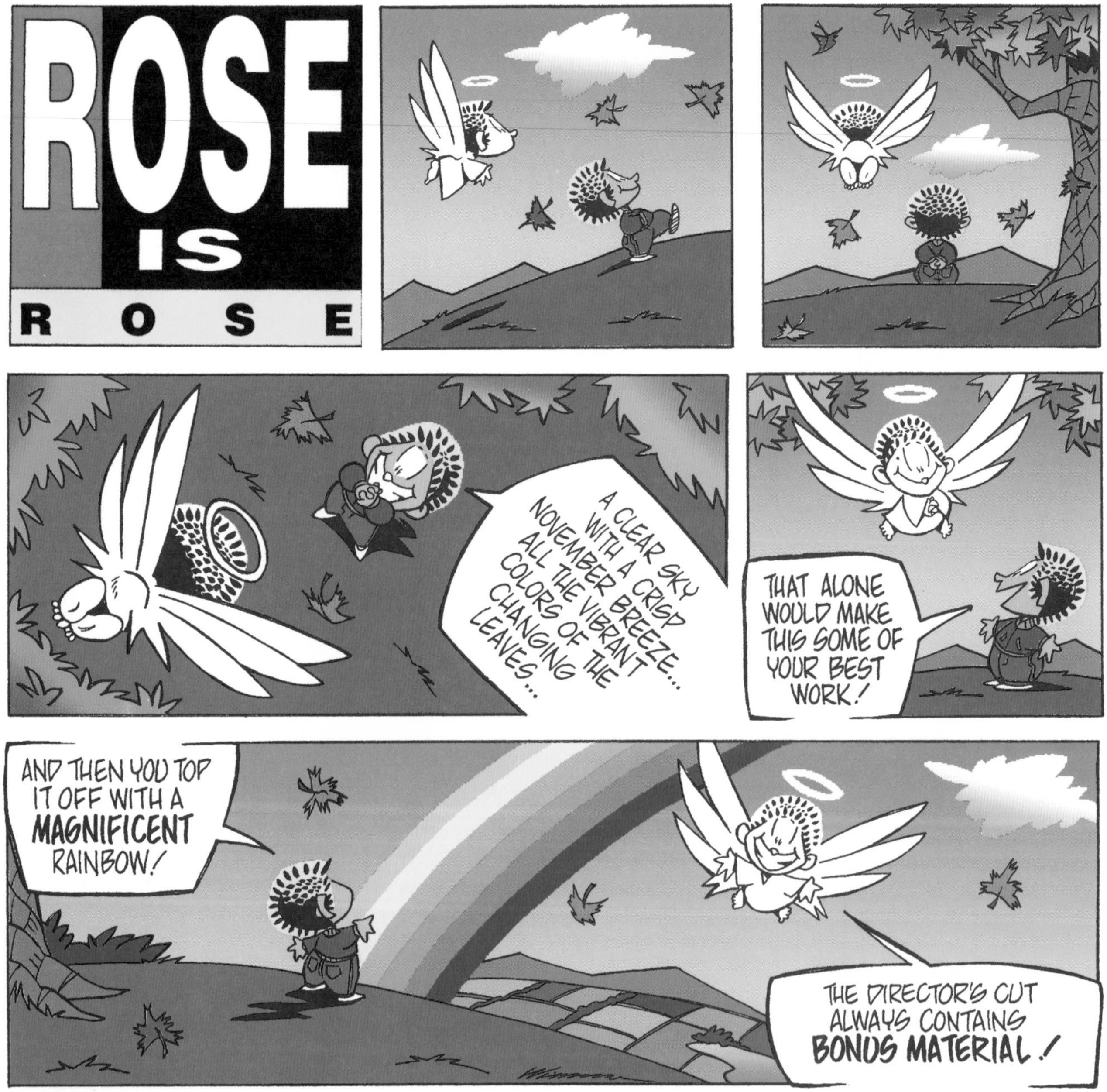
ROSE IS ROSE
A CLEAR SKY WITH A CRISP NOVEMBER BREEZE... ALL THE VIBRANT COLORS OF THE CHANGING LEAVES...
THAT ALONE WOULD MAKE THIS SOME OF YOUR BEST WORK!
AND THEN YOU TOP IT OFF WITH A **MAGNIFICENT** RAINBOW!
THE DIRECTOR'S CUT ALWAYS CONTAINS **BONUS MATERIAL**!

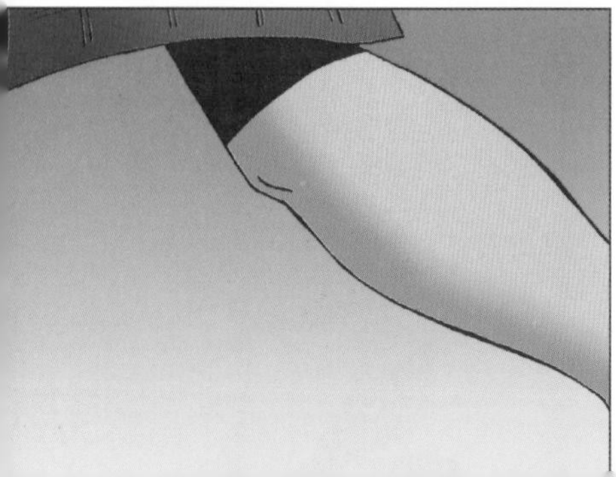

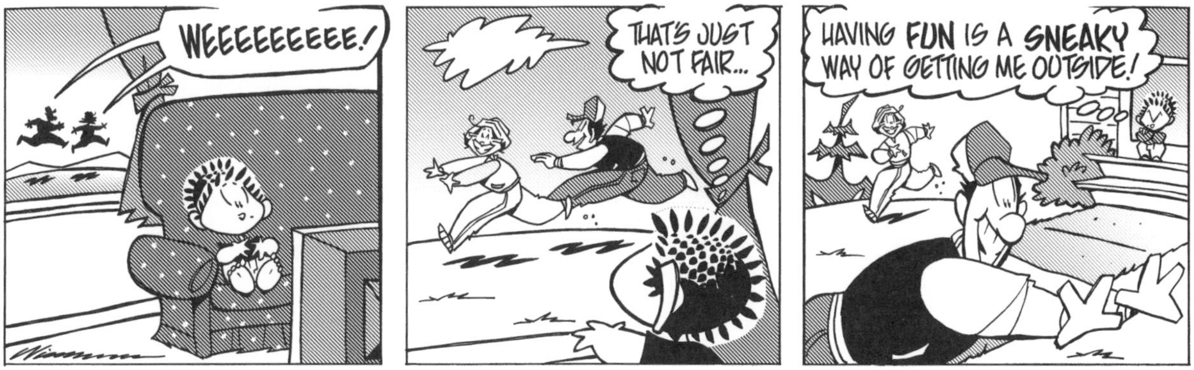
WEEEEEEEEE!
THAT'S JUST NOT FAIR...
HAVING FUN IS A SNEAKY WAY OF GETTING ME OUTSIDE!

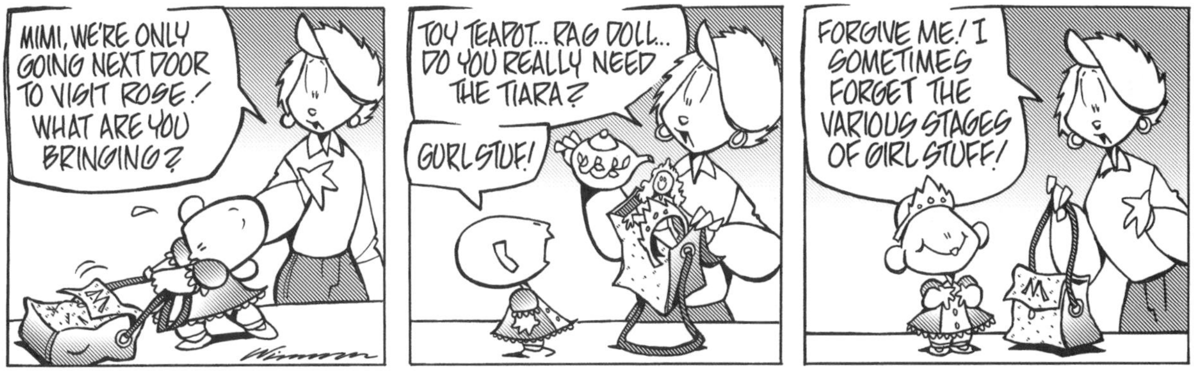
MIMI, WE'RE ONLY GOING NEXT DOOR TO VISIT ROSE! WHAT ARE YOU BRINGING?
TOY TEAPOT... RAG DOLL... DO YOU REALLY NEED THE TIARA?
GURL STUF!
FORGIVE ME! I SOMETIMES FORGET THE VARIOUS STAGES OF GIRL STUFF!

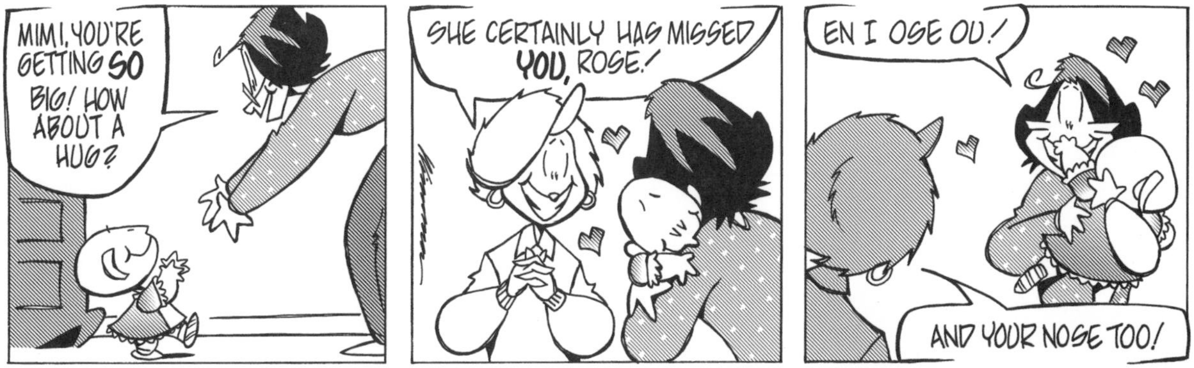
MIMI, YOU'RE GETTING SO BIG! HOW ABOUT A HUG?
SHE CERTAINLY HAS MISSED YOU, ROSE!
EN I OSE OU!
AND YOUR NOSE TOO!

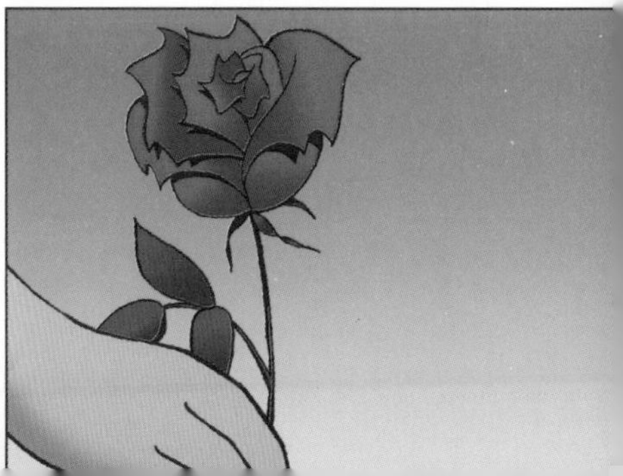

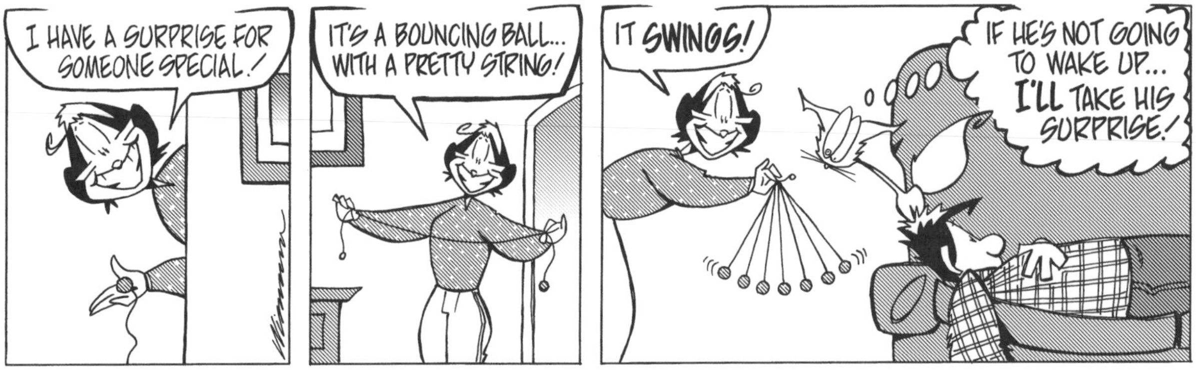
I HAVE A SURPRISE FOR SOMEONE SPECIAL!
IT'S A BOUNCING BALL... WITH A PRETTY STRING!
IT SWINGS!
IF HE'S NOT GOING TO WAKE UP... I'LL TAKE HIS SURPRISE!

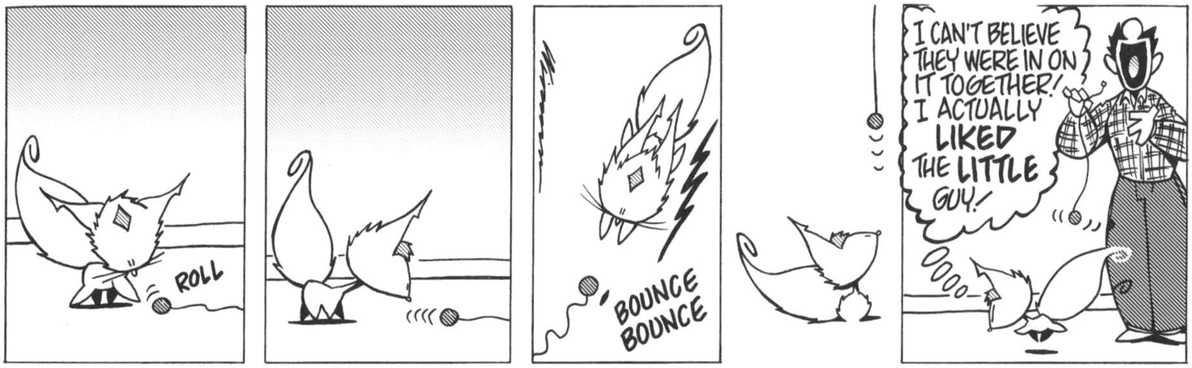
ROLL
BOUNCE BOUNCE
I CAN'T BELIEVE THEY WERE IN ON IT TOGETHER! I ACTUALLY LIKED THE LITTLE GUY!

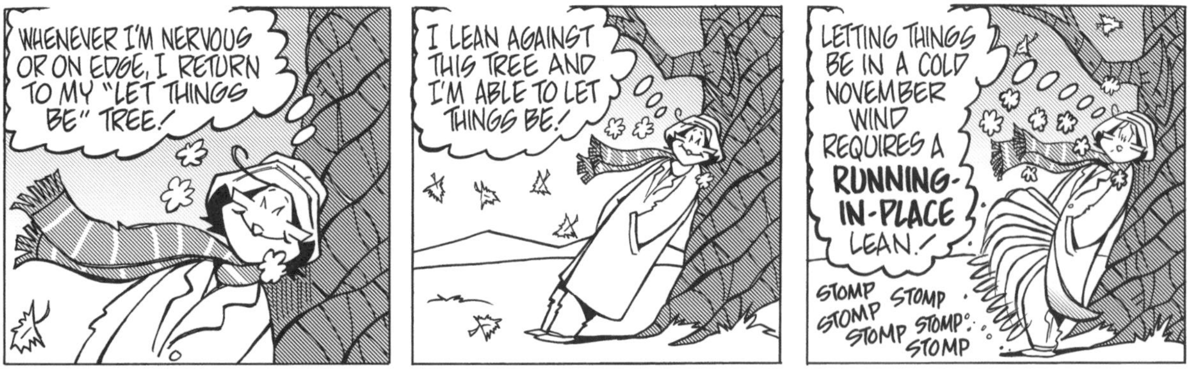
WHENEVER I'M NERVOUS OR ON EDGE, I RETURN TO MY "LET THINGS BE" TREE!
I LEAN AGAINST THIS TREE AND I'M ABLE TO LET THINGS BE!
LETTING THINGS BE IN A COLD NOVEMBER WIND REQUIRES A RUNNING-IN-PLACE LEAN!
STOMP STOMP STOMP STOMP STOMP STOMP STOMP

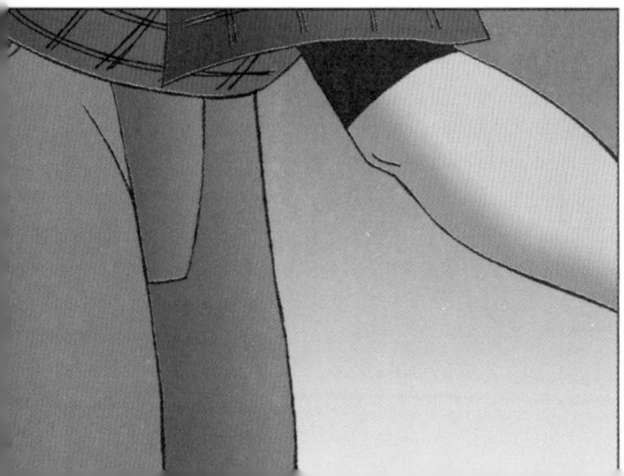

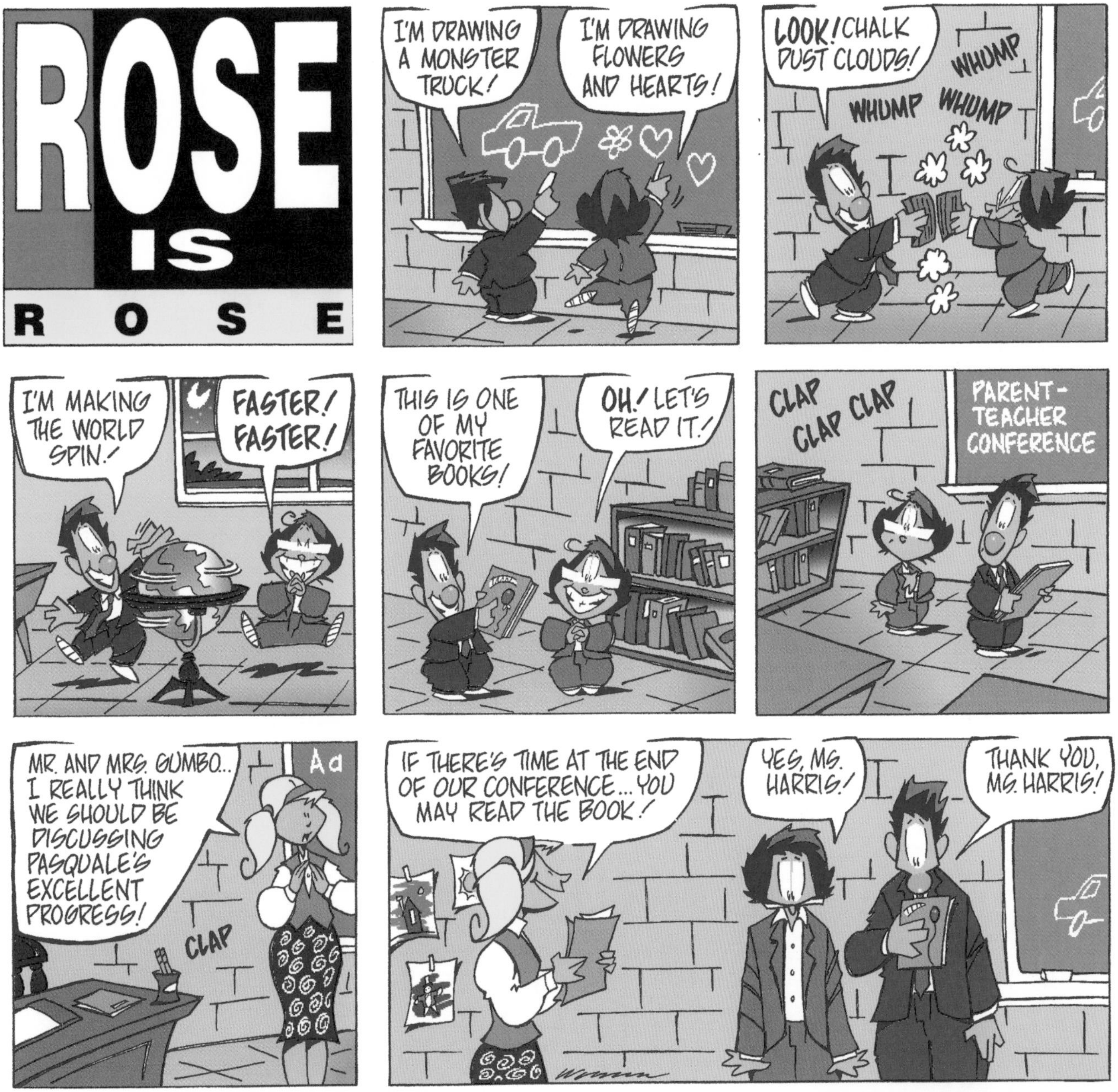
ROSE IS ROSE
I'M DRAWING A MONSTER TRUCK!
I'M DRAWING FLOWERS AND HEARTS!
LOOK! CHALK DUST CLOUDS!
WHUMP WHUMP WHUMP
I'M MAKING THE WORLD SPIN!
FASTER! FASTER!
THIS IS ONE OF MY FAVORITE BOOKS!
OH! LET'S READ IT!
CLAP CLAP CLAP
PARENT-TEACHER CONFERENCE
MR. AND MRS. GUMBO... I REALLY THINK WE SHOULD BE DISCUSSING PASQUALE'S EXCELLENT PROGRESS!
Aa
CLAP
IF THERE'S TIME AT THE END OF OUR CONFERENCE... YOU MAY READ THE BOOK!
YES, MS. HARRIS!
THANK YOU, MS. HARRIS!

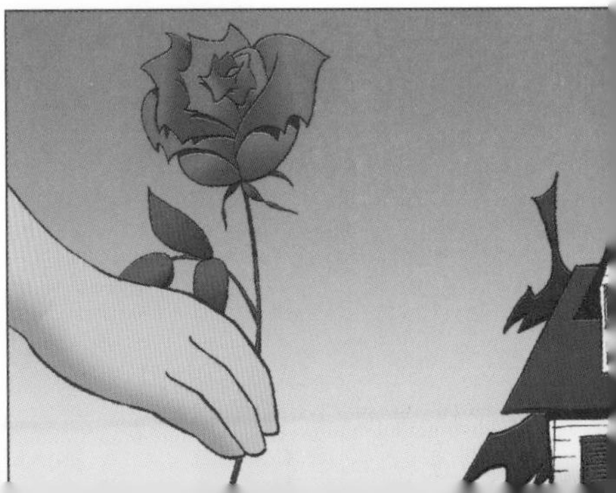

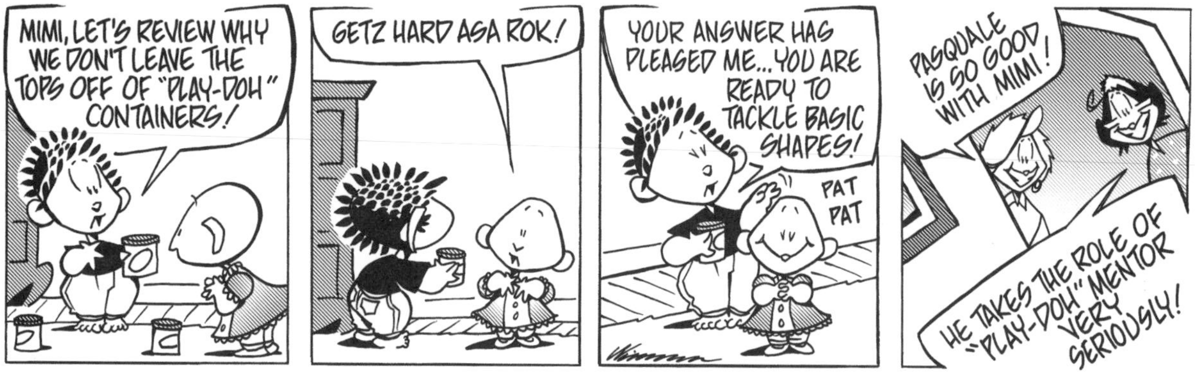
MIMI, LET'S REVIEW WHY WE DON'T LEAVE THE TOPS OFF OF "PLAY-DOH" CONTAINERS!
GETZ HARD ASA ROK!
YOUR ANSWER HAS PLEASED ME... YOU ARE READY TO TACKLE BASIC SHAPES!
PAT PAT
PASQUALE IS SO GOOD WITH MIMI!
HE TAKES THE ROLE OF "PLAY-DOH" MENTOR VERY SERIOUSLY!

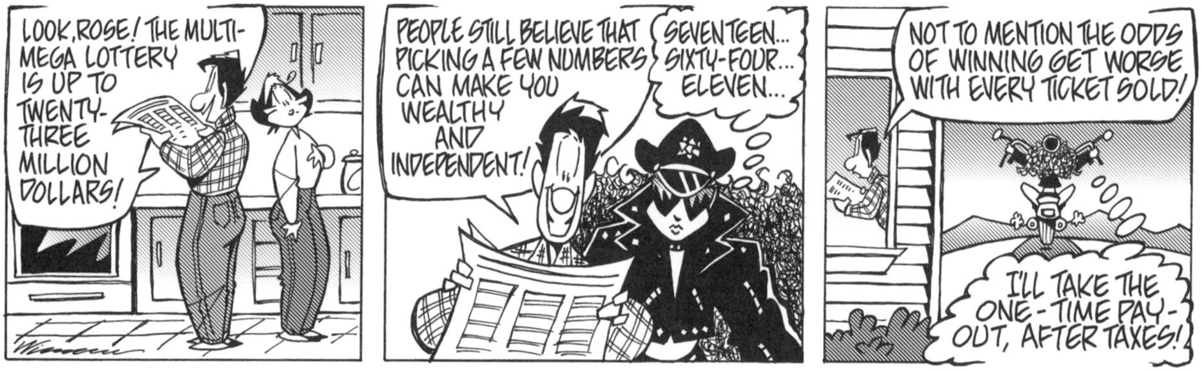
LOOK, ROSE! THE MULTI-MEGA LOTTERY IS UP TO TWENTY-THREE MILLION DOLLARS!
PEOPLE STILL BELIEVE THAT PICKING A FEW NUMBERS CAN MAKE YOU WEALTHY AND INDEPENDENT!
SEVENTEEN... SIXTY-FOUR... ELEVEN...
NOT TO MENTION THE ODDS OF WINNING GET WORSE WITH EVERY TICKET SOLD!
I'LL TAKE THE ONE-TIME PAY-OUT, AFTER TAXES!

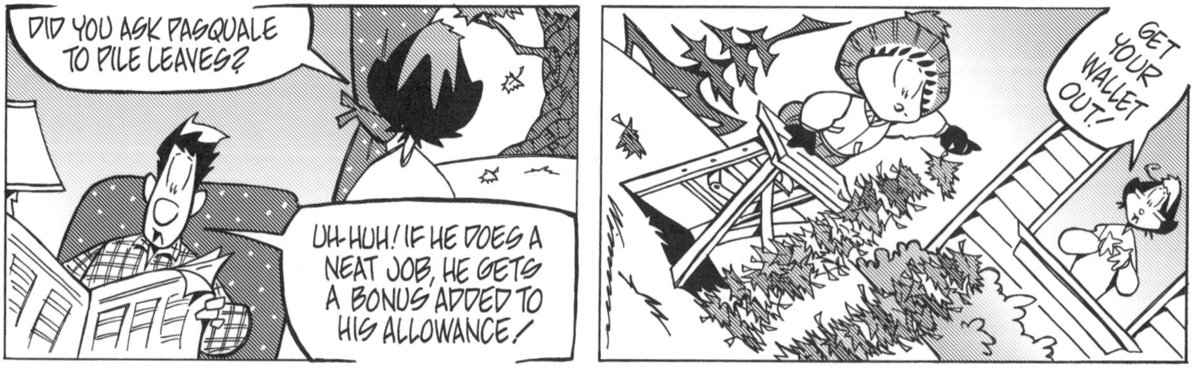
DID YOU ASK PASQUALE TO PILE LEAVES?
UH-HUH! IF HE DOES A NEAT JOB, HE GETS A BONUS ADDED TO HIS ALLOWANCE!
GET YOUR WALLET OUT!

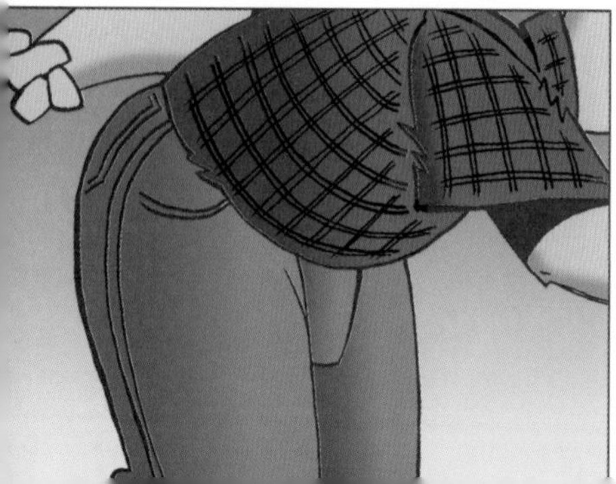

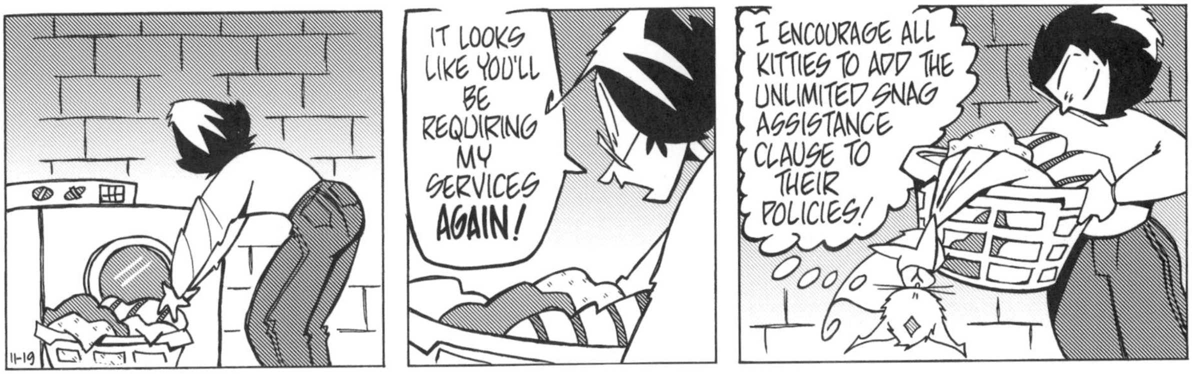
IT LOOKS LIKE YOU'LL BE REQUIRING MY SERVICES AGAIN!
I ENCOURAGE ALL KITTIES TO ADD THE UNLIMITED SNAG ASSISTANCE CLAUSE TO THEIR POLICIES!

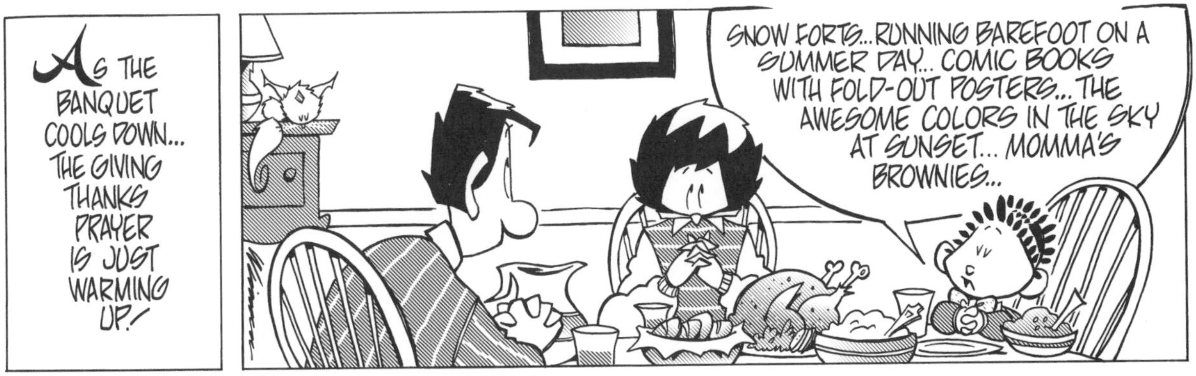
AS THE BANQUET COOLS DOWN... THE GIVING THANKS PRAYER IS JUST WARMING UP!
SNOW FORTS...RUNNING BAREFOOT ON A SUMMER DAY... COMIC BOOKS WITH FOLD-OUT POSTERS... THE AWESOME COLORS IN THE SKY AT SUNSET... MOMMA'S BROWNIES...

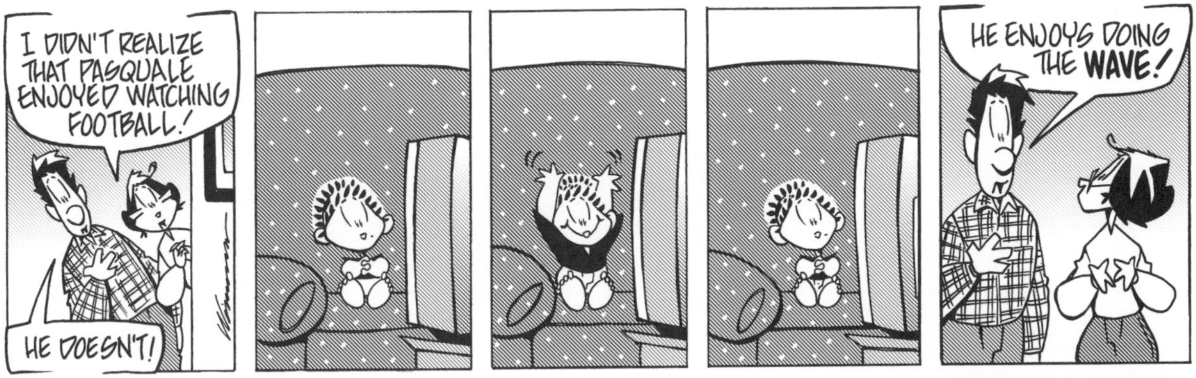
I DIDN'T REALIZE THAT PASQUALE ENJOYED WATCHING FOOTBALL!
HE DOESN'T!
HE ENJOYS DOING THE WAVE!

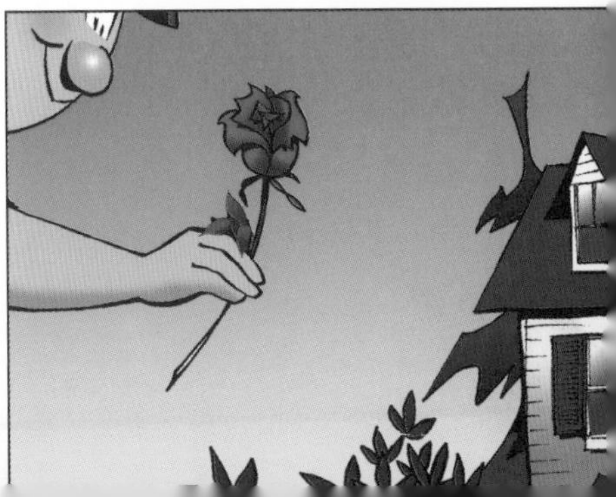

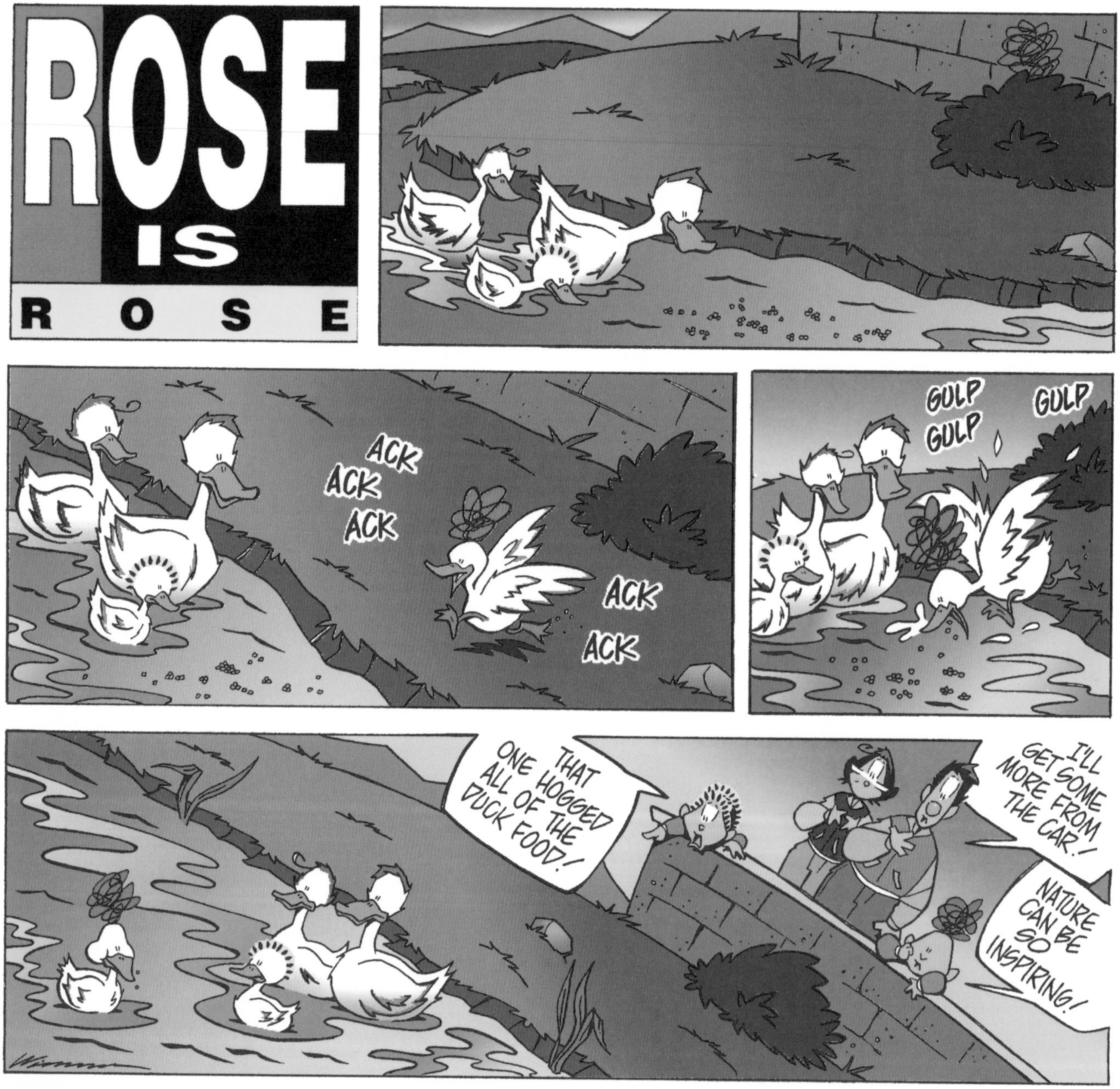
ROSE IS ROSE
ACK ACK ACK
ACK ACK
GULP GULP
GULP
THAT ONE HOGGED ALL OF THE DUCK FOOD!
I'LL GET SOME MORE FROM THE CAR!
NATURE CAN BE SO INSPIRING!

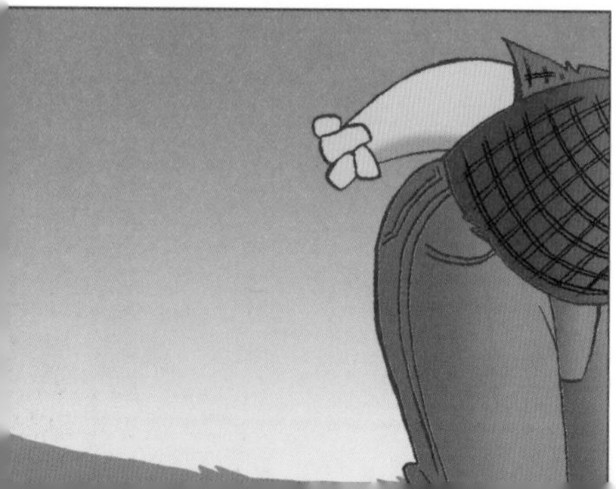

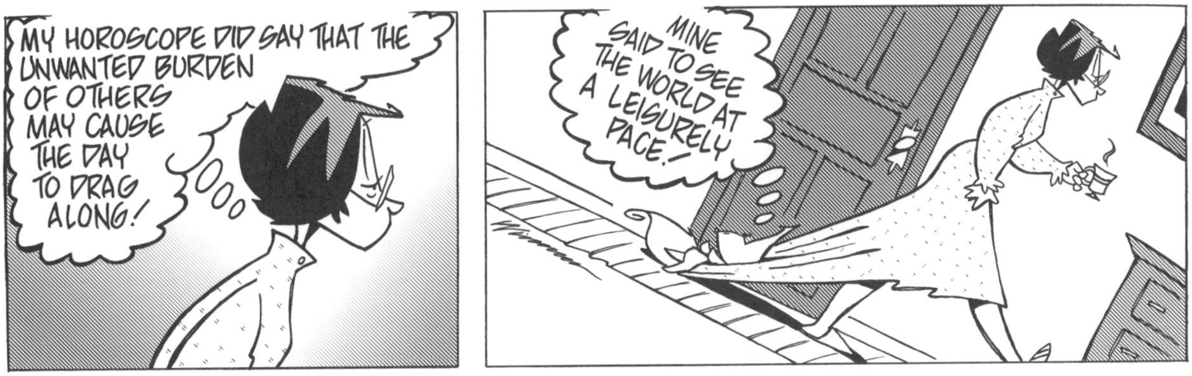
MY HOROSCOPE DID SAY THAT THE UNWANTED BURDEN OF OTHERS MAY CAUSE THE DAY TO DRAG ALONG!
MINE SAID TO SEE THE WORLD AT A LEISURELY PACE!

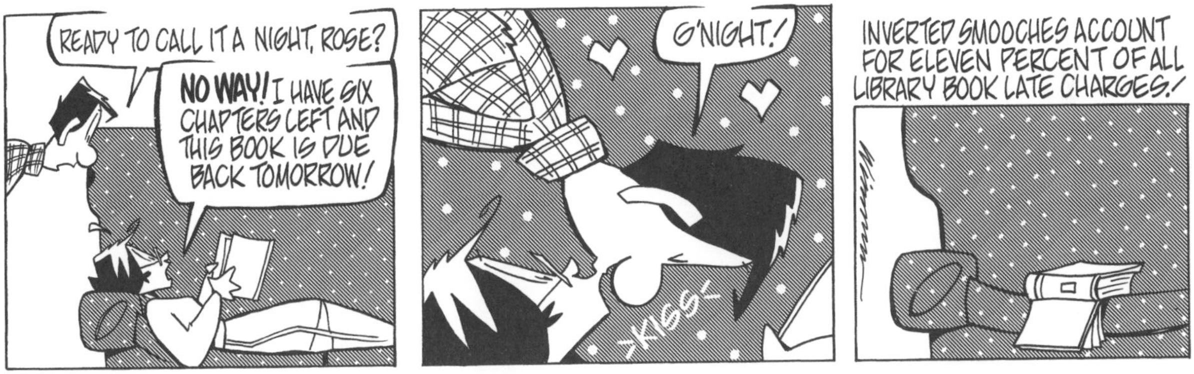
READY TO CALL IT A NIGHT, ROSE?
NO WAY! I HAVE SIX CHAPTERS LEFT AND THIS BOOK IS DUE BACK TOMORROW!
G'NIGHT!
>KISS<
INVERTED SMOOCHES ACCOUNT FOR ELEVEN PERCENT OF ALL LIBRARY BOOK LATE CHARGES!

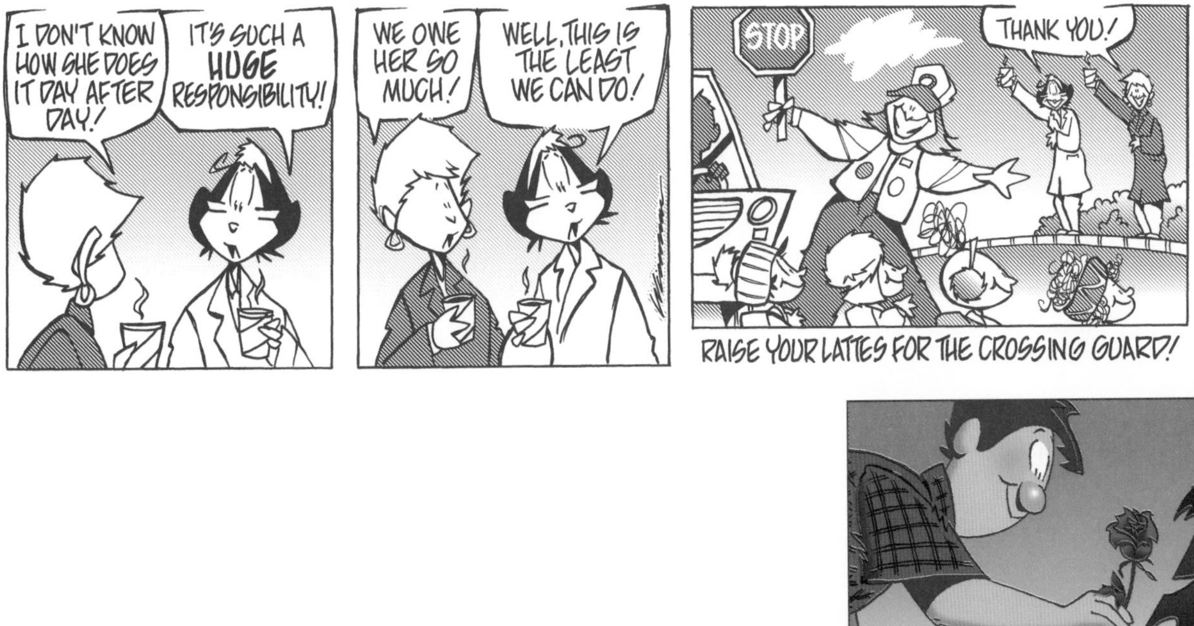
I DON'T KNOW HOW SHE DOES IT DAY AFTER DAY!
IT'S SUCH A HUGE RESPONSIBILITY!
WE OWE HER SO MUCH!
WELL, THIS IS THE LEAST WE CAN DO!
STOP
THANK YOU!
RAISE YOUR LATTES FOR THE CROSSING GUARD!

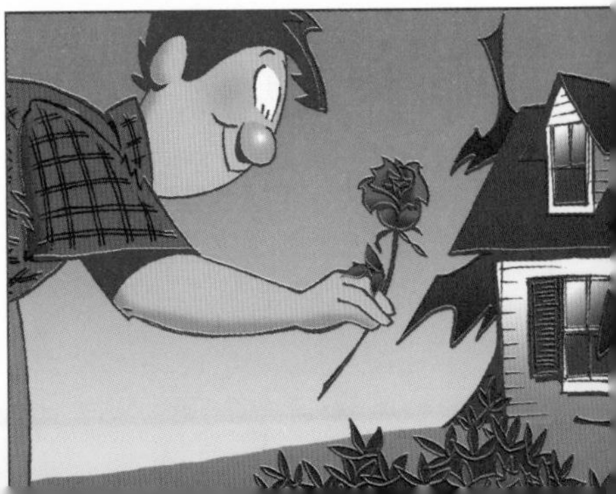

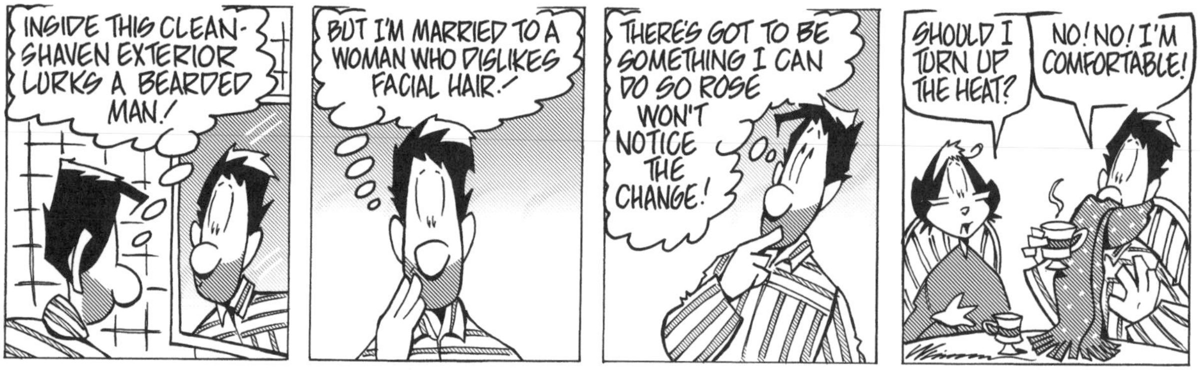
INSIDE THIS CLEAN-SHAVEN EXTERIOR LURKS A BEARDED MAN!
BUT I'M MARRIED TO A WOMAN WHO DISLIKES FACIAL HAIR!
THERE'S GOT TO BE SOMETHING I CAN DO SO ROSE WON'T NOTICE THE CHANGE!
SHOULD I TURN UP THE HEAT?
NO! NO! I'M COMFORTABLE!

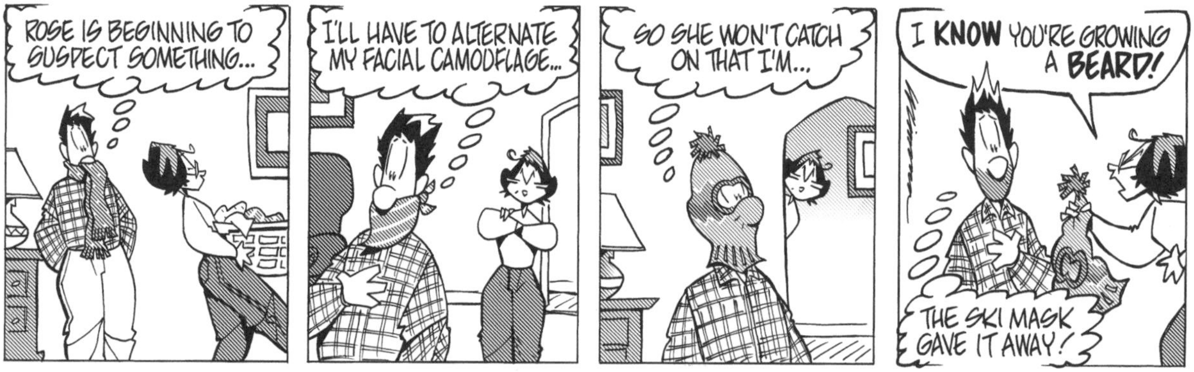
ROSE IS BEGINNING TO SUSPECT SOMETHING...
I'LL HAVE TO ALTERNATE MY FACIAL CAMOUFLAGE...
SO SHE WON'T CATCH ON THAT I'M...
I KNOW YOU'RE GROWING A BEARD!
THE SKI MASK GAVE IT AWAY!

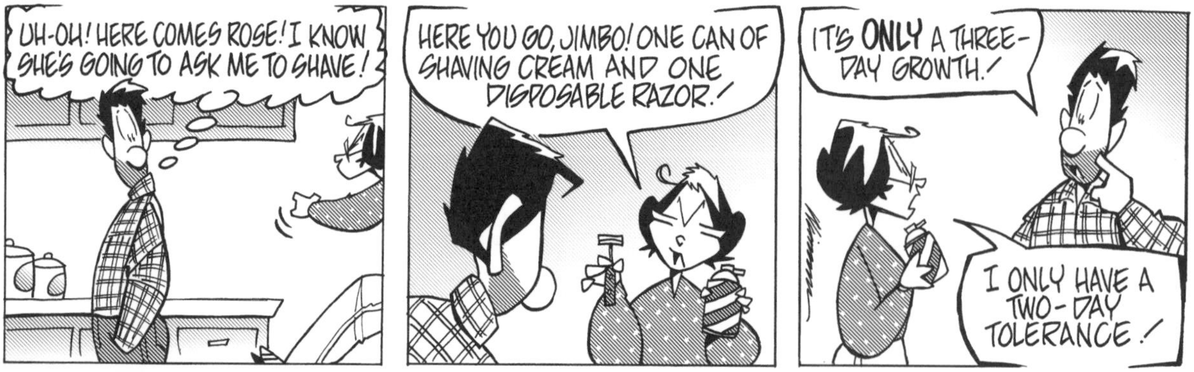
UH-OH! HERE COMES ROSE! I KNOW SHE'S GOING TO ASK ME TO SHAVE!
HERE YOU GO, JIMBO! ONE CAN OF SHAVING CREAM AND ONE DISPOSABLE RAZOR!
IT'S ONLY A THREE-DAY GROWTH!
I ONLY HAVE A TWO-DAY TOLERANCE!

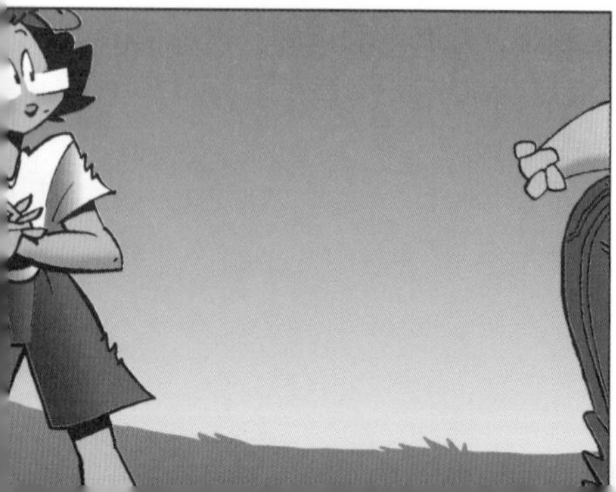

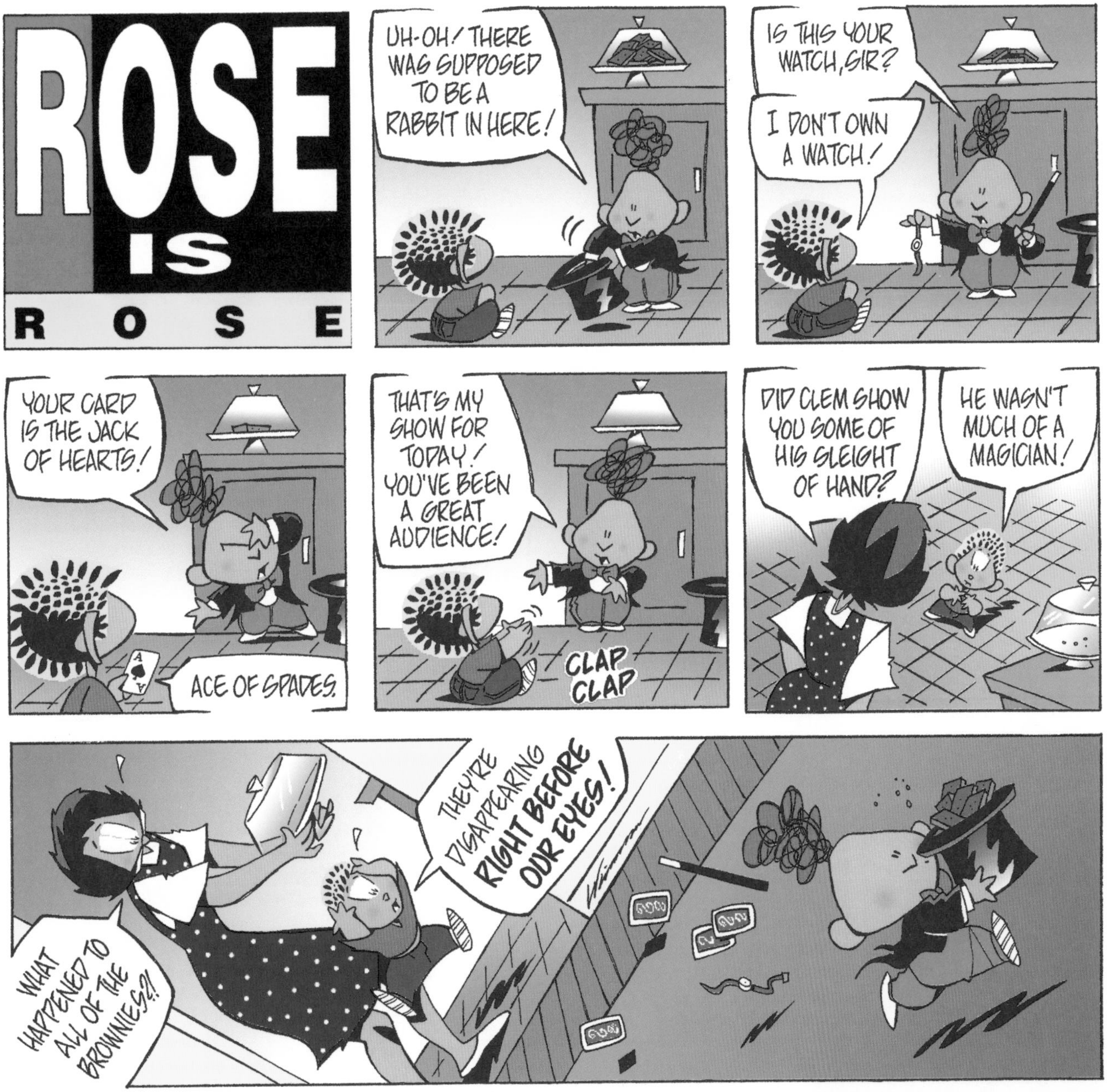
ROSE IS ROSE
UH-OH! THERE WAS SUPPOSED TO BE A RABBIT IN HERE!
IS THIS YOUR WATCH, SIR?
I DON'T OWN A WATCH!
YOUR CARD IS THE JACK OF HEARTS!
ACE OF SPADES.
THAT'S MY SHOW FOR TODAY! YOU'VE BEEN A GREAT AUDIENCE!
CLAP CLAP
DID CLEM SHOW YOU SOME OF HIS SLEIGHT OF HAND?
HE WASN'T MUCH OF A MAGICIAN!
WHAT HAPPENED TO ALL OF THE BROWNIES?!
THEY'RE DISAPPEARING RIGHT BEFORE OUR EYES!

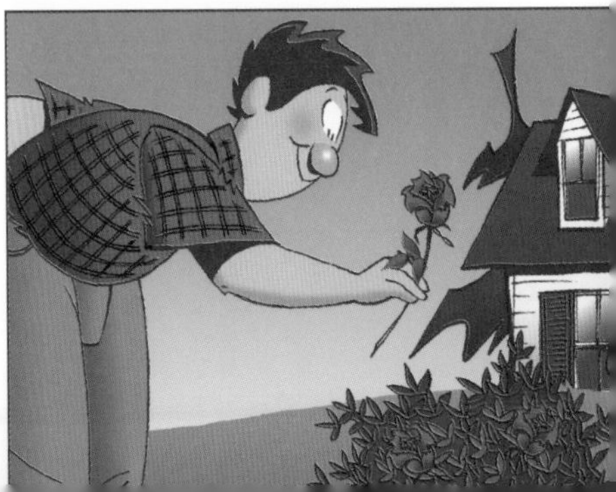

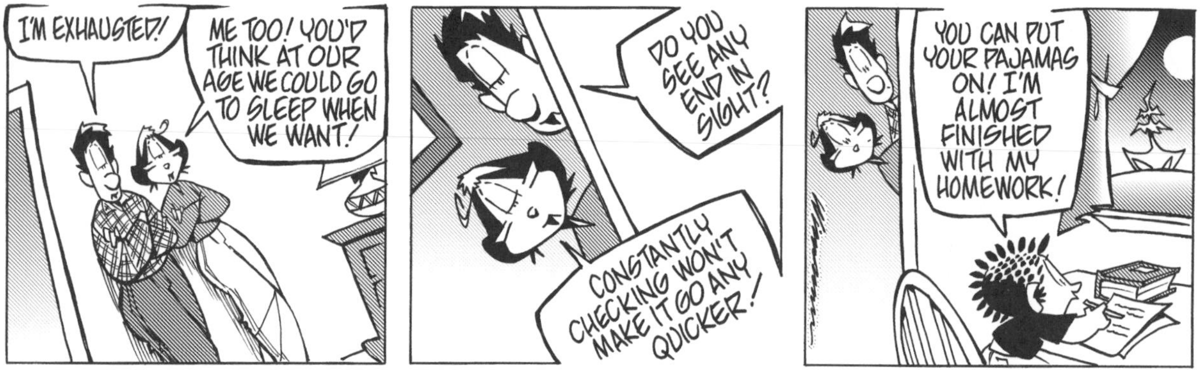
I'M EXHAUSTED!
ME TOO! YOU'D THINK AT OUR AGE WE COULD GO TO SLEEP WHEN WE WANT!
DO YOU SEE ANY END IN SIGHT?
CONSTANTLY CHECKING WON'T MAKE IT GO ANY QUICKER!
YOU CAN PUT YOUR PAJAMAS ON! I'M ALMOST FINISHED WITH MY HOMEWORK!

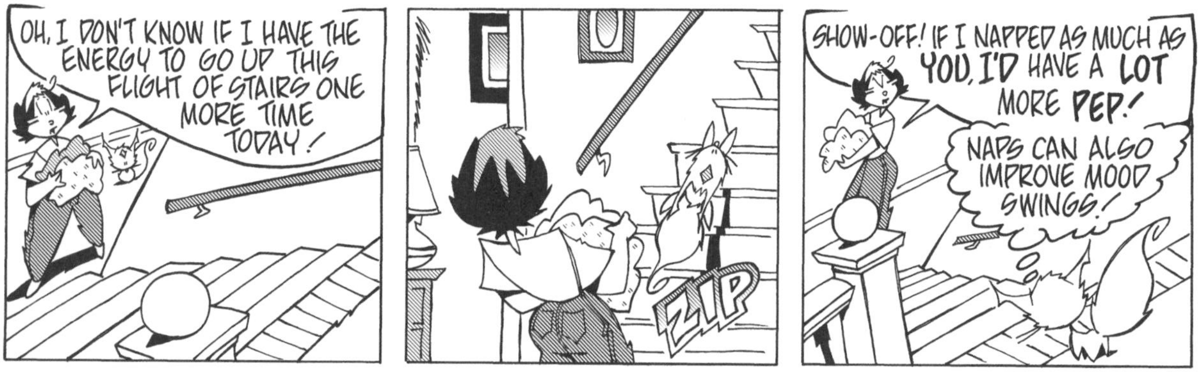
OH, I DON'T KNOW IF I HAVE THE ENERGY TO GO UP THIS FLIGHT OF STAIRS ONE MORE TIME TODAY!
ZIP
SHOW-OFF! IF I NAPPED AS MUCH AS YOU, I'D HAVE A LOT MORE PEP!
NAPS CAN ALSO IMPROVE MOOD SWINGS!

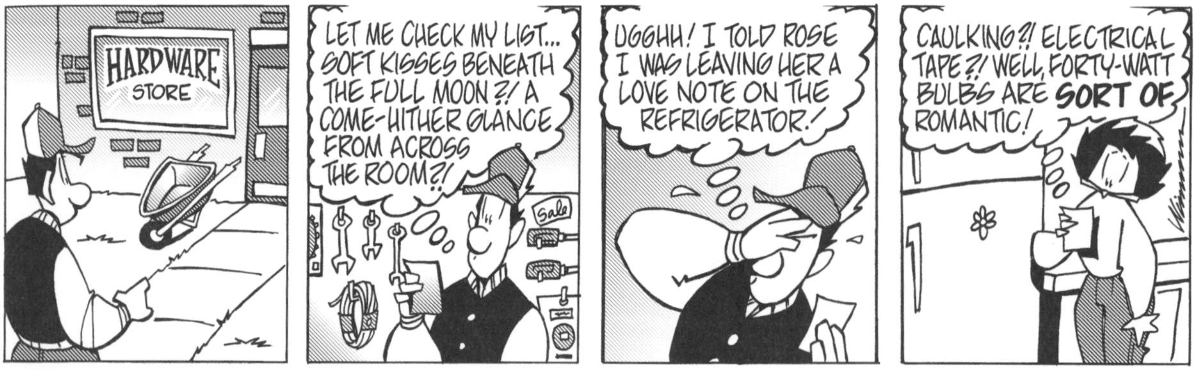
HARDWARE STORE
LET ME CHECK MY LIST... SOFT KISSES BENEATH THE FULL MOON?! A COME-HITHER GLANCE FROM ACROSS THE ROOM?!
SALE
UGGHH! I TOLD ROSE I WAS LEAVING HER A LOVE NOTE ON THE REFRIGERATOR!
CAULKING?! ELECTRICAL TAPE?! WELL, FORTY-WATT BULBS ARE SORT OF ROMANTIC!

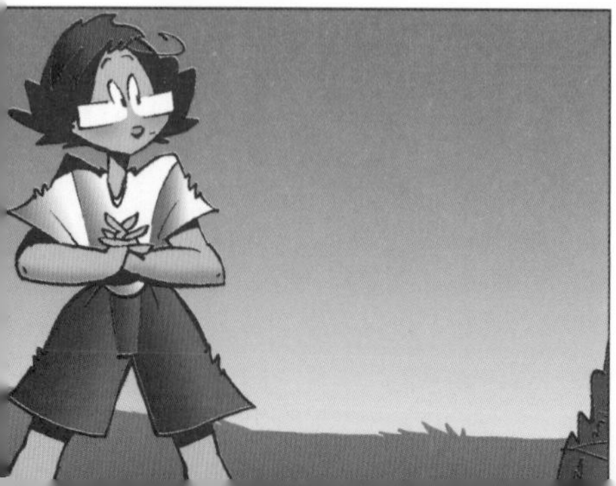

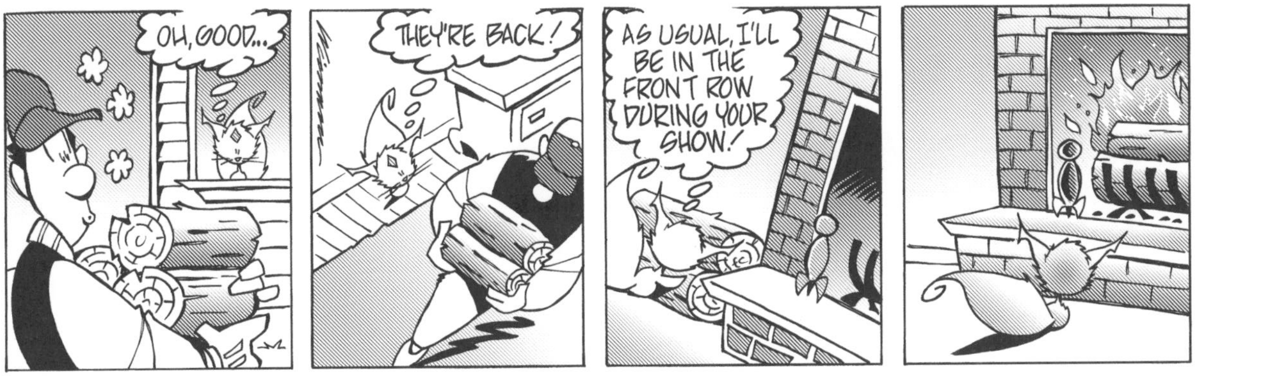
OH, GOOD...
THEY'RE BACK!
AS USUAL, I'LL BE IN THE FRONT ROW DURING YOUR SHOW!

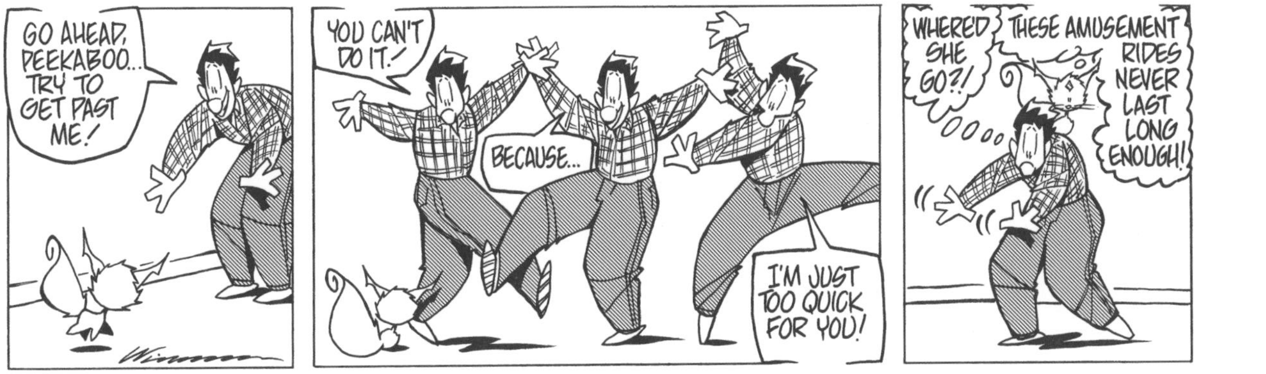
GO AHEAD, PEEKABOO... TRY TO GET PAST ME!
YOU CAN'T DO IT!
BECAUSE...
I'M JUST TOO QUICK FOR YOU!
WHERE'D SHE GO?!
THESE AMUSEMENT RIDES NEVER LAST LONG ENOUGH!

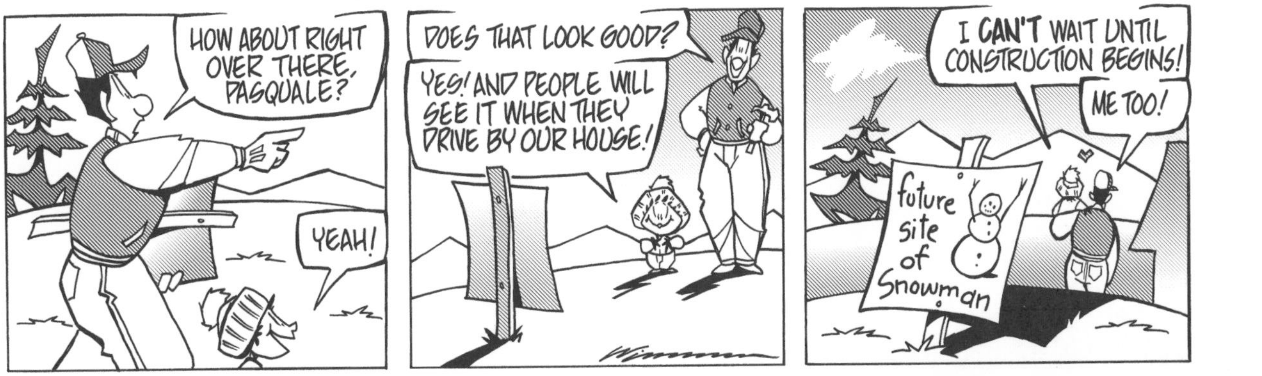
HOW ABOUT RIGHT OVER THERE, PASQUALE?
YEAH!
DOES THAT LOOK GOOD?
YES! AND PEOPLE WILL SEE IT WHEN THEY DRIVE BY OUR HOUSE!
future site of Snowman
I **CAN'T** WAIT UNTIL CONSTRUCTION BEGINS!
ME TOO!

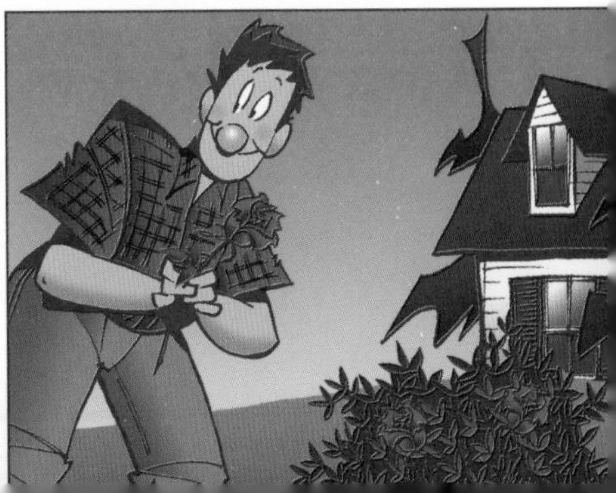

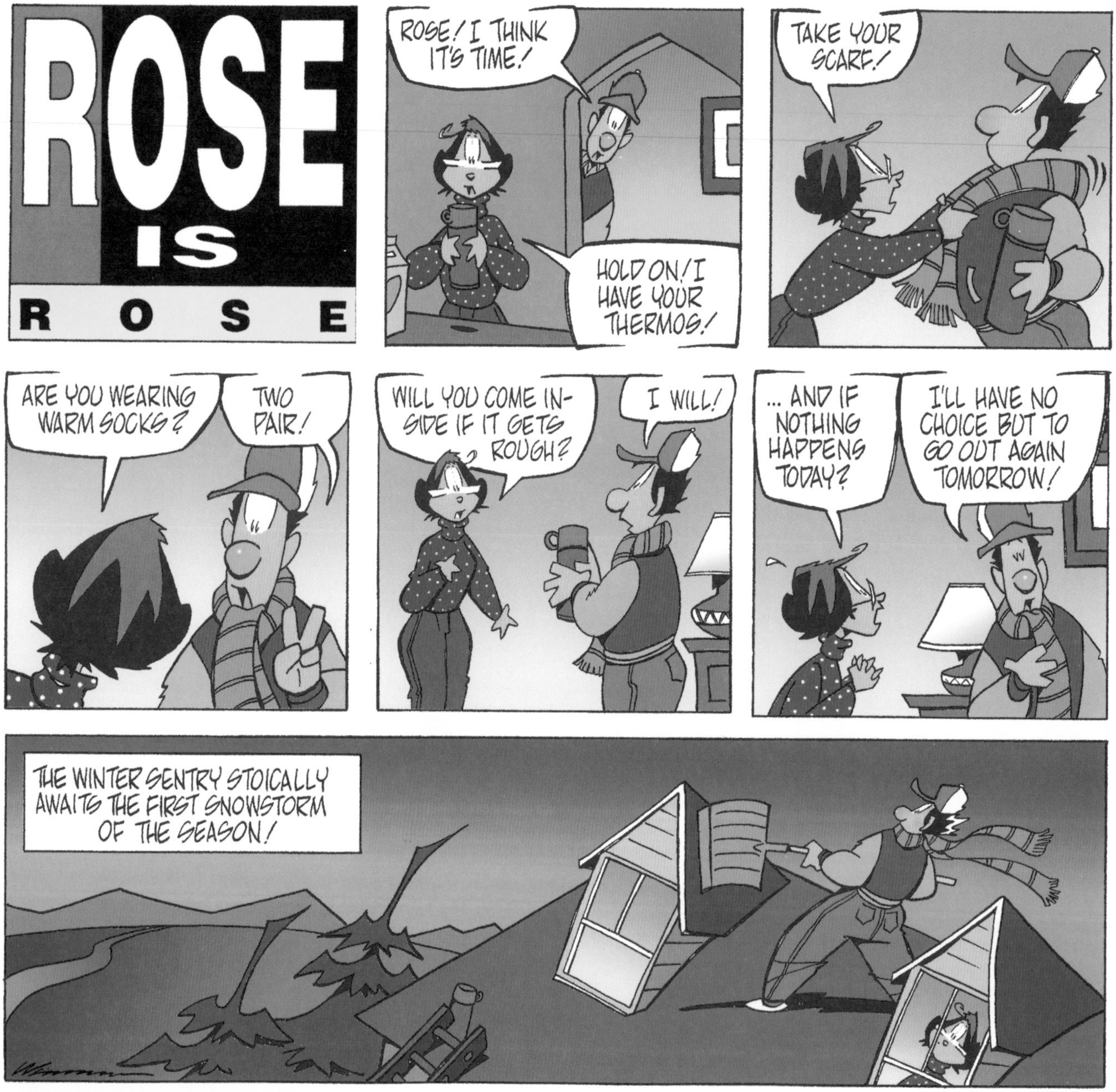
ROSE IS ROSE
ROSE! I THINK IT'S TIME!
HOLD ON! I HAVE YOUR THERMOS!
TAKE YOUR SCARF!
ARE YOU WEARING WARM SOCKS?
TWO PAIR!
WILL YOU COME IN-SIDE IF IT GETS ROUGH?
I WILL!
... AND IF NOTHING HAPPENS TODAY?
I'LL HAVE NO CHOICE BUT TO GO OUT AGAIN TOMORROW!
THE WINTER SENTRY STOICALLY AWAITS THE FIRST SNOWSTORM OF THE SEASON!

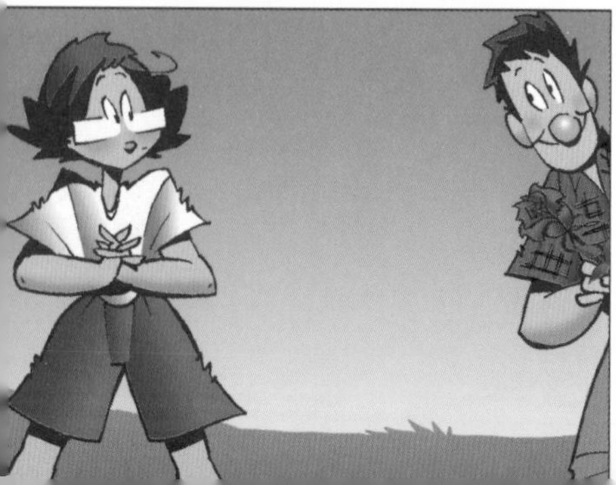

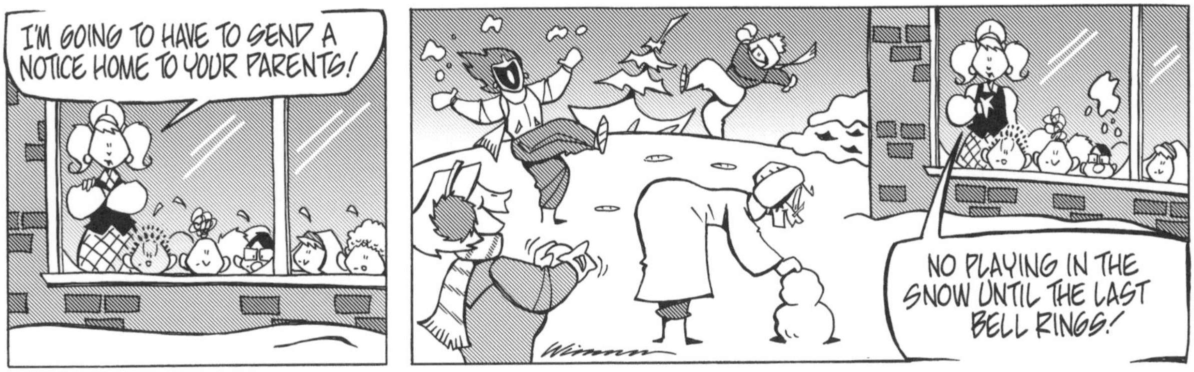
I'M GOING TO HAVE TO SEND A NOTICE HOME TO YOUR PARENTS!
NO PLAYING IN THE SNOW UNTIL THE LAST BELL RINGS!
Wimmer

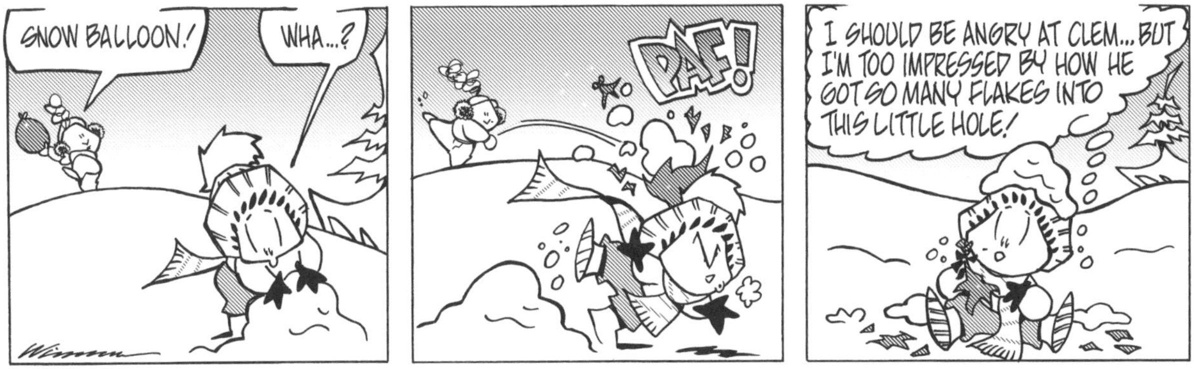
SNOW BALLOON!
WHA...?
PAF!
I SHOULD BE ANGRY AT CLEM...BUT I'M TOO IMPRESSED BY HOW HE GOT SO MANY FLAKES INTO THIS LITTLE HOLE!
Wimmer

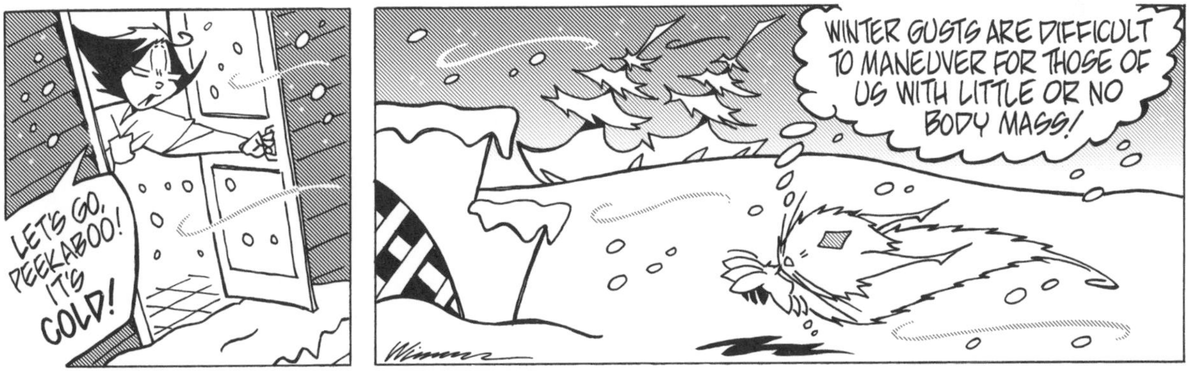
LET'S GO, PEEKABOO! IT'S COLD!
WINTER GUSTS ARE DIFFICULT TO MANEUVER FOR THOSE OF US WITH LITTLE OR NO BODY MASS!
Wimmer

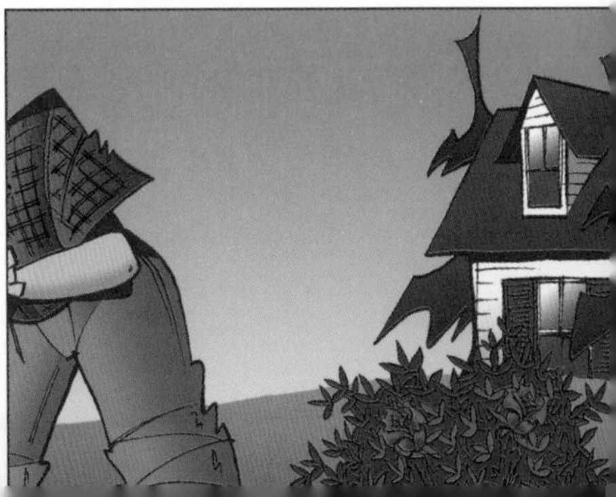

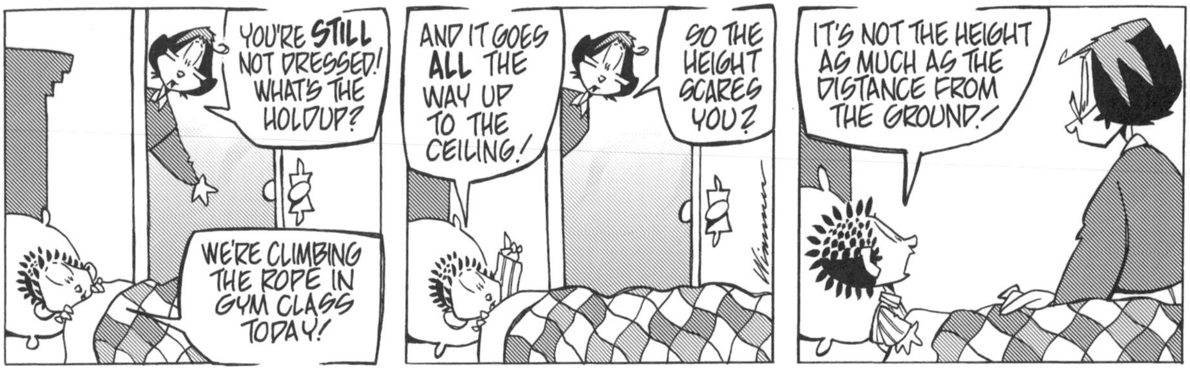
YOU'RE **STILL** NOT DRESSED! WHAT'S THE HOLDUP?
WE'RE CLIMBING THE ROPE IN GYM CLASS TODAY!
AND IT GOES **ALL** THE WAY UP TO THE CEILING!
SO THE HEIGHT SCARES YOU?
IT'S NOT THE HEIGHT AS MUCH AS THE DISTANCE FROM THE GROUND!

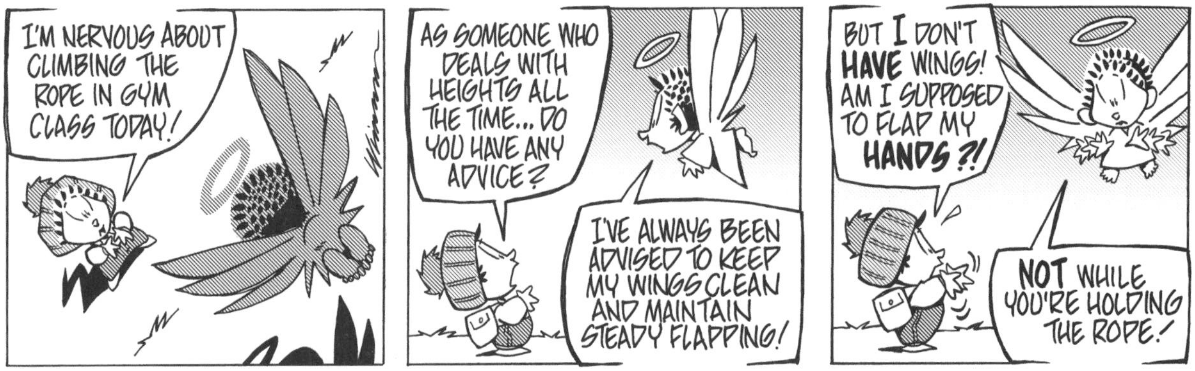
I'M NERVOUS ABOUT CLIMBING THE ROPE IN GYM CLASS TODAY!
AS SOMEONE WHO DEALS WITH HEIGHTS ALL THE TIME... DO YOU HAVE ANY ADVICE?
I'VE ALWAYS BEEN ADVISED TO KEEP MY WINGS CLEAN AND MAINTAIN STEADY FLAPPING!
BUT **I** DON'T **HAVE** WINGS! AM I SUPPOSED TO FLAP MY **HANDS** ?!
NOT WHILE YOU'RE HOLDING THE ROPE!

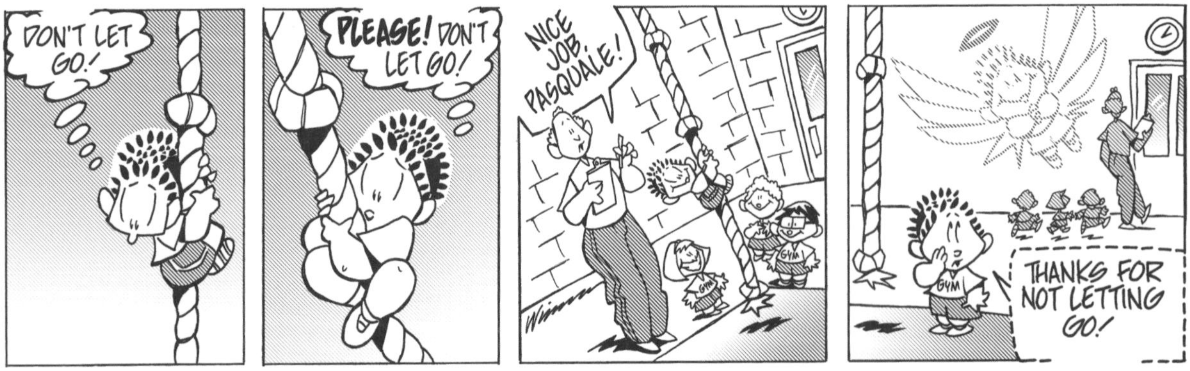
DON'T LET GO!
PLEASE! DON'T LET GO!
NICE JOB, PASQUALE!
THANKS FOR NOT LETTING GO!

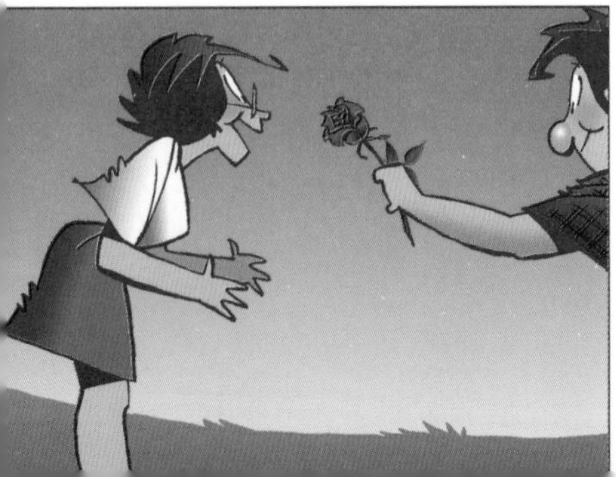

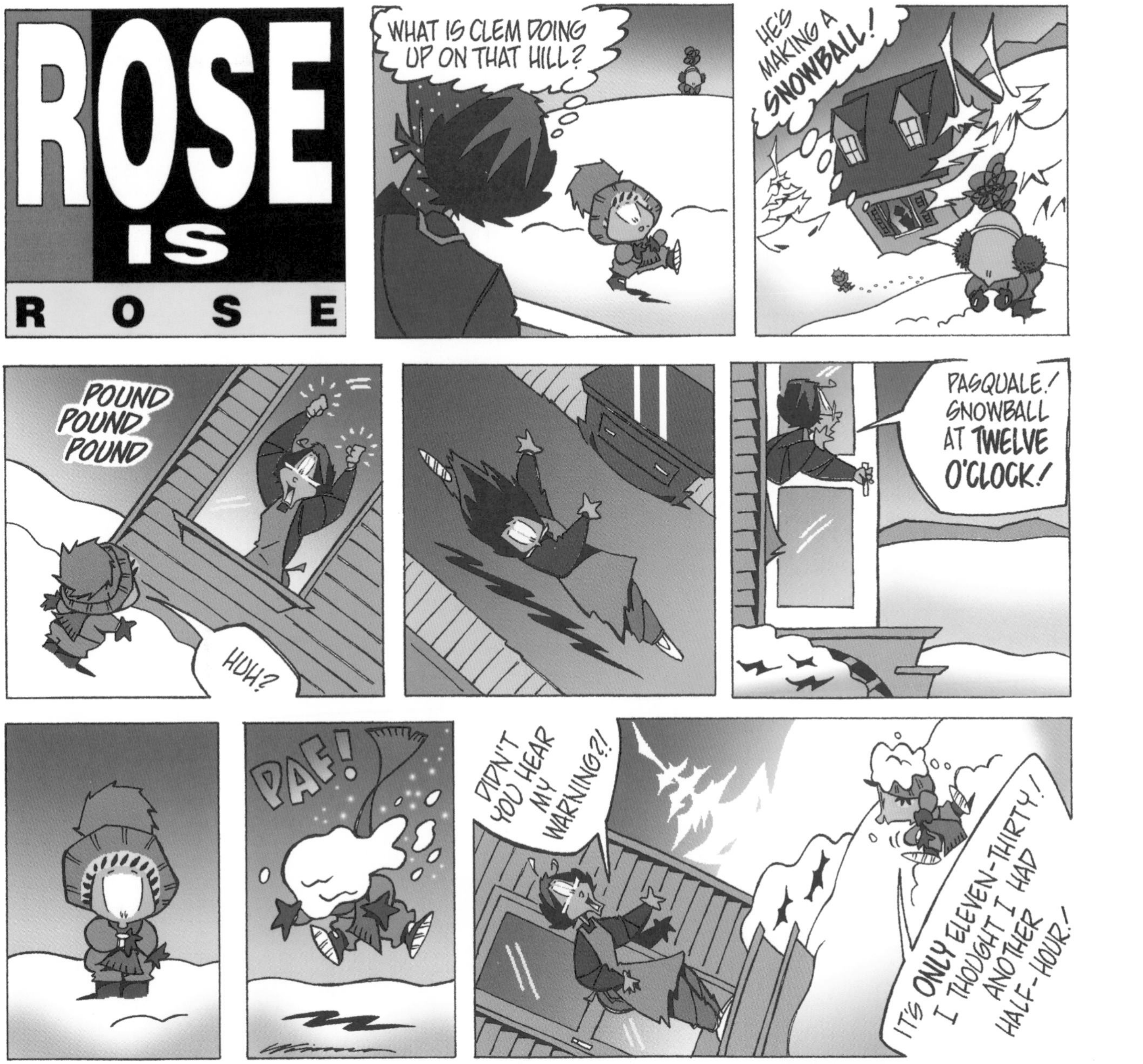
ROSE IS ROSE
WHAT IS CLEM DOING UP ON THAT HILL?
HE'S MAKING A SNOWBALL!
POUND POUND POUND
HUH?
PASQUALE! SNOWBALL AT TWELVE O'CLOCK!
PAF!
DIDN'T YOU HEAR MY WARNING?!
IT'S ONLY ELEVEN-THIRTY! I THOUGHT I HAD ANOTHER HALF-HOUR!

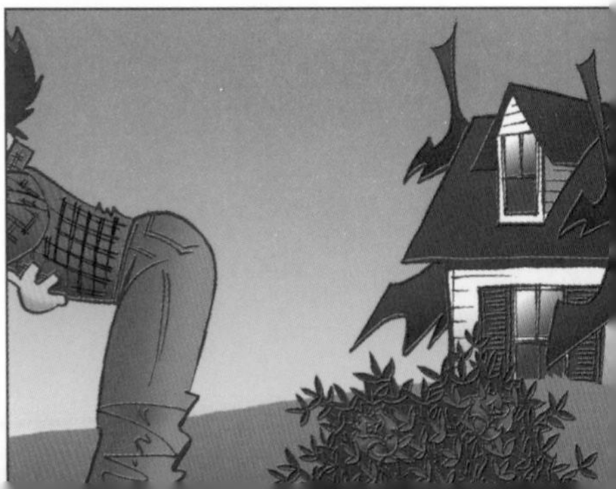

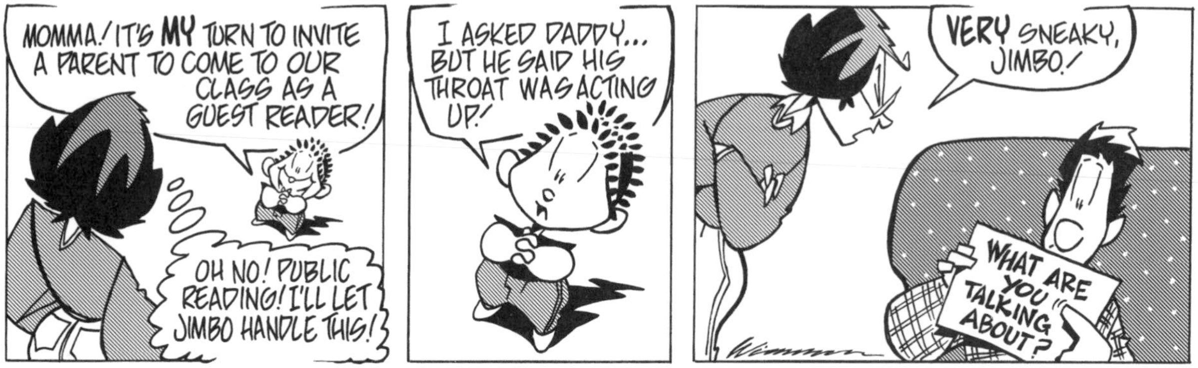
MOMMA! IT'S MY TURN TO INVITE A PARENT TO COME TO OUR CLASS AS A GUEST READER!
OH NO! PUBLIC READING! I'LL LET JIMBO HANDLE THIS!
I ASKED DADDY... BUT HE SAID HIS THROAT WAS ACTING UP!
VERY SNEAKY, JIMBO!
WHAT ARE YOU TALKING ABOUT?

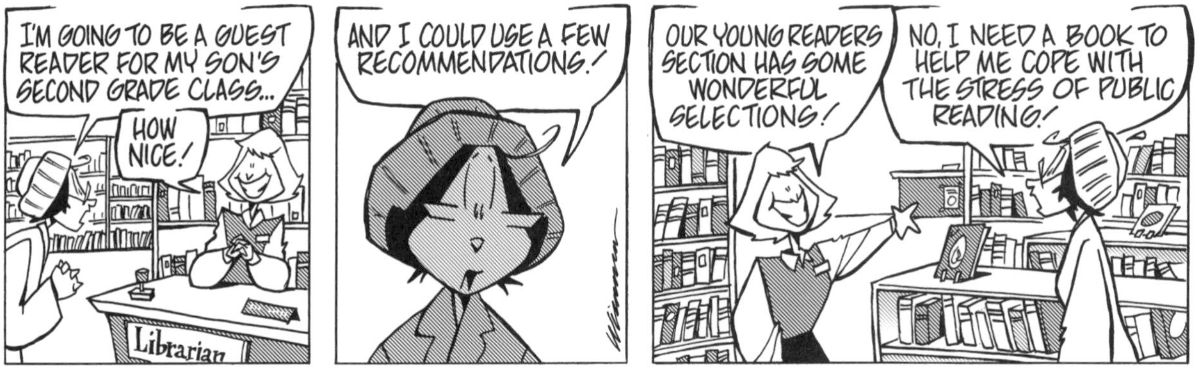
I'M GOING TO BE A GUEST READER FOR MY SON'S SECOND GRADE CLASS...
HOW NICE!
Librarian
AND I COULD USE A FEW RECOMMENDATIONS!
OUR YOUNG READERS SECTION HAS SOME WONDERFUL SELECTIONS!
NO, I NEED A BOOK TO HELP ME COPE WITH THE STRESS OF PUBLIC READING!

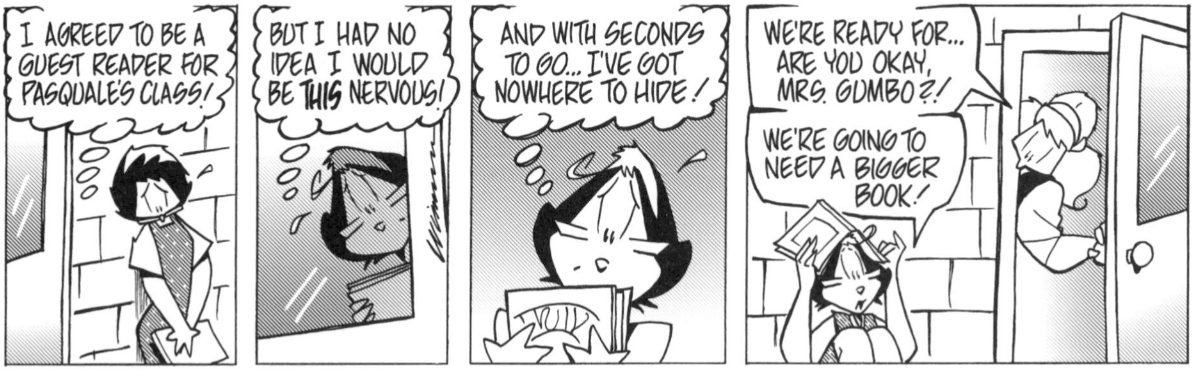
I AGREED TO BE A GUEST READER FOR PASQUALE'S CLASS!
BUT I HAD NO IDEA I WOULD BE THIS NERVOUS!
AND WITH SECONDS TO GO... I'VE GOT NOWHERE TO HIDE!
WE'RE READY FOR... ARE YOU OKAY, MRS. GUMBO?!
WE'RE GOING TO NEED A BIGGER BOOK!

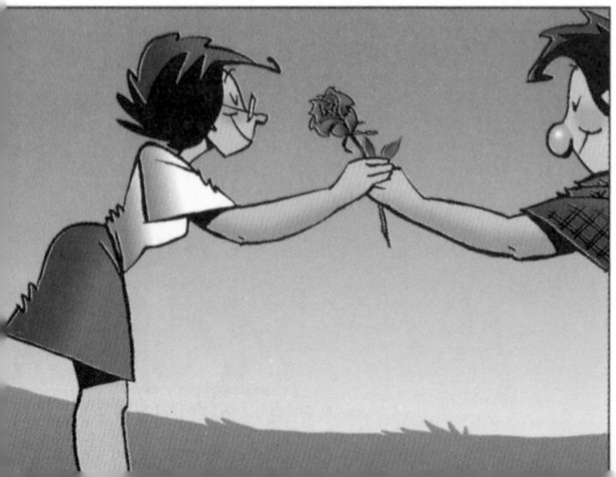

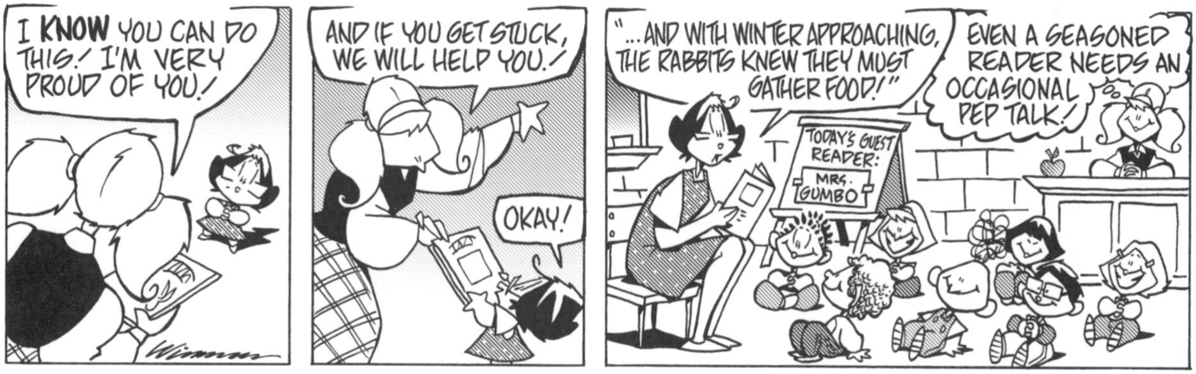
I KNOW YOU CAN DO THIS! I'M VERY PROUD OF YOU!
AND IF YOU GET STUCK, WE WILL HELP YOU.!
OKAY!
"...AND WITH WINTER APPROACHING, THE RABBITS KNEW THEY MUST GATHER FOOD!"
TODAY'S GUEST READER: MRS. GUMBO
EVEN A SEASONED READER NEEDS AN OCCASIONAL PEP TALK!

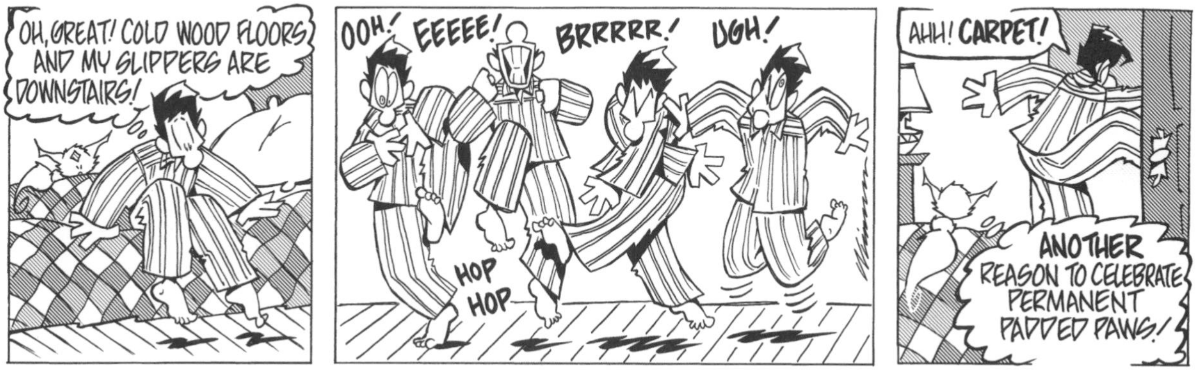
OH, GREAT! COLD WOOD FLOORS AND MY SLIPPERS ARE DOWNSTAIRS!
OOH!
EEEEE!
BRRRRR!
UGH!
HOP
HOP
AHH! CARPET!
ANOTHER REASON TO CELEBRATE PERMANENT PADDED PAWS!

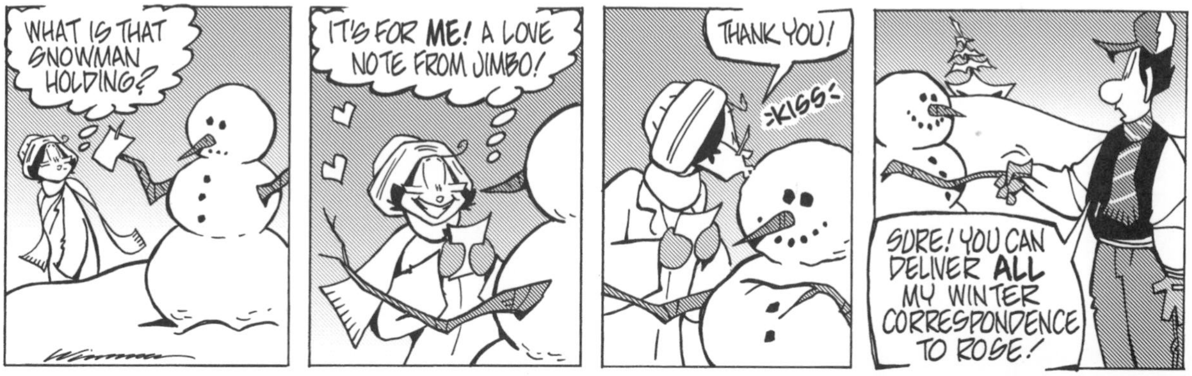
WHAT IS THAT SNOWMAN HOLDING?
IT'S FOR ME! A LOVE NOTE FROM JIMBO!
THANK YOU!
KISS
SURE! YOU CAN DELIVER ALL MY WINTER CORRESPONDENCE TO ROSE!

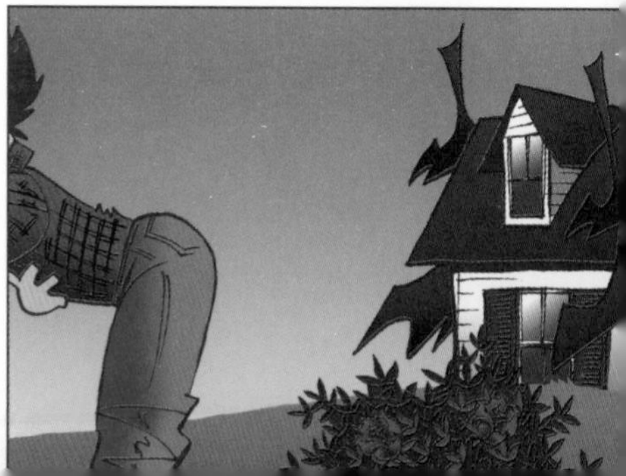

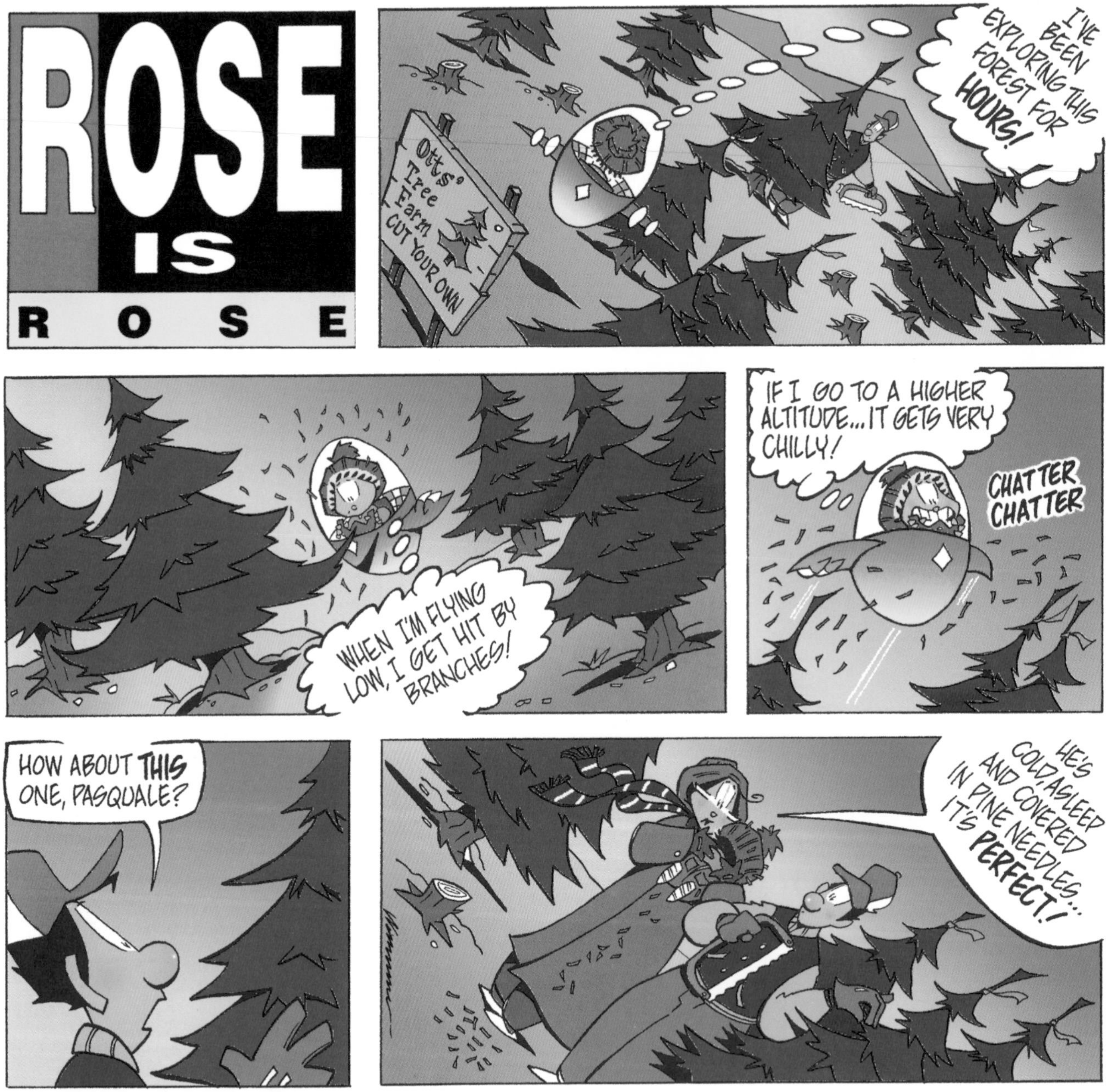
ROSE IS ROSE
Otts' Tree Farm
CUT YOUR OWN
I'VE BEEN EXPLORING THIS FOREST FOR HOURS!
WHEN I'M FLYING LOW, I GET HIT BY BRANCHES!
IF I GO TO A HIGHER ALTITUDE... IT GETS VERY CHILLY!
CHATTER CHATTER
HOW ABOUT THIS ONE, PASQUALE?
HE'S COLD, ASLEEP AND COVERED IN PINE NEEDLES... IT'S PERFECT!

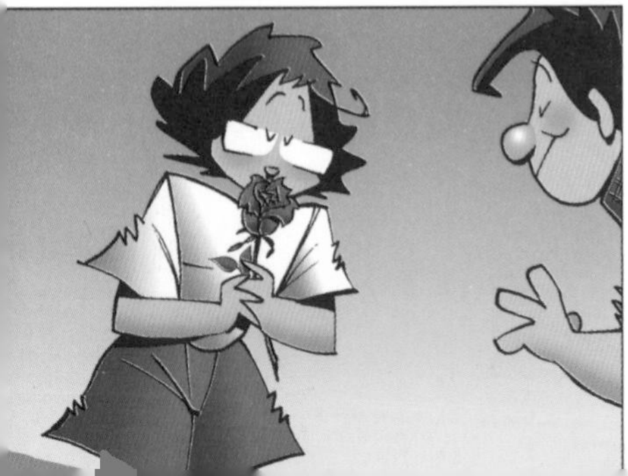

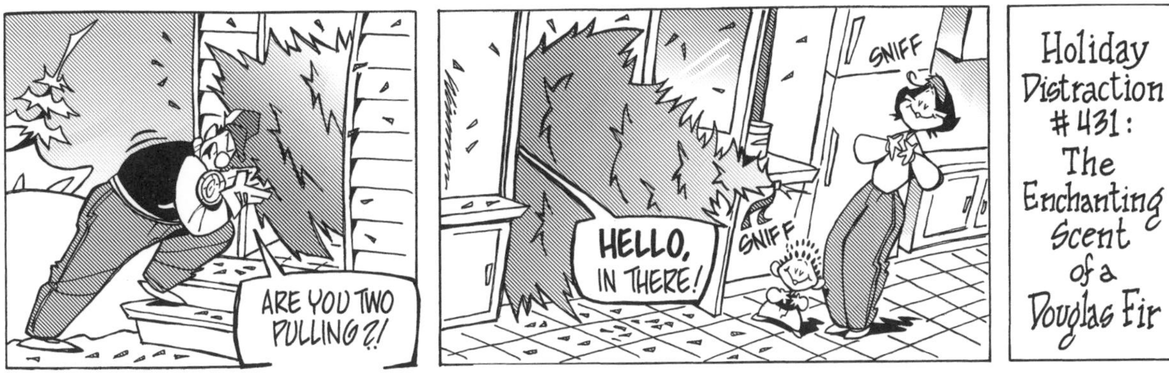
ARE YOU TWO PULLING?!
HELLO, IN THERE!
SNIFF
SNIFF
Holiday Distraction #431: The Enchanting Scent of a Douglas Fir

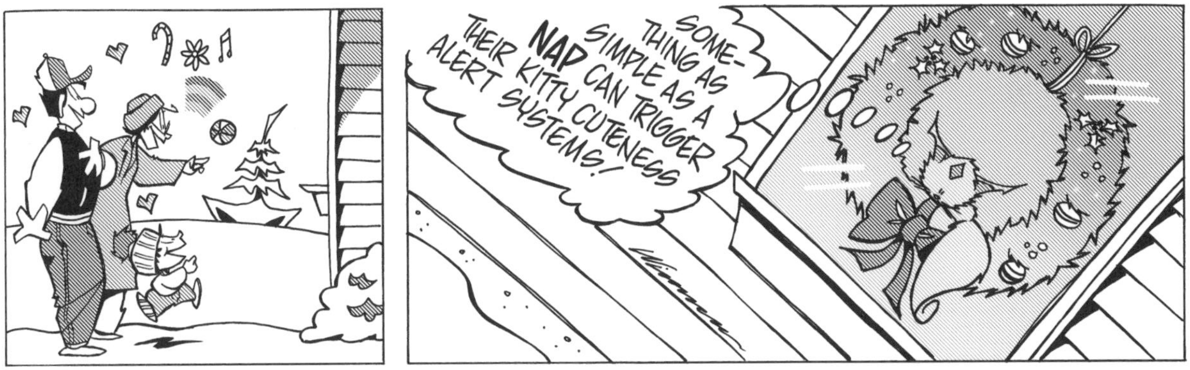
SOME-THING AS SIMPLE AS A NAP CAN TRIGGER THEIR KITTY CUTENESS ALERT SYSTEMS!

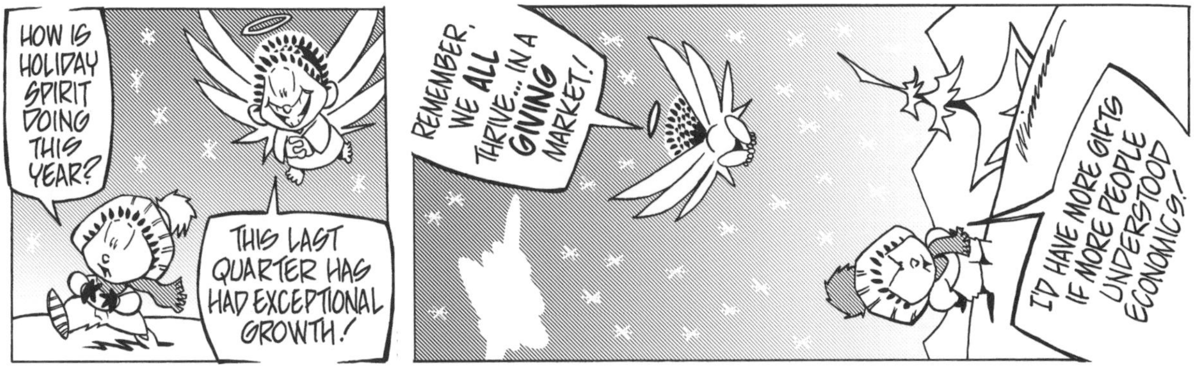
HOW IS HOLIDAY SPIRIT DOING THIS YEAR?
THIS LAST QUARTER HAS HAD EXCEPTIONAL GROWTH!
REMEMBER. WE ALL THRIVE... IN A GIVING MARKET!
I'D HAVE MORE GIFTS IF MORE PEOPLE UNDERSTOOD ECONOMICS!

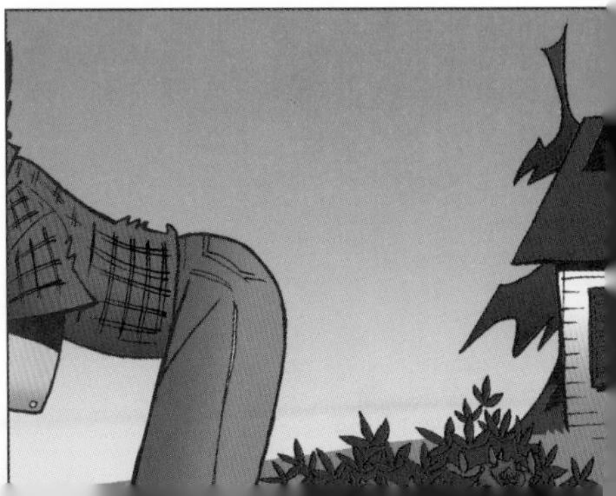

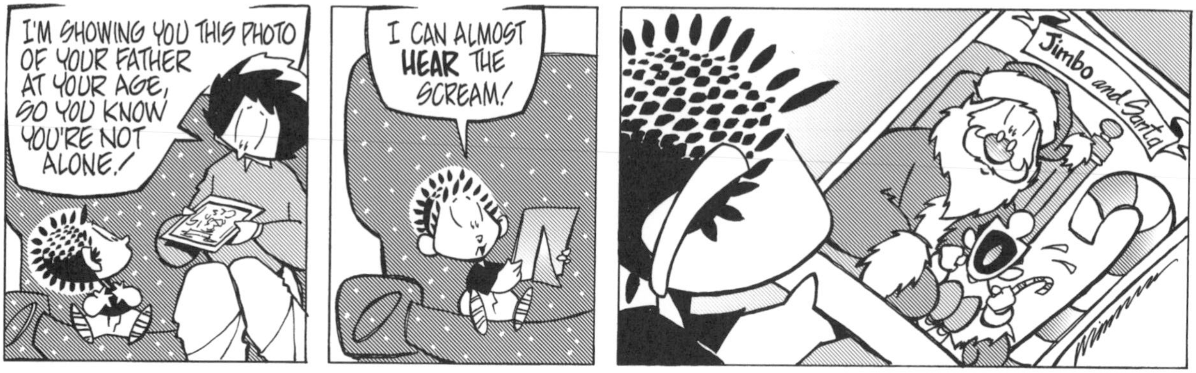
I'M SHOWING YOU THIS PHOTO OF YOUR FATHER AT YOUR AGE, SO YOU KNOW YOU'RE NOT ALONE!
I CAN ALMOST **HEAR** THE SCREAM!
Jimbo and Santa

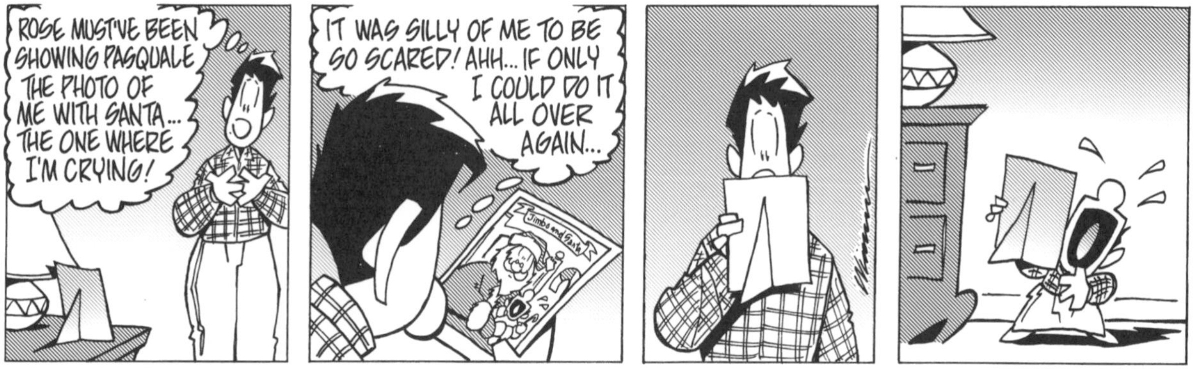
ROSE MUST'VE BEEN SHOWING PASQUALE THE PHOTO OF ME WITH SANTA... THE ONE WHERE I'M CRYING!
IT WAS SILLY OF ME TO BE SO SCARED! AHH... IF ONLY I COULD DO IT ALL OVER AGAIN...

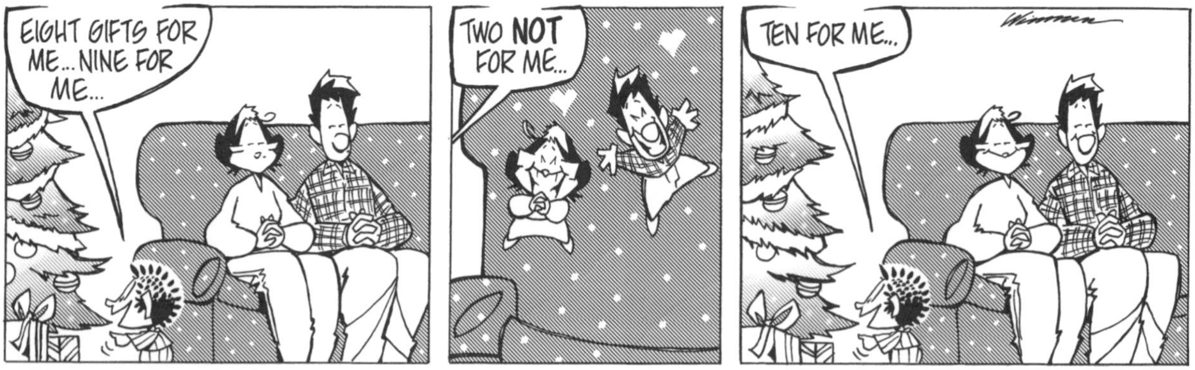
EIGHT GIFTS FOR ME... NINE FOR ME...
TWO **NOT** FOR ME...
TEN FOR ME...

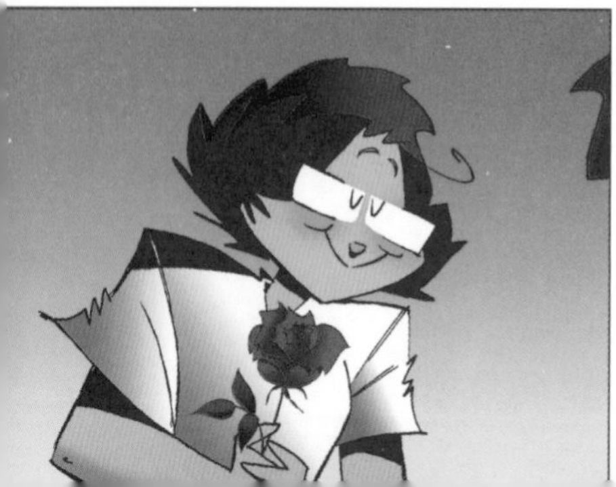

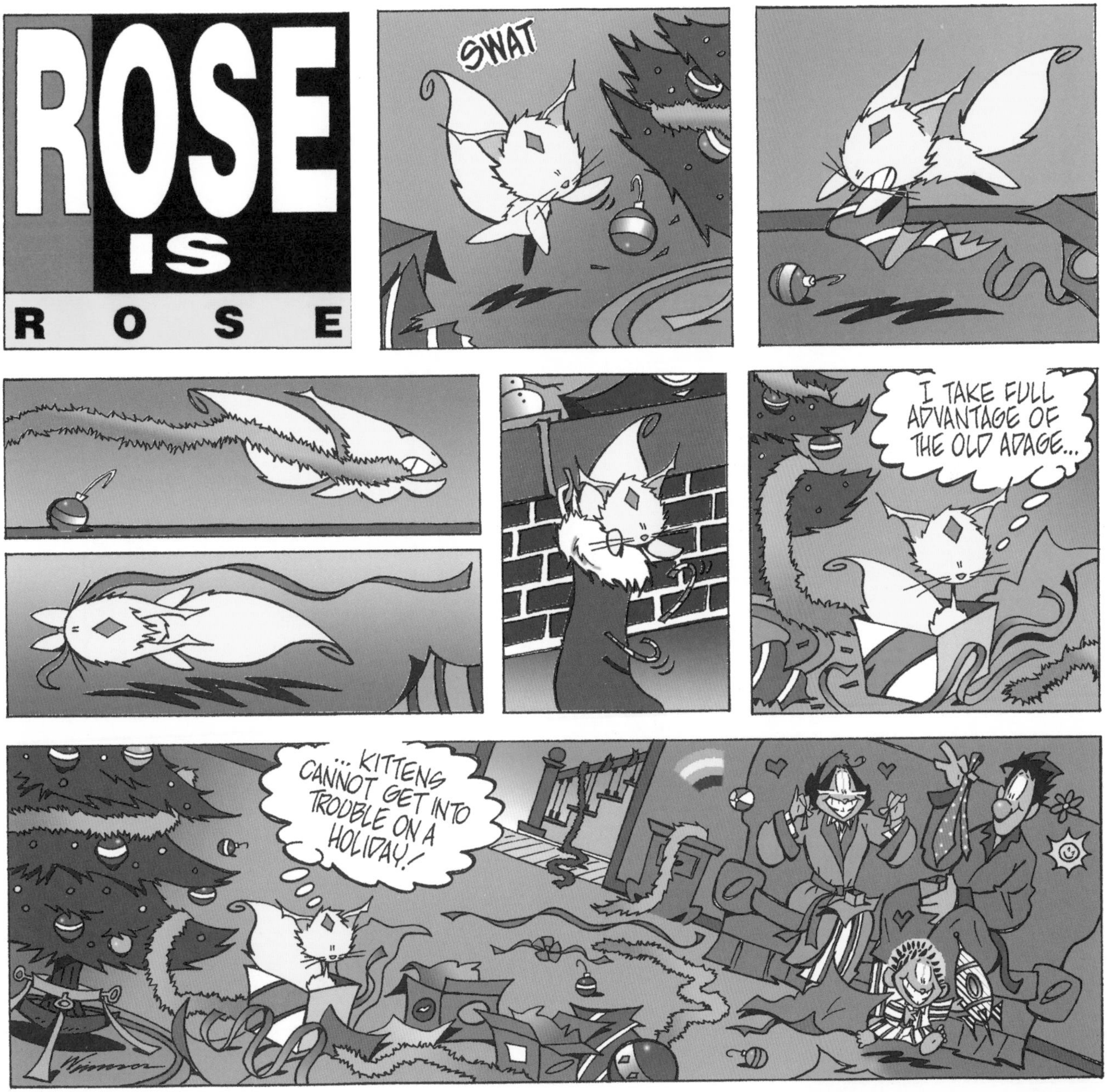
ROSE IS ROSE
SWAT
I TAKE FULL ADVANTAGE OF THE OLD ADAGE...
...KITTENS CANNOT GET INTO TROUBLE ON A HOLIDAY!

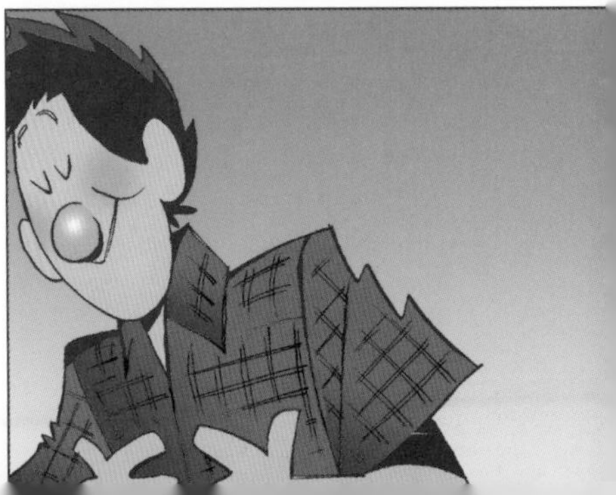

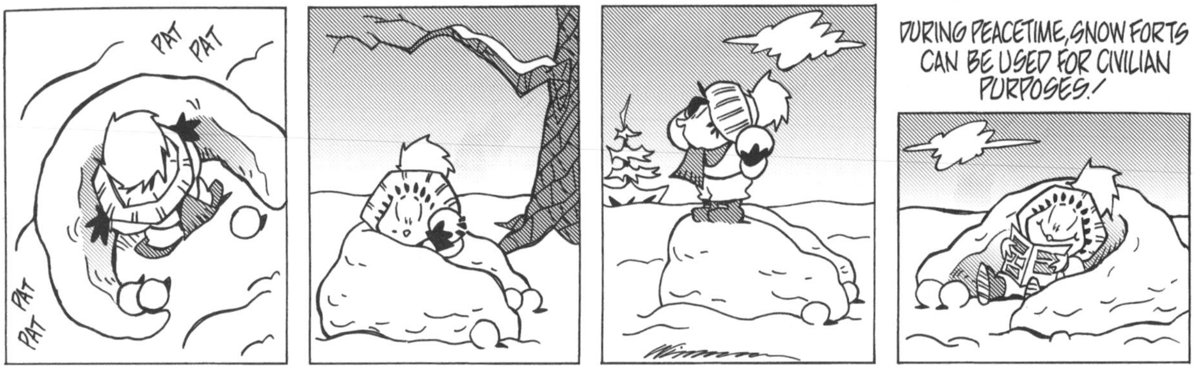
PAT PAT
PAT PAT
DURING PEACETIME, SNOW FORTS CAN BE USED FOR CIVILIAN PURPOSES!

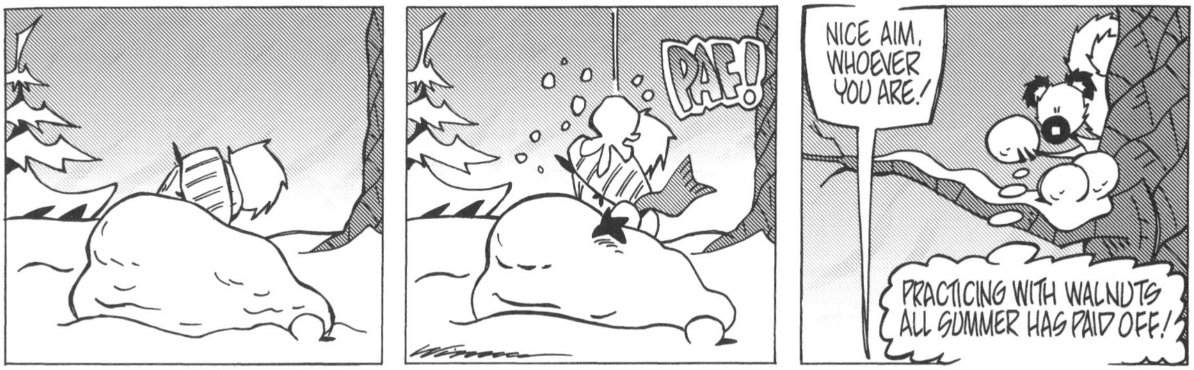
PAF!
NICE AIM, WHOEVER YOU ARE!
PRACTICING WITH WALNUTS ALL SUMMER HAS PAID OFF!

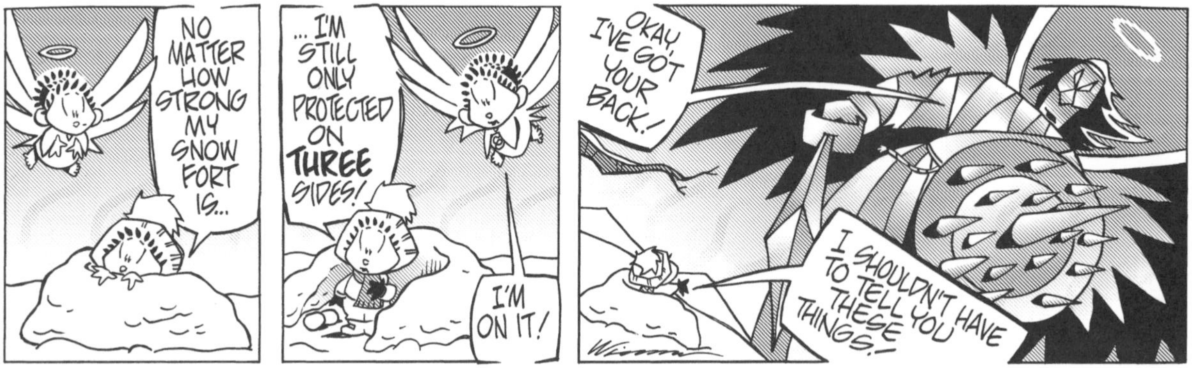
NO MATTER HOW STRONG MY SNOW FORT IS...
...I'M STILL ONLY PROTECTED ON **THREE** SIDES!
I'M ON IT!
OKAY, I'VE GOT YOUR BACK!
I SHOULDN'T HAVE TO TELL YOU THESE THINGS!

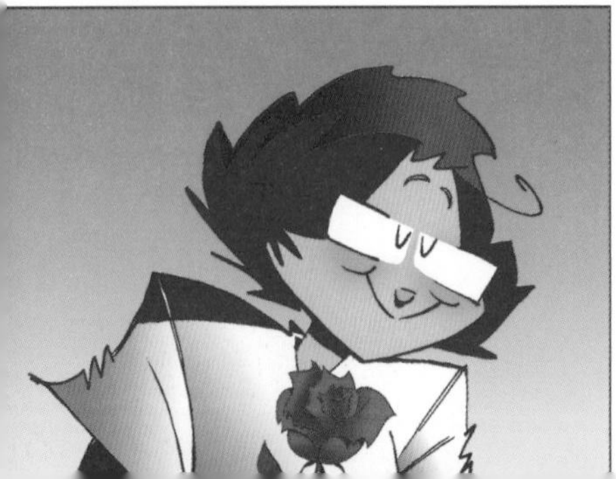

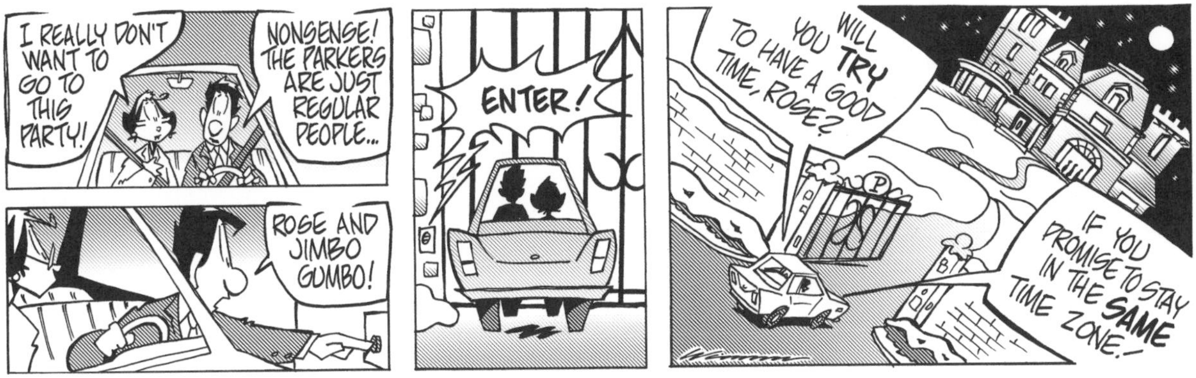
I REALLY DON'T WANT TO GO TO THIS PARTY!
NONSENSE! THE PARKERS ARE JUST REGULAR PEOPLE...
ROSE AND JIMBO GUMBO!
ENTER!
WILL YOU TRY TO HAVE A GOOD TIME, ROSE?
IF YOU PROMISE TO STAY IN THE SAME TIME ZONE!

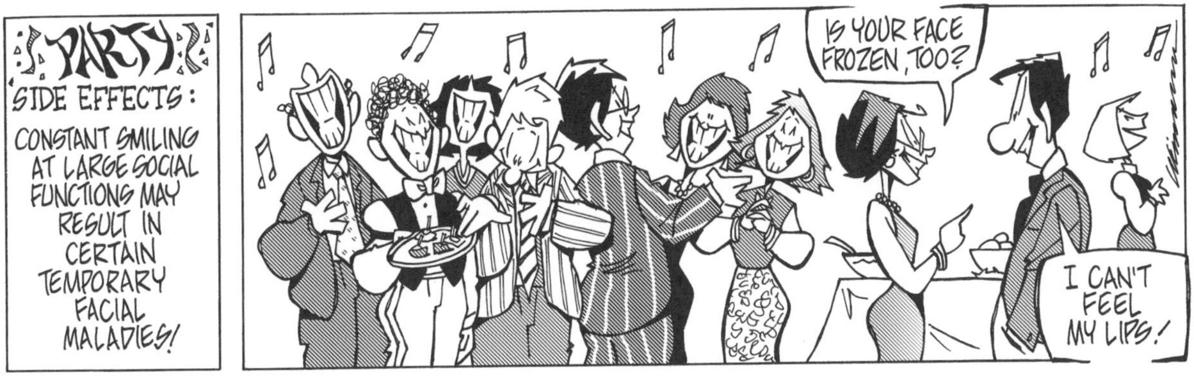
PARTY
SIDE EFFECTS:
CONSTANT SMILING AT LARGE SOCIAL FUNCTIONS MAY RESULT IN CERTAIN TEMPORARY FACIAL MALADIES!
IS YOUR FACE FROZEN, TOO?
I CAN'T FEEL MY LIPS!

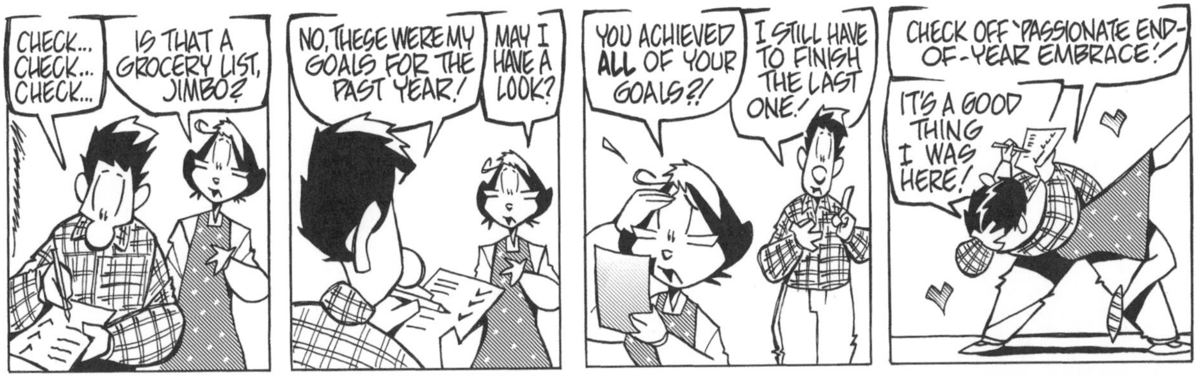
CHECK... CHECK... CHECK...
IS THAT A GROCERY LIST, JIMBO?
NO, THESE WERE MY GOALS FOR THE PAST YEAR!
MAY I HAVE A LOOK?
YOU ACHIEVED ALL OF YOUR GOALS?!
I STILL HAVE TO FINISH THE LAST ONE!
CHECK OFF 'PASSIONATE END-OF-YEAR EMBRACE'!
IT'S A GOOD THING I WAS HERE!

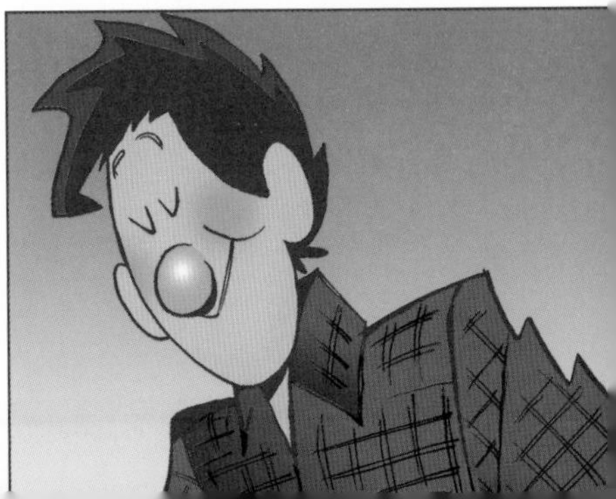

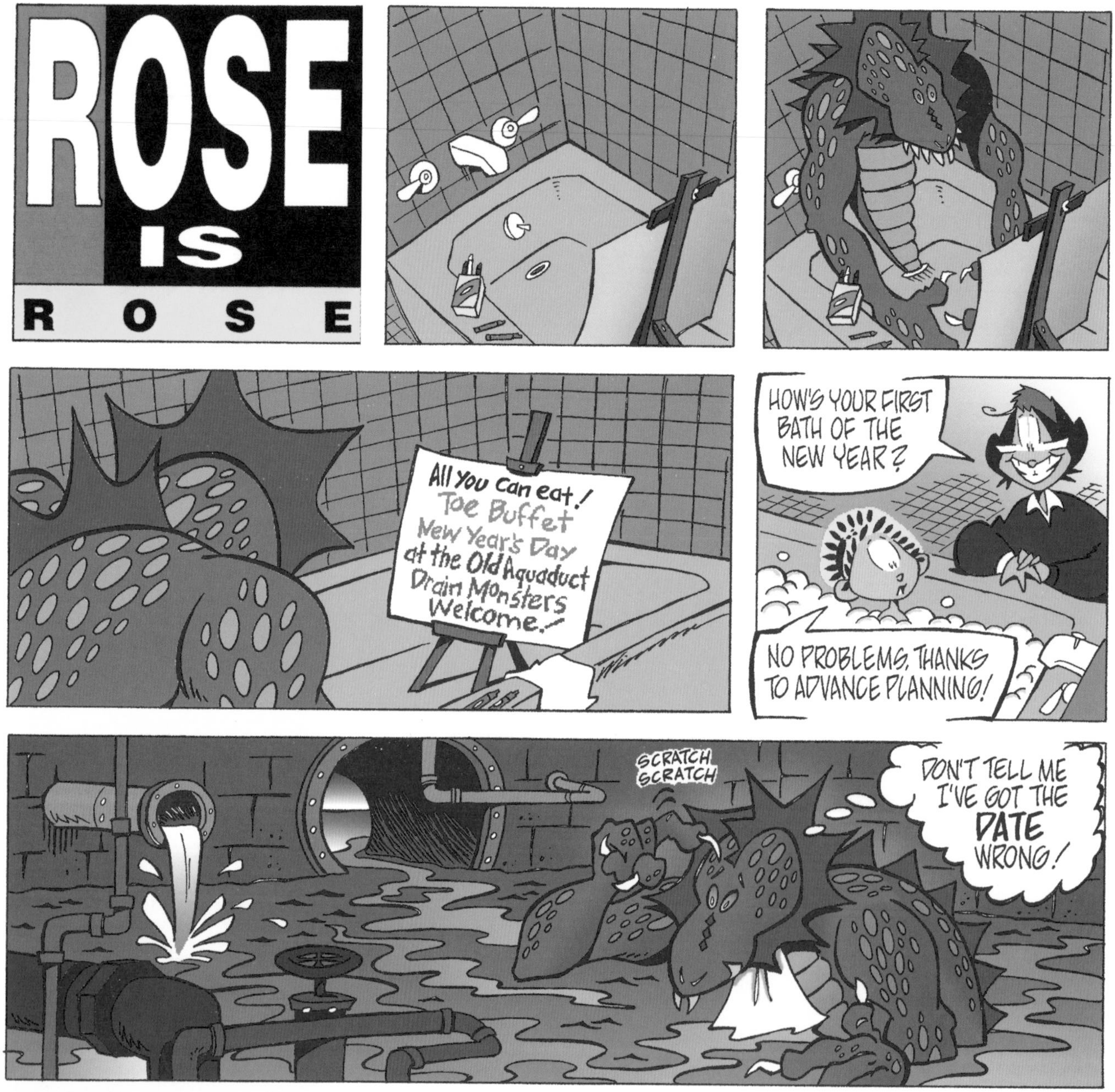
ROSE IS ROSE
All You Can eat!
Toe Buffet
New Year's Day
at the Old Aquaduct
Drain Monsters
Welcome.!
HOW'S YOUR FIRST BATH OF THE NEW YEAR?
NO PROBLEMS, THANKS TO ADVANCE PLANNING!
SCRATCH SCRATCH
DON'T TELL ME I'VE GOT THE DATE WRONG!

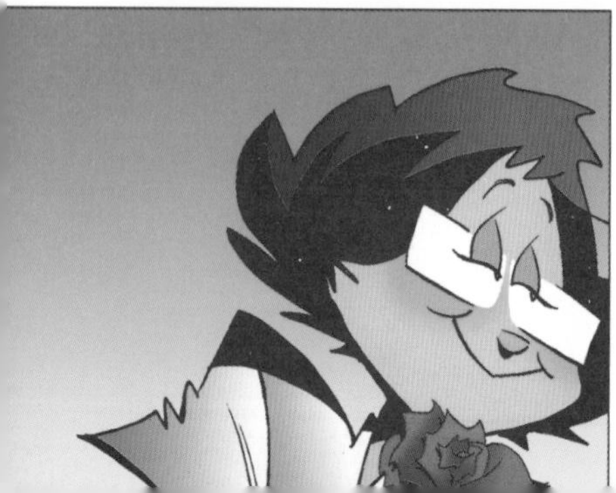

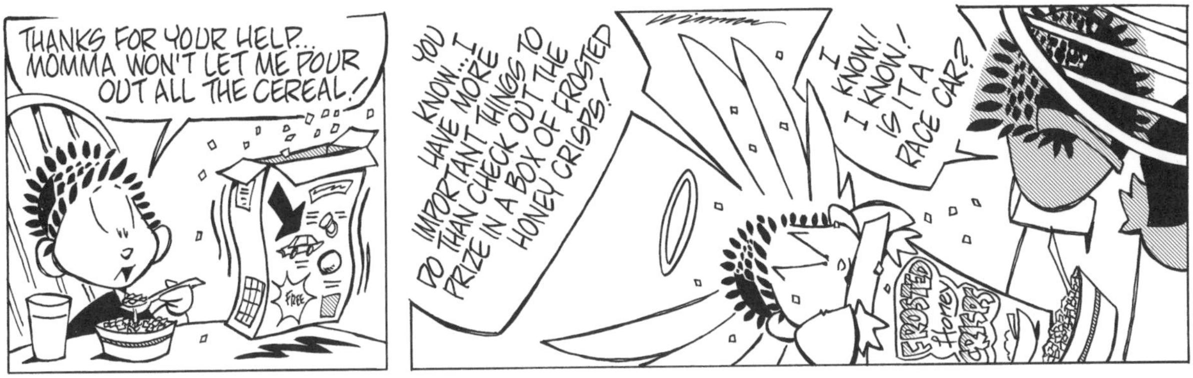
THANKS FOR YOUR HELP... MOMMA WON'T LET ME POUR OUT ALL THE CEREAL!
YOU KNOW... I HAVE MORE IMPORTANT THINGS TO DO THAN CHECK OUT THE PRIZE IN A BOX OF FROSTED HONEY CRISPS!
I KNOW! I KNOW! IS IT A RACE CAR?
FROSTED Honey CRISPS

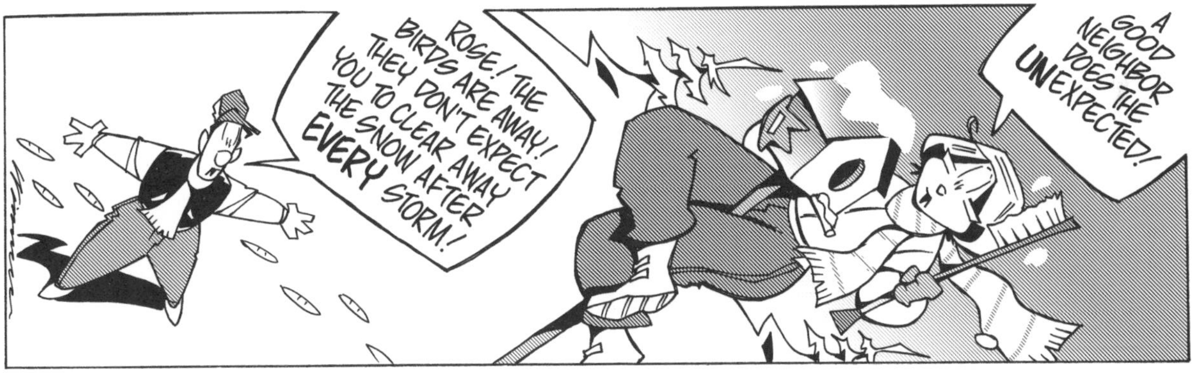
ROSE! THE BIRDS ARE AWAY! THEY DON'T EXPECT YOU TO CLEAR AWAY THE SNOW AFTER **EVERY** STORM!
A GOOD NEIGHBOR DOES THE **UN**EXPECTED!

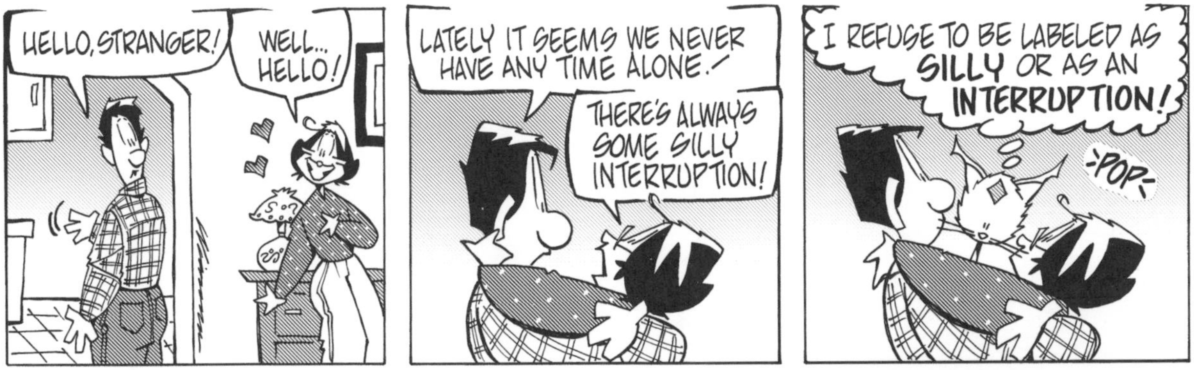
HELLO, STRANGER!
WELL... HELLO!
LATELY IT SEEMS WE NEVER HAVE ANY TIME ALONE.
THERE'S ALWAYS SOME SILLY INTERRUPTION!
I REFUSE TO BE LABELED AS **SILLY** OR AS AN **INTERRUPTION!**
POP

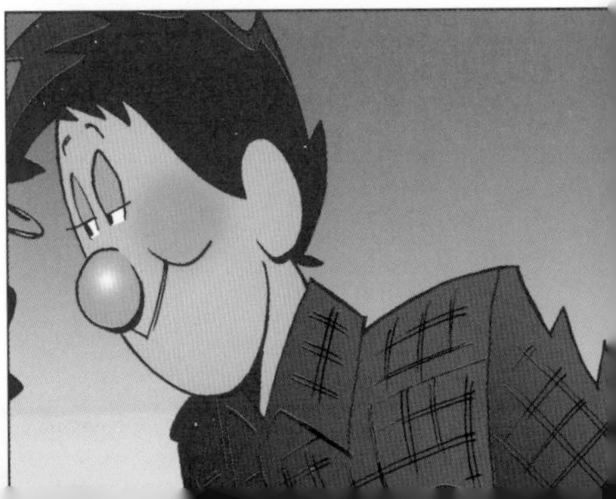

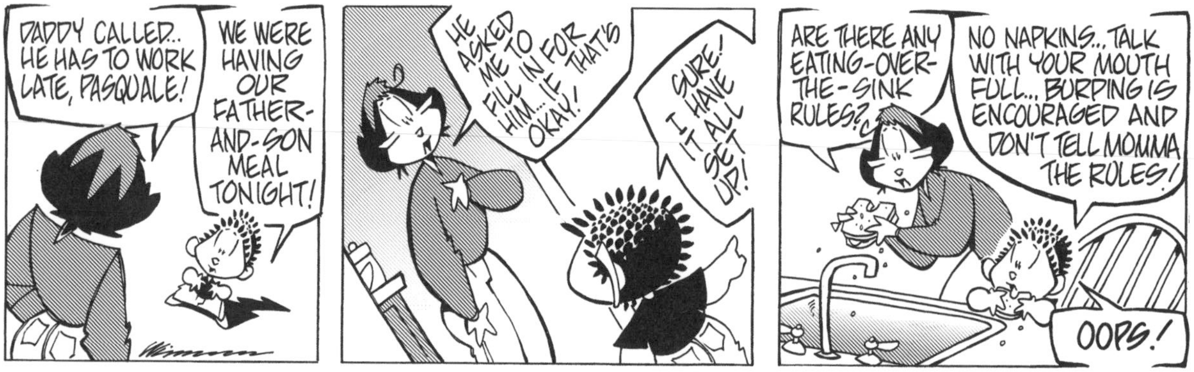
DADDY CALLED.. HE HAS TO WORK LATE, PASQUALE!
WE WERE HAVING OUR FATHER-AND-SON MEAL TONIGHT!
HE ASKED ME TO FILL IN FOR HIM... IF THAT'S OKAY!
SURE! I HAVE IT ALL SET UP!
ARE THERE ANY EATING-OVER-THE-SINK RULES?
NO NAPKINS... TALK WITH YOUR MOUTH FULL... BURPING IS ENCOURAGED AND DON'T TELL MOMMA THE RULES!
OOPS!

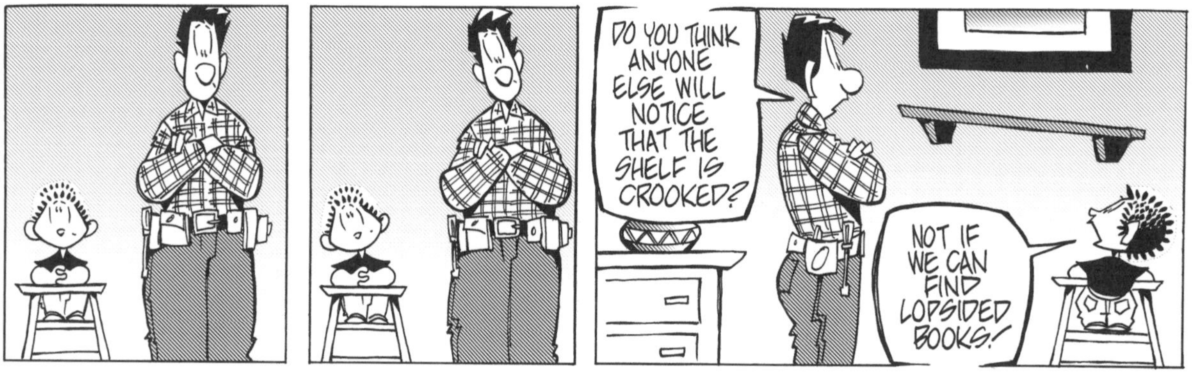
DO YOU THINK ANYONE ELSE WILL NOTICE THAT THE SHELF IS CROOKED?
NOT IF WE CAN FIND LOPSIDED BOOKS!

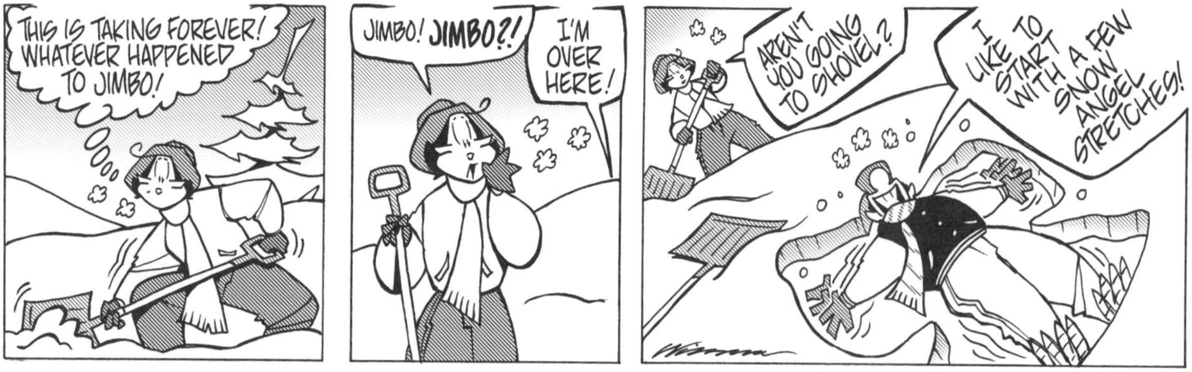
THIS IS TAKING FOREVER! WHATEVER HAPPENED TO JIMBO!
JIMBO! **JIMBO?!**
I'M OVER HERE!
AREN'T YOU GOING TO SHOVEL?
I LIKE TO START WITH A FEW SNOW ANGEL STRETCHES!

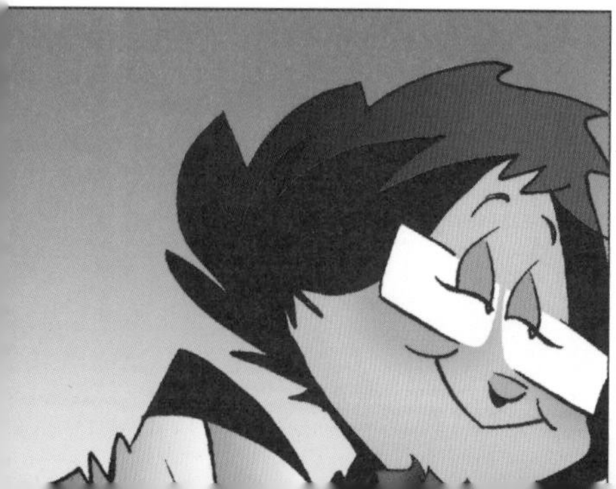

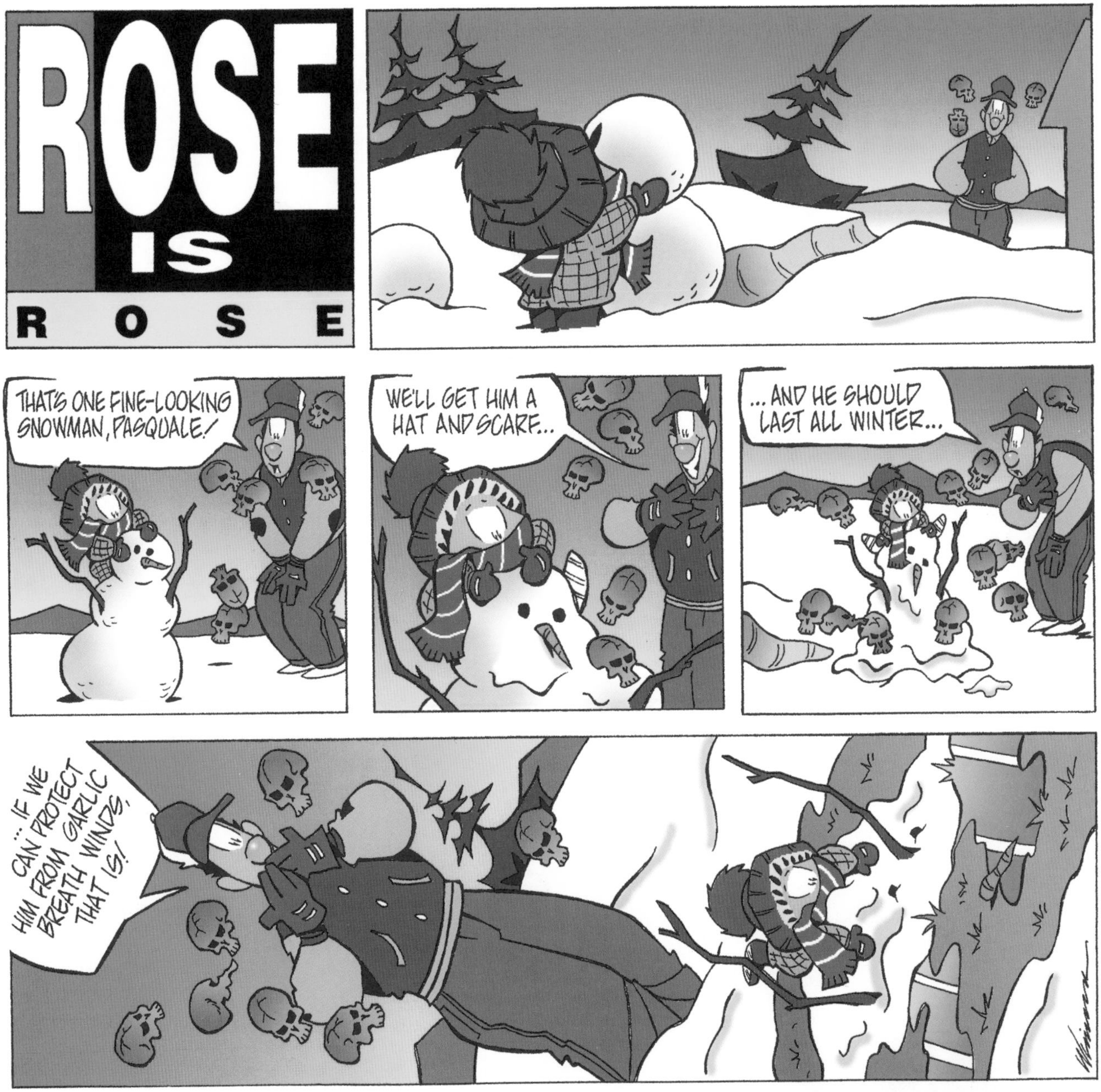
ROSE IS ROSE
THAT'S ONE FINE-LOOKING SNOWMAN, PASQUALE!
WE'LL GET HIM A HAT AND SCARF...
...AND HE SHOULD LAST ALL WINTER...
...IF WE CAN PROTECT HIM FROM GARLIC BREATH WINDS, THAT IS!

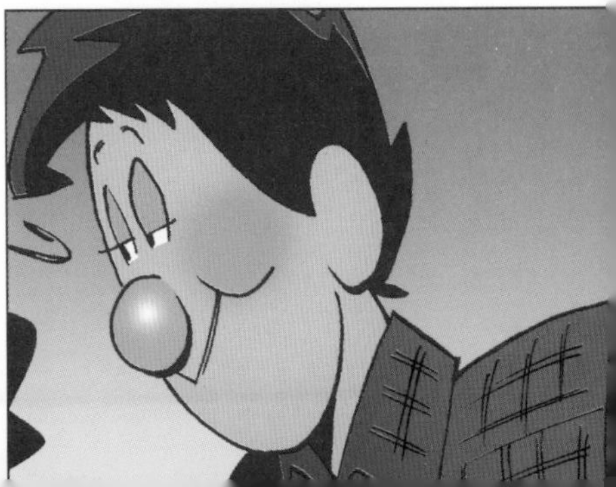

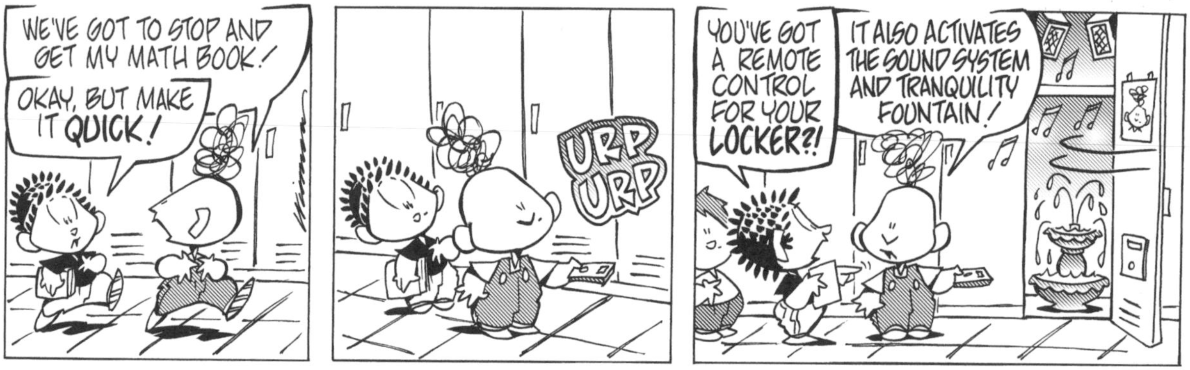
WE'VE GOT TO STOP AND GET MY MATH BOOK!
OKAY, BUT MAKE IT QUICK!
URP URP
YOU'VE GOT A REMOTE CONTROL FOR YOUR LOCKER?!
IT ALSO ACTIVATES THE SOUND SYSTEM AND TRANQUILITY FOUNTAIN!

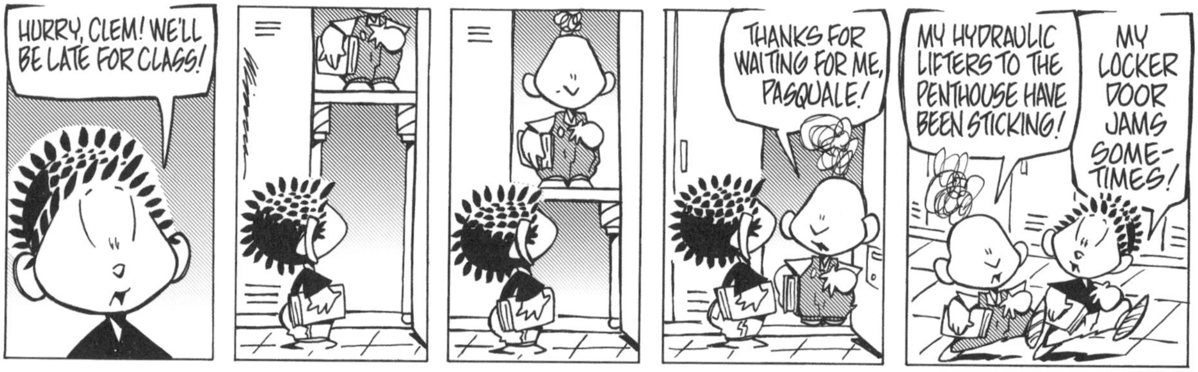
HURRY, CLEM! WE'LL BE LATE FOR CLASS!
THANKS FOR WAITING FOR ME, PASQUALE!
MY HYDRAULIC LIFTERS TO THE PENTHOUSE HAVE BEEN STICKING!
MY LOCKER DOOR JAMS SOME-TIMES!

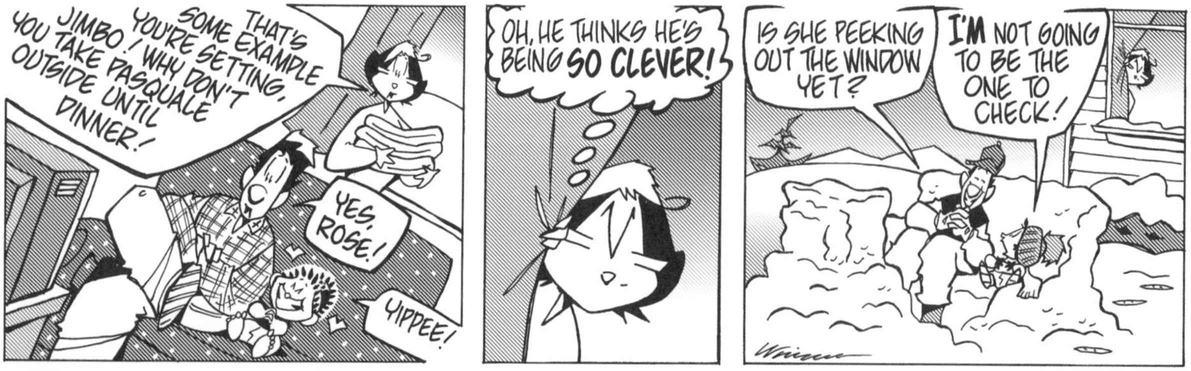
THAT'S SOME EXAMPLE YOU'RE SETTING, JIMBO! WHY DON'T YOU TAKE PASQUALE OUTSIDE UNTIL DINNER!
YES, ROSE!
YIPPEE!
OH, HE THINKS HE'S BEING SO CLEVER!
IS SHE PEEKING OUT THE WINDOW YET?
I'M NOT GOING TO BE THE ONE TO CHECK!

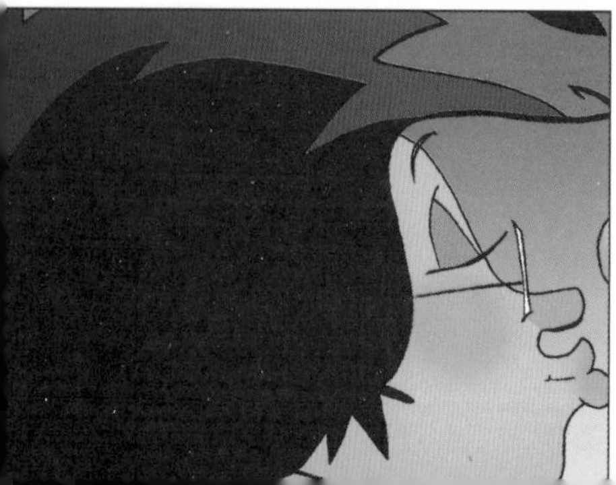

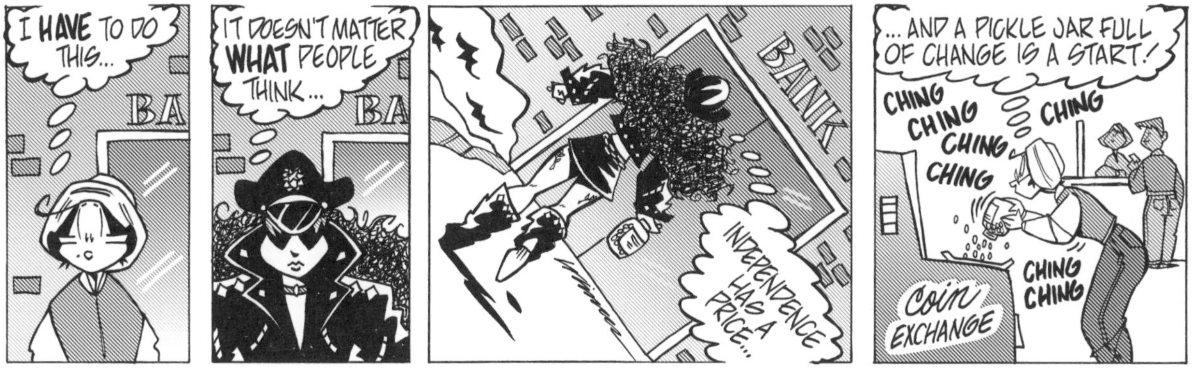
I HAVE TO DO THIS...
IT DOESN'T MATTER WHAT PEOPLE THINK...
BANK
INDEPENDENCE HAS A PRICE...
... AND A PICKLE JAR FULL OF CHANGE IS A START!
CHING CHING CHING CHING
CHING
CHING CHING
Coin EXCHANGE

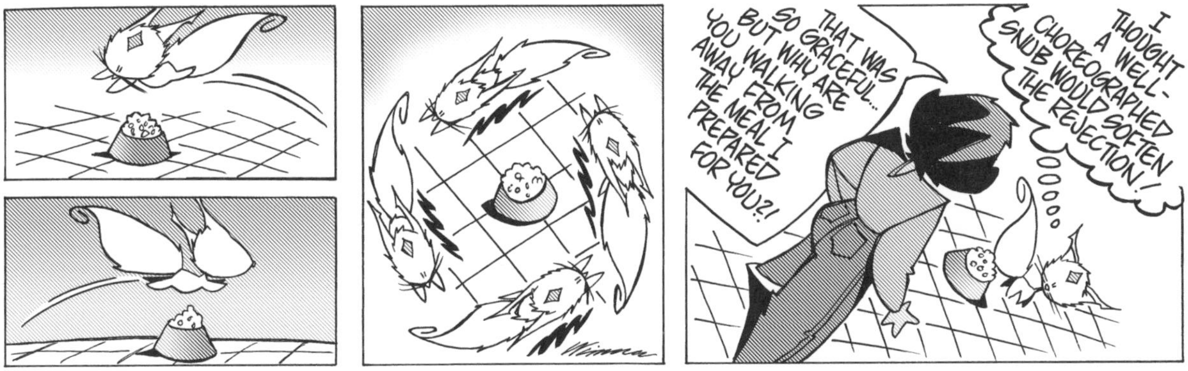
THAT WAS SO GRACEFUL... BUT WHY ARE YOU WALKING AWAY FROM THE MEAL I PREPARED FOR YOU?!
I THOUGHT A WELL-CHOREOGRAPHED SNUB WOULD SOFTEN THE REJECTION!

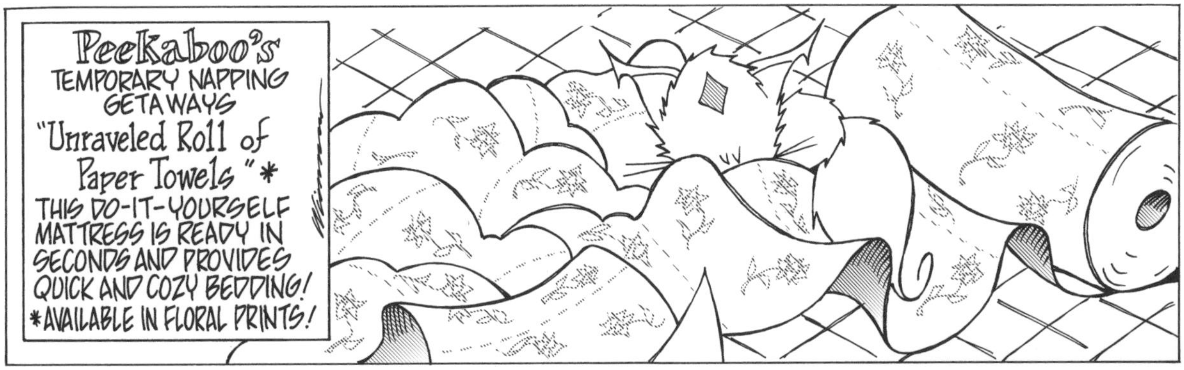
Peekaboo's
TEMPORARY NAPPING GETAWAYS
"Unraveled Roll of Paper Towels"*
THIS DO-IT-YOURSELF MATTRESS IS READY IN SECONDS AND PROVIDES QUICK AND COZY BEDDING!
*AVAILABLE IN FLORAL PRINTS!

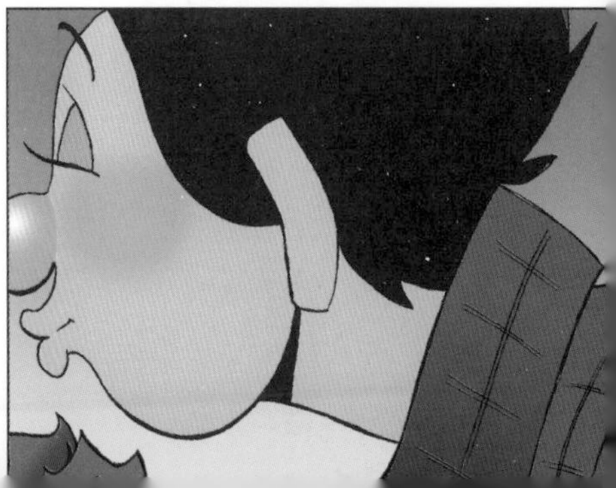

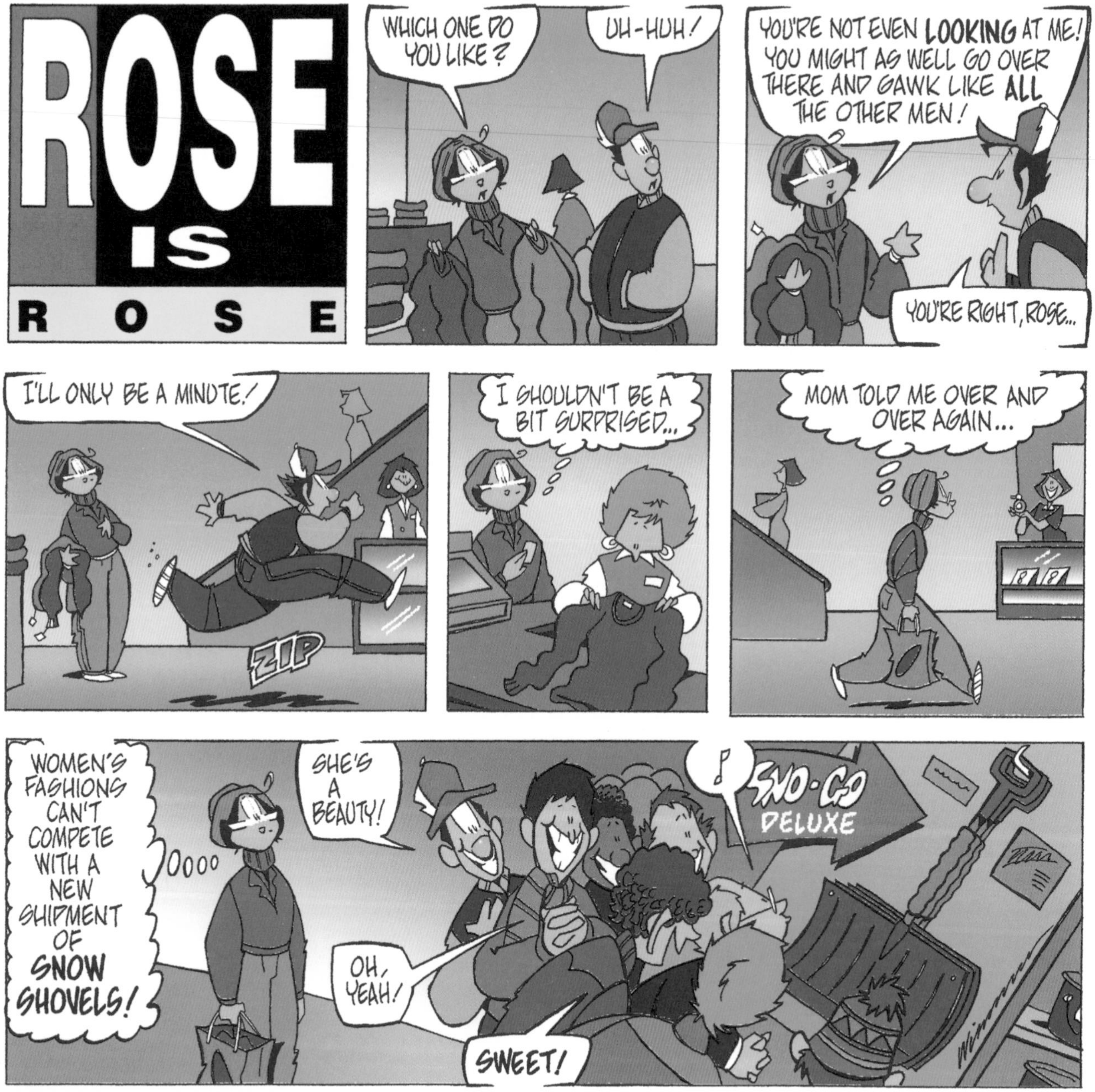
ROSE IS ROSE
WHICH ONE DO YOU LIKE?
UH-HUH!
YOU'RE NOT EVEN LOOKING AT ME! YOU MIGHT AS WELL GO OVER THERE AND GAWK LIKE ALL THE OTHER MEN!
YOU'RE RIGHT, ROSE...
I'LL ONLY BE A MINUTE!
ZIP
I SHOULDN'T BE A BIT SURPRISED...
MOM TOLD ME OVER AND OVER AGAIN...
WOMEN'S FASHIONS CAN'T COMPETE WITH A NEW SHIPMENT OF SNOW SHOVELS!
Oooo
SHE'S A BEAUTY!
SNO-GO DELUXE
OH, YEAH!
SWEET!

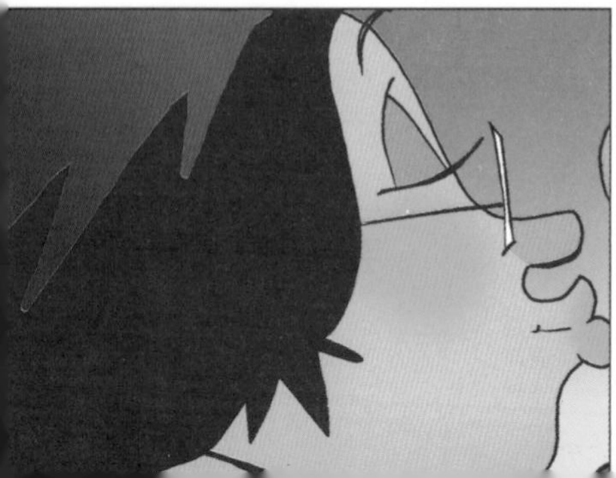

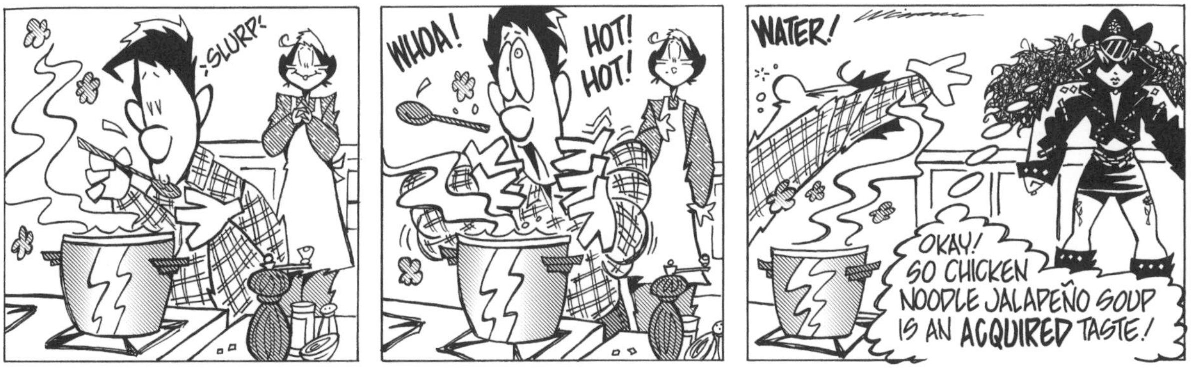
SLURP!
WHOA!
HOT! HOT!
WATER!
OKAY! SO CHICKEN NOODLE JALAPEÑO SOUP IS AN ACQUIRED TASTE!

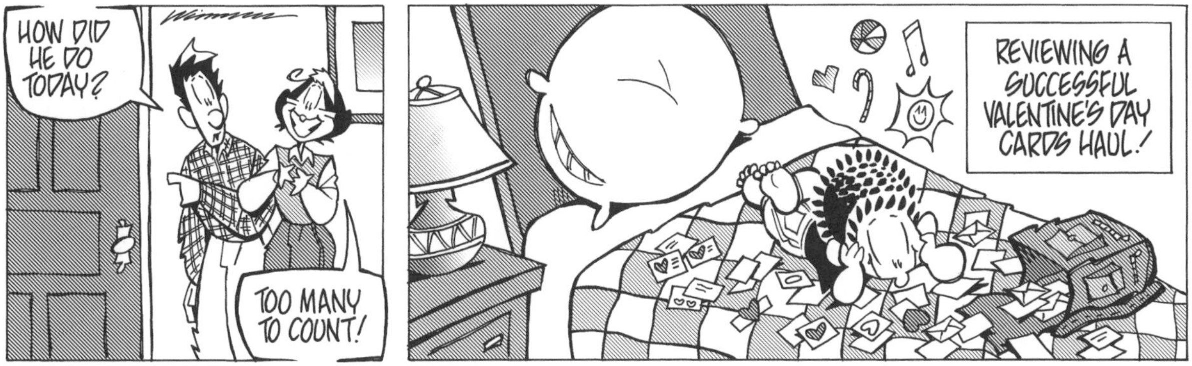
HOW DID HE DO TODAY?
TOO MANY TO COUNT!
REVIEWING A SUCCESSFUL VALENTINE'S DAY CARDS HAUL!

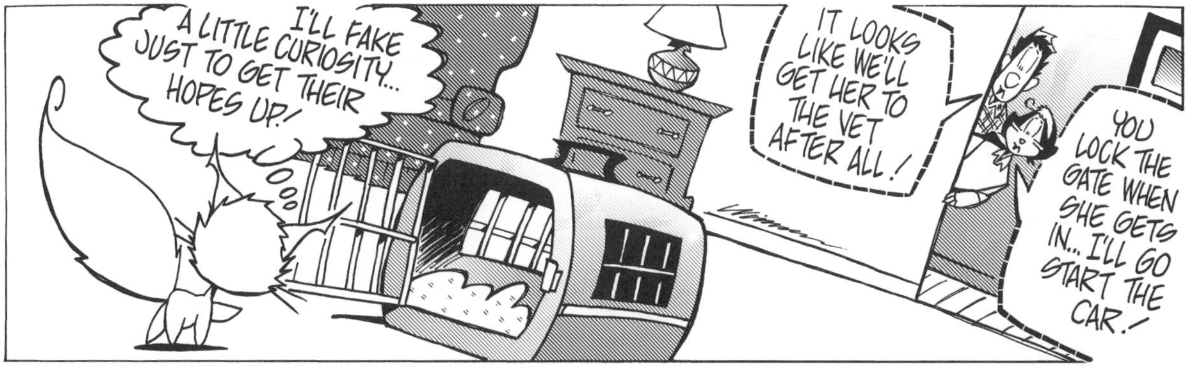
I'LL FAKE A LITTLE CURIOSITY... JUST TO GET THEIR HOPES UP!
IT LOOKS LIKE WE'LL GET HER TO THE VET AFTER ALL!
YOU LOCK THE GATE WHEN SHE GETS IN... I'LL GO START THE CAR!

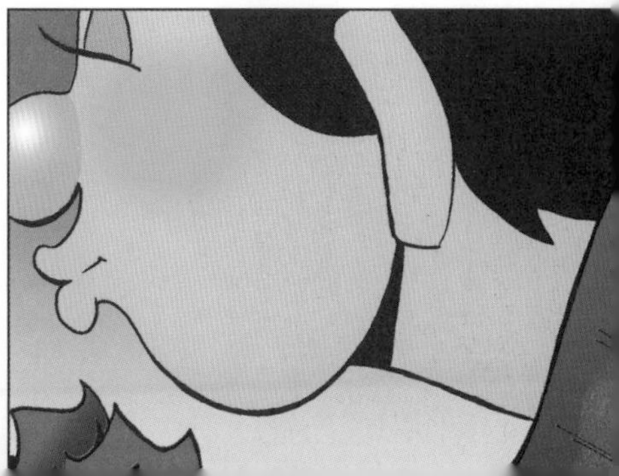

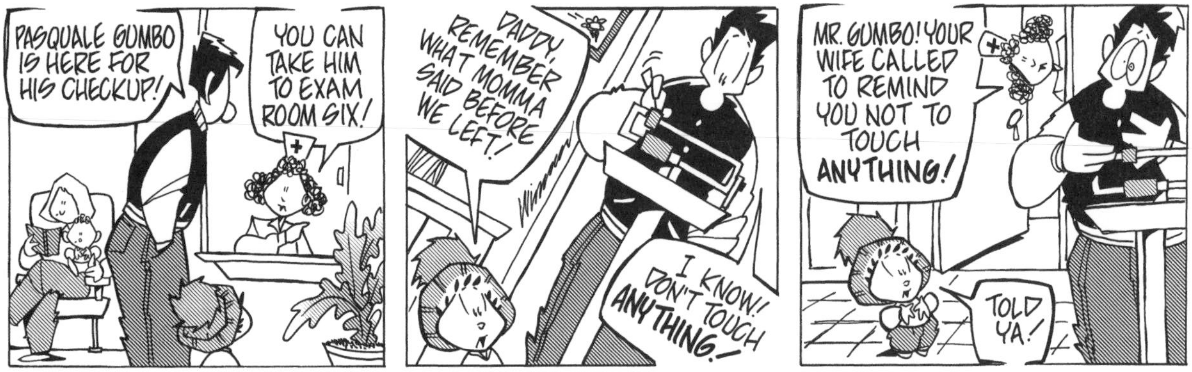
PASQUALE GUMBO IS HERE FOR HIS CHECKUP!
YOU CAN TAKE HIM TO EXAM ROOM SIX!
DADDY, REMEMBER WHAT MOMMA SAID BEFORE WE LEFT!
I KNOW! DON'T TOUCH ANYTHING!
MR. GUMBO! YOUR WIFE CALLED TO REMIND YOU NOT TO TOUCH ANYTHING!
TOLD YA!

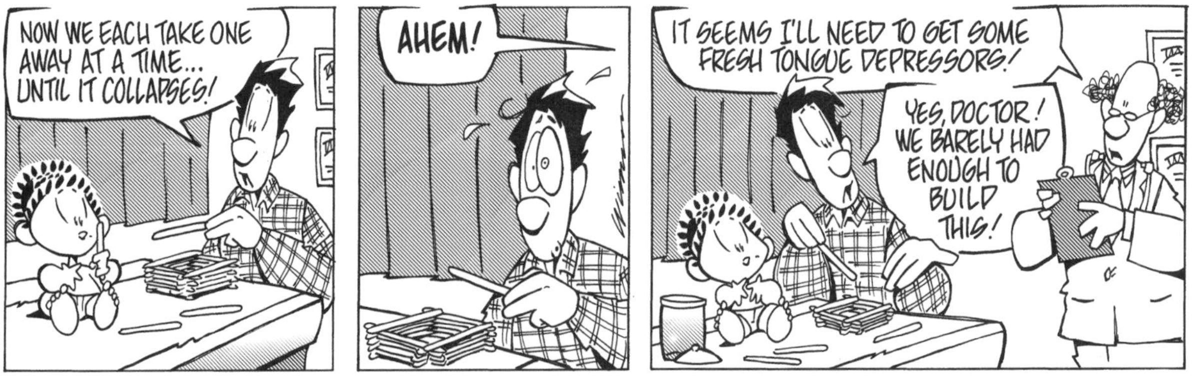
NOW WE EACH TAKE ONE AWAY AT A TIME... UNTIL IT COLLAPSES!
AHEM!
IT SEEMS I'LL NEED TO GET SOME FRESH TONGUE DEPRESSORS!
YES, DOCTOR! WE BARELY HAD ENOUGH TO BUILD THIS!

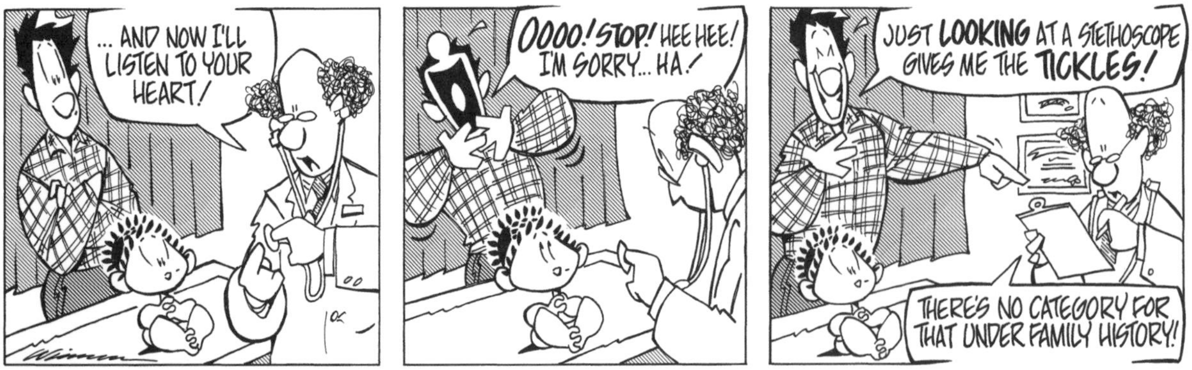
... AND NOW I'LL LISTEN TO YOUR HEART!
OOOO! STOP! HEE HEE! I'M SORRY... HA!
JUST LOOKING AT A STETHOSCOPE GIVES ME THE TICKLES!
THERE'S NO CATEGORY FOR THAT UNDER FAMILY HISTORY!

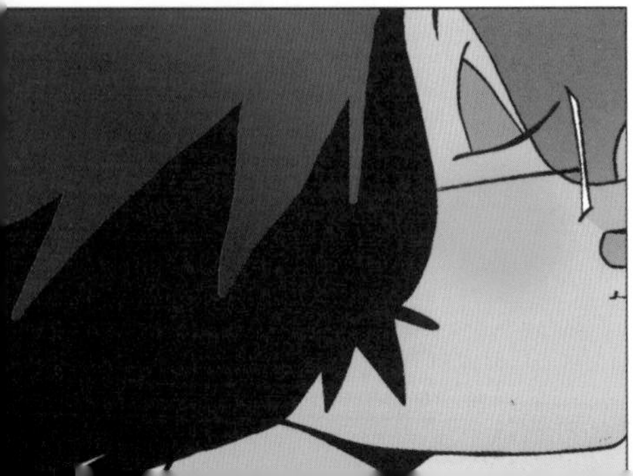

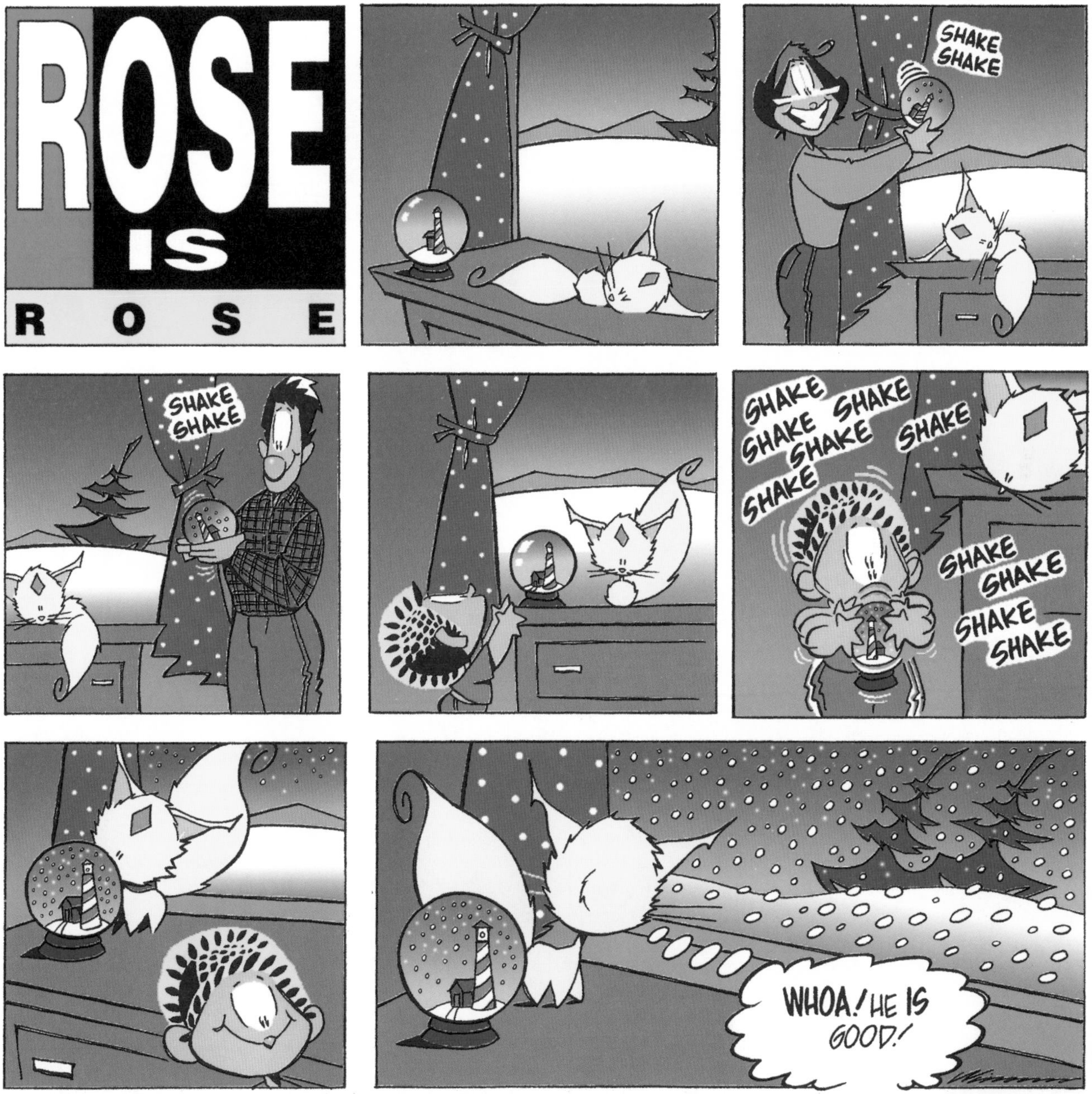
ROSE IS ROSE
SHAKE SHAKE
SHAKE SHAKE
SHAKE SHAKE SHAKE SHAKE SHAKE SHAKE
SHAKE SHAKE SHAKE SHAKE
WHOA! HE IS GOOD!

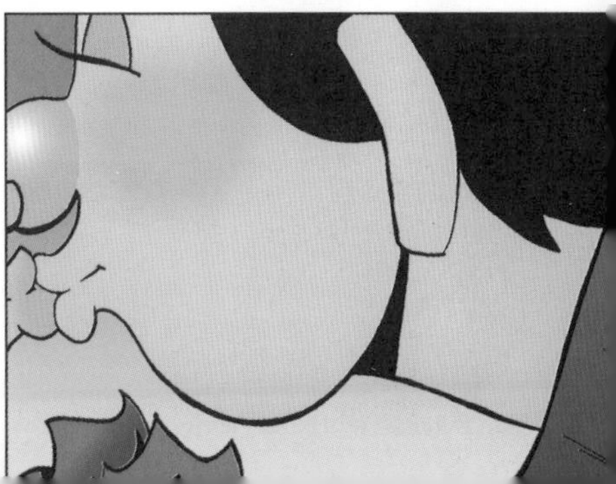

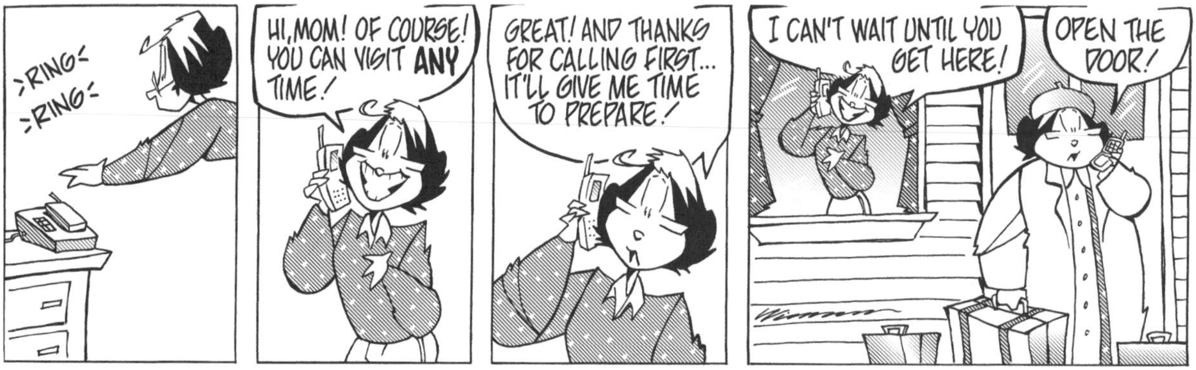
RING
RING
HI, MOM! OF COURSE! YOU CAN VISIT ANY TIME!
GREAT! AND THANKS FOR CALLING FIRST... IT'LL GIVE ME TIME TO PREPARE!
I CAN'T WAIT UNTIL YOU GET HERE!
OPEN THE DOOR!

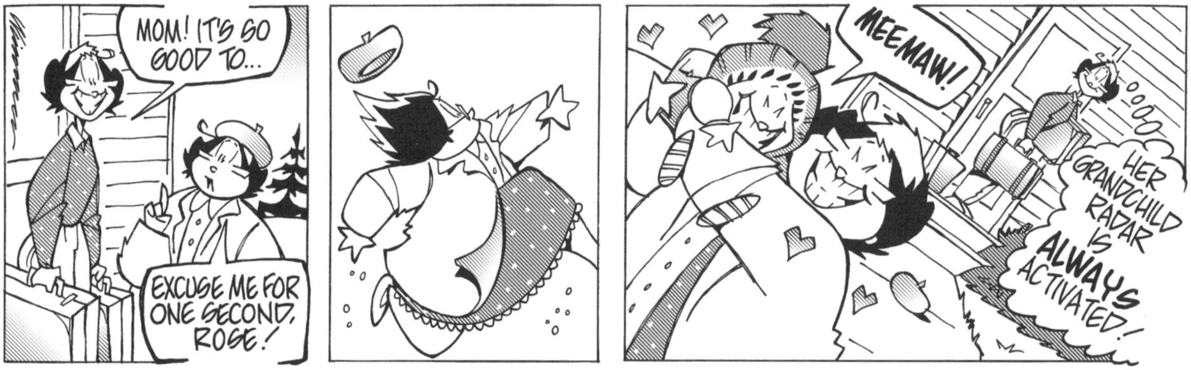
MOM! IT'S SO GOOD TO...
EXCUSE ME FOR ONE SECOND, ROSE!
MEEMAW!
OOOO
HER GRANDCHILD RADAR IS ALWAYS ACTIVATED!

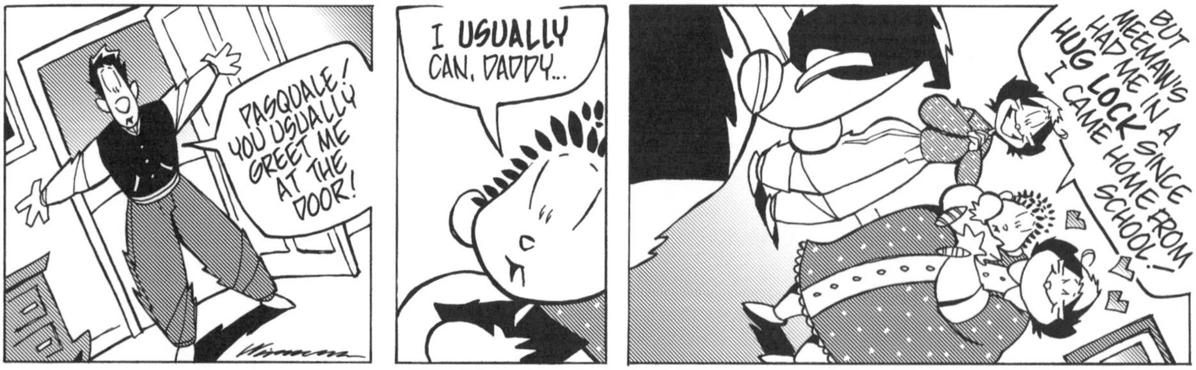
PASQUALE! YOU USUALLY GREET ME AT THE DOOR!
I USUALLY CAN, DADDY...
BUT MEEMAW'S HAD ME IN A HUG LOCK SINCE I CAME HOME FROM SCHOOL!

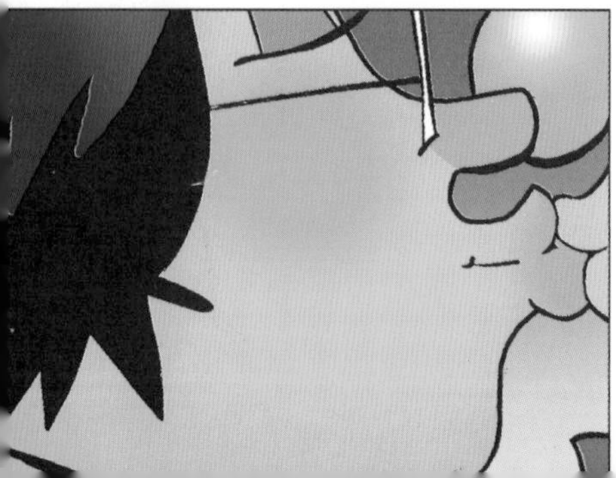

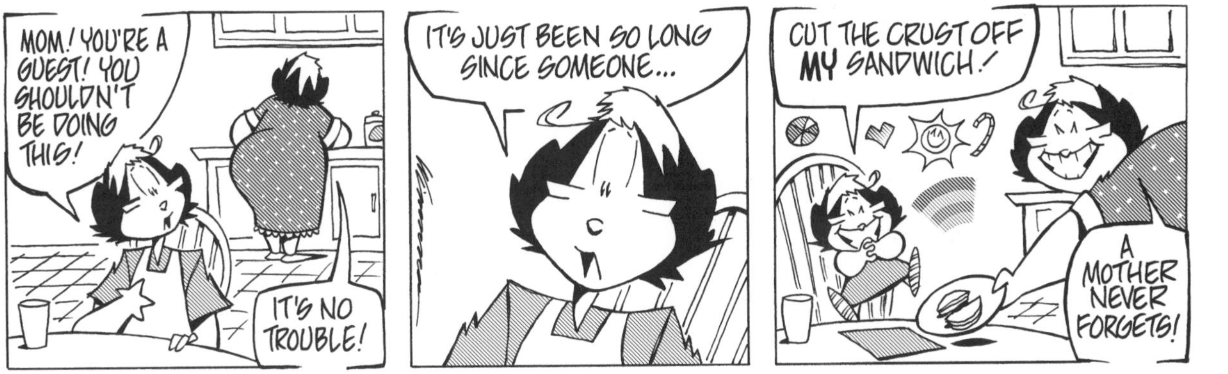
MOM! YOU'RE A GUEST! YOU SHOULDN'T BE DOING THIS!
IT'S NO TROUBLE!
IT'S JUST BEEN SO LONG SINCE SOMEONE...
CUT THE CRUST OFF **MY** SANDWICH!
A MOTHER NEVER FORGETS!

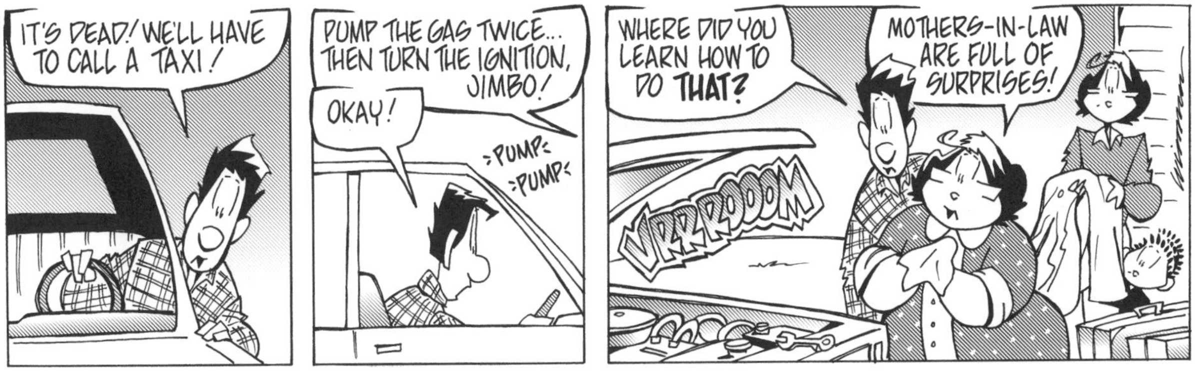
IT'S DEAD! WE'LL HAVE TO CALL A TAXI!
PUMP THE GAS TWICE... THEN TURN THE IGNITION, JIMBO!
OKAY!
PUMP
PUMP
WHERE DID YOU LEARN HOW TO DO **THAT?**
MOTHERS-IN-LAW ARE FULL OF SURPRISES!

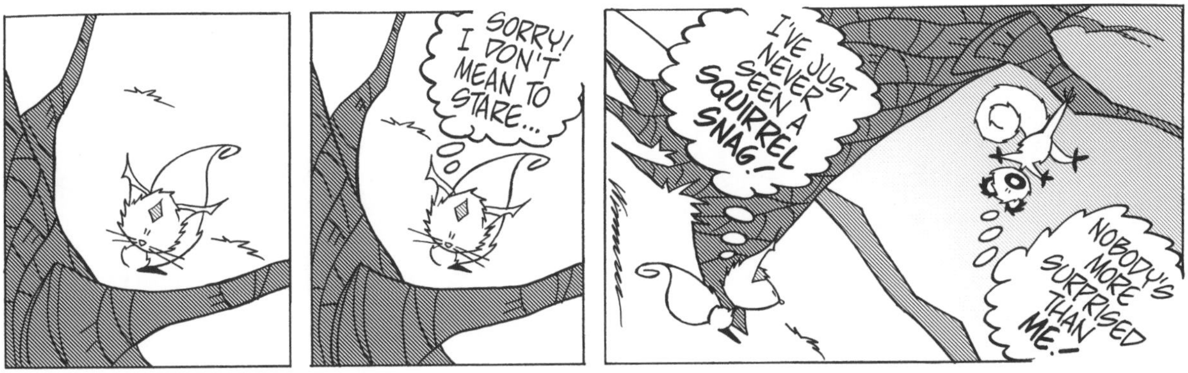
SORRY! I DON'T MEAN TO STARE...
I'VE JUST NEVER SEEN A **SQUIRREL SNAG!**
NOBODY'S MORE SURPRISED THAN **ME!**

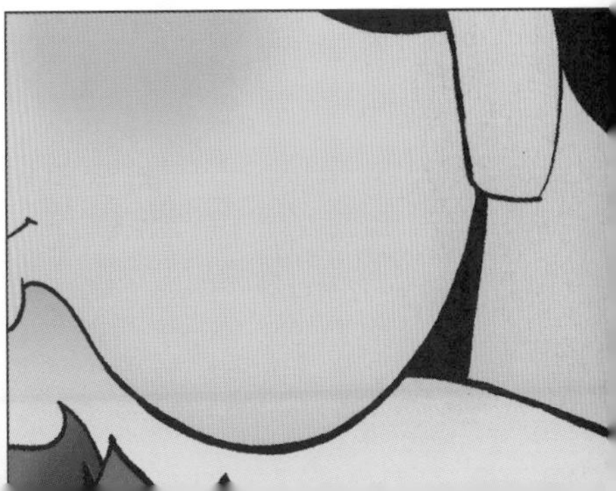

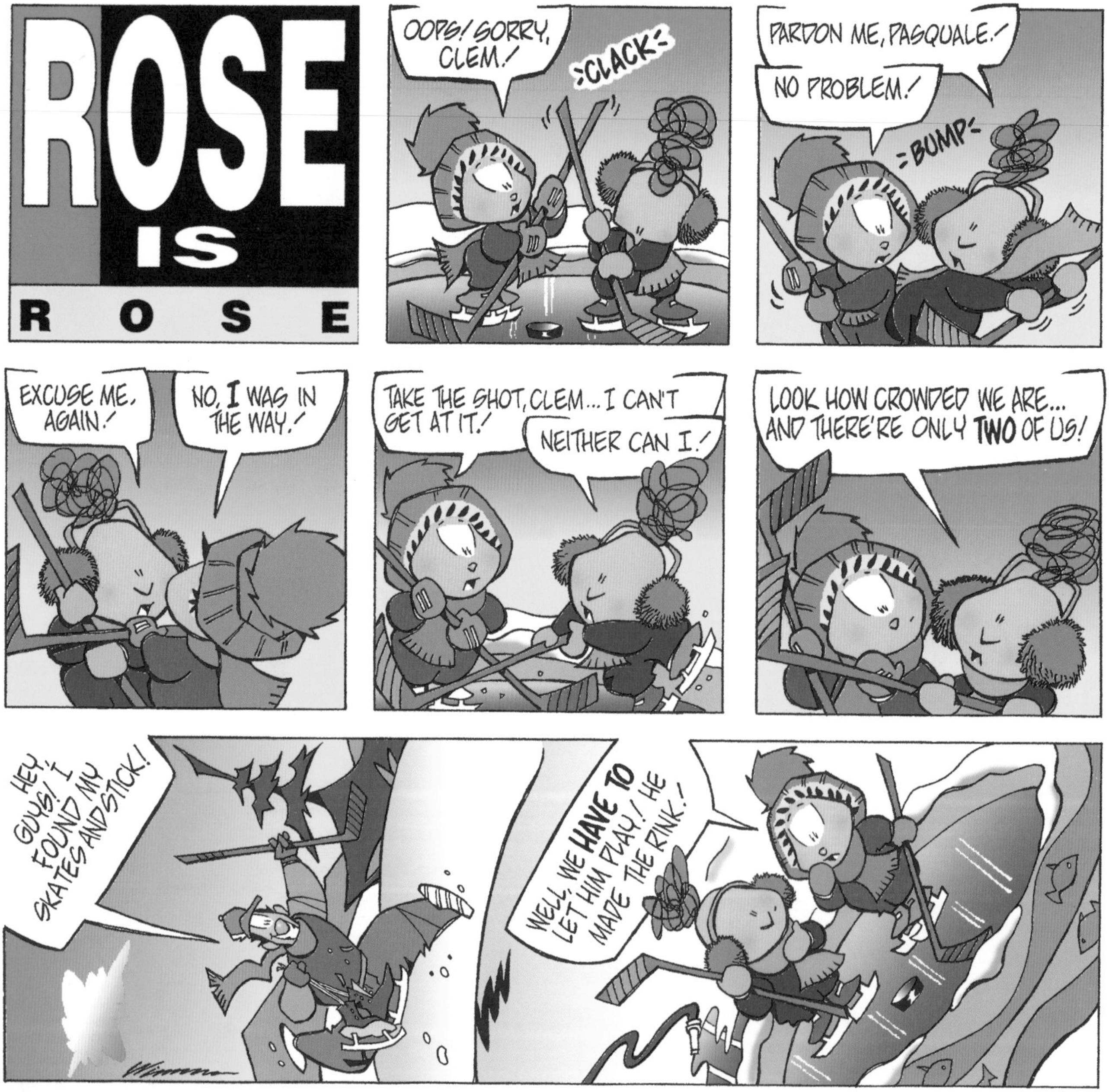
ROSE IS ROSE
OOPS! SORRY, CLEM!
CLACK
PARDON ME, PASQUALE!
NO PROBLEM!
BUMP
EXCUSE ME, AGAIN!
NO, I WAS IN THE WAY!
TAKE THE SHOT, CLEM... I CAN'T GET AT IT!
NEITHER CAN I!
LOOK HOW CROWDED WE ARE... AND THERE'RE ONLY TWO OF US!
HEY, GUYS! I FOUND MY SKATES AND STICK!
WELL, WE HAVE TO LET HIM PLAY! HE MADE THE RINK!

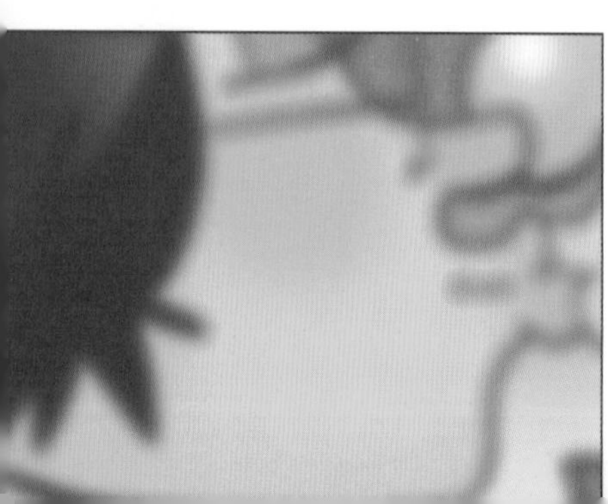

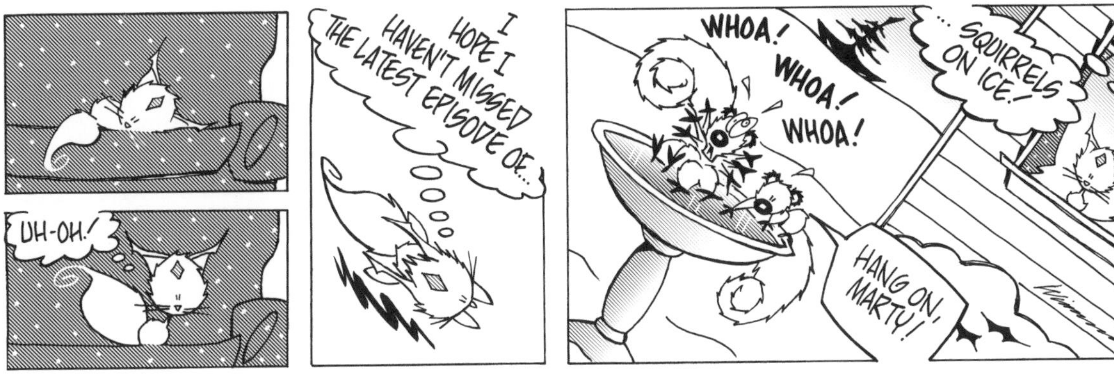
UH-OH!
I HOPE I HAVEN'T MISSED THE LATEST EPISODE OF...
WHOA! WHOA! WHOA!
... SQUIRRELS ON ICE!
HANG ON, MARTY!

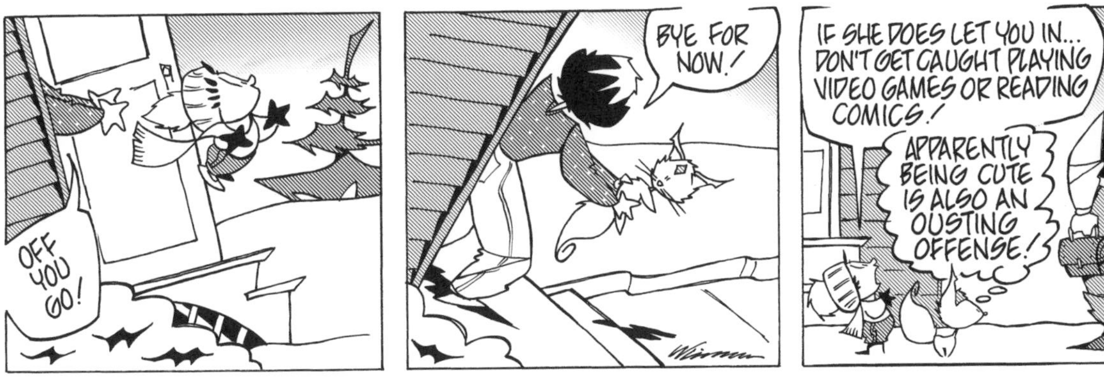
OFF YOU GO!
BYE FOR NOW!
IF SHE DOES LET YOU IN... DON'T GET CAUGHT PLAYING VIDEO GAMES OR READING COMICS!
APPARENTLY BEING CUTE IS ALSO AN OUSTING OFFENSE!

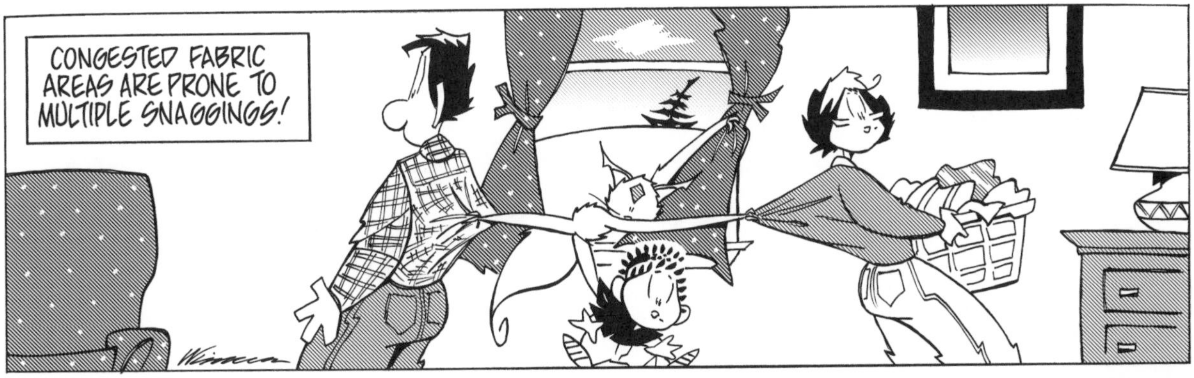
CONGESTED FABRIC AREAS ARE PRONE TO MULTIPLE SNAGGINGS!

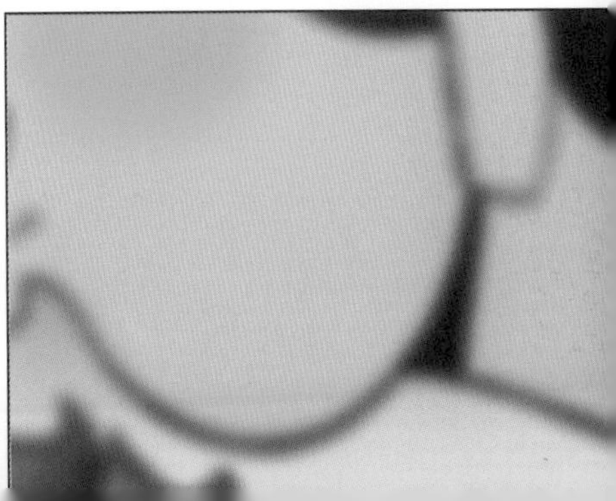

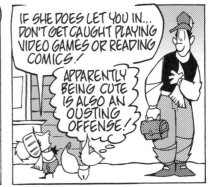

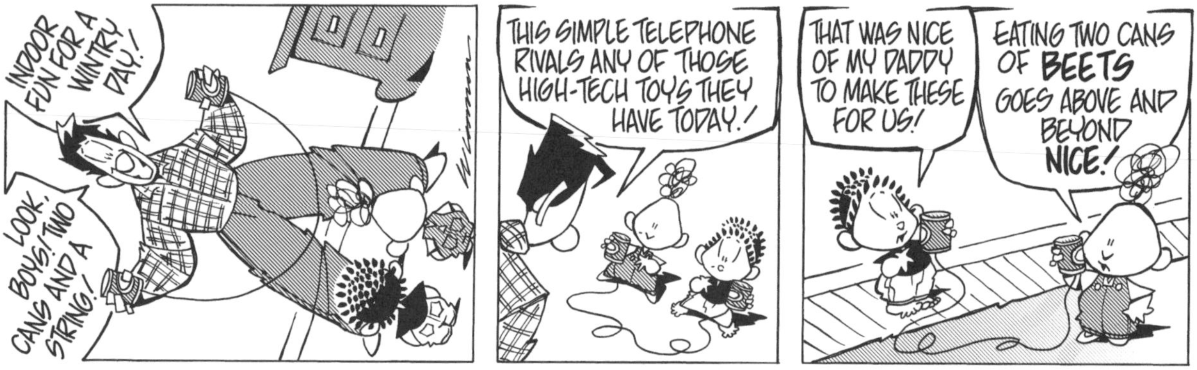
INDOOR FUN FOR A WINTRY DAY!
LOOK, BOYS! TWO CANS AND A STRING!
THIS SIMPLE TELEPHONE RIVALS ANY OF THOSE HIGH-TECH TOYS THEY HAVE TODAY!
THAT WAS NICE OF MY DADDY TO MAKE THESE FOR US!
EATING TWO CANS OF **BEETS** GOES ABOVE AND BEYOND **NICE!**

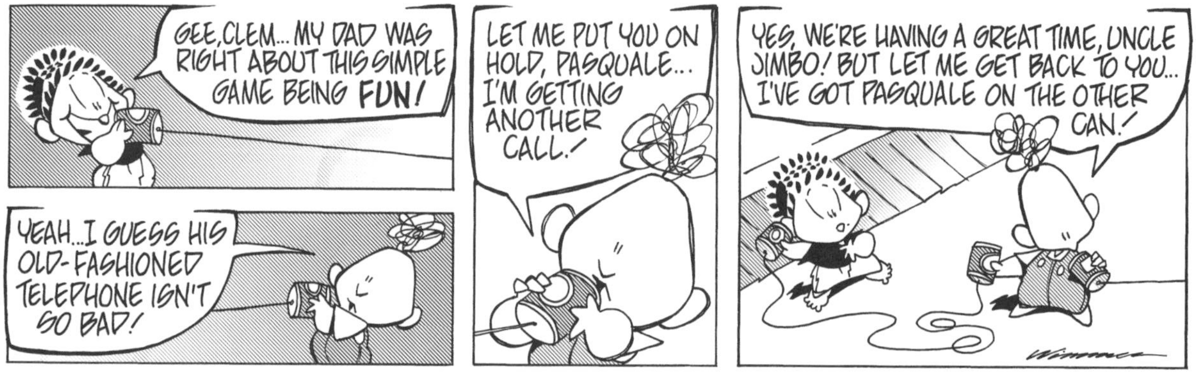
GEE, CLEM... MY DAD WAS RIGHT ABOUT THIS SIMPLE GAME BEING **FUN!**
YEAH...I GUESS HIS OLD-FASHIONED TELEPHONE ISN'T SO BAD!
LET ME PUT YOU ON HOLD, PASQUALE... I'M GETTING ANOTHER CALL!
YES, WE'RE HAVING A GREAT TIME, UNCLE JIMBO! BUT LET ME GET BACK TO YOU... I'VE GOT PASQUALE ON THE OTHER CAN!

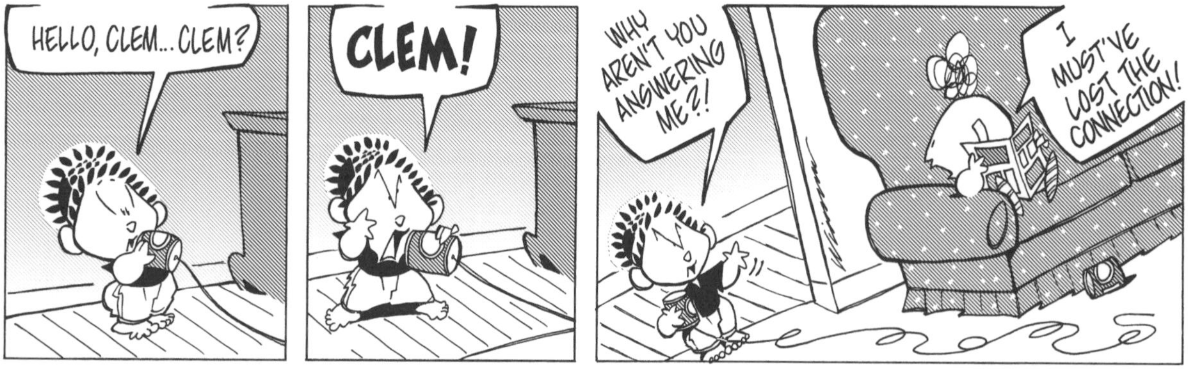
HELLO, CLEM... CLEM?
CLEM!
WHY AREN'T YOU ANSWERING ME?!
I MUST'VE LOST THE CONNECTION!

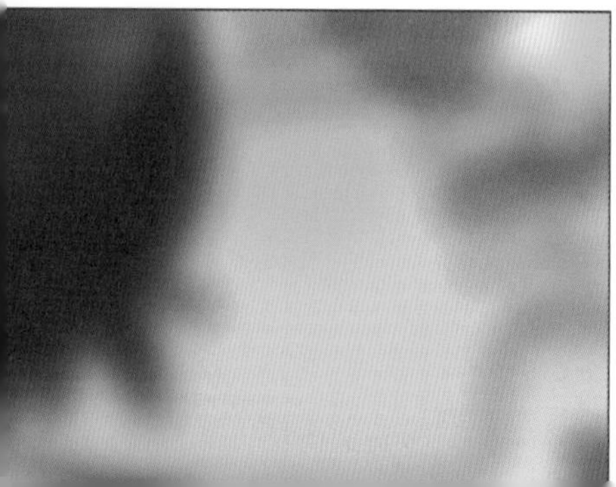

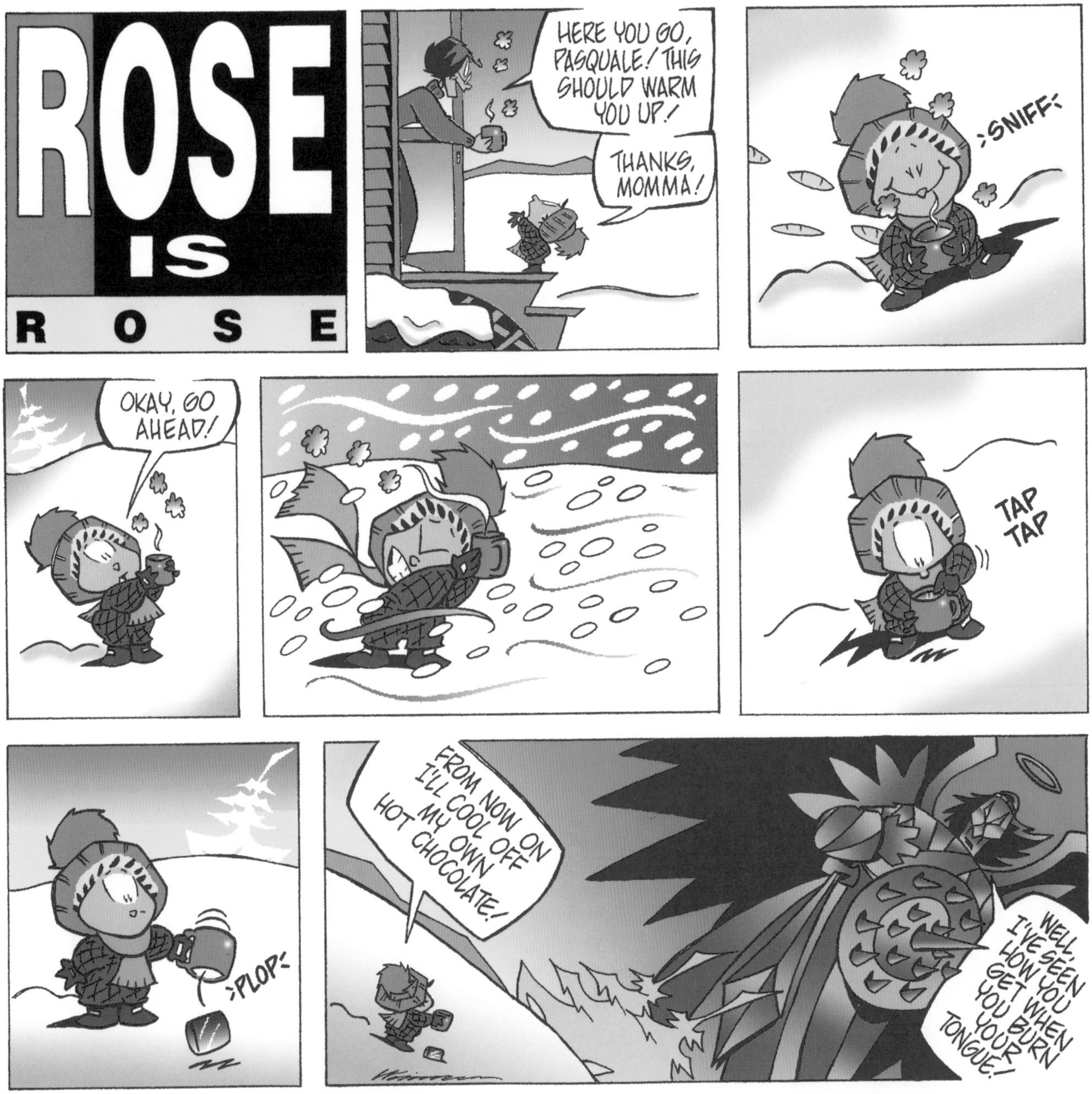
ROSE IS ROSE
HERE YOU GO, PASQUALE! THIS SHOULD WARM YOU UP!
THANKS, MOMMA!
SNIFF
OKAY, GO AHEAD!
TAP TAP
PLOP
FROM NOW ON I'LL COOL OFF MY OWN HOT CHOCOLATE!
WELL, I'VE SEEN HOW YOU GET WHEN YOU BURN YOUR TONGUE!

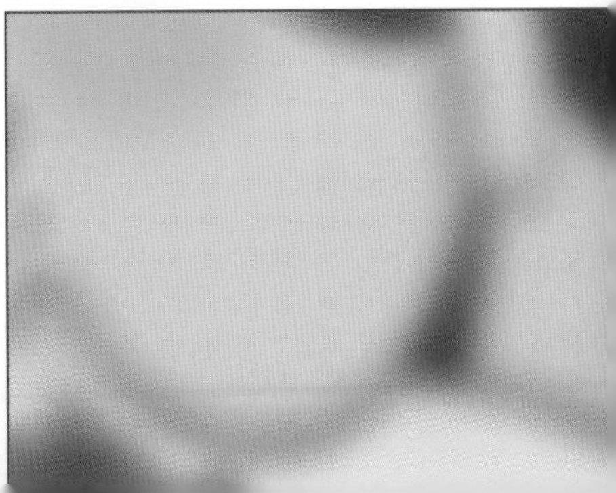

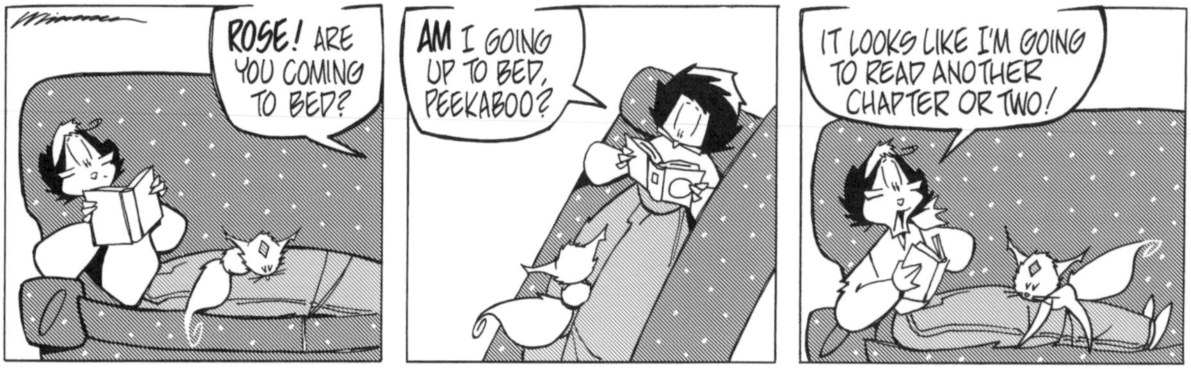
ROSE! ARE YOU COMING TO BED?
AM I GOING UP TO BED, PEEKABOO?
IT LOOKS LIKE I'M GOING TO READ ANOTHER CHAPTER OR TWO!

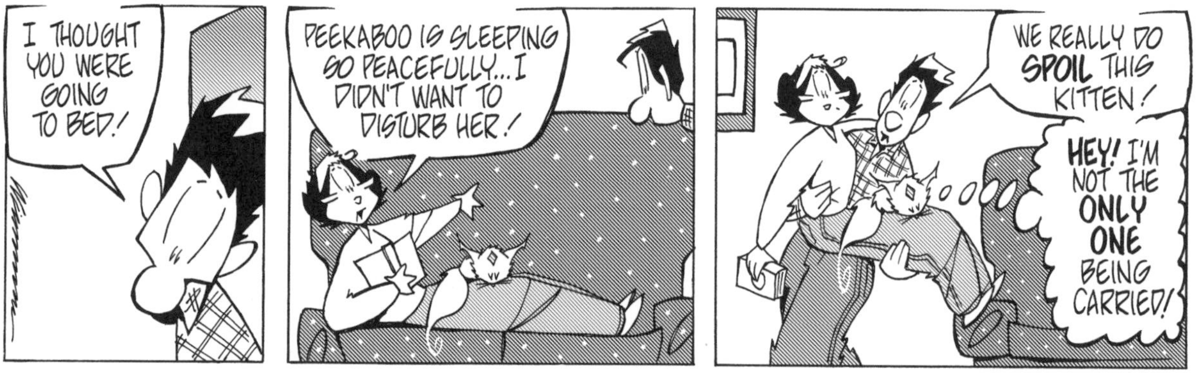
I THOUGHT YOU WERE GOING TO BED!
PEEKABOO IS SLEEPING SO PEACEFULLY... I DIDN'T WANT TO DISTURB HER!
WE REALLY DO SPOIL THIS KITTEN!
HEY! I'M NOT THE ONLY ONE BEING CARRIED!

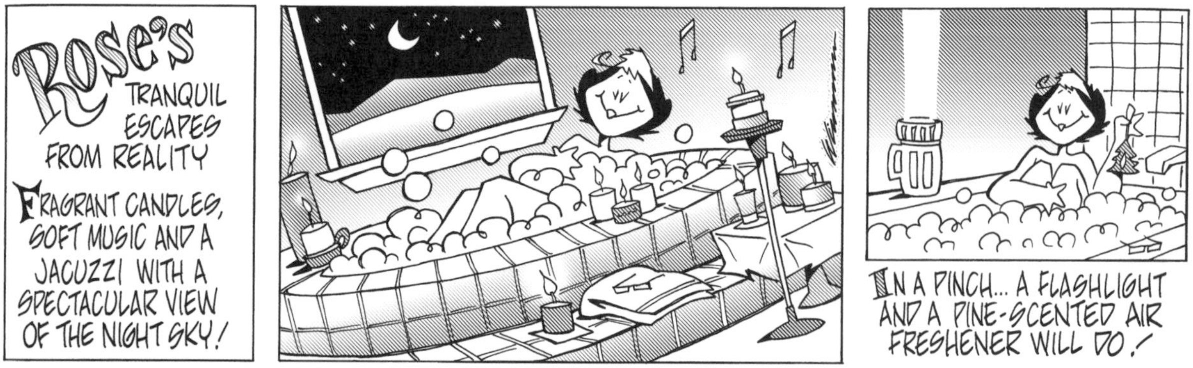
Rose's TRANQUIL ESCAPES FROM REALITY
FRAGRANT CANDLES, SOFT MUSIC AND A JACUZZI WITH A SPECTACULAR VIEW OF THE NIGHT SKY!
IN A PINCH... A FLASHLIGHT AND A PINE-SCENTED AIR FRESHENER WILL DO!

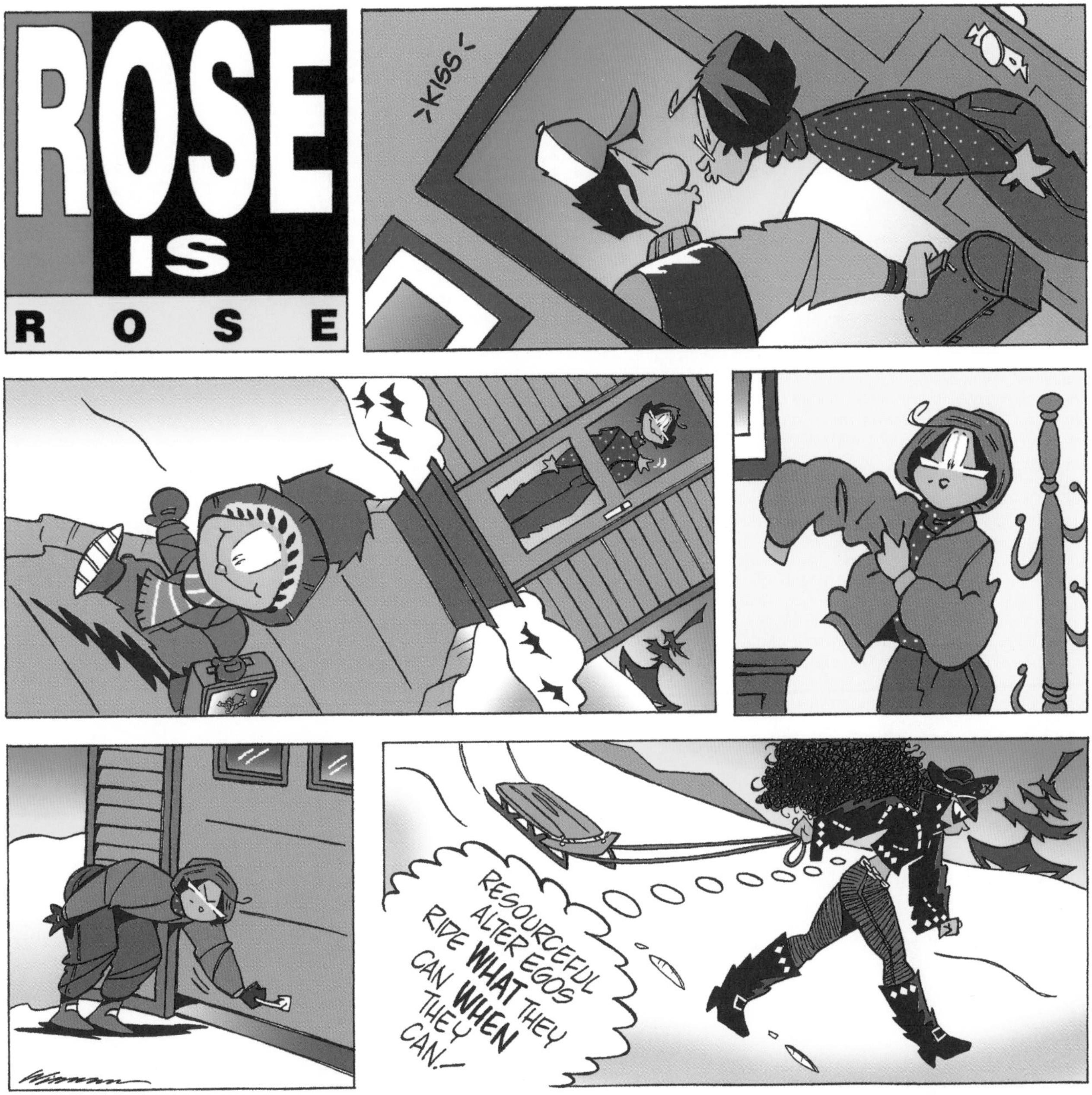
ROSE IS ROSE
KISS
RESOURCEFUL ALTER EGOS RIDE WHAT THEY CAN WHEN THEY CAN!

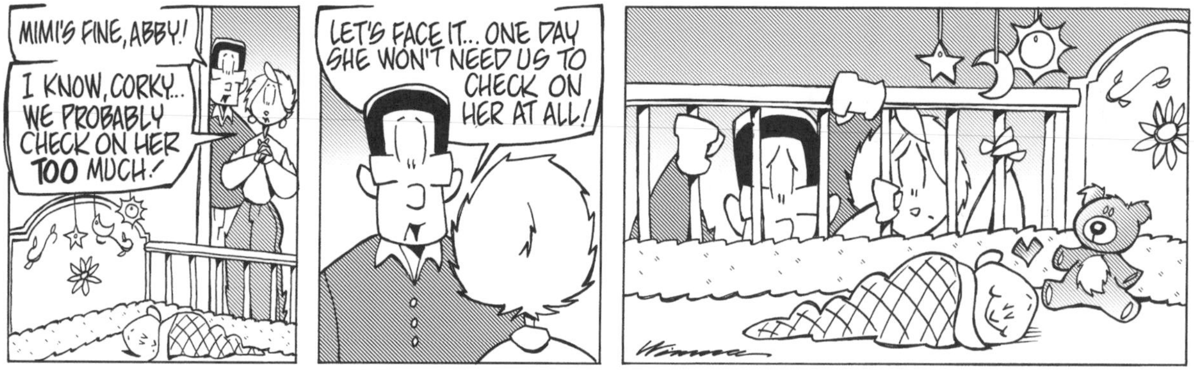
MIMI'S FINE, ABBY!
I KNOW, CORKY... WE PROBABLY CHECK ON HER TOO MUCH!
LET'S FACE IT... ONE DAY SHE WON'T NEED US TO CHECK ON HER AT ALL!

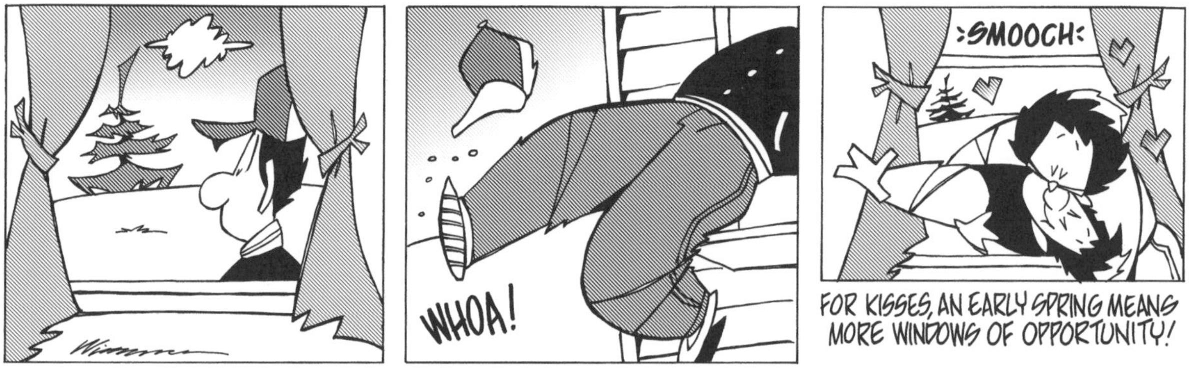
WHOA!
:SMOOCH:
FOR KISSES, AN EARLY SPRING MEANS MORE WINDOWS OF OPPORTUNITY!

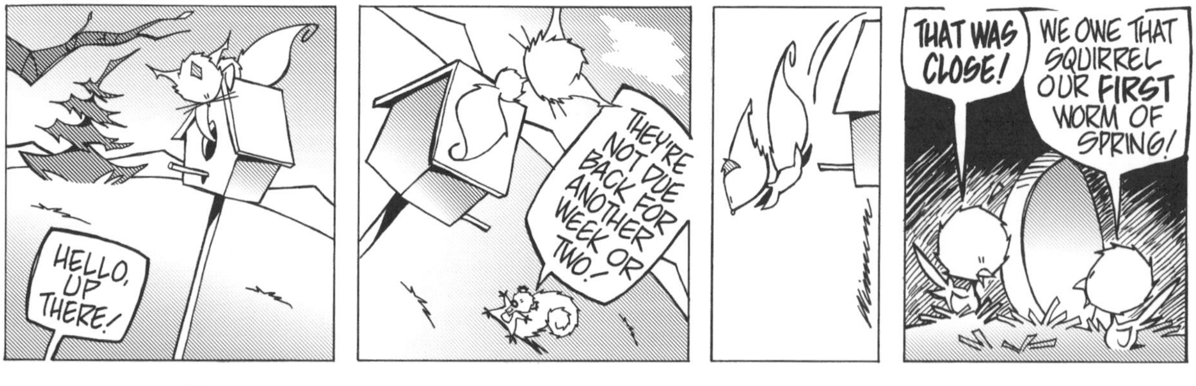
HELLO, UP THERE!
THEY'RE NOT DUE BACK FOR ANOTHER WEEK OR TWO!
THAT WAS CLOSE!
WE OWE THAT SQUIRREL OUR FIRST WORM OF SPRING!

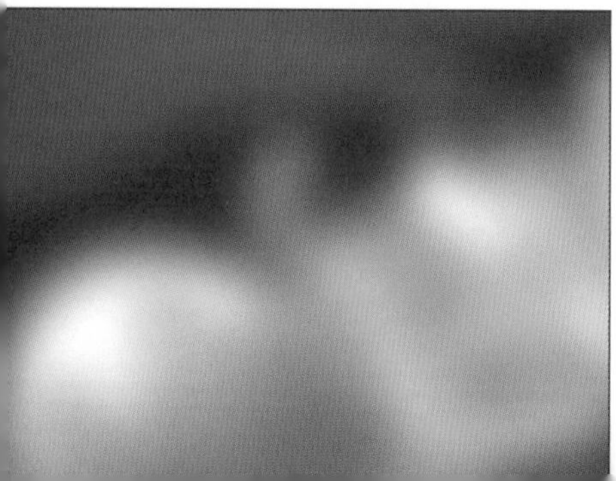

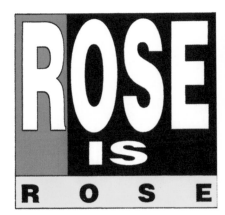

ROSE IS ROSE

LET'S HEAR IT FOR THE RISK-TAKERS!

THOSE FEARLESS ADVENTURERS WHO ATTEMPT THE DIFFICULT AND UNKNOWN...

MEETING CHALLENGES HEAD-ON, UNCERTAIN OF THE OUTCOME!

WE MUST CHEER FOR THEIR INSPIRING ACCOMPLISHMENTS...

AND ENCOURAGE THEIR FUTURE ENDEAVORS...

BECAUSE THEY TRY THEIR **BEST**!

I DID IT!

DID DADDY BAKE A CAKE?

LET'S LET **HIM** TELL **US** WHAT IT IS!

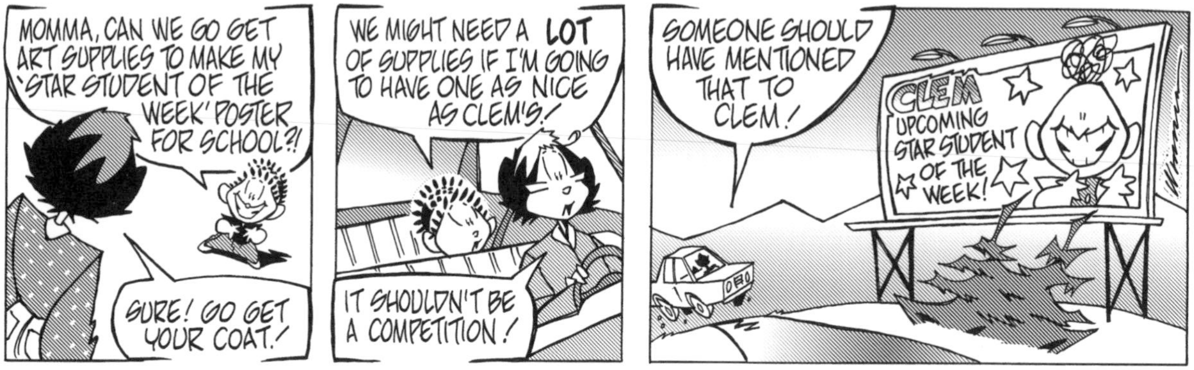
MOMMA, CAN WE GO GET ART SUPPLIES TO MAKE MY 'STAR STUDENT OF THE WEEK' POSTER FOR SCHOOL?!
SURE! GO GET YOUR COAT.!
WE MIGHT NEED A LOT OF SUPPLIES IF I'M GOING TO HAVE ONE AS NICE AS CLEM'S!
IT SHOULDN'T BE A COMPETITION!
SOMEONE SHOULD HAVE MENTIONED THAT TO CLEM!
CLEM
UPCOMING STAR STUDENT OF THE WEEK!

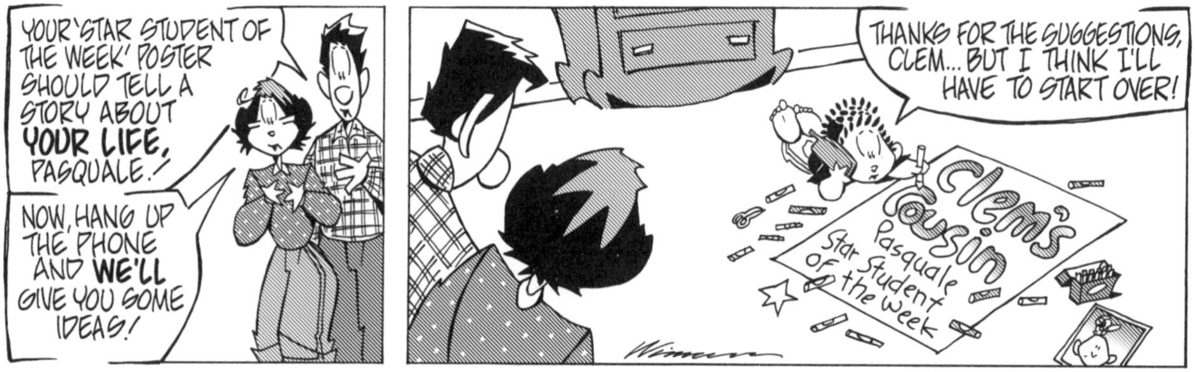
YOUR 'STAR STUDENT OF THE WEEK' POSTER SHOULD TELL A STORY ABOUT YOUR LIFE, PASQUALE!
NOW, HANG UP THE PHONE AND WE'LL GIVE YOU SOME IDEAS!
THANKS FOR THE SUGGESTIONS, CLEM... BUT I THINK I'LL HAVE TO START OVER!
Clem's Cousin
Pasquale
Star Student of the week

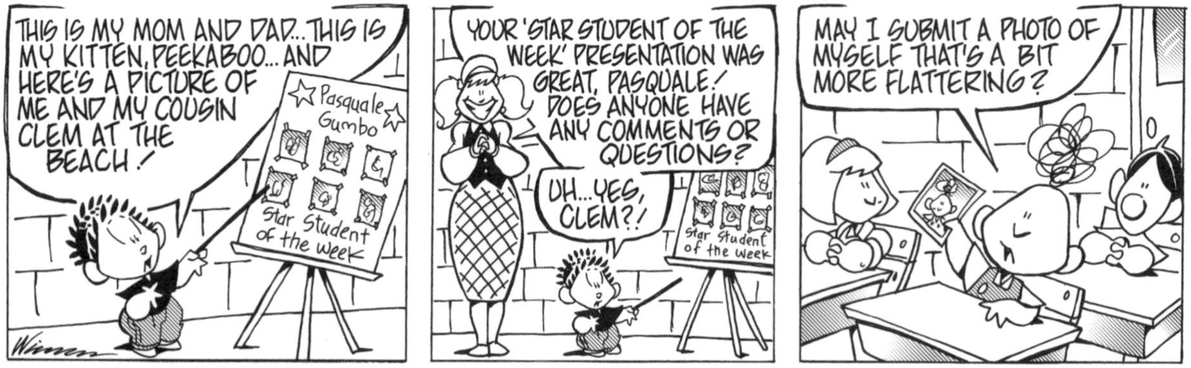
THIS IS MY MOM AND DAD... THIS IS MY KITTEN, PEEKABOO... AND HERE'S A PICTURE OF ME AND MY COUSIN CLEM AT THE BEACH!
Pasquale Gumbo
Star Student of the week
YOUR 'STAR STUDENT OF THE WEEK' PRESENTATION WAS GREAT, PASQUALE! DOES ANYONE HAVE ANY COMMENTS OR QUESTIONS?
UH... YES, CLEM?!
Star Student of the week
MAY I SUBMIT A PHOTO OF MYSELF THAT'S A BIT MORE FLATTERING?

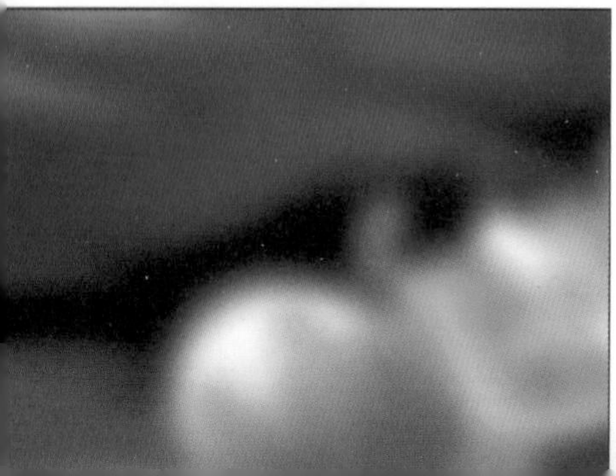

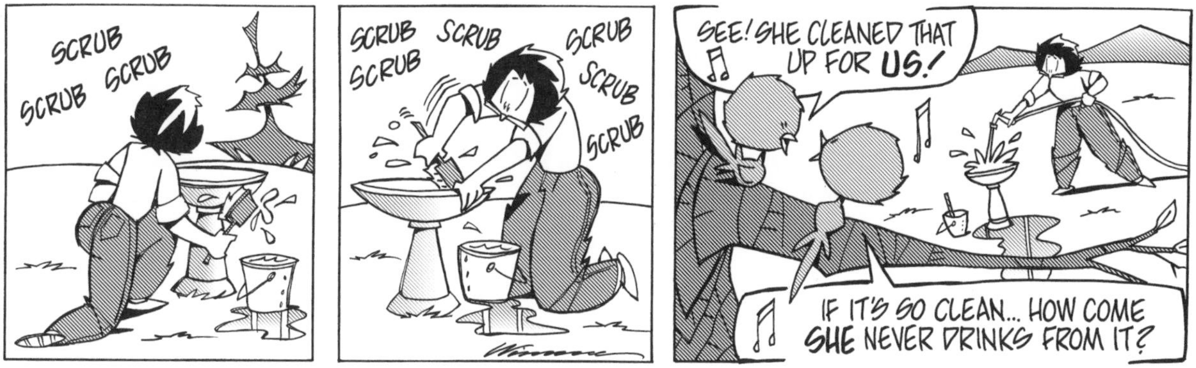
SCRUB
SCRUB SCRUB
SCRUB SCRUB
SCRUB SCRUB
SCRUB SCRUB
SCRUB
SEE! SHE CLEANED THAT UP FOR **US!**
IF IT'S SO CLEAN... HOW COME **SHE** NEVER DRINKS FROM IT?

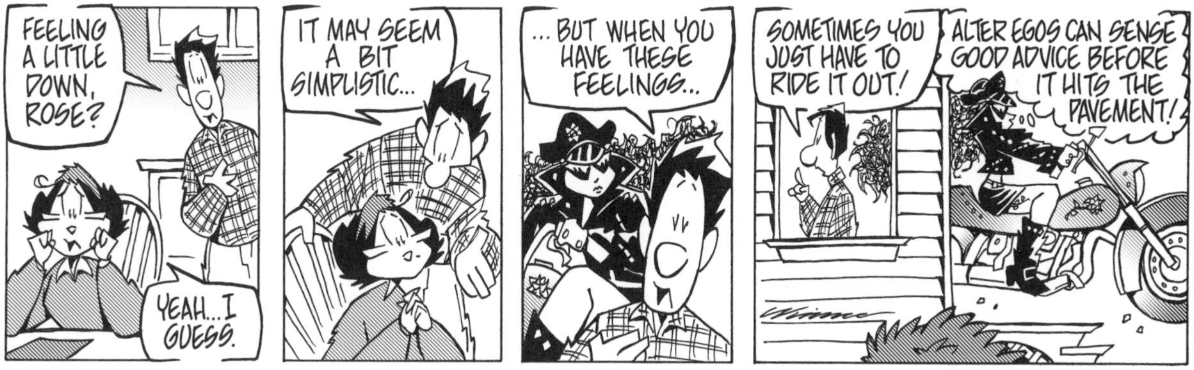
FEELING A LITTLE DOWN, ROSE?
YEAH...I GUESS.
IT MAY SEEM A BIT SIMPLISTIC...
...BUT WHEN YOU HAVE THESE FEELINGS...
SOMETIMES YOU JUST HAVE TO RIDE IT OUT!
ALTER EGOS CAN SENSE GOOD ADVICE BEFORE IT HITS THE PAVEMENT!

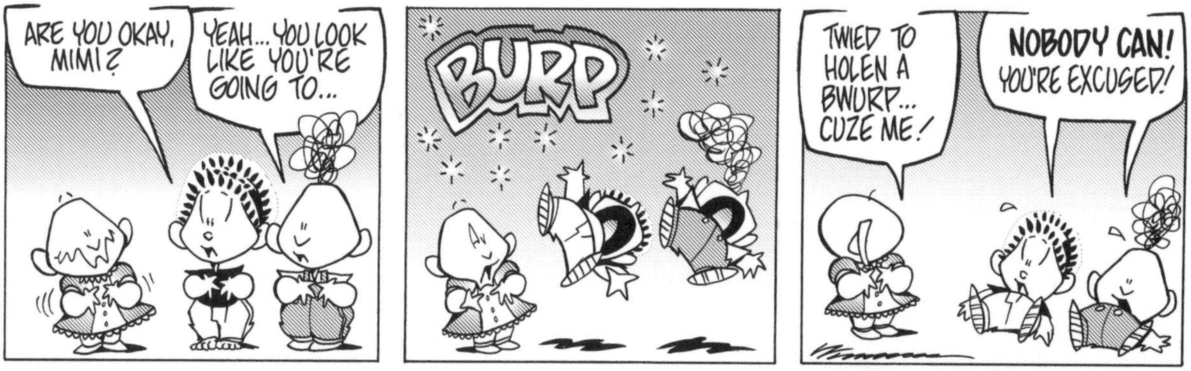
ARE YOU OKAY, MIMI?
YEAH...YOU LOOK LIKE YOU'RE GOING TO...
BURP
TWIED TO HOLEN A BWURP... CUZE ME!
NOBODY CAN! YOU'RE EXCUSED!

FLIP THE PAGE CORNERS FROM FRONT TO BACK AND WATCH BOTH SIDES TOGETHER!

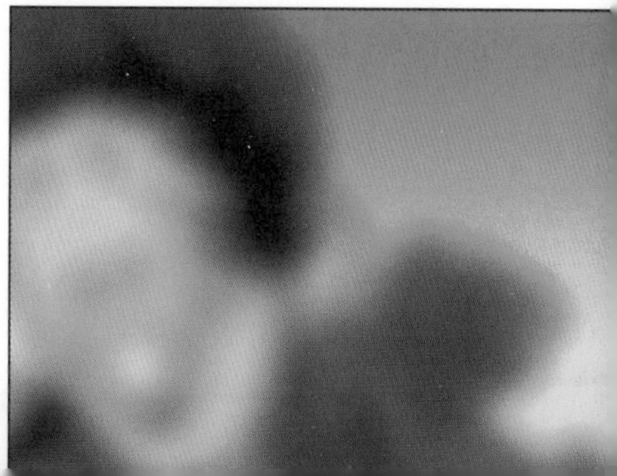

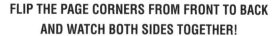

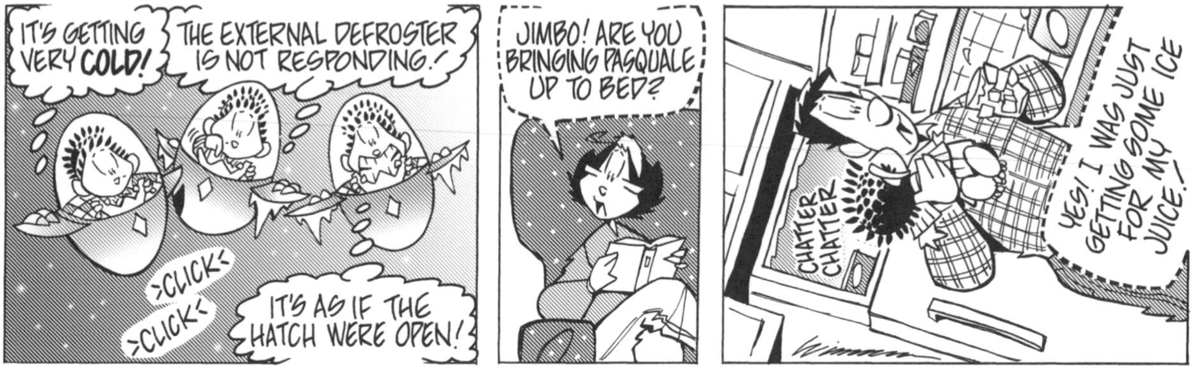
IT'S GETTING VERY **COLD**!
THE EXTERNAL DEFROSTER IS NOT RESPONDING!
>CLICK<
>CLICK<
IT'S AS IF THE HATCH WERE OPEN!
JIMBO! ARE YOU BRINGING PASQUALE UP TO BED?
CHATTER CHATTER
YES! I WAS JUST GETTING SOME ICE FOR MY JUICE!

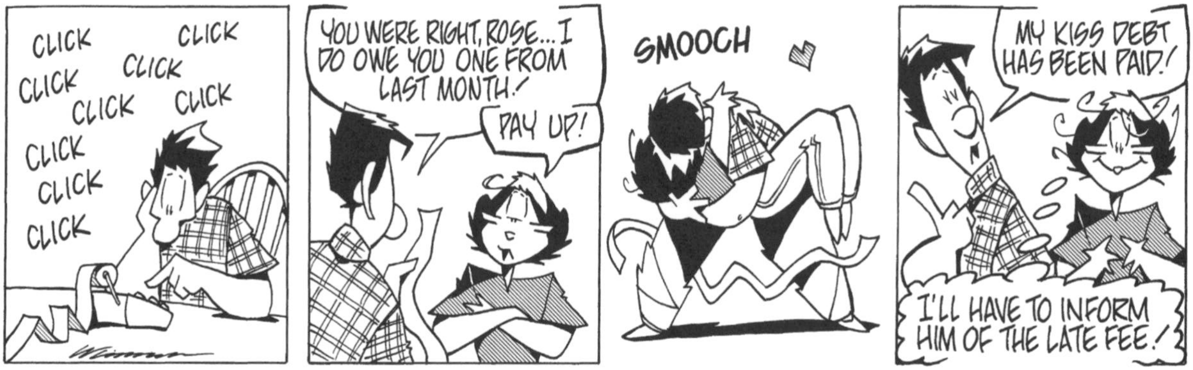
CLICK CLICK CLICK CLICK CLICK CLICK CLICK CLICK CLICK
YOU WERE RIGHT, ROSE... I DO OWE YOU ONE FROM LAST MONTH!
PAY UP!
SMOOCH
MY KISS DEBT HAS BEEN PAID!
I'LL HAVE TO INFORM HIM OF THE LATE FEE!

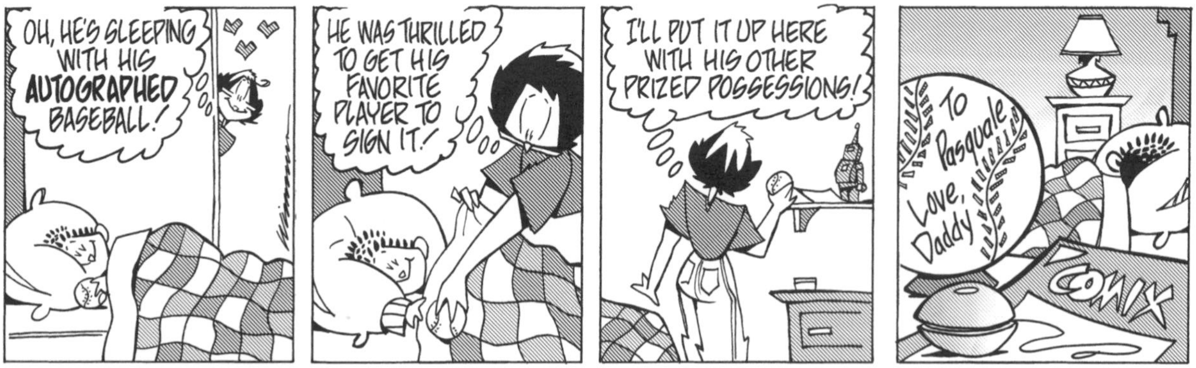
OH, HE'S SLEEPING WITH HIS **AUTOGRAPHED** BASEBALL!
HE WAS THRILLED TO GET HIS FAVORITE PLAYER TO SIGN IT!
I'LL PUT IT UP HERE WITH HIS OTHER PRIZED POSSESSIONS!
To Pasquale
Love, Daddy
CONIX

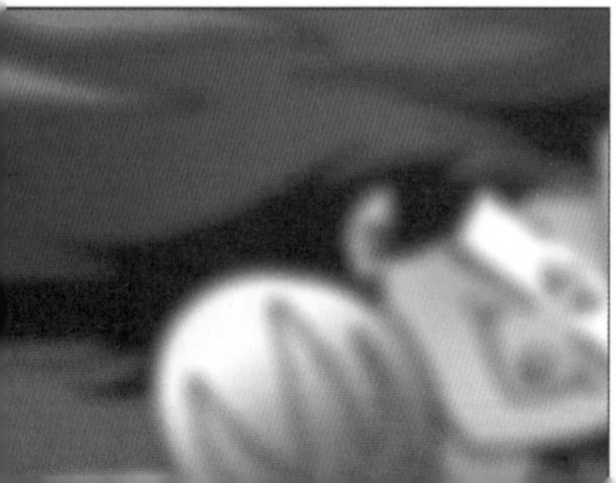

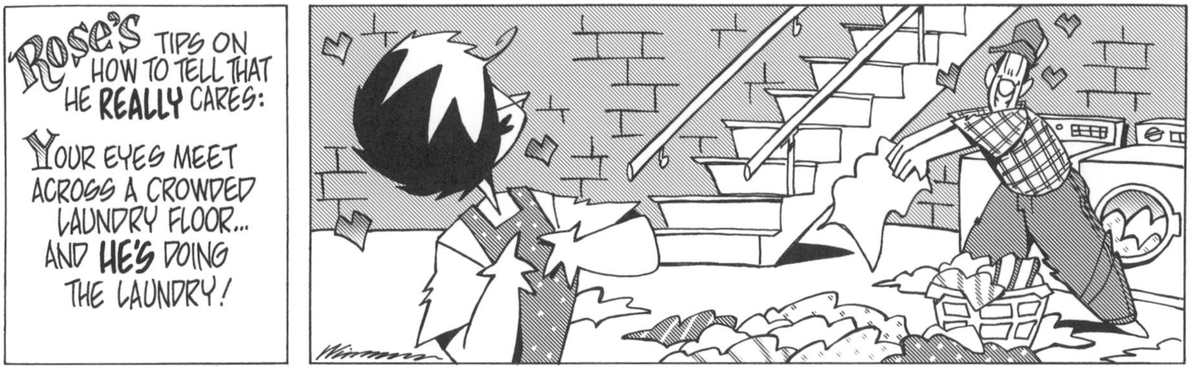
ROSE'S TIPS ON HOW TO TELL THAT HE REALLY CARES:
YOUR EYES MEET ACROSS A CROWDED LAUNDRY FLOOR... AND HE'S DOING THE LAUNDRY!

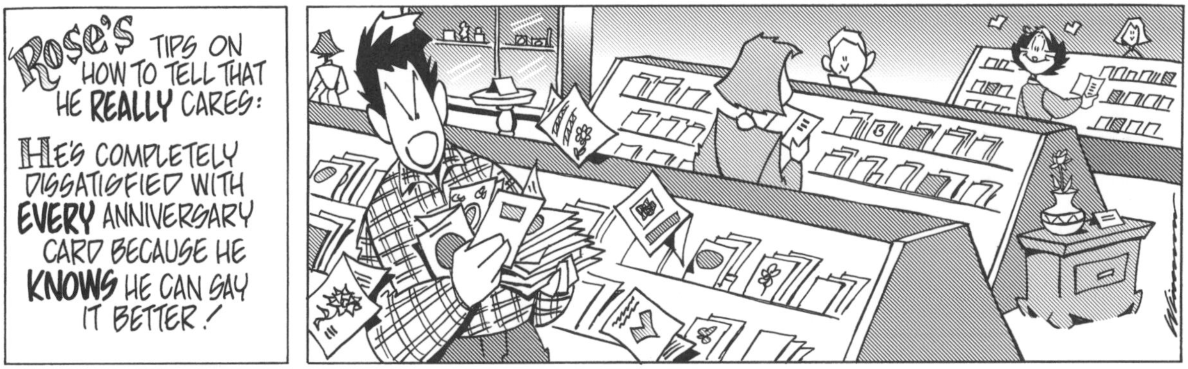
ROSE'S TIPS ON HOW TO TELL THAT HE REALLY CARES:
HE'S COMPLETELY DISSATISFIED WITH EVERY ANNIVERSARY CARD BECAUSE HE KNOWS HE CAN SAY IT BETTER!

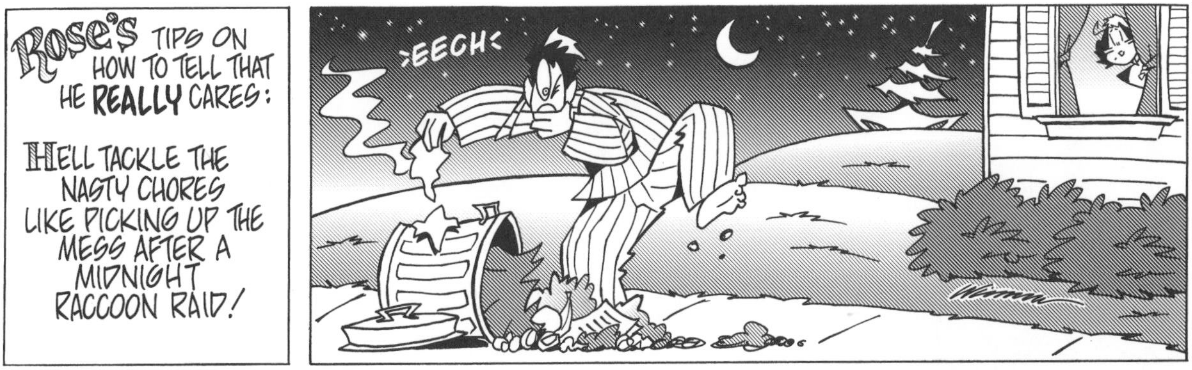
ROSE'S TIPS ON HOW TO TELL THAT HE REALLY CARES:
HE'LL TACKLE THE NASTY CHORES LIKE PICKING UP THE MESS AFTER A MIDNIGHT RACCOON RAID!
>EECH<

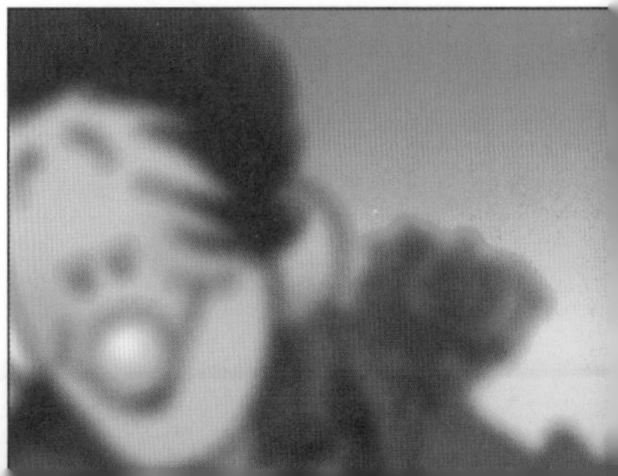

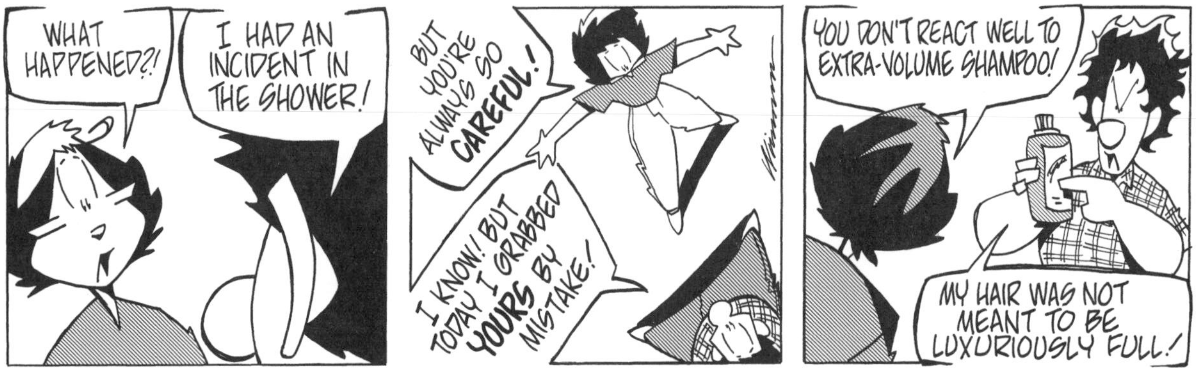
WHAT HAPPENED?!
I HAD AN INCIDENT IN THE SHOWER!
BUT YOU'RE ALWAYS SO CAREFUL!
I KNOW! BUT TODAY I GRABBED YOURS BY MISTAKE!
YOU DON'T REACT WELL TO EXTRA-VOLUME SHAMPOO!
MY HAIR WAS NOT MEANT TO BE LUXURIOUSLY FULL!

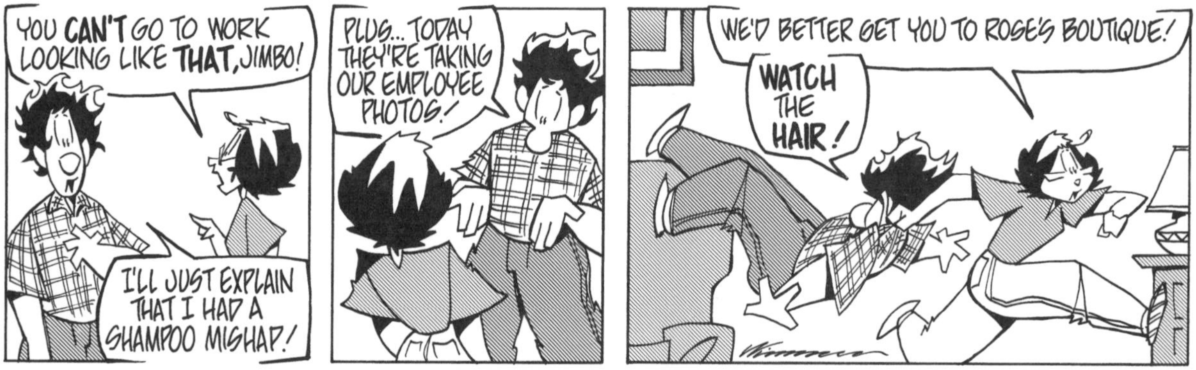
YOU CAN'T GO TO WORK LOOKING LIKE THAT, JIMBO!
I'LL JUST EXPLAIN THAT I HAD A SHAMPOO MISHAP!
PLUS... TODAY THEY'RE TAKING OUR EMPLOYEE PHOTOS!
WE'D BETTER GET YOU TO ROSE'S BOUTIQUE!
WATCH THE HAIR!

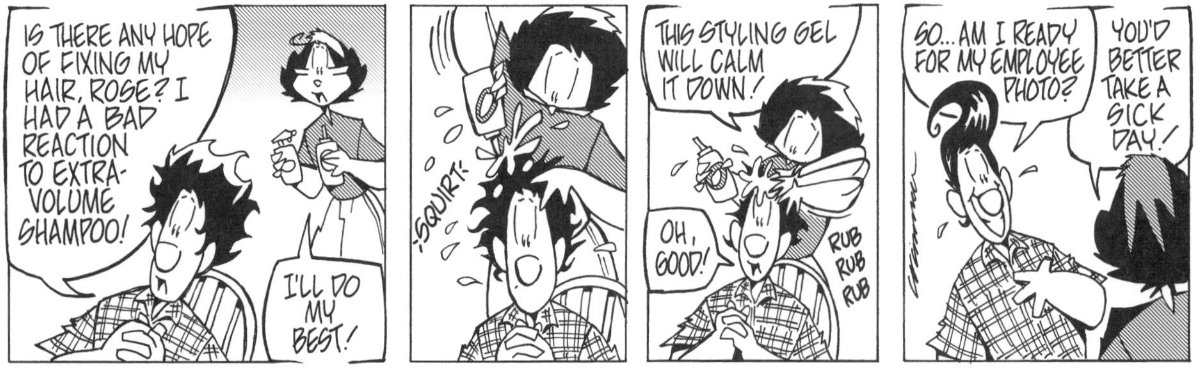
IS THERE ANY HOPE OF FIXING MY HAIR, ROSE? I HAD A BAD REACTION TO EXTRA-VOLUME SHAMPOO!
I'LL DO MY BEST!
-SQUIRT-
THIS STYLING GEL WILL CALM IT DOWN!
OH, GOOD!
RUB RUB RUB
SO... AM I READY FOR MY EMPLOYEE PHOTO?
YOU'D BETTER TAKE A SICK DAY!

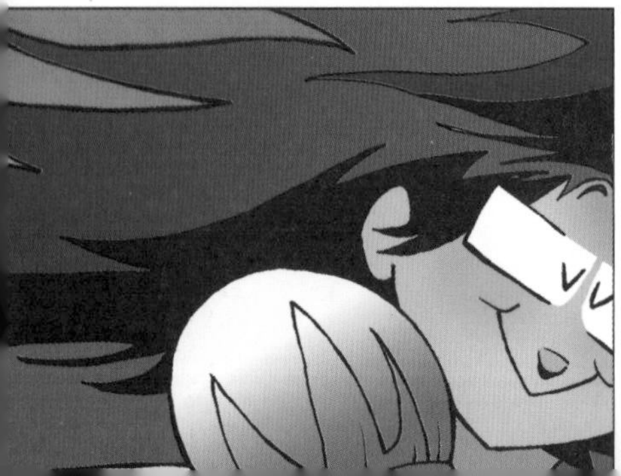

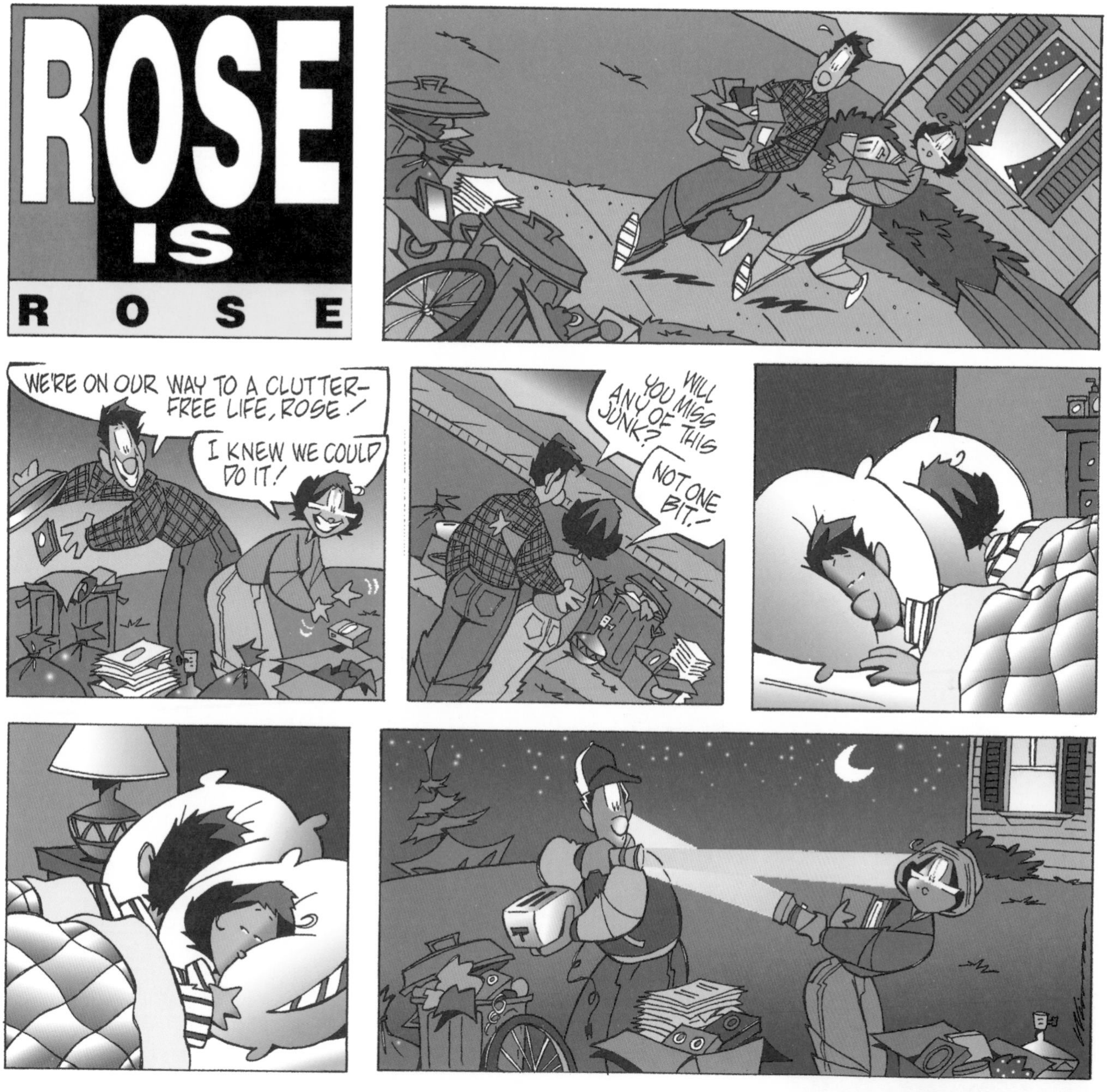
ROSE IS ROSE
WE'RE ON OUR WAY TO A CLUTTER-FREE LIFE, ROSE!
I KNEW WE COULD DO IT!
WILL YOU MISS ANY OF THIS JUNK?
NOT ONE BIT!

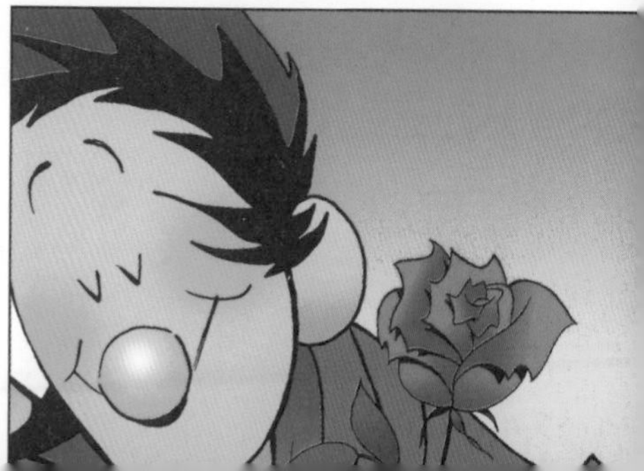

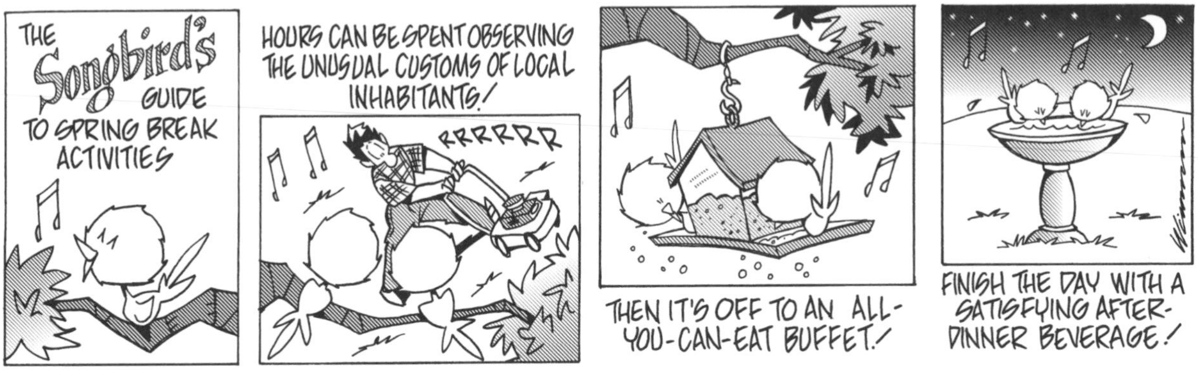
THE Songbird's GUIDE TO SPRING BREAK ACTIVITIES
HOURS CAN BE SPENT OBSERVING THE UNUSUAL CUSTOMS OF LOCAL INHABITANTS!
RRRRRR
THEN IT'S OFF TO AN ALL-YOU-CAN-EAT BUFFET!
FINISH THE DAY WITH A SATISFYING AFTER-DINNER BEVERAGE!

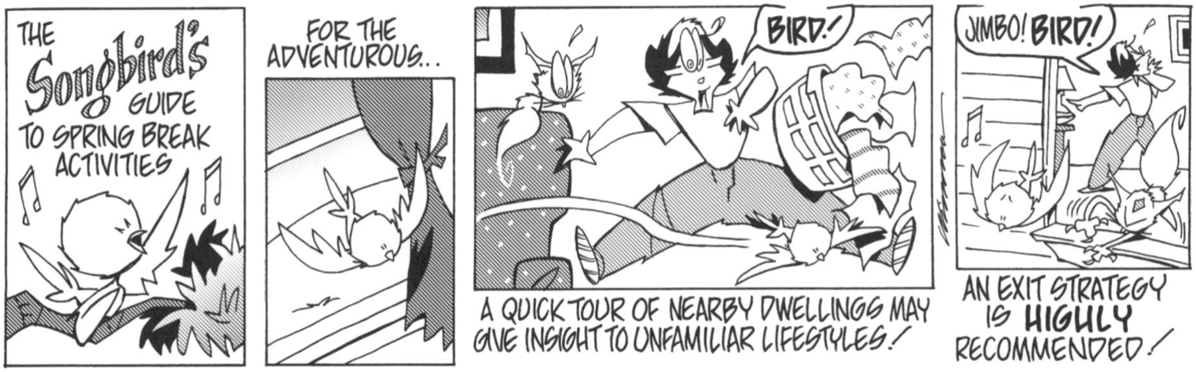
THE Songbird's GUIDE TO SPRING BREAK ACTIVITIES
FOR THE ADVENTUROUS...
BIRD!
A QUICK TOUR OF NEARBY DWELLINGS MAY GIVE INSIGHT TO UNFAMILIAR LIFESTYLES!
JIMBO! BIRD!
AN EXIT STRATEGY IS HIGHLY RECOMMENDED!

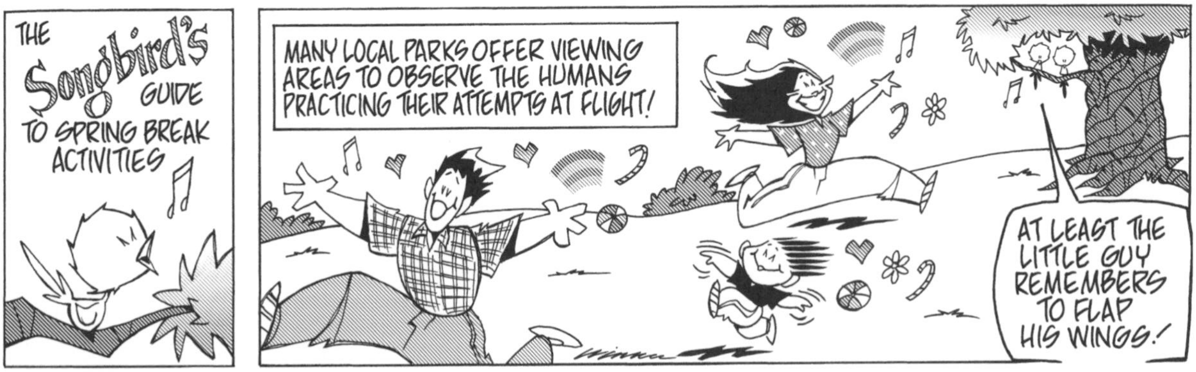
THE Songbird's GUIDE TO SPRING BREAK ACTIVITIES
MANY LOCAL PARKS OFFER VIEWING AREAS TO OBSERVE THE HUMANS PRACTICING THEIR ATTEMPTS AT FLIGHT!
AT LEAST THE LITTLE GUY REMEMBERS TO FLAP HIS WINGS!

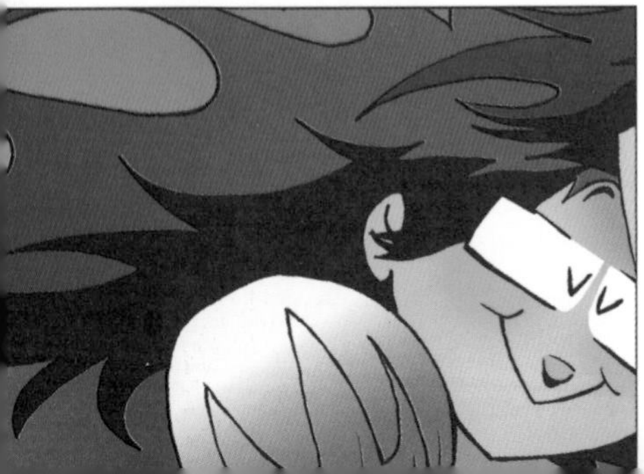

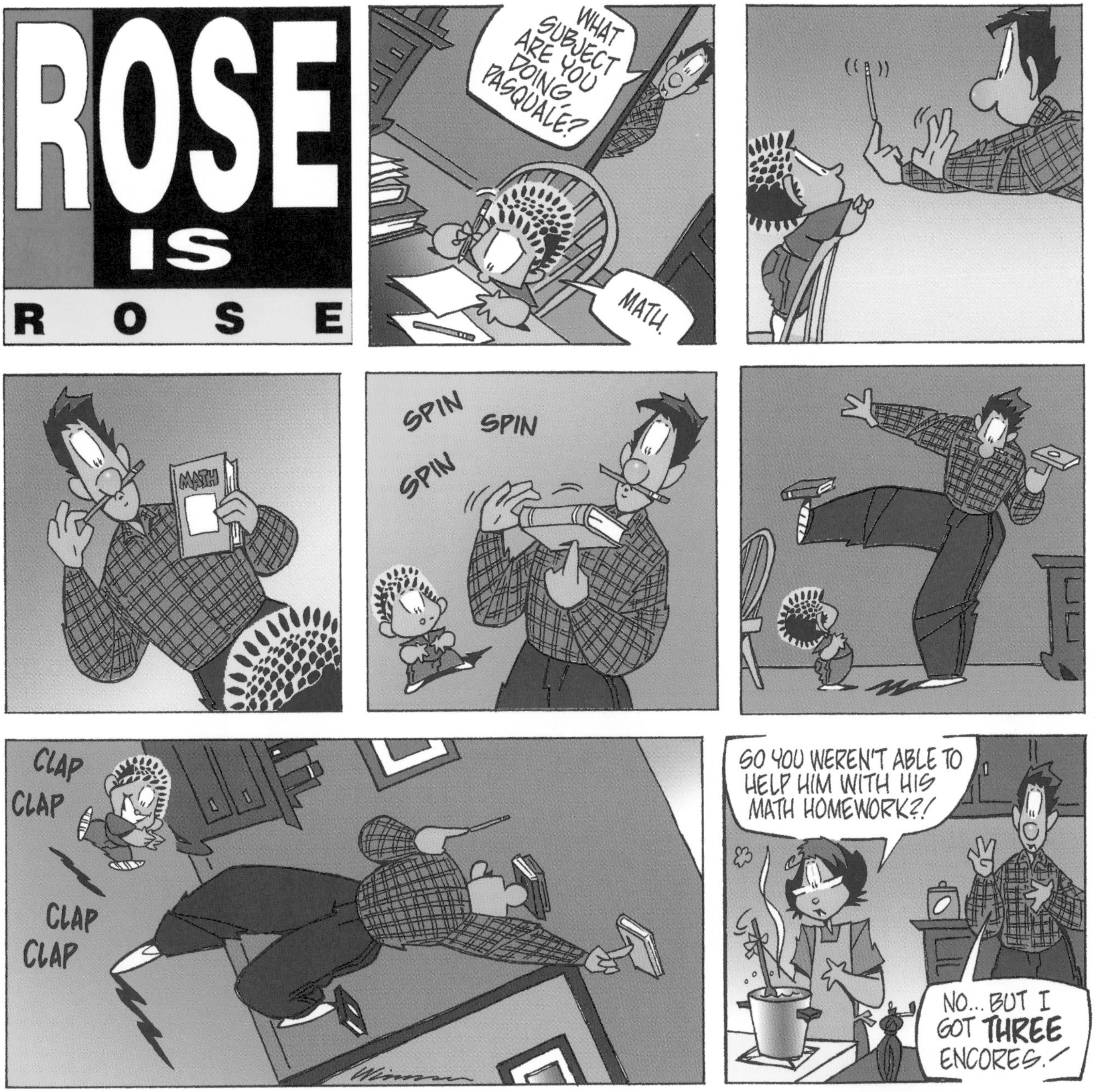
ROSE IS ROSE
WHAT SUBJECT ARE YOU DOING, PASQUALE?
MATH.
MATH
SPIN
SPIN
SPIN
CLAP
CLAP
CLAP
CLAP
SO YOU WEREN'T ABLE TO HELP HIM WITH HIS MATH HOMEWORK?!
NO... BUT I GOT **THREE** ENCORES.!

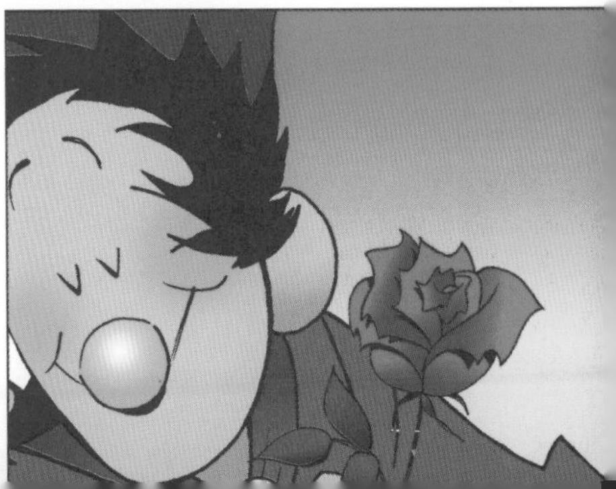

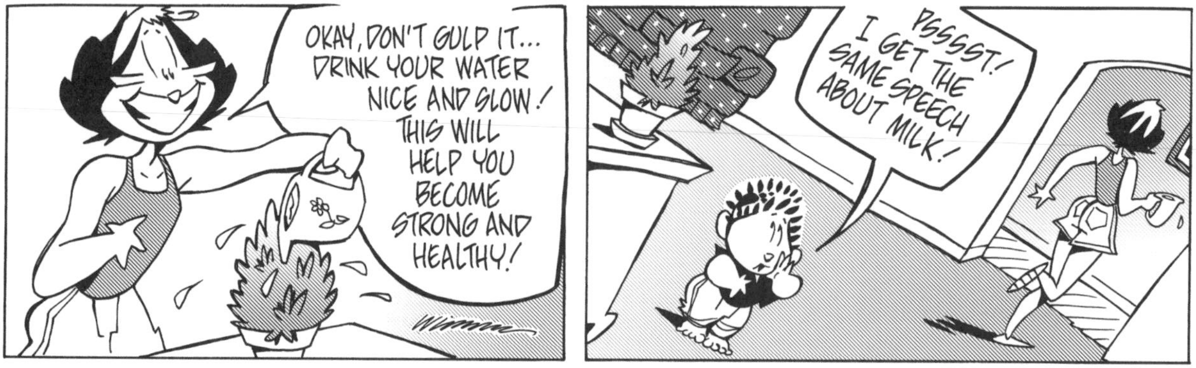
OKAY, DON'T GULP IT... DRINK YOUR WATER NICE AND SLOW! THIS WILL HELP YOU BECOME STRONG AND HEALTHY!
PSSSST! I GET THE SAME SPEECH ABOUT MILK!

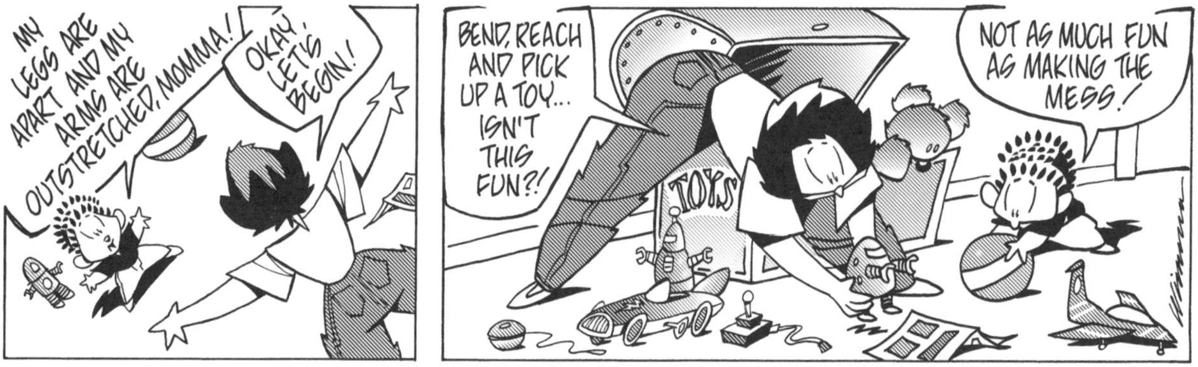
MY LEGS ARE APART AND MY ARMS ARE OUTSTRETCHED, MOMMA!
OKAY, LET'S BEGIN!
BEND, REACH AND PICK UP A TOY... ISN'T THIS FUN?!
NOT AS MUCH FUN AS MAKING THE MESS!
TOYS

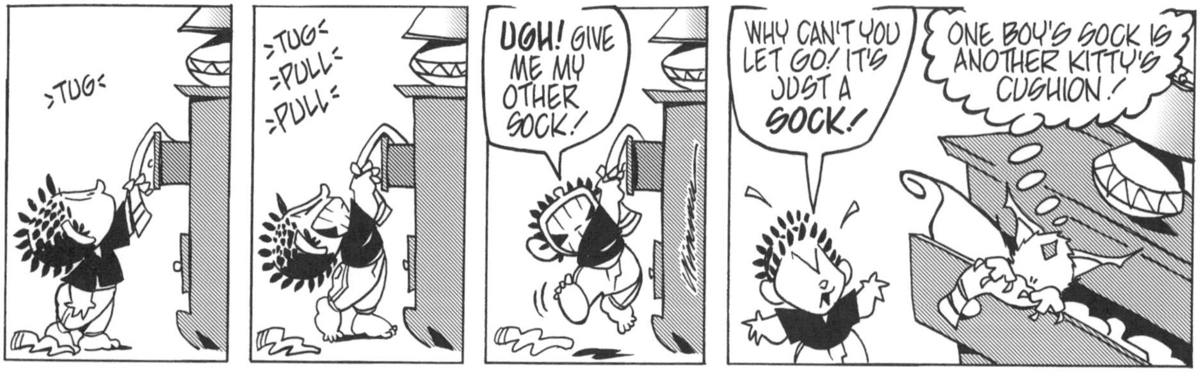
>TUG<
>TUG<
>PULL<
>PULL<
UGH! GIVE ME MY OTHER SOCK!
WHY CAN'T YOU LET GO! IT'S JUST A SOCK!
ONE BOY'S SOCK IS ANOTHER KITTY'S CUSHION!

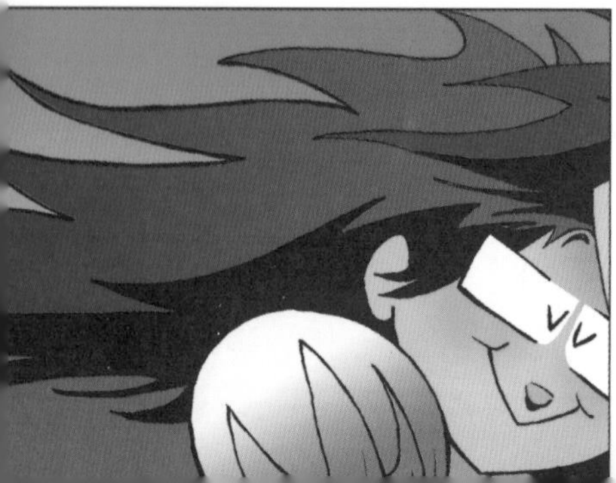

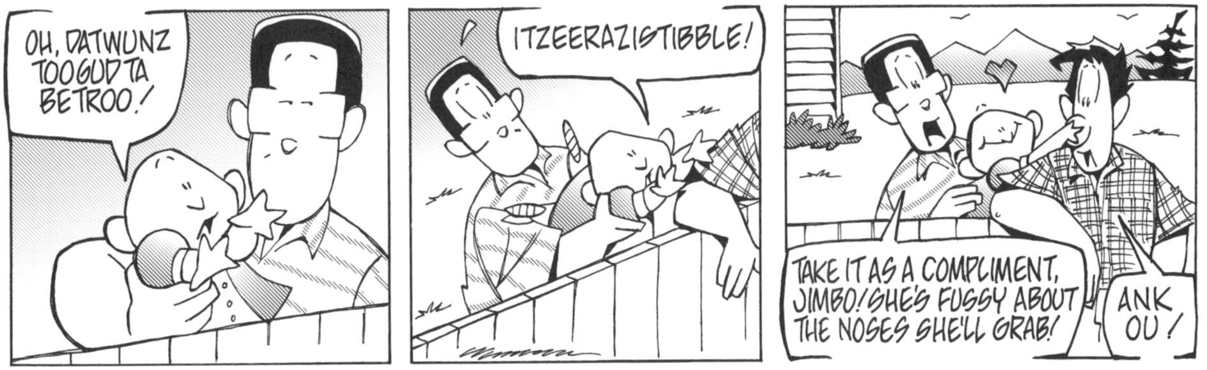
OH, DATWUNZ TOOGUDTA BETROO!
ITZEERAZISTIBBLE!
TAKE IT AS A COMPLIMENT, JIMBO! SHE'S FUSSY ABOUT THE NOSES SHE'LL GRAB!
ANK OU!

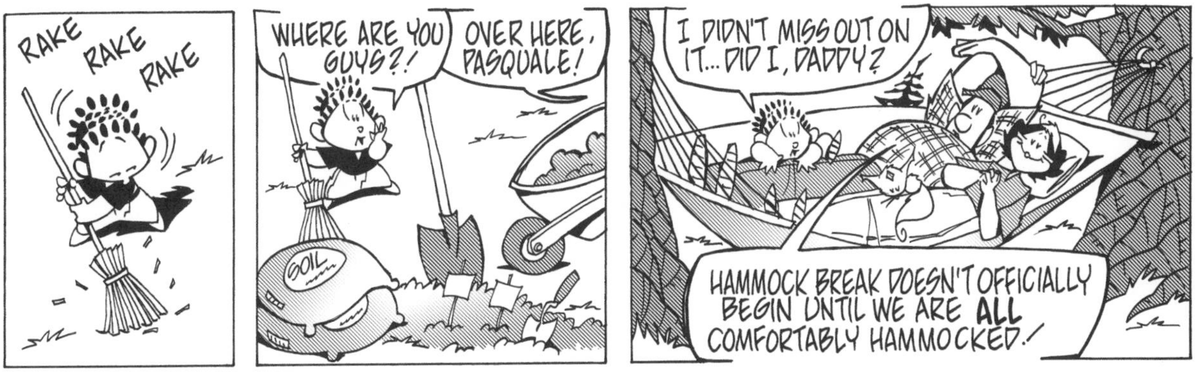
RAKE RAKE RAKE
WHERE ARE YOU GUYS?!
OVER HERE, PASQUALE!
SOIL
I DIDN'T MISS OUT ON IT... DID I, DADDY?
HAMMOCK BREAK DOESN'T OFFICIALLY BEGIN UNTIL WE ARE **ALL** COMFORTABLY HAMMOCKED!

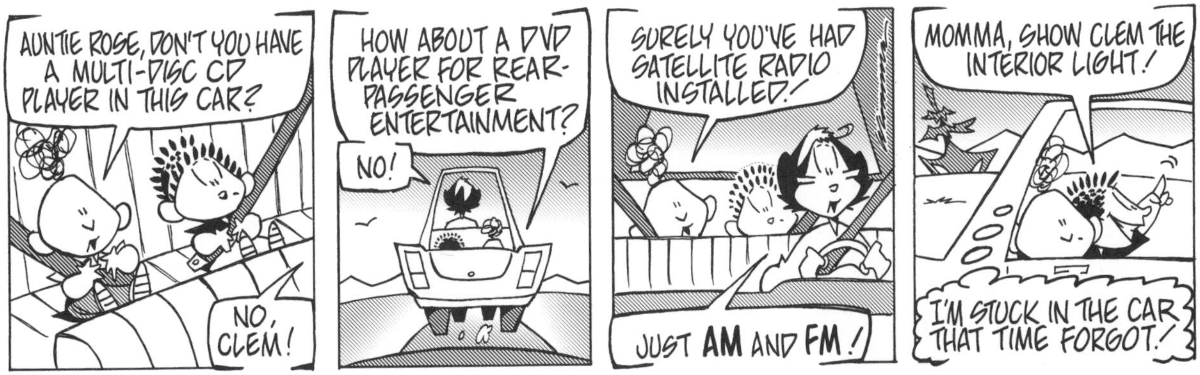
AUNTIE ROSE, DON'T YOU HAVE A MULTI-DISC CD PLAYER IN THIS CAR?
NO, CLEM!
HOW ABOUT A DVD PLAYER FOR REAR-PASSENGER ENTERTAINMENT?
NO!
SURELY YOU'VE HAD SATELLITE RADIO INSTALLED!
JUST **AM** AND **FM**!
MOMMA, SHOW CLEM THE INTERIOR LIGHT!
I'M STUCK IN THE CAR THAT TIME FORGOT!

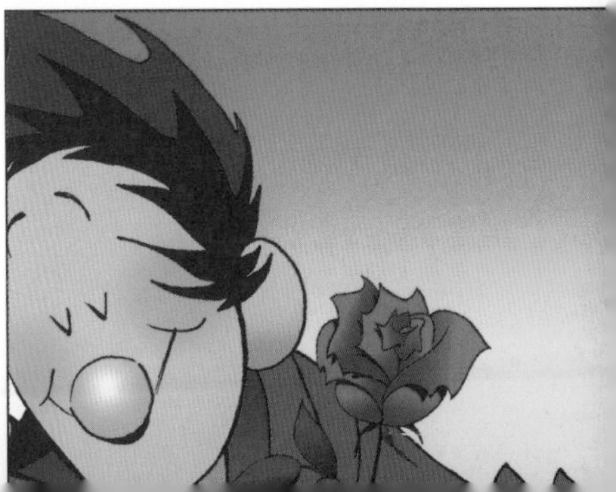

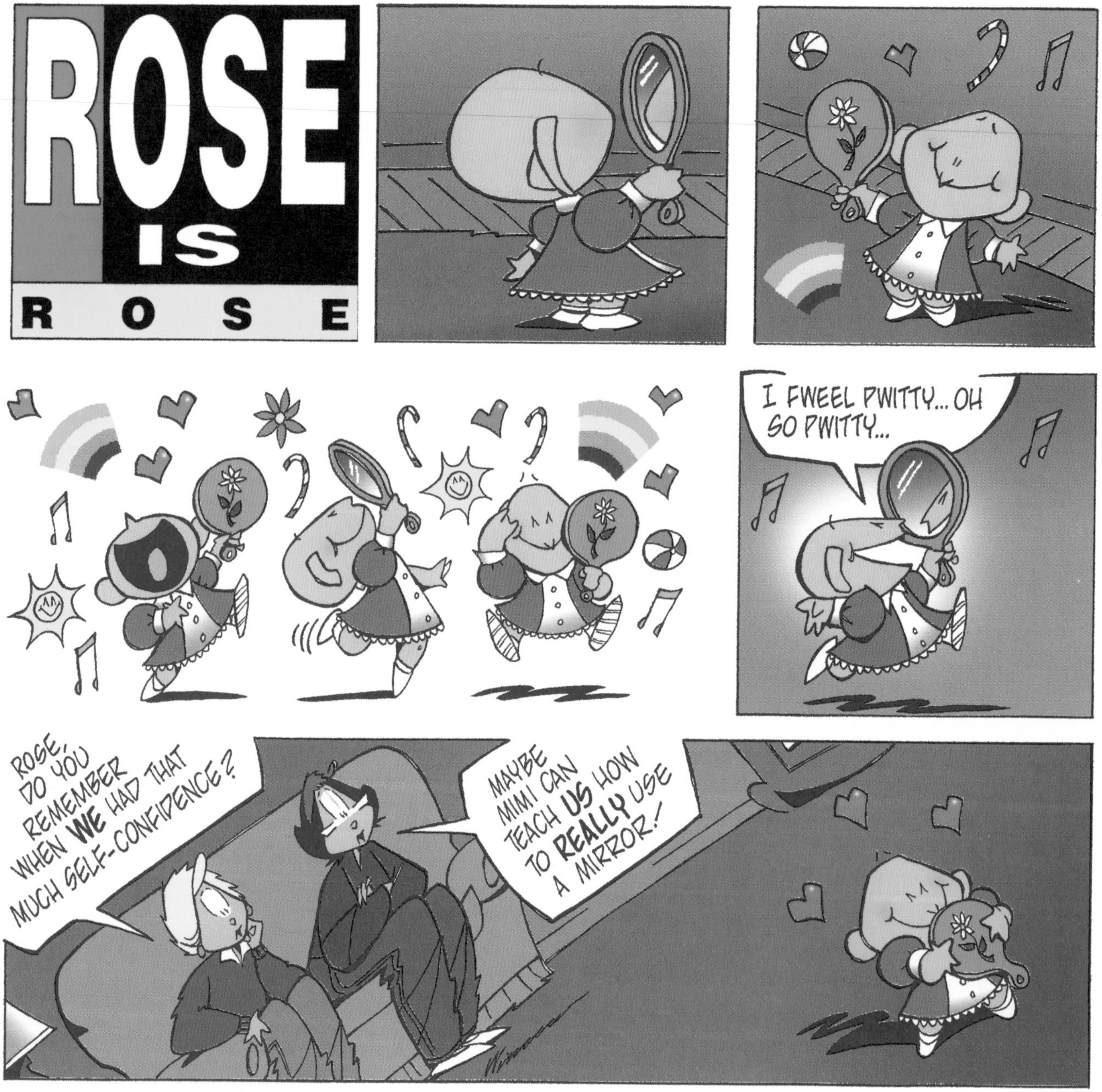
ROSE IS ROSE
I FWEEL PWITTY... OH SO PWITTY...
ROSE, DO YOU REMEMBER WHEN WE HAD THAT MUCH SELF-CONFIDENCE?
MAYBE MIMI CAN TEACH US HOW TO REALLY USE A MIRROR!

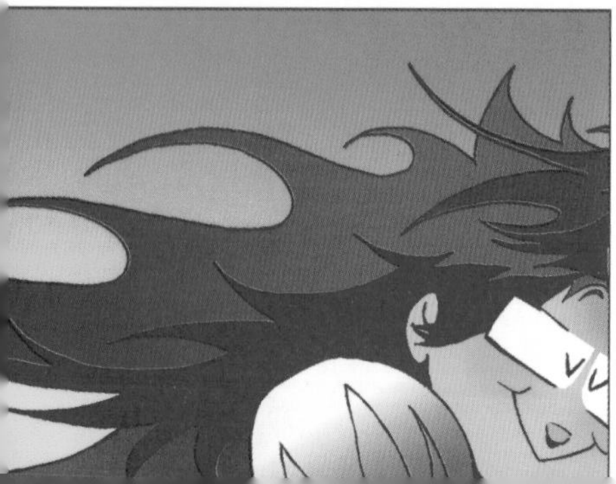

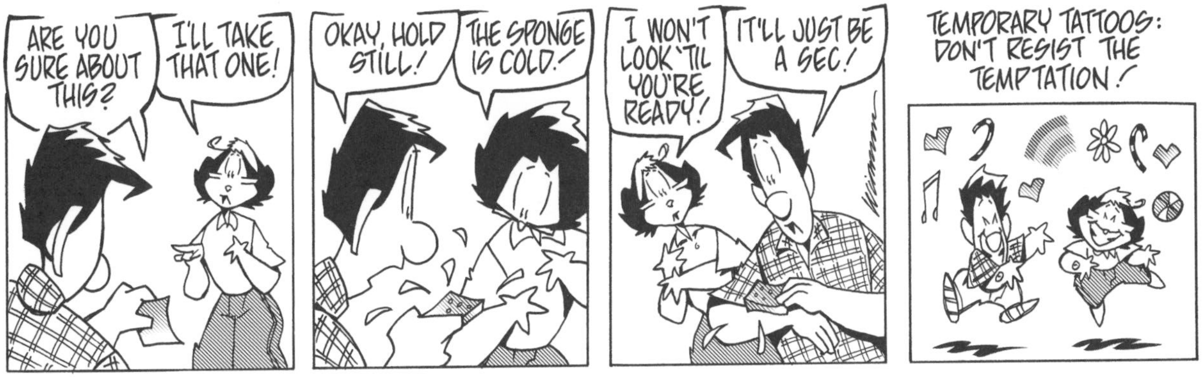
ARE YOU SURE ABOUT THIS?
I'LL TAKE THAT ONE!
OKAY, HOLD STILL!
THE SPONGE IS COLD!
I WON'T LOOK 'TIL YOU'RE READY!
IT'LL JUST BE A SEC!
TEMPORARY TATTOOS: DON'T RESIST THE TEMPTATION!

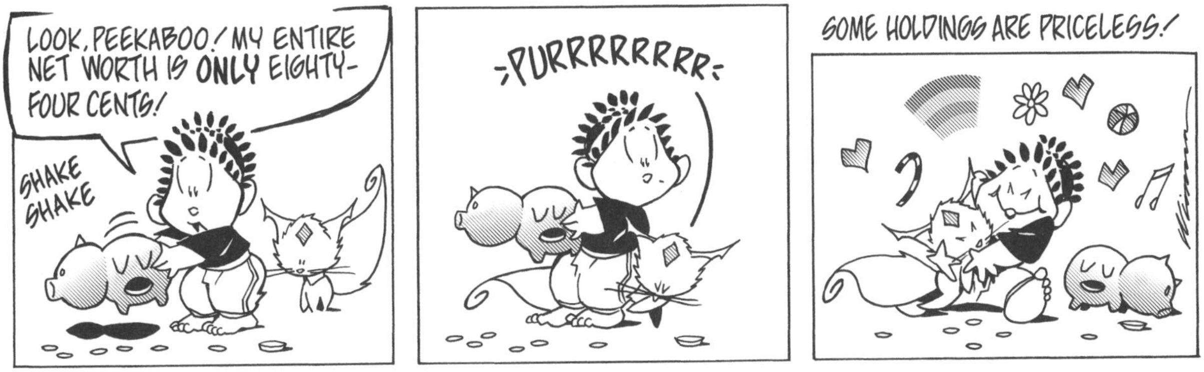
LOOK, PEEKABOO! MY ENTIRE NET WORTH IS ONLY EIGHTY-FOUR CENTS!
SHAKE SHAKE
PURRRRRRRR
SOME HOLDINGS ARE PRICELESS!

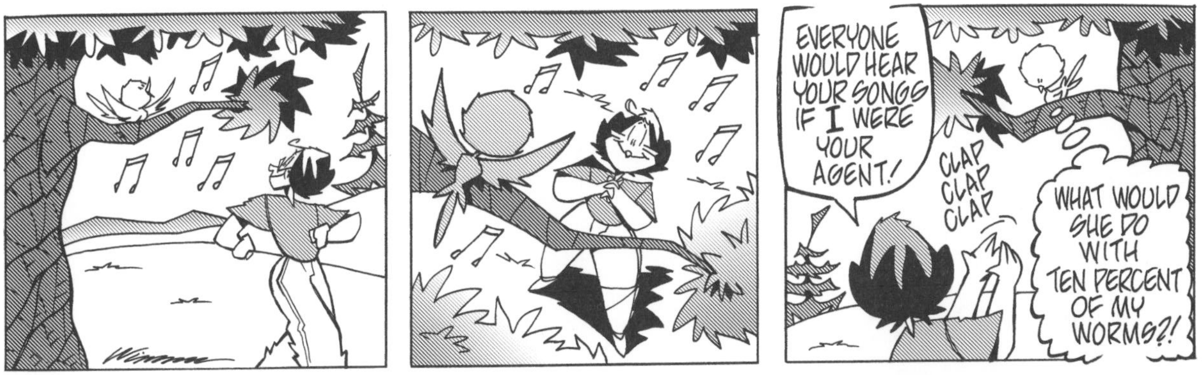
EVERYONE WOULD HEAR YOUR SONGS IF I WERE YOUR AGENT!
CLAP CLAP CLAP
WHAT WOULD SHE DO WITH TEN PERCENT OF MY WORMS?!

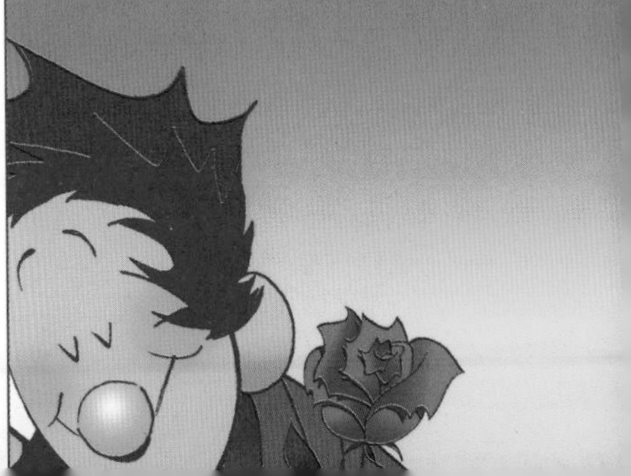

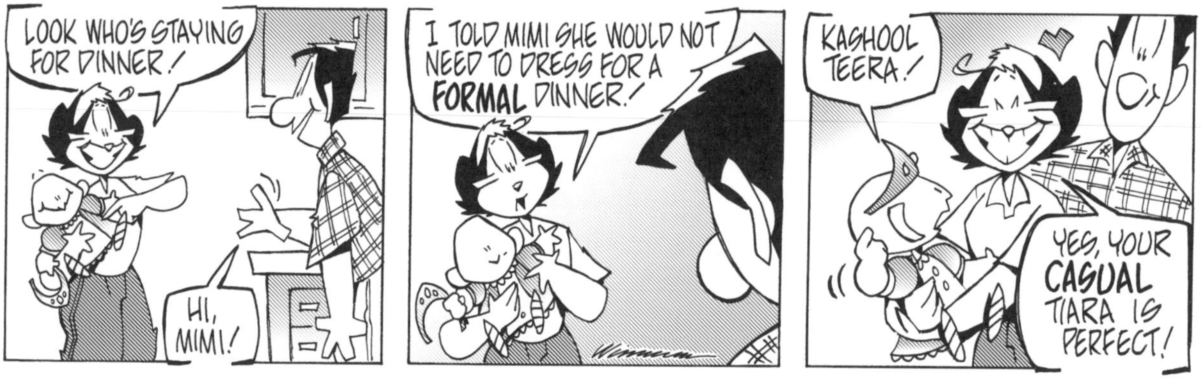
LOOK WHO'S STAYING FOR DINNER!
HI, MIMI!
I TOLD MIMI SHE WOULD NOT NEED TO DRESS FOR A **FORMAL** DINNER!
KASHOOL TEERA!
YES, YOUR **CASUAL** TIARA IS PERFECT!

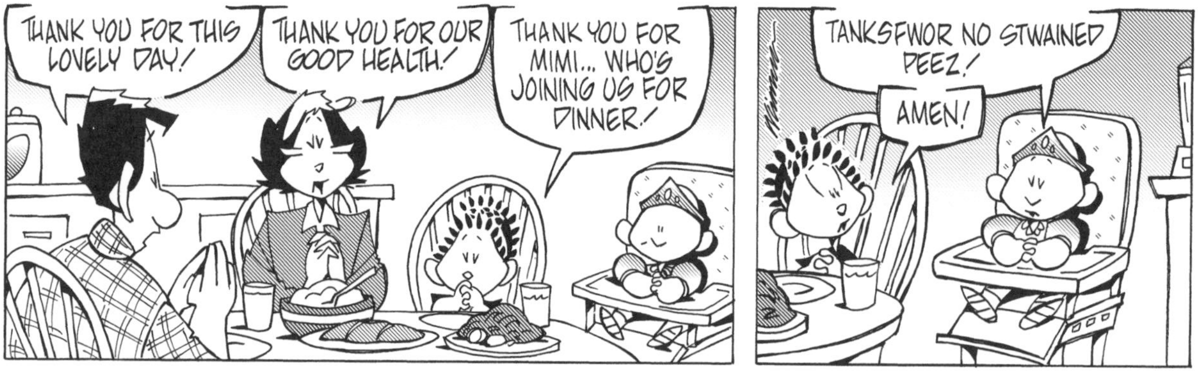
THANK YOU FOR THIS LOVELY DAY!
THANK YOU FOR OUR GOOD HEALTH!
THANK YOU FOR MIMI... WHO'S JOINING US FOR DINNER!
TANKSFWOR NO STWAINED PEEZ!
AMEN!

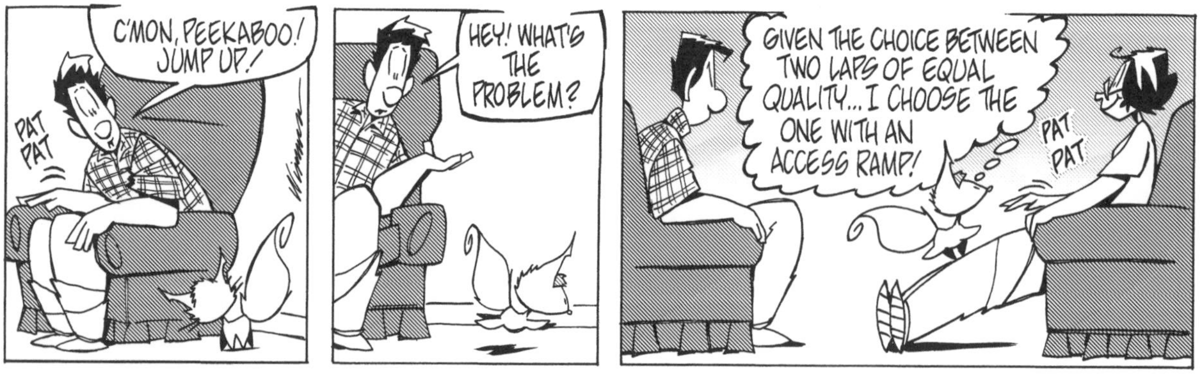
C'MON, PEEKABOO! JUMP UP!
PAT PAT
HEY! WHAT'S THE PROBLEM?
GIVEN THE CHOICE BETWEEN TWO LAPS OF EQUAL QUALITY... I CHOOSE THE ONE WITH AN ACCESS RAMP!
PAT PAT

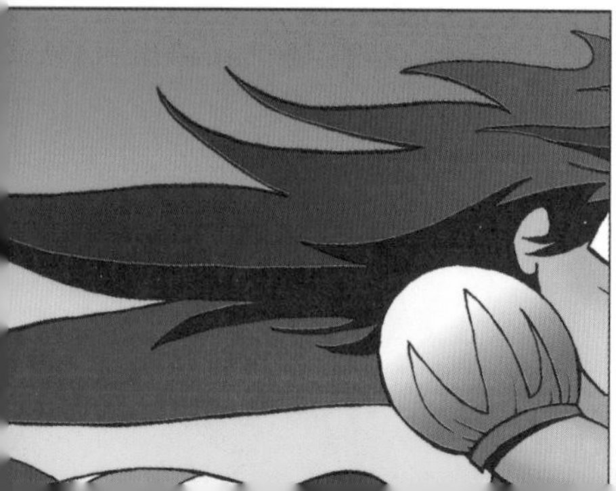

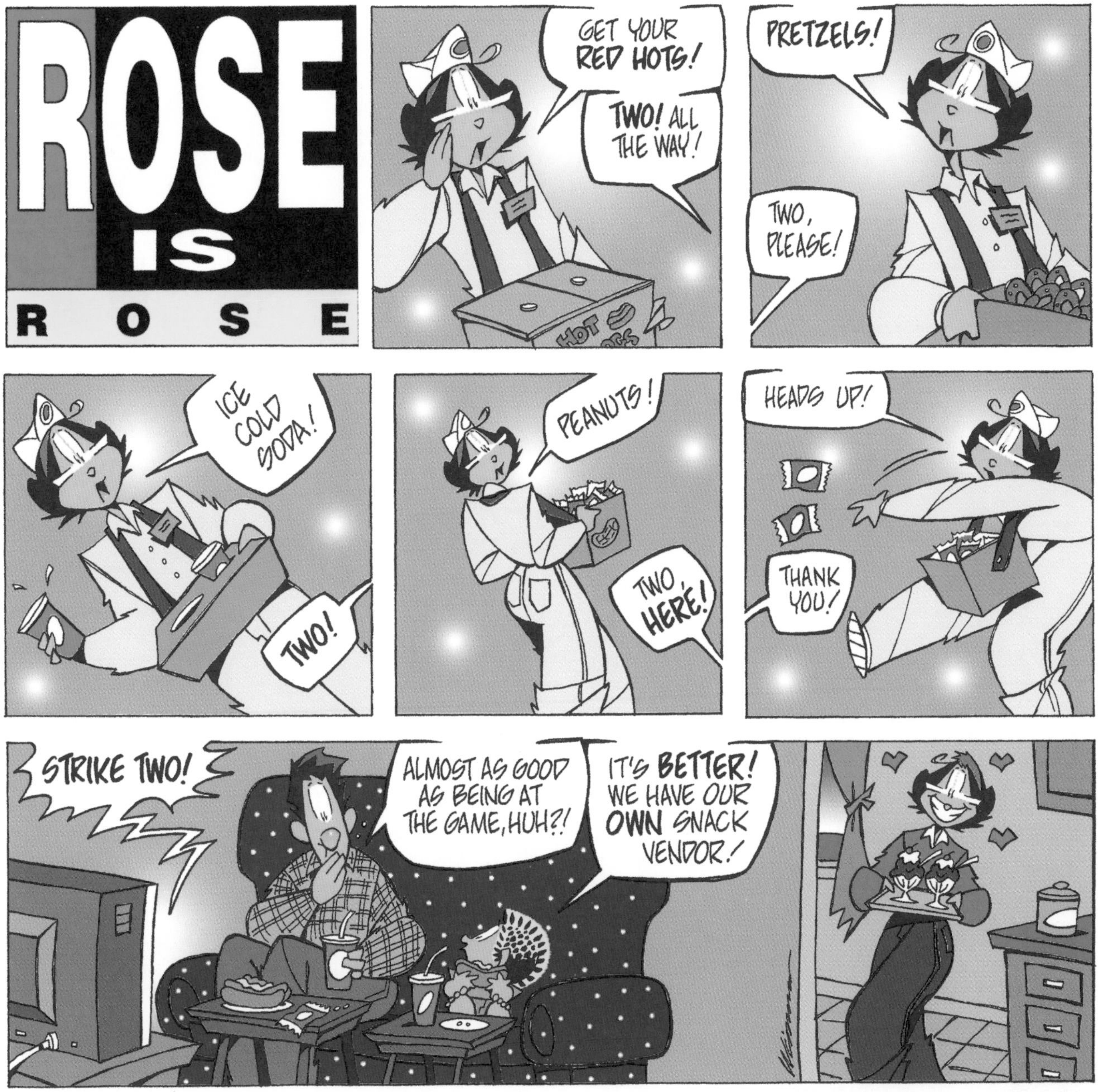
ROSE IS ROSE
GET YOUR RED HOTS!
TWO! ALL THE WAY!
PRETZELS!
TWO, PLEASE!
ICE COLD SODA!
TWO!
PEANUTS!
TWO, HERE!
HEADS UP!
THANK YOU!
STRIKE TWO!
ALMOST AS GOOD AS BEING AT THE GAME, HUH?!
IT'S BETTER! WE HAVE OUR OWN SNACK VENDOR!

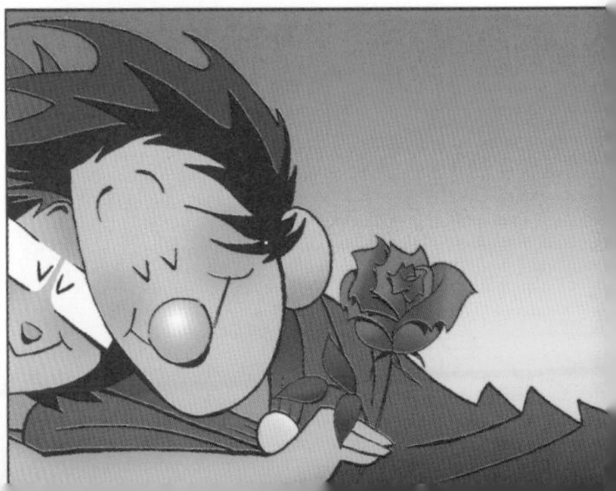

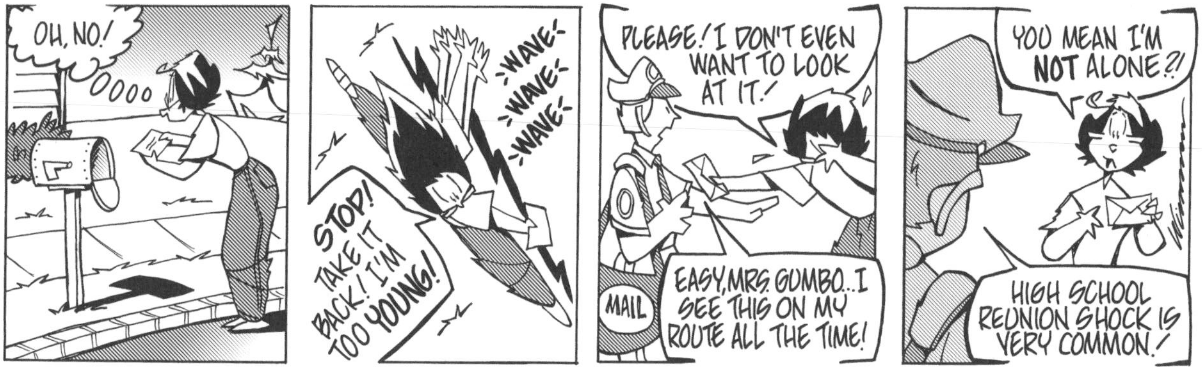
OH, NO!
OOOO
STOP! TAKE IT BACK! I'M TOO YOUNG!
WAVE WAVE WAVE
PLEASE! I DON'T EVEN WANT TO LOOK AT IT!
EASY, MRS. GUMBO... I SEE THIS ON MY ROUTE ALL THE TIME!
MAIL
YOU MEAN I'M NOT ALONE?!
HIGH SCHOOL REUNION SHOCK IS VERY COMMON!

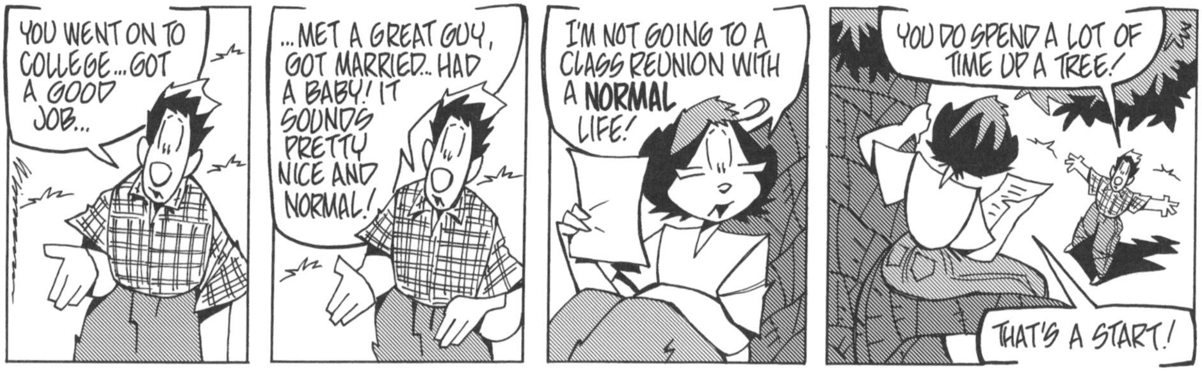
YOU WENT ON TO COLLEGE... GOT A GOOD JOB...
...MET A GREAT GUY, GOT MARRIED... HAD A BABY! IT SOUNDS PRETTY NICE AND NORMAL!
I'M NOT GOING TO A CLASS REUNION WITH A NORMAL LIFE!
YOU DO SPEND A LOT OF TIME UP A TREE!
THAT'S A START!

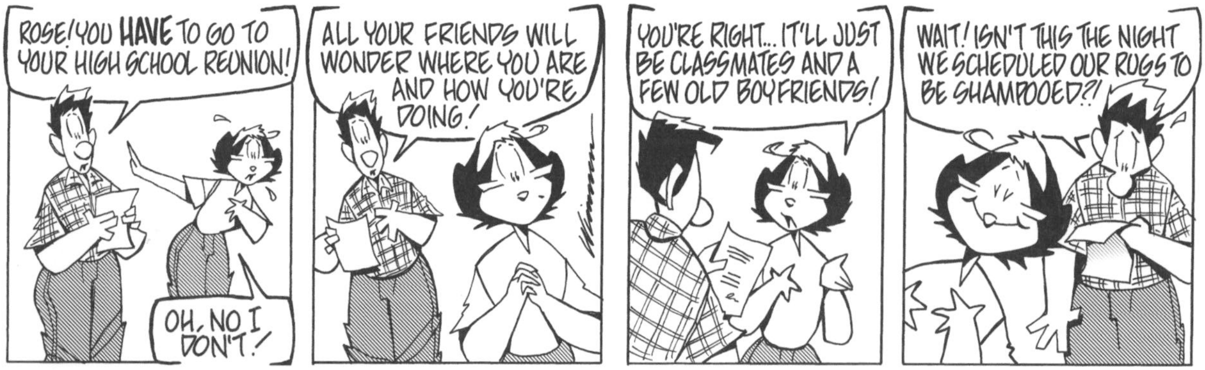
ROSE! YOU HAVE TO GO TO YOUR HIGH SCHOOL REUNION!
OH, NO I DON'T!
ALL YOUR FRIENDS WILL WONDER WHERE YOU ARE AND HOW YOU'RE DOING!
YOU'RE RIGHT... IT'LL JUST BE CLASSMATES AND A FEW OLD BOYFRIENDS!
WAIT! ISN'T THIS THE NIGHT WE SCHEDULED OUR RUGS TO BE SHAMPOOED?!

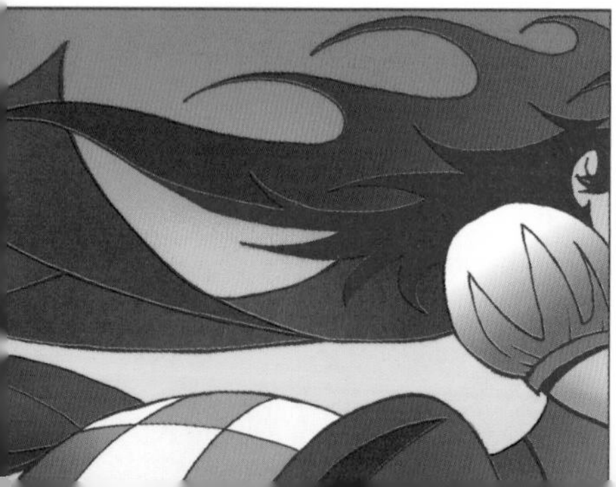

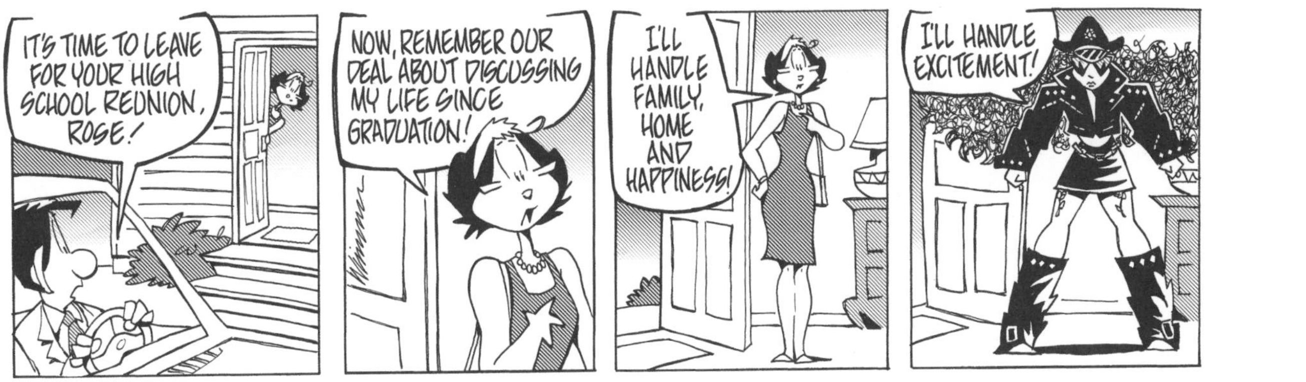
IT'S TIME TO LEAVE FOR YOUR HIGH SCHOOL REUNION, ROSE!
NOW, REMEMBER OUR DEAL ABOUT DISCUSSING MY LIFE SINCE GRADUATION!
I'LL HANDLE FAMILY, HOME AND HAPPINESS!
I'LL HANDLE EXCITEMENT!

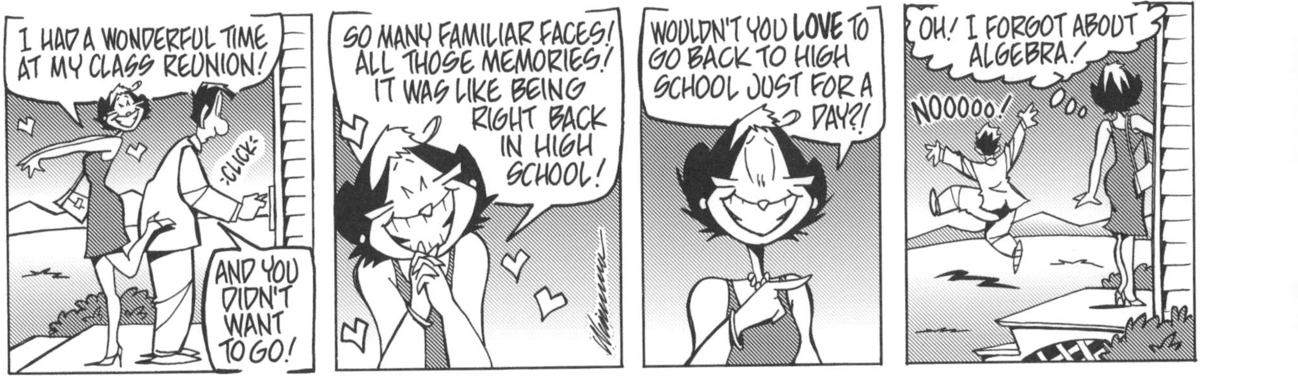
I HAD A WONDERFUL TIME AT MY CLASS REUNION!
CLICK
AND YOU DIDN'T WANT TO GO!
SO MANY FAMILIAR FACES! ALL THOSE MEMORIES! IT WAS LIKE BEING RIGHT BACK IN HIGH SCHOOL!
WOULDN'T YOU LOVE TO GO BACK TO HIGH SCHOOL JUST FOR A DAY?!
OH! I FORGOT ABOUT ALGEBRA!
NOOOOO!

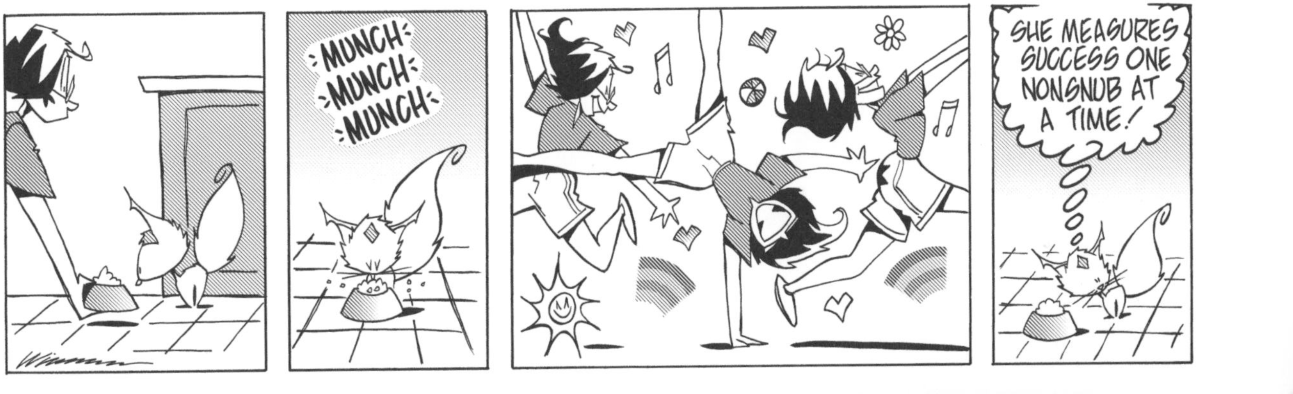
MUNCH MUNCH MUNCH
SHE MEASURES SUCCESS ONE NONSNUB AT A TIME!

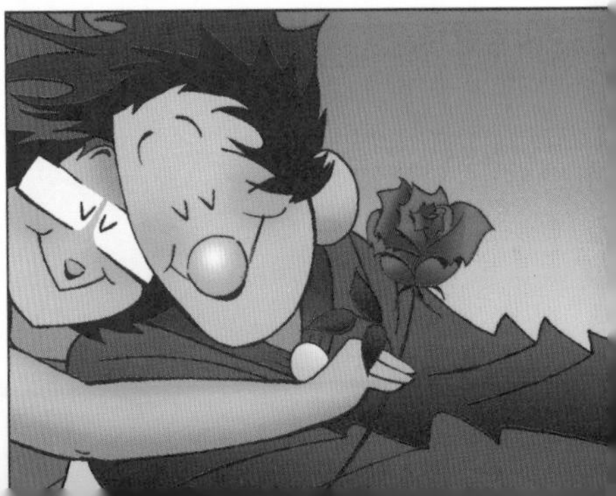

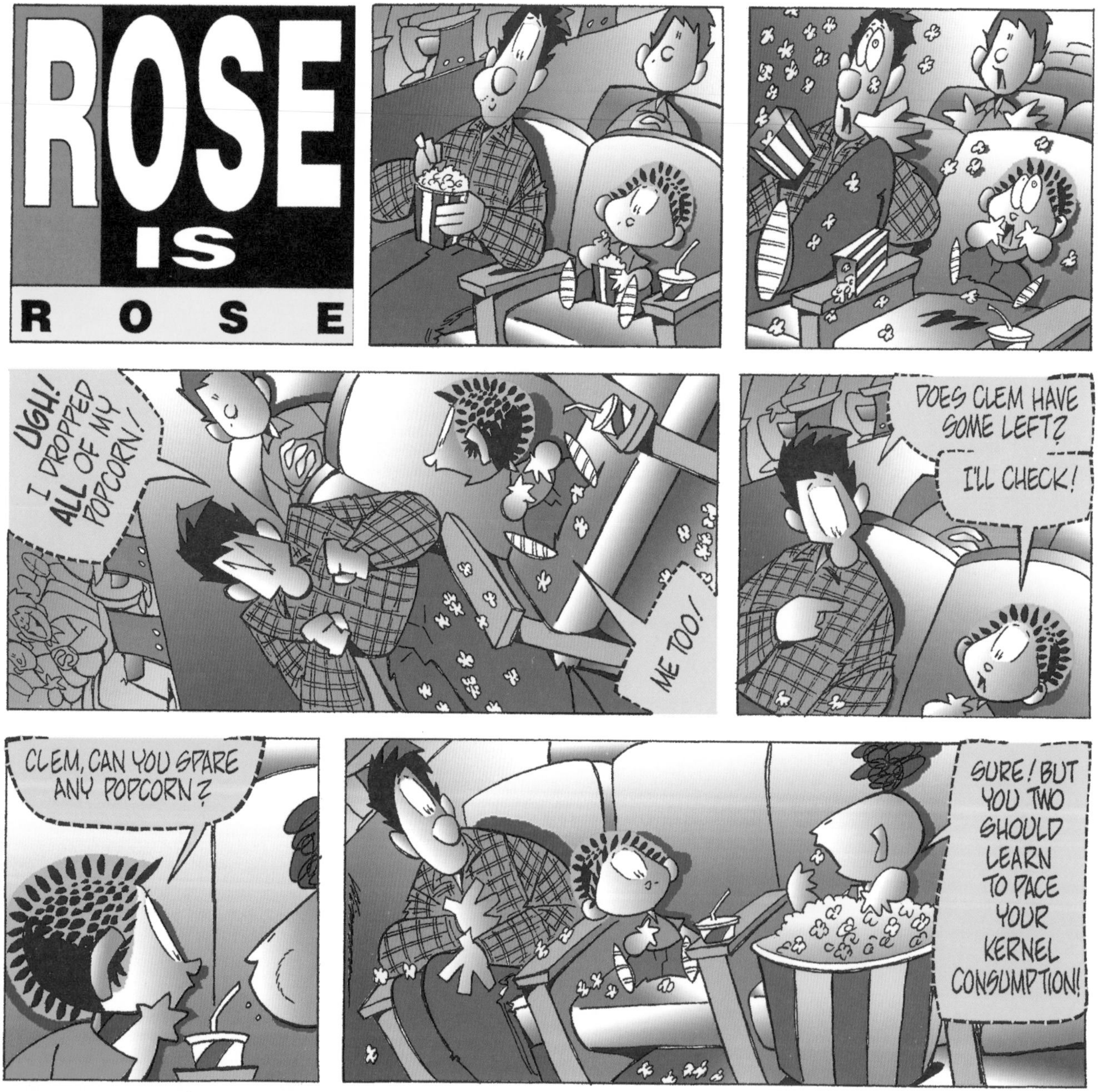
ROSE IS ROSE
UGH! I DROPPED ALL OF MY POPCORN!
ME TOO!
DOES CLEM HAVE SOME LEFT?
I'LL CHECK!
CLEM, CAN YOU SPARE ANY POPCORN?
SURE! BUT YOU TWO SHOULD LEARN TO PACE YOUR KERNEL CONSUMPTION!

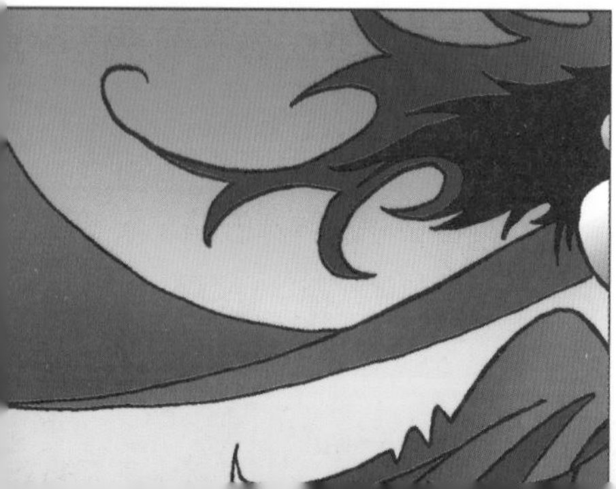

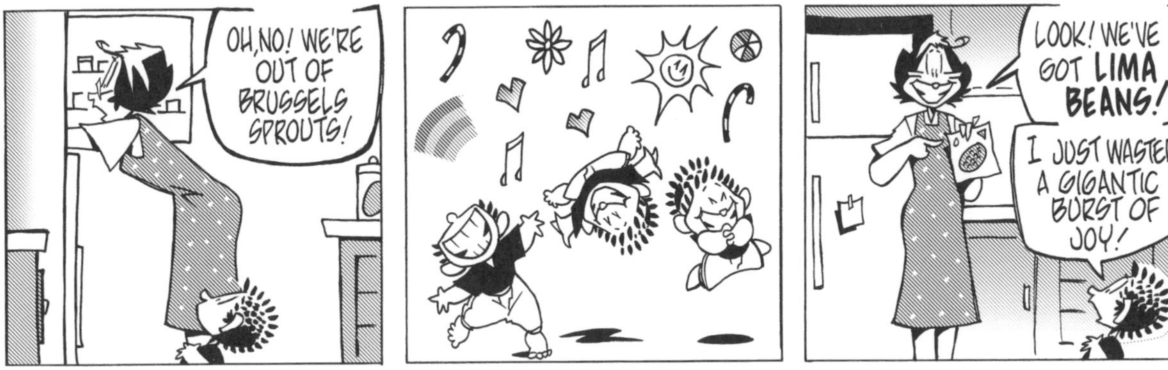
OH, NO! WE'RE OUT OF BRUSSELS SPROUTS!
LOOK! WE'VE GOT **LIMA BEANS**!
I JUST WASTED A GIGANTIC BURST OF JOY!

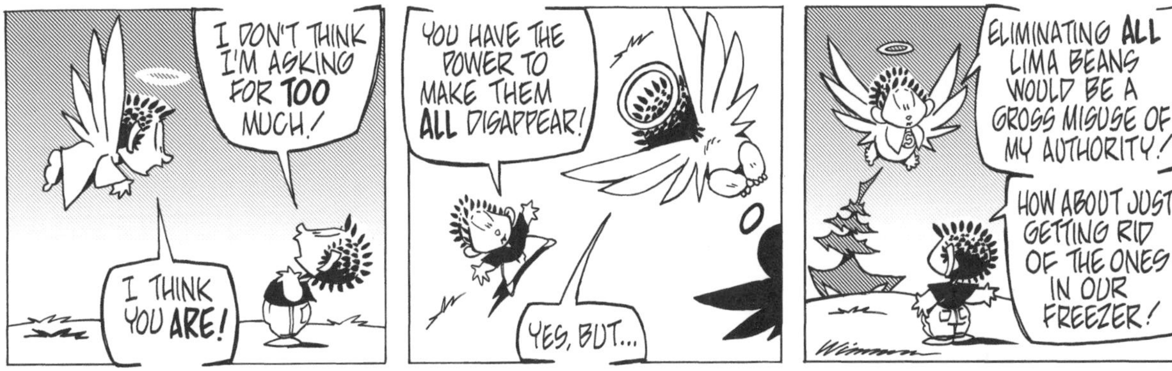
I DON'T THINK I'M ASKING FOR **TOO** MUCH!
I THINK YOU **ARE**!
YOU HAVE THE POWER TO MAKE THEM **ALL** DISAPPEAR!
YES, BUT...
ELIMINATING **ALL** LIMA BEANS WOULD BE A GROSS MISUSE OF MY AUTHORITY!
HOW ABOUT JUST GETTING RID OF THE ONES IN OUR FREEZER!

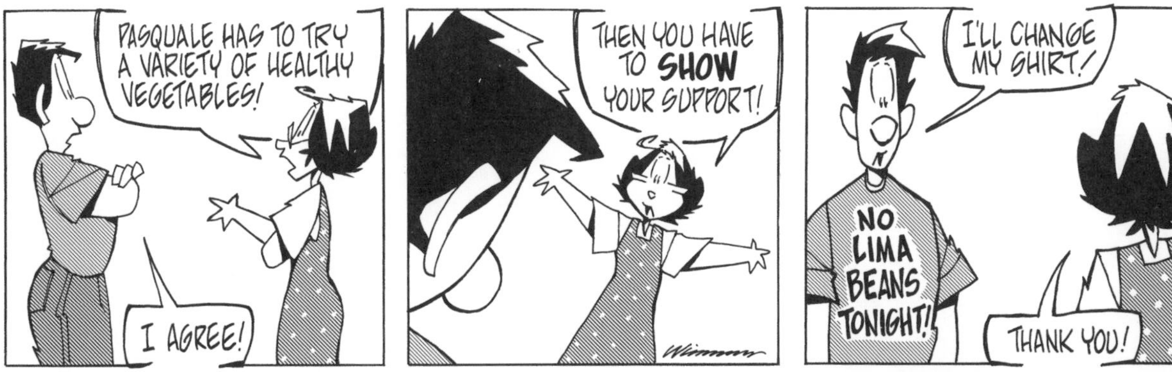
PASQUALE HAS TO TRY A VARIETY OF HEALTHY VEGETABLES!
I AGREE!
THEN YOU HAVE TO **SHOW** YOUR SUPPORT!
I'LL CHANGE MY SHIRT!
NO LIMA BEANS TONIGHT!
THANK YOU!

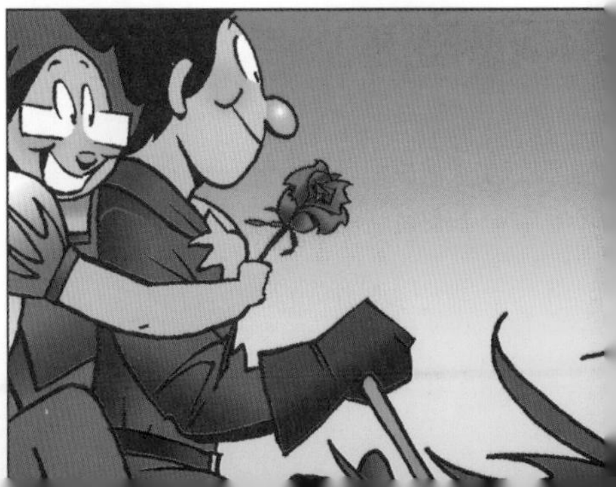

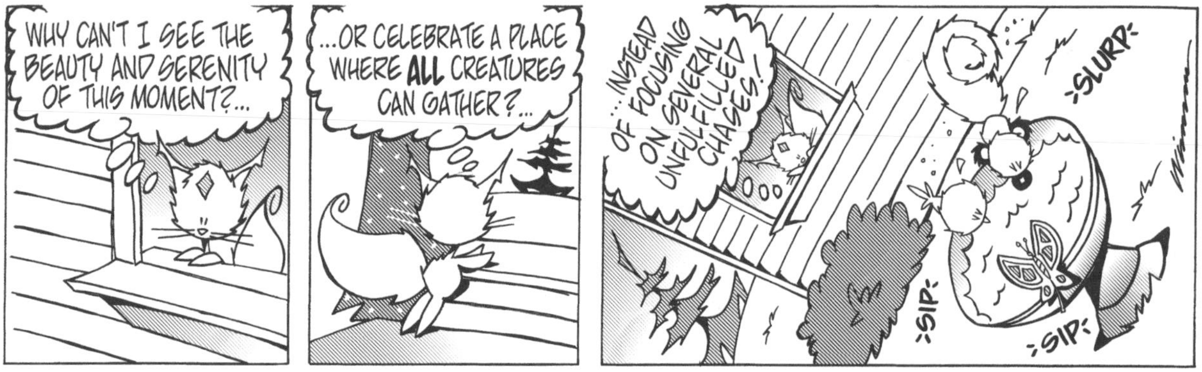
WHY CAN'T I SEE THE BEAUTY AND SERENITY OF THIS MOMENT?...
...OR CELEBRATE A PLACE WHERE ALL CREATURES CAN GATHER?...
...INSTEAD OF FOCUSING ON SEVERAL UNFULFILLED CHASES!
SLURP
SIP
SIP

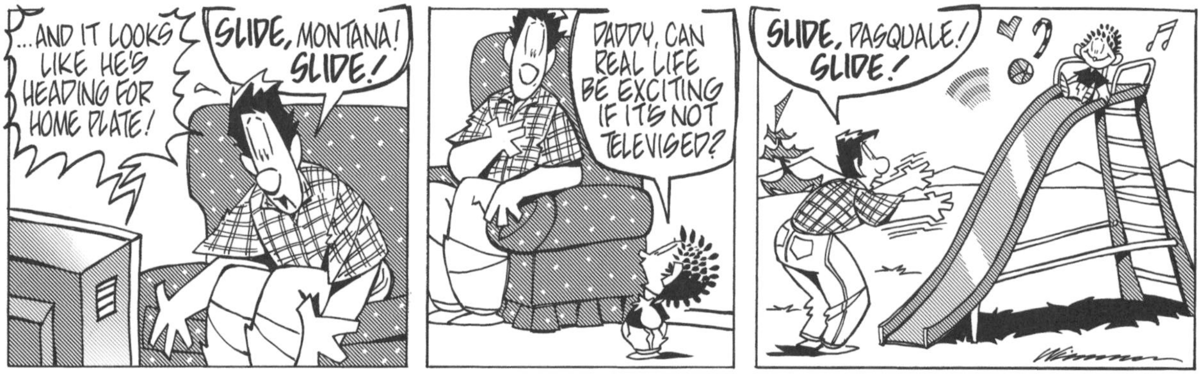
...AND IT LOOKS LIKE HE'S HEADING FOR HOME PLATE!
SLIDE, MONTANA! SLIDE!
DADDY, CAN REAL LIFE BE EXCITING IF IT'S NOT TELEVISED?
SLIDE, PASQUALE! SLIDE!

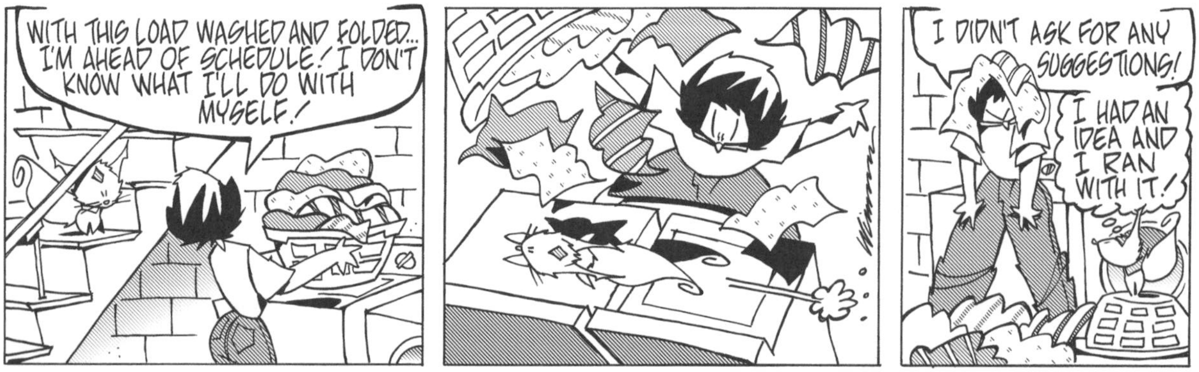
WITH THIS LOAD WASHED AND FOLDED... I'M AHEAD OF SCHEDULE! I DON'T KNOW WHAT I'LL DO WITH MYSELF!
I DIDN'T ASK FOR ANY SUGGESTIONS!
I HAD AN IDEA AND I RAN WITH IT!

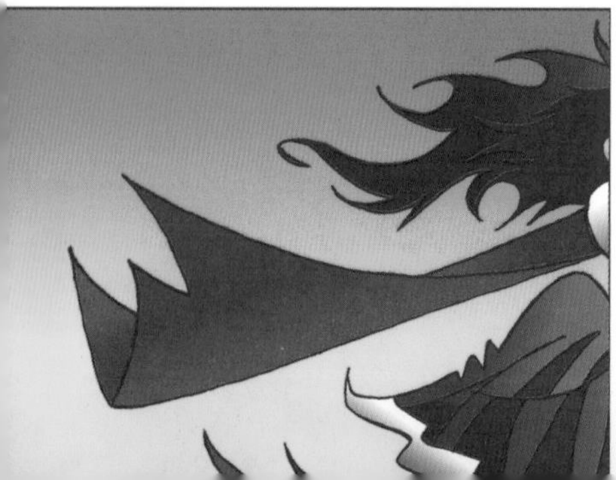

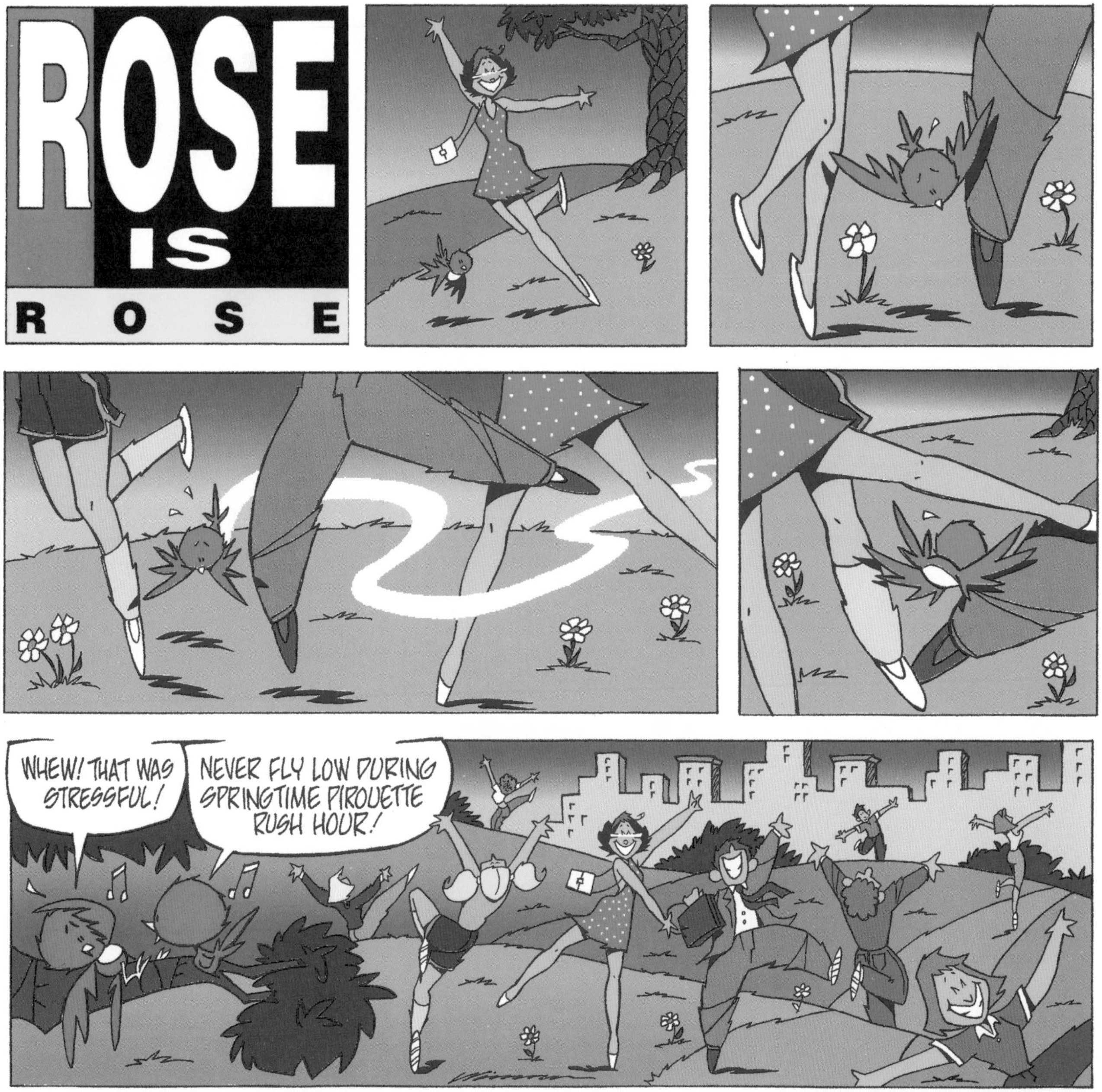
ROSE IS ROSE
WHEW! THAT WAS STRESSFUL!
NEVER FLY LOW DURING SPRINGTIME PIROUETTE RUSH HOUR!

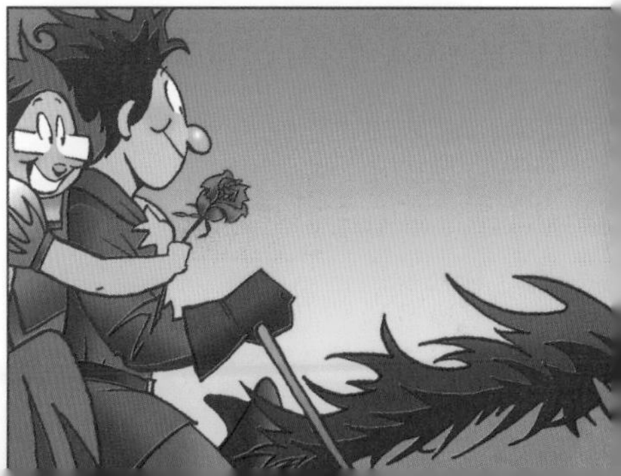

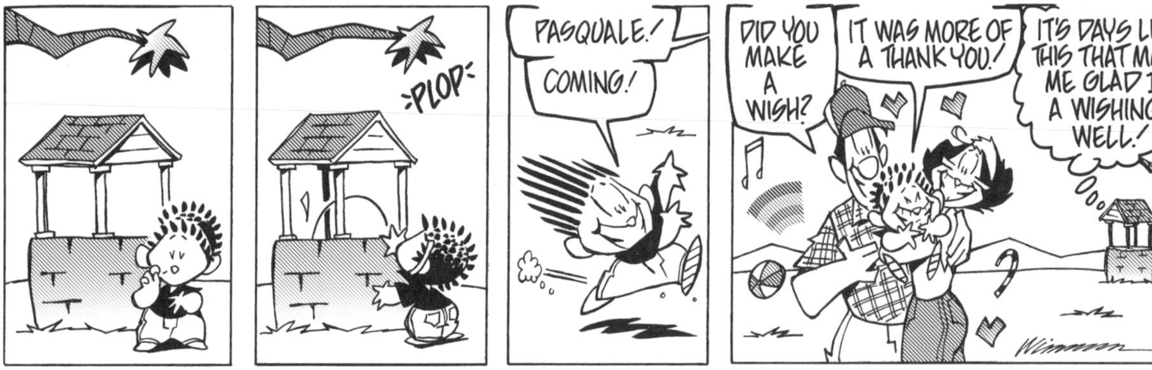
PLOP
PASQUALE!
COMING!
DID YOU MAKE A WISH?
IT WAS MORE OF A THANK YOU!
IT'S DAYS LIKE THIS THAT MAKE ME GLAD I'M A WISHING WELL!

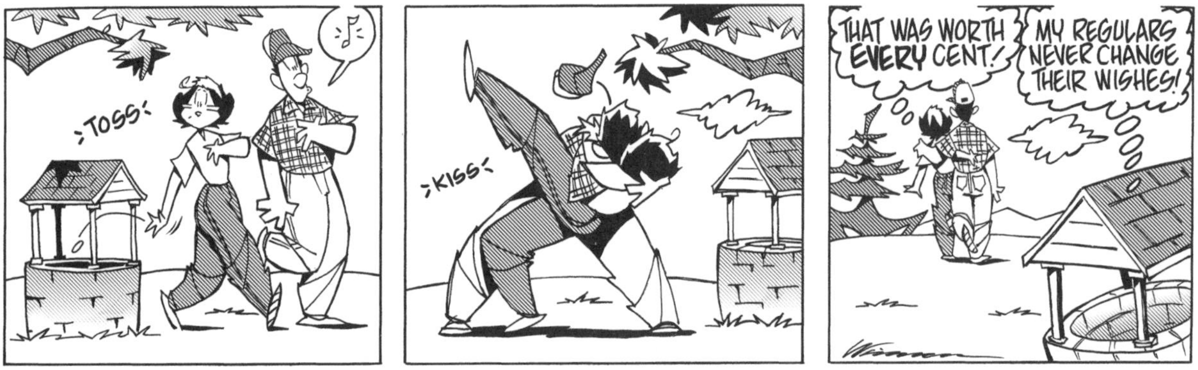
TOSS
KISS
THAT WAS WORTH EVERY CENT!
MY REGULARS NEVER CHANGE THEIR WISHES!

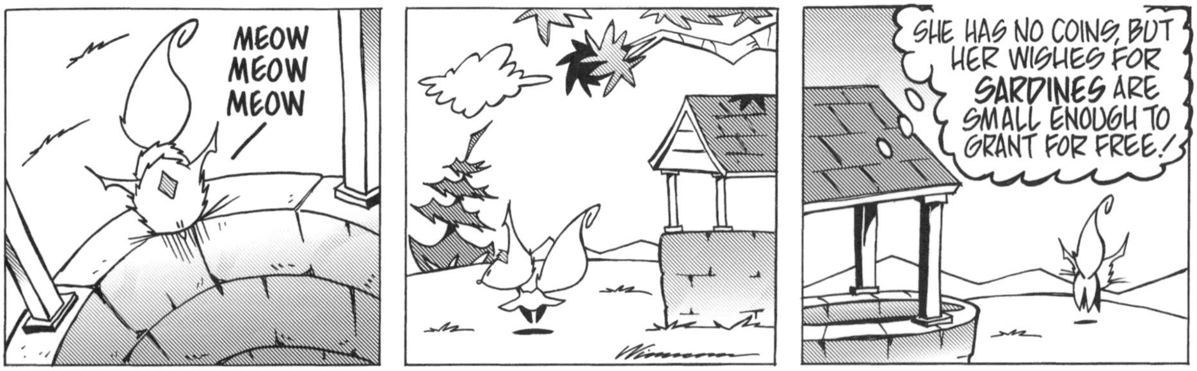
MEOW MEOW MEOW
SHE HAS NO COINS, BUT HER WISHES FOR SARDINES ARE SMALL ENOUGH TO GRANT FOR FREE!

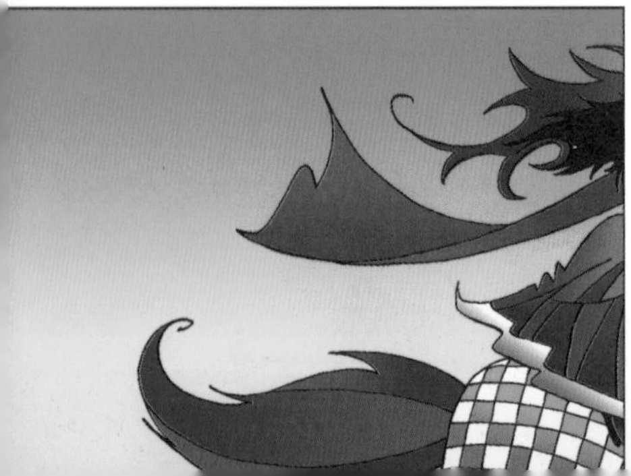

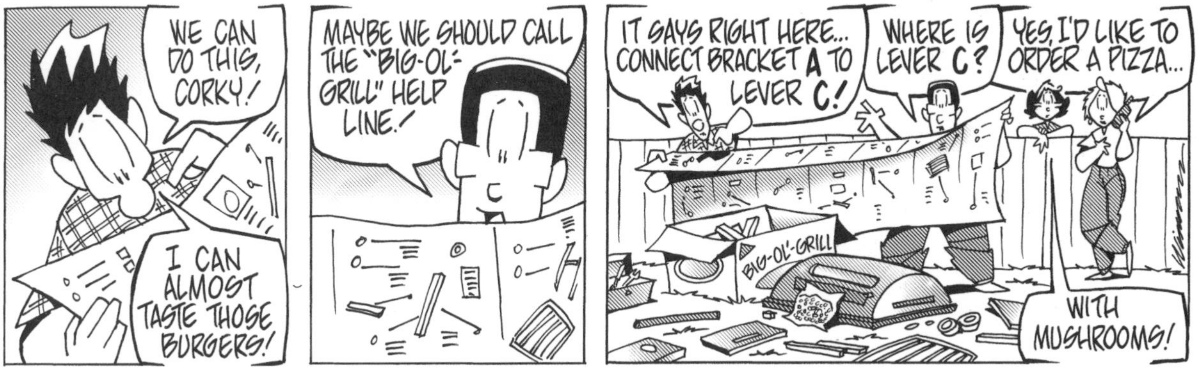
WE CAN DO THIS, CORKY!
I CAN ALMOST TASTE THOSE BURGERS!
MAYBE WE SHOULD CALL THE "BIG-OL'-GRILL" HELP LINE!
IT SAYS RIGHT HERE... CONNECT BRACKET A TO LEVER C!
WHERE IS LEVER C?
BIG-OL'-GRILL
YES, I'D LIKE TO ORDER A PIZZA...
WITH MUSHROOMS!

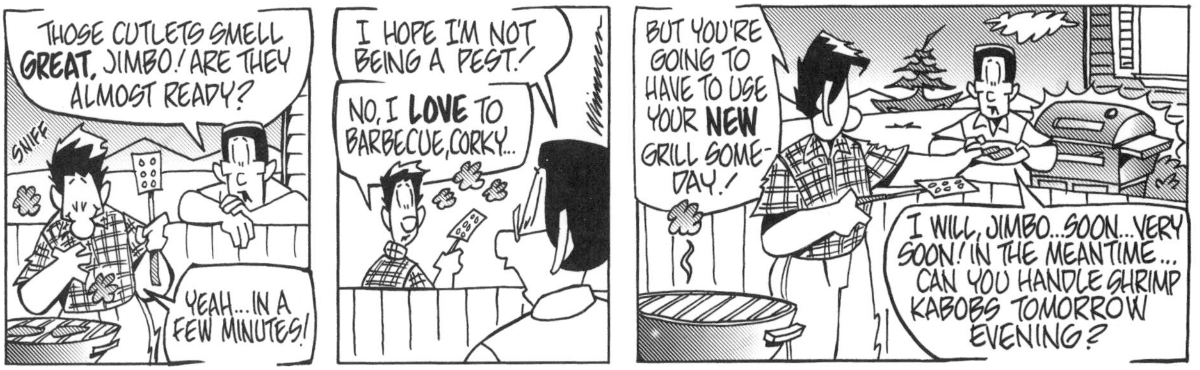
THOSE CUTLETS SMELL GREAT, JIMBO! ARE THEY ALMOST READY?
SNIFF
YEAH... IN A FEW MINUTES!
I HOPE I'M NOT BEING A PEST!
NO, I LOVE TO BARBECUE, CORKY...
BUT YOU'RE GOING TO HAVE TO USE YOUR NEW GRILL SOME-DAY!
I WILL, JIMBO...SOON...VERY SOON! IN THE MEANTIME... CAN YOU HANDLE SHRIMP KABOBS TOMORROW EVENING?

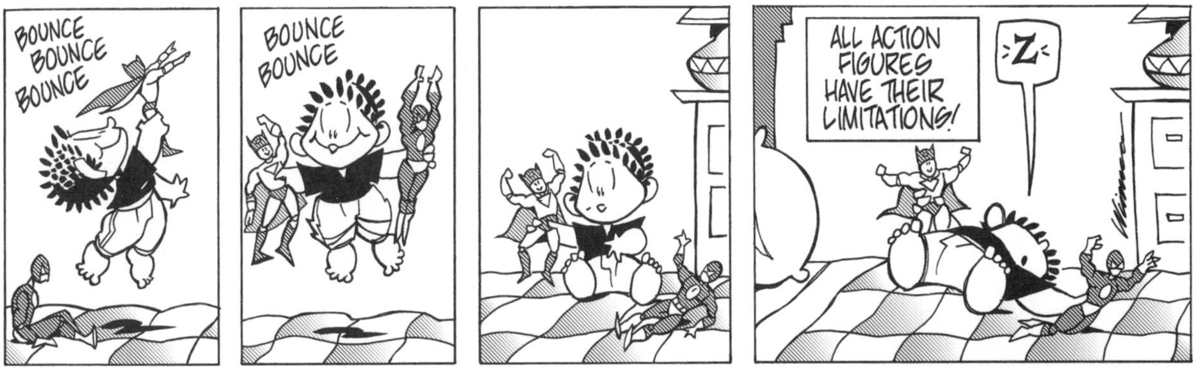
BOUNCE BOUNCE BOUNCE
BOUNCE BOUNCE
ALL ACTION FIGURES HAVE THEIR LIMITATIONS!
Z

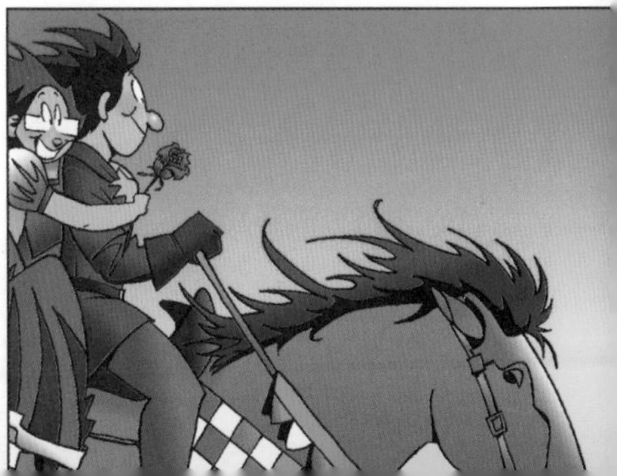

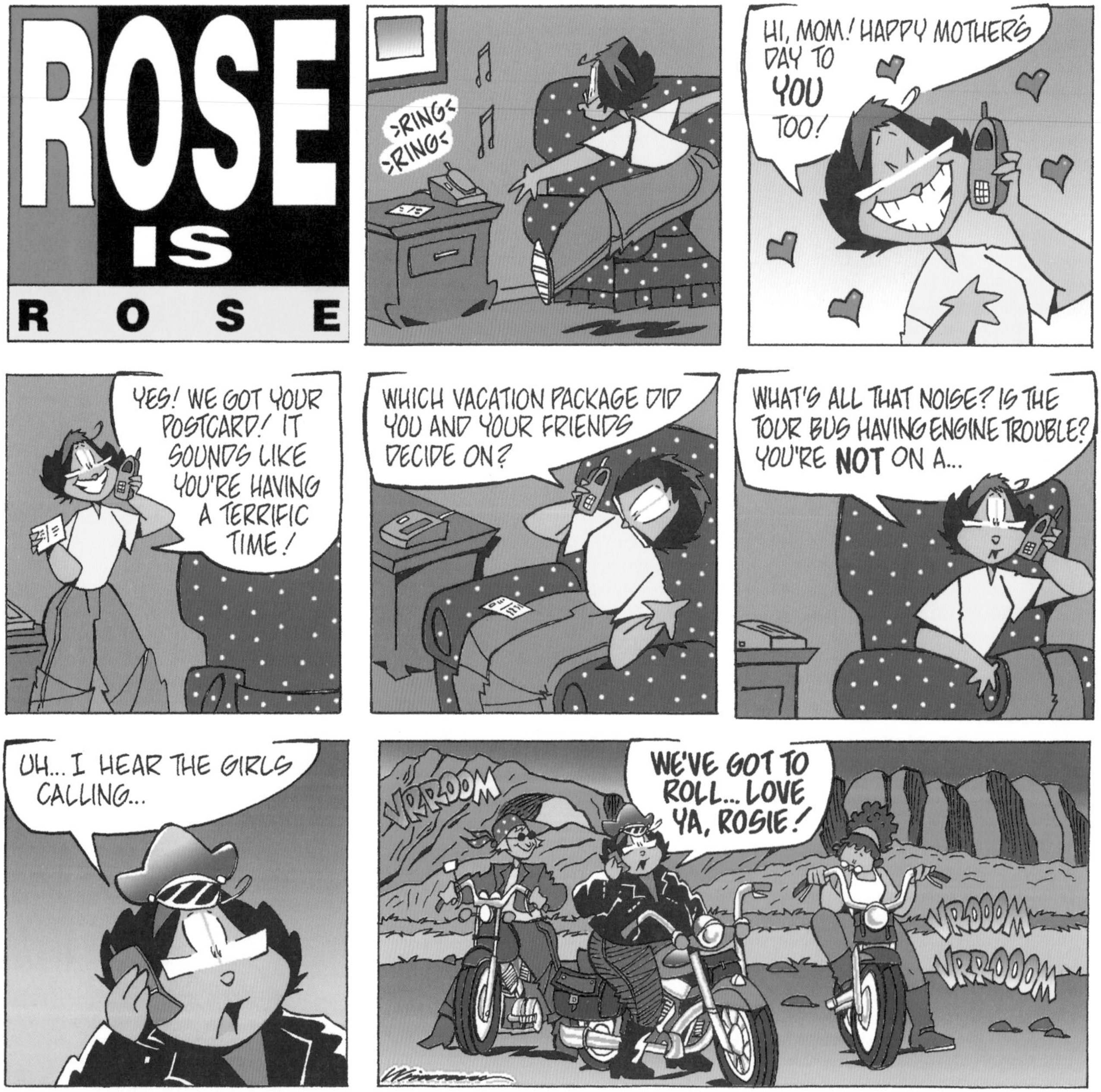
ROSE IS ROSE
>RING< >RING<
HI, MOM! HAPPY MOTHER'S DAY TO YOU TOO!
YES! WE GOT YOUR POSTCARD! IT SOUNDS LIKE YOU'RE HAVING A TERRIFIC TIME!
WHICH VACATION PACKAGE DID YOU AND YOUR FRIENDS DECIDE ON?
WHAT'S ALL THAT NOISE? IS THE TOUR BUS HAVING ENGINE TROUBLE? YOU'RE NOT ON A...
UH... I HEAR THE GIRLS CALLING...
VRROOM
WE'VE GOT TO ROLL... LOVE YA, ROSIE!
VRROOOM
VRROOOM

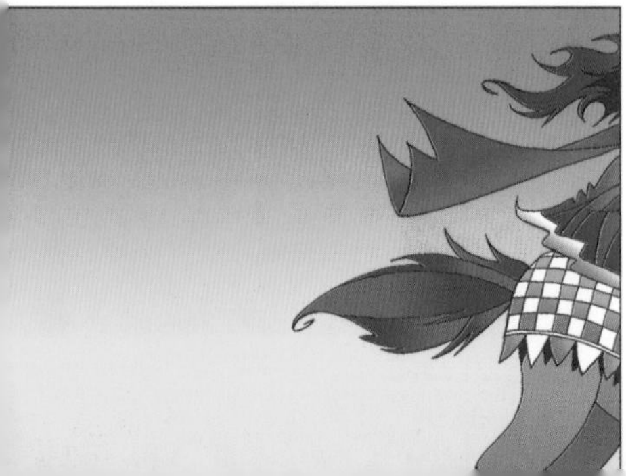

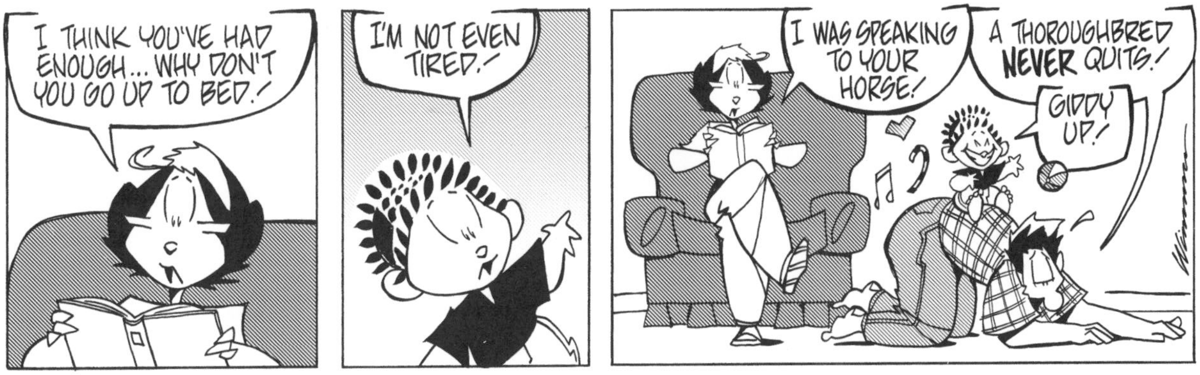
I THINK YOU'VE HAD ENOUGH... WHY DON'T YOU GO UP TO BED!
I'M NOT EVEN TIRED!
I WAS SPEAKING TO YOUR HORSE!
A THOROUGHBRED **NEVER** QUITS!
GIDDY UP!

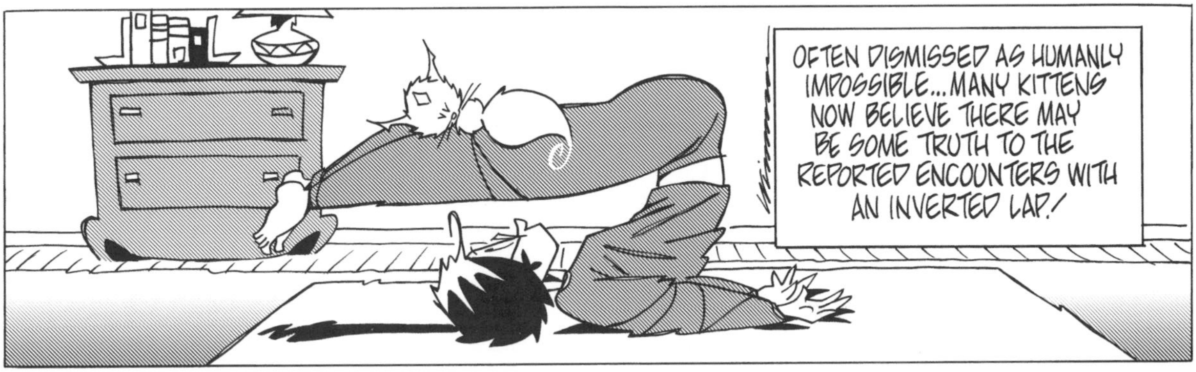
OFTEN DISMISSED AS HUMANLY IMPOSSIBLE... MANY KITTENS NOW BELIEVE THERE MAY BE SOME TRUTH TO THE REPORTED ENCOUNTERS WITH AN INVERTED LAP!

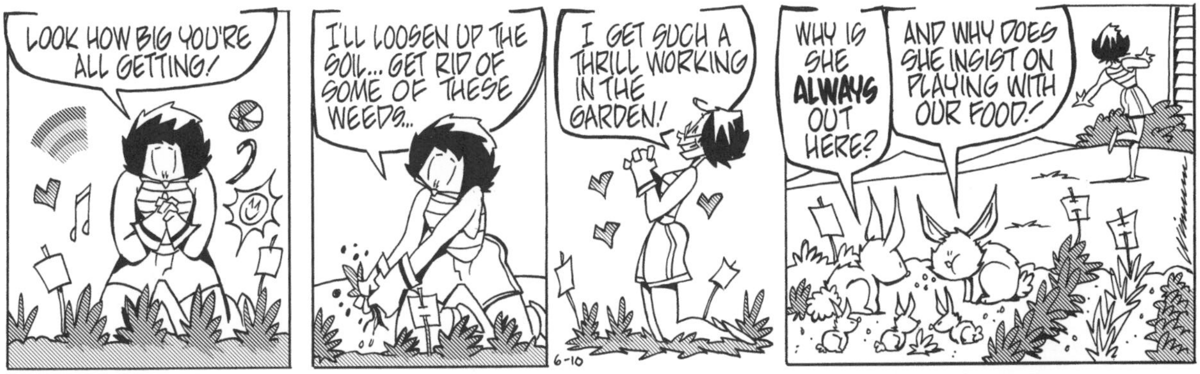
LOOK HOW BIG YOU'RE ALL GETTING!
I'LL LOOSEN UP THE SOIL... GET RID OF SOME OF THESE WEEDS...
I GET SUCH A THRILL WORKING IN THE GARDEN!
6-10
WHY IS SHE **ALWAYS** OUT HERE?
AND WHY DOES SHE INSIST ON PLAYING WITH OUR FOOD!

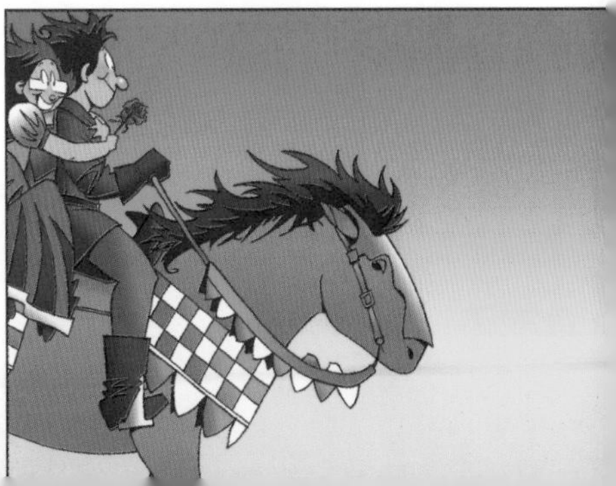

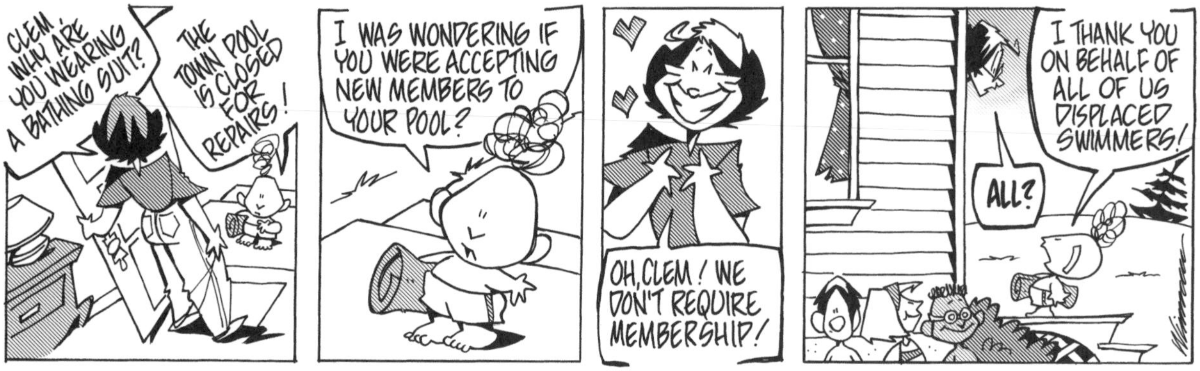
CLEM, WHY ARE YOU WEARING A BATHING SUIT?
THE TOWN POOL IS CLOSED FOR REPAIRS!
I WAS WONDERING IF YOU WERE ACCEPTING NEW MEMBERS TO YOUR POOL?
OH, CLEM! WE DON'T REQUIRE MEMBERSHIP!
I THANK YOU ON BEHALF OF ALL OF US DISPLACED SWIMMERS!
ALL?

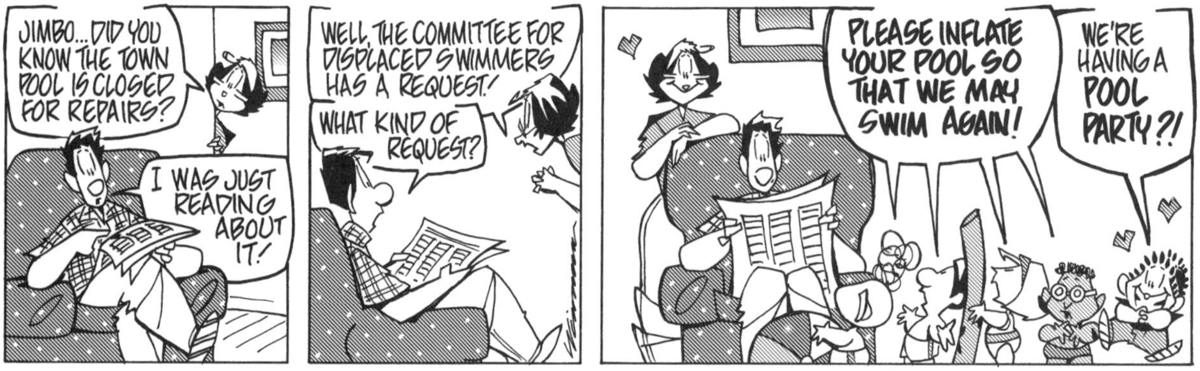
JIMBO... DID YOU KNOW THE TOWN POOL IS CLOSED FOR REPAIRS?
I WAS JUST READING ABOUT IT!
WELL, THE COMMITTEE FOR DISPLACED SWIMMERS HAS A REQUEST!
WHAT KIND OF REQUEST?
PLEASE INFLATE YOUR POOL SO THAT WE MAY SWIM AGAIN!
WE'RE HAVING A POOL PARTY?!

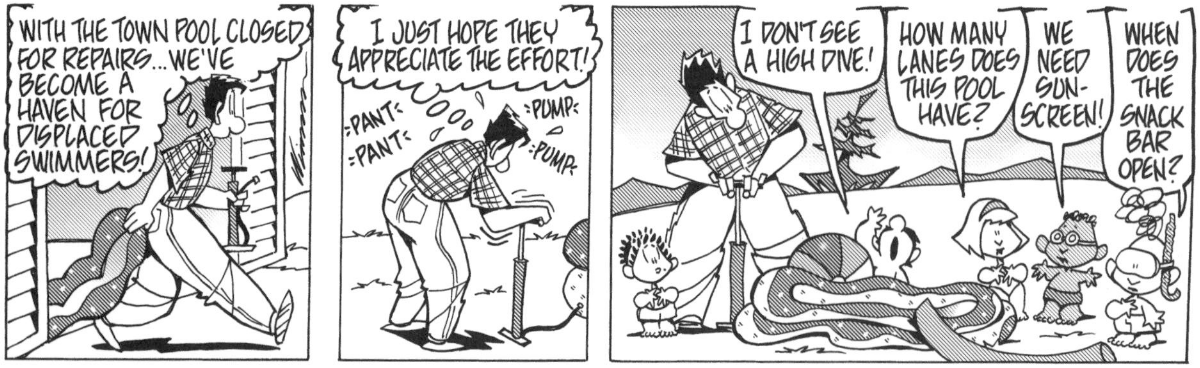
WITH THE TOWN POOL CLOSED FOR REPAIRS... WE'VE BECOME A HAVEN FOR DISPLACED SWIMMERS!
I JUST HOPE THEY APPRECIATE THE EFFORT!
PANT PANT
PUMP PUMP
I DON'T SEE A HIGH DIVE!
HOW MANY LANES DOES THIS POOL HAVE?
WE NEED SUN-SCREEN!
WHEN DOES THE SNACK BAR OPEN?

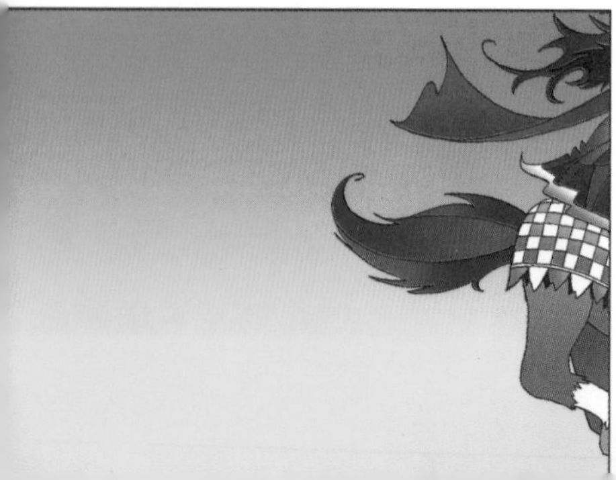

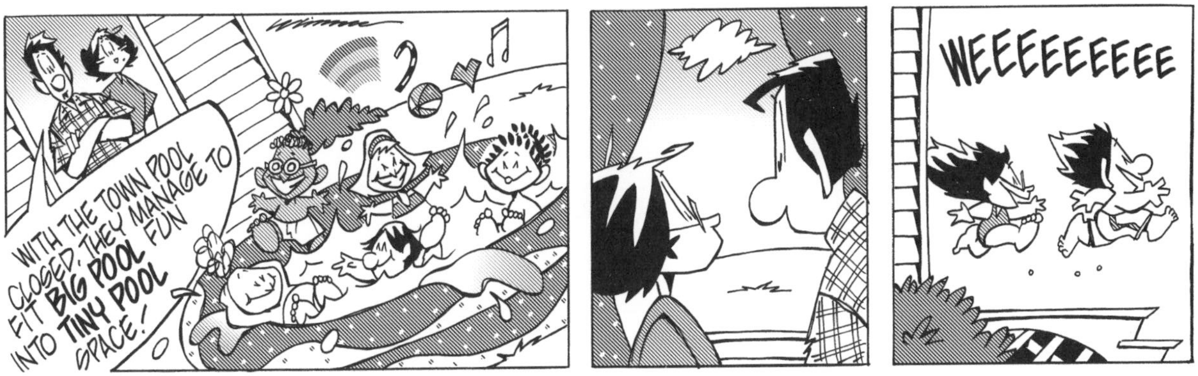
WITH THE TOWN POOL CLOSED, THEY MANAGE TO FIT BIG POOL FUN INTO TINY POOL SPACE!
WEEEEEEEEE

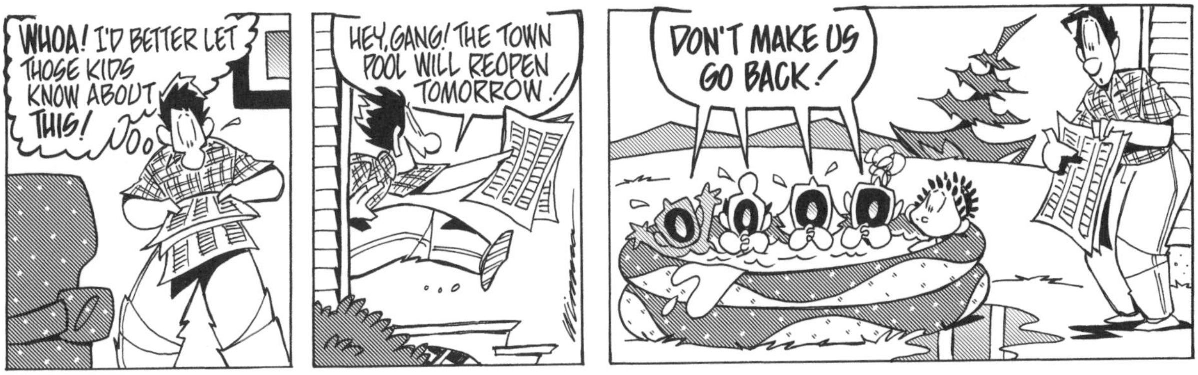
WHOA! I'D BETTER LET THOSE KIDS KNOW ABOUT THIS!
HEY, GANG! THE TOWN POOL WILL REOPEN TOMORROW!
DON'T MAKE US GO BACK!

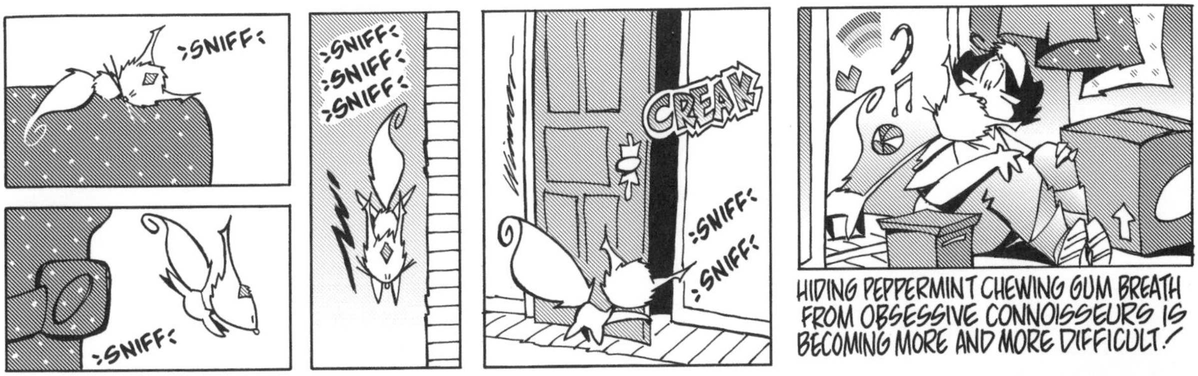
:SNIFF:
:SNIFF:
:SNIFF:
:SNIFF:
:SNIFF:
CREAK
:SNIFF:
:SNIFF:
HIDING PEPPERMINT CHEWING GUM BREATH FROM OBSESSIVE CONNOISSEURS IS BECOMING MORE AND MORE DIFFICULT!

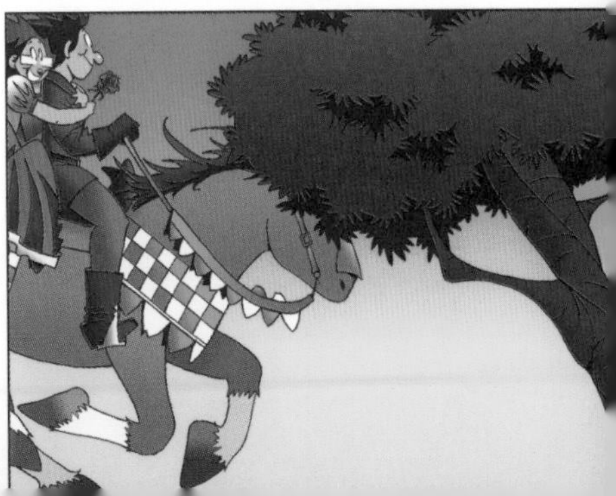

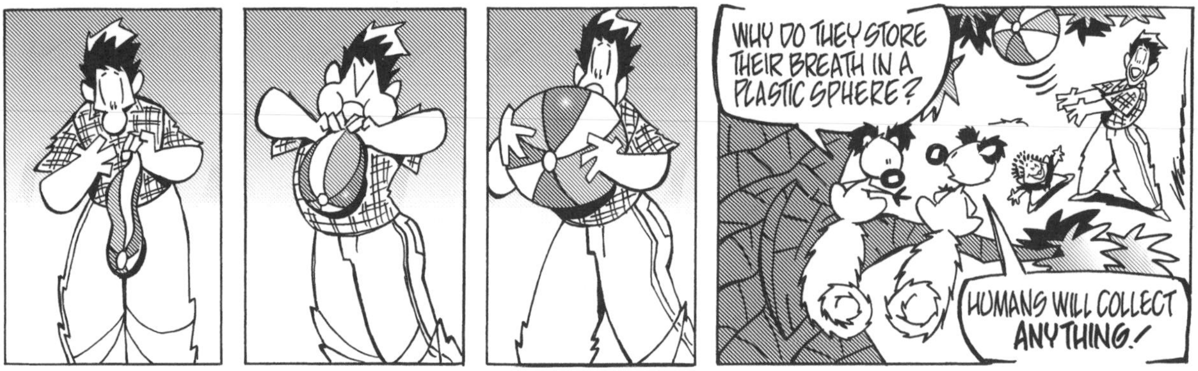
WHY DO THEY STORE THEIR BREATH IN A PLASTIC SPHERE?
HUMANS WILL COLLECT ANYTHING!

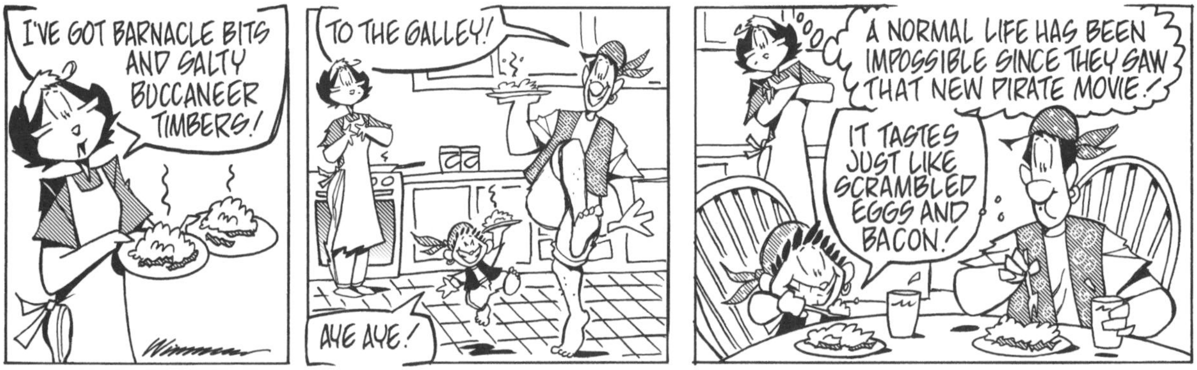
I'VE GOT BARNACLE BITS AND SALTY BUCCANEER TIMBERS!
TO THE GALLEY!
AYE AYE!
A NORMAL LIFE HAS BEEN IMPOSSIBLE SINCE THEY SAW THAT NEW PIRATE MOVIE!
IT TASTES JUST LIKE SCRAMBLED EGGS AND BACON!

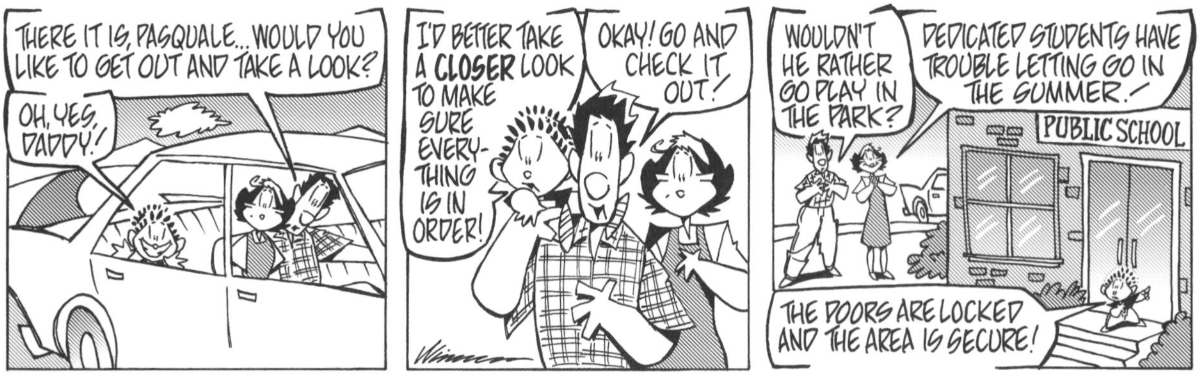
THERE IT IS, PASQUALE... WOULD YOU LIKE TO GET OUT AND TAKE A LOOK?
OH, YES, DADDY!
I'D BETTER TAKE A CLOSER LOOK TO MAKE SURE EVERYTHING IS IN ORDER!
OKAY! GO AND CHECK IT OUT!
WOULDN'T HE RATHER GO PLAY IN THE PARK?
DEDICATED STUDENTS HAVE TROUBLE LETTING GO IN THE SUMMER.
PUBLIC SCHOOL
THE DOORS ARE LOCKED AND THE AREA IS SECURE!

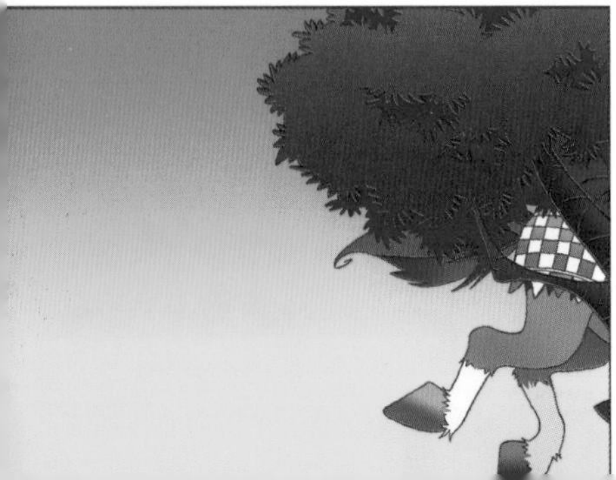

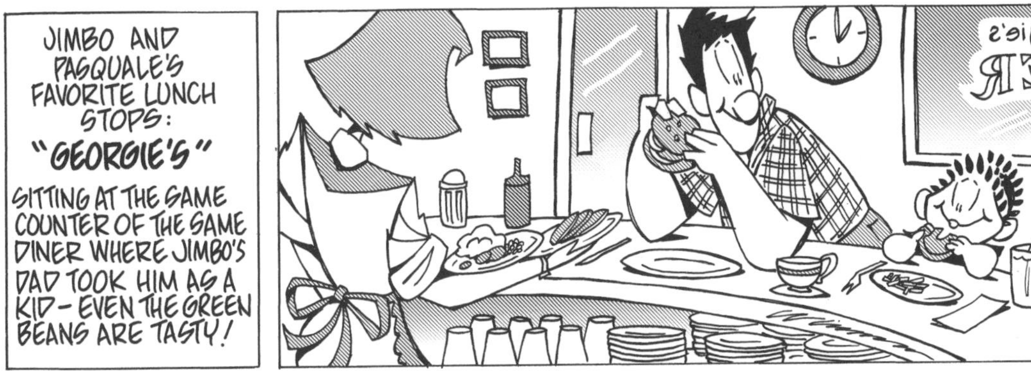
JIMBO AND PASQUALE'S FAVORITE LUNCH STOPS:
"GEORGIE'S"
SITTING AT THE SAME COUNTER OF THE SAME DINER WHERE JIMBO'S DAD TOOK HIM AS A KID - EVEN THE GREEN BEANS ARE TASTY!
Georgie's DINER

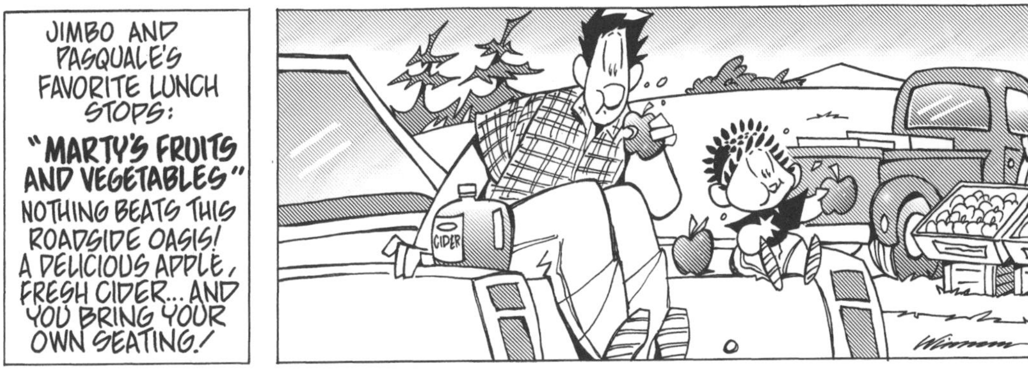
JIMBO AND PASQUALE'S FAVORITE LUNCH STOPS:
"MARTY'S FRUITS AND VEGETABLES"
NOTHING BEATS THIS ROADSIDE OASIS! A DELICIOUS APPLE, FRESH CIDER... AND YOU BRING YOUR OWN SEATING!
CIDER

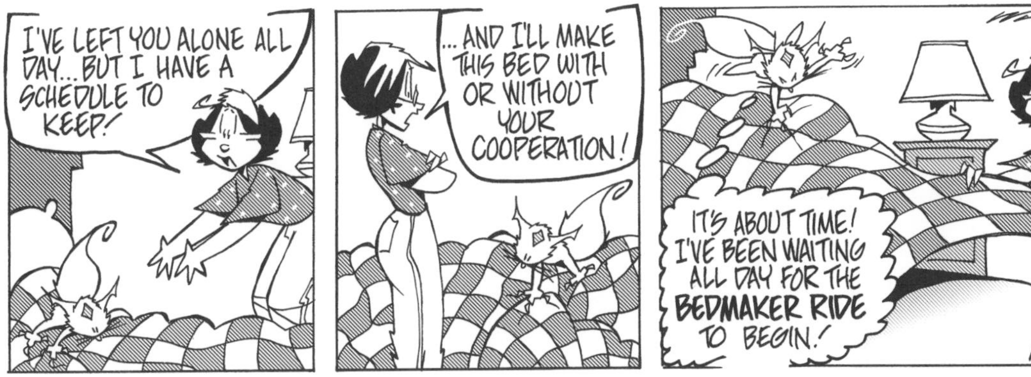
I'VE LEFT YOU ALONE ALL DAY... BUT I HAVE A SCHEDULE TO KEEP!
...AND I'LL MAKE THIS BED WITH OR WITHOUT YOUR COOPERATION!
IT'S ABOUT TIME! I'VE BEEN WAITING ALL DAY FOR THE BEDMAKER RIDE TO BEGIN!

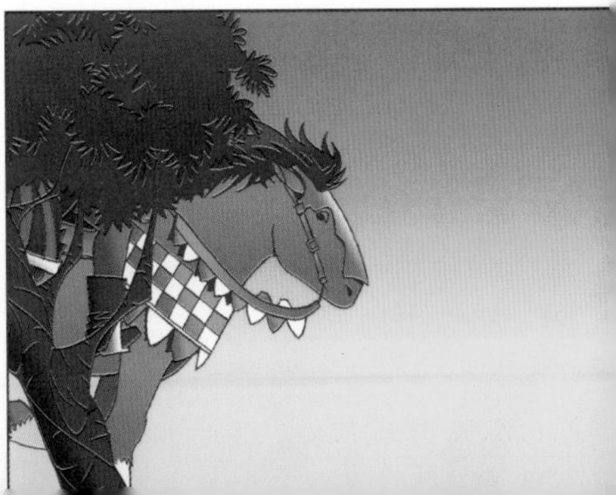

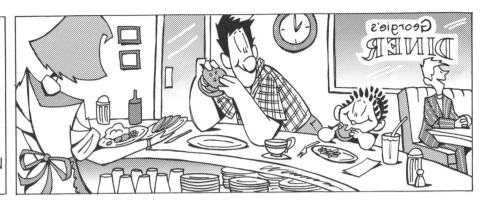

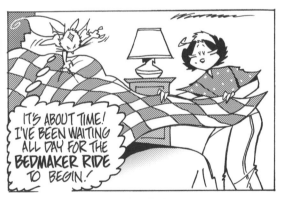

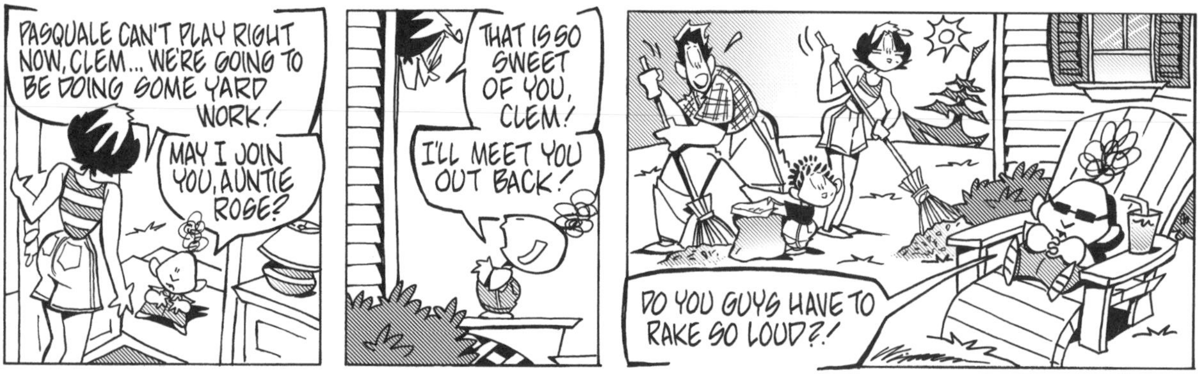
PASQUALE CAN'T PLAY RIGHT NOW, CLEM... WE'RE GOING TO BE DOING SOME YARD WORK!
MAY I JOIN YOU, AUNTIE ROSE?
THAT IS SO SWEET OF YOU, CLEM!
I'LL MEET YOU OUT BACK!
DO YOU GUYS HAVE TO RAKE SO LOUD?!

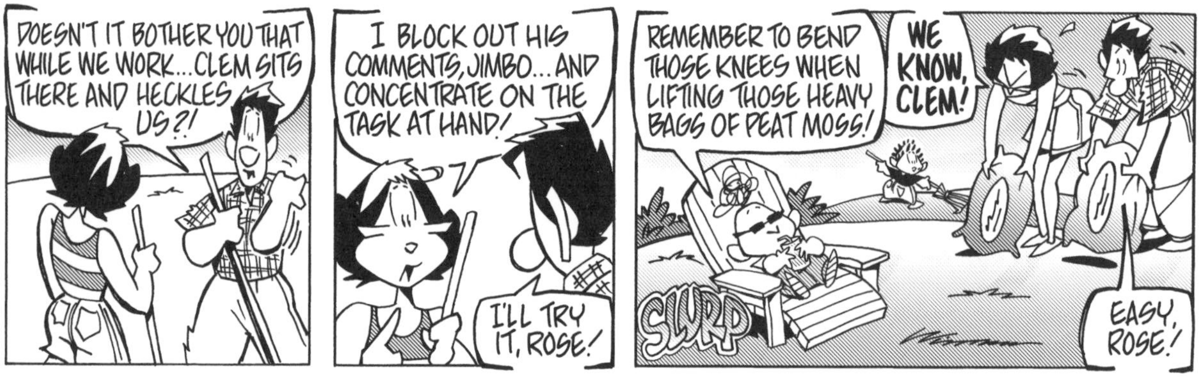
DOESN'T IT BOTHER YOU THAT WHILE WE WORK... CLEM SITS THERE AND HECKLES US?!
I BLOCK OUT HIS COMMENTS, JIMBO... AND CONCENTRATE ON THE TASK AT HAND!
I'LL TRY IT, ROSE!
REMEMBER TO BEND THOSE KNEES WHEN LIFTING THOSE HEAVY BAGS OF PEAT MOSS!
WE KNOW, CLEM!
SLURP
EASY, ROSE!

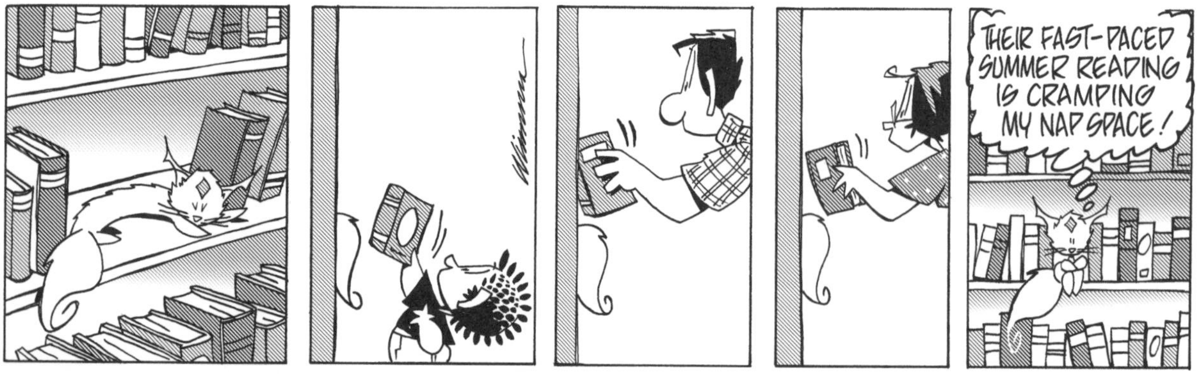
THEIR FAST-PACED SUMMER READING IS CRAMPING MY NAP SPACE!

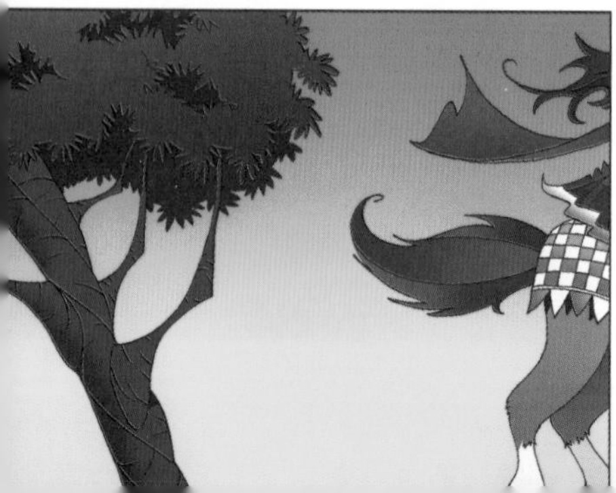

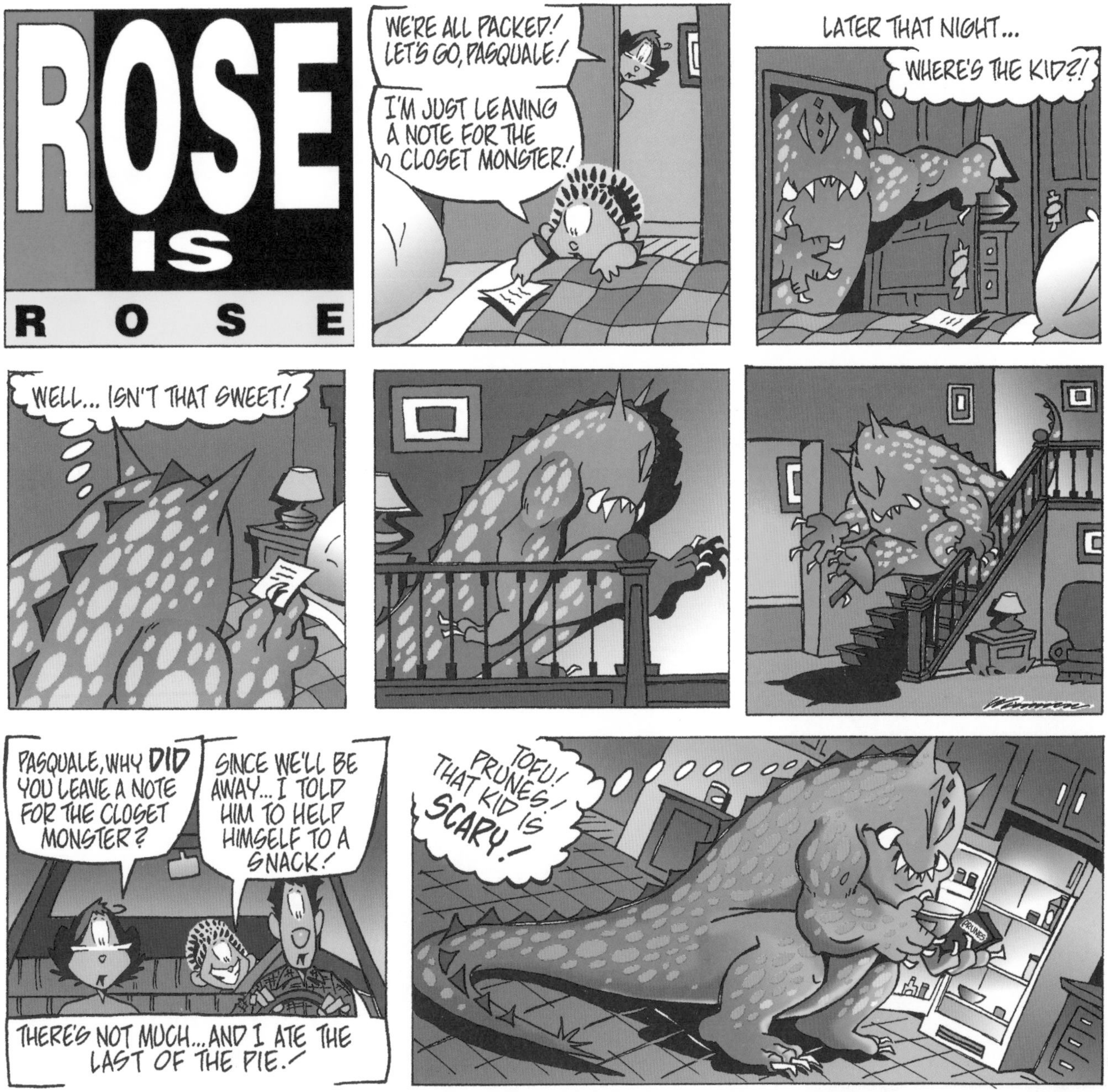
ROSE IS ROSE
WE'RE ALL PACKED! LET'S GO, PASQUALE!
I'M JUST LEAVING A NOTE FOR THE CLOSET MONSTER!
LATER THAT NIGHT...
WHERE'S THE KID?!
WELL... ISN'T THAT SWEET!
PASQUALE, WHY **DID** YOU LEAVE A NOTE FOR THE CLOSET MONSTER?
SINCE WE'LL BE AWAY... I TOLD HIM TO HELP HIMSELF TO A SNACK!
THERE'S NOT MUCH... AND I ATE THE LAST OF THE PIE!
TOFU! PRUNES! THAT KID IS SCARY!
PRUNES

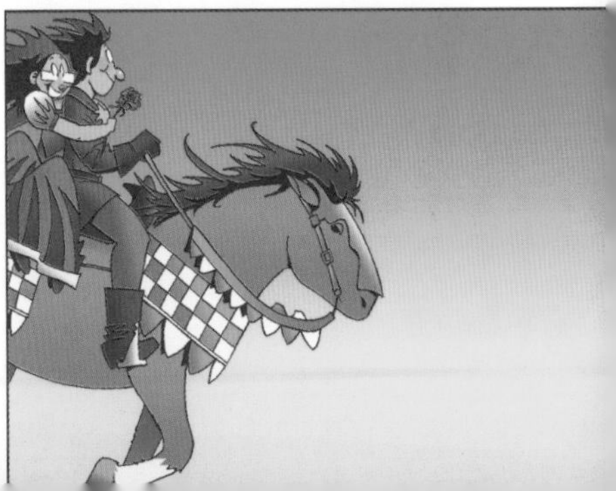

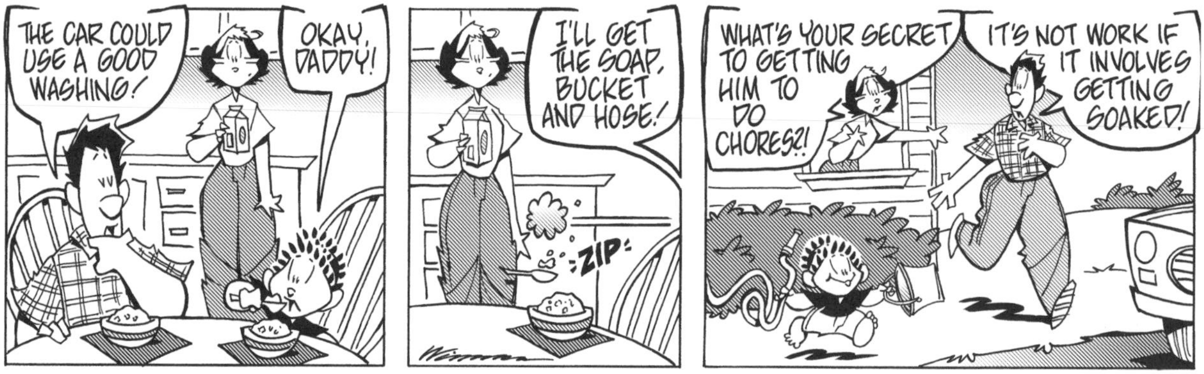
THE CAR COULD USE A GOOD WASHING!
OKAY, DADDY!
I'LL GET THE SOAP, BUCKET AND HOSE!
ZIP
WHAT'S YOUR SECRET TO GETTING HIM TO DO CHORES?!
IT'S NOT WORK IF IT INVOLVES GETTING SOAKED!

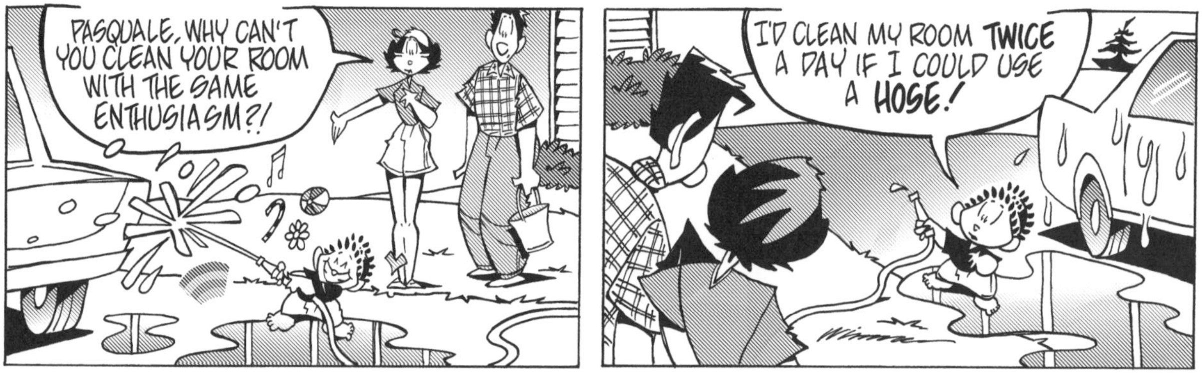
PASQUALE, WHY CAN'T YOU CLEAN YOUR ROOM WITH THE SAME ENTHUSIASM?!
I'D CLEAN MY ROOM TWICE A DAY IF I COULD USE A HOSE!

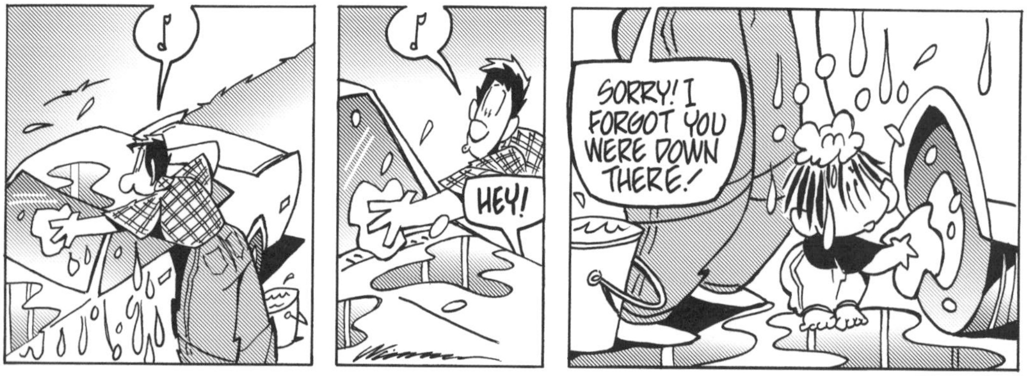
HEY!
SORRY! I FORGOT YOU WERE DOWN THERE!
LOWER LEVEL EMPLOYEES OFTEN HAVE TO RAISE THEIR VOICE IF THEY WANT THEIR POSITION TO BE UNDERSTOOD!

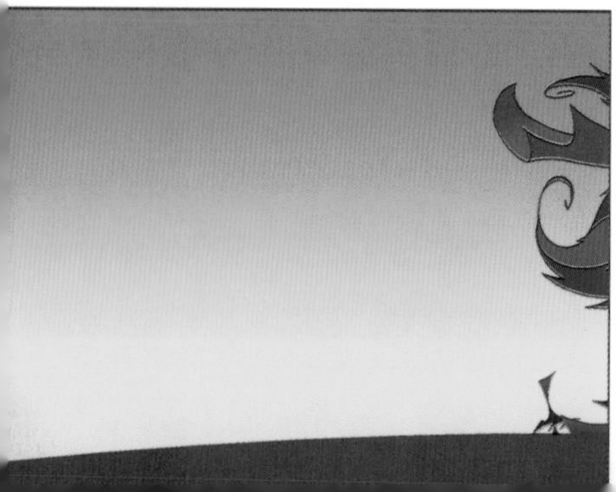

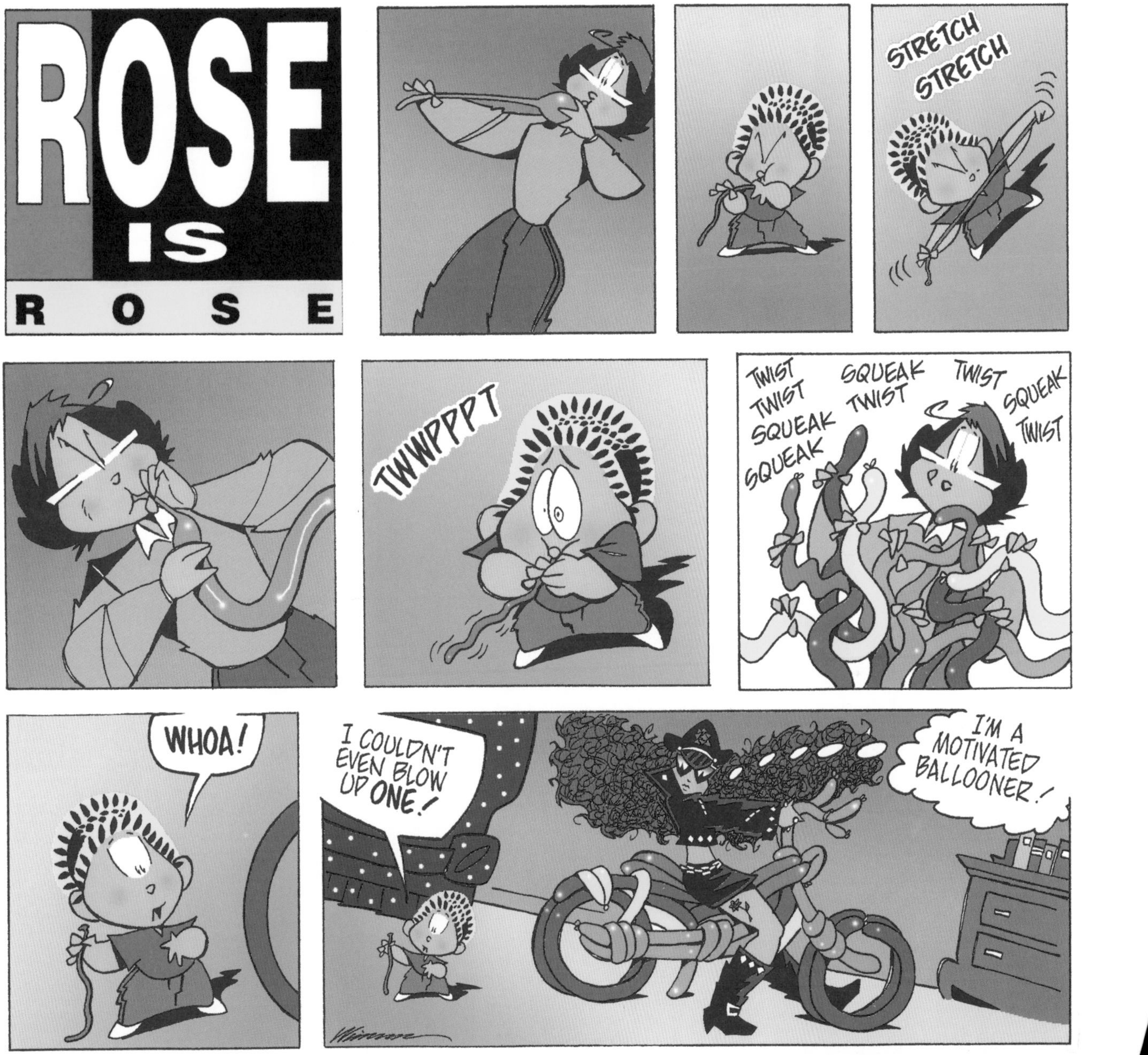
ROSE IS ROSE
STRETCH
STRETCH
TWWPPPT
TWIST
TWIST
SQUEAK
SQUEAK
SQUEAK
TWIST
TWIST
SQUEAK
TWIST
WHOA!
I COULDN'T EVEN BLOW UP ONE!
I'M A MOTIVATED BALLOONER!

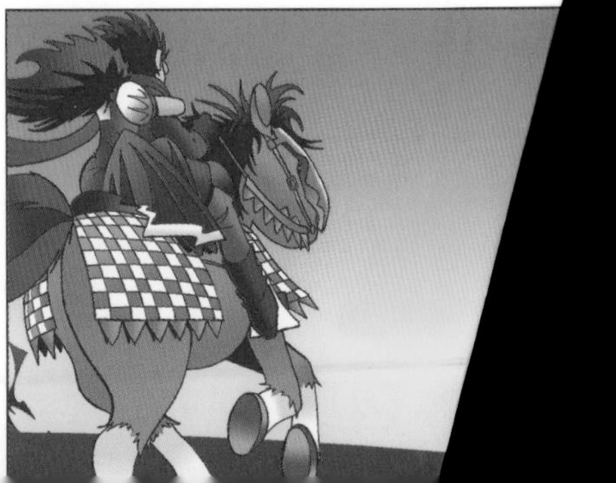

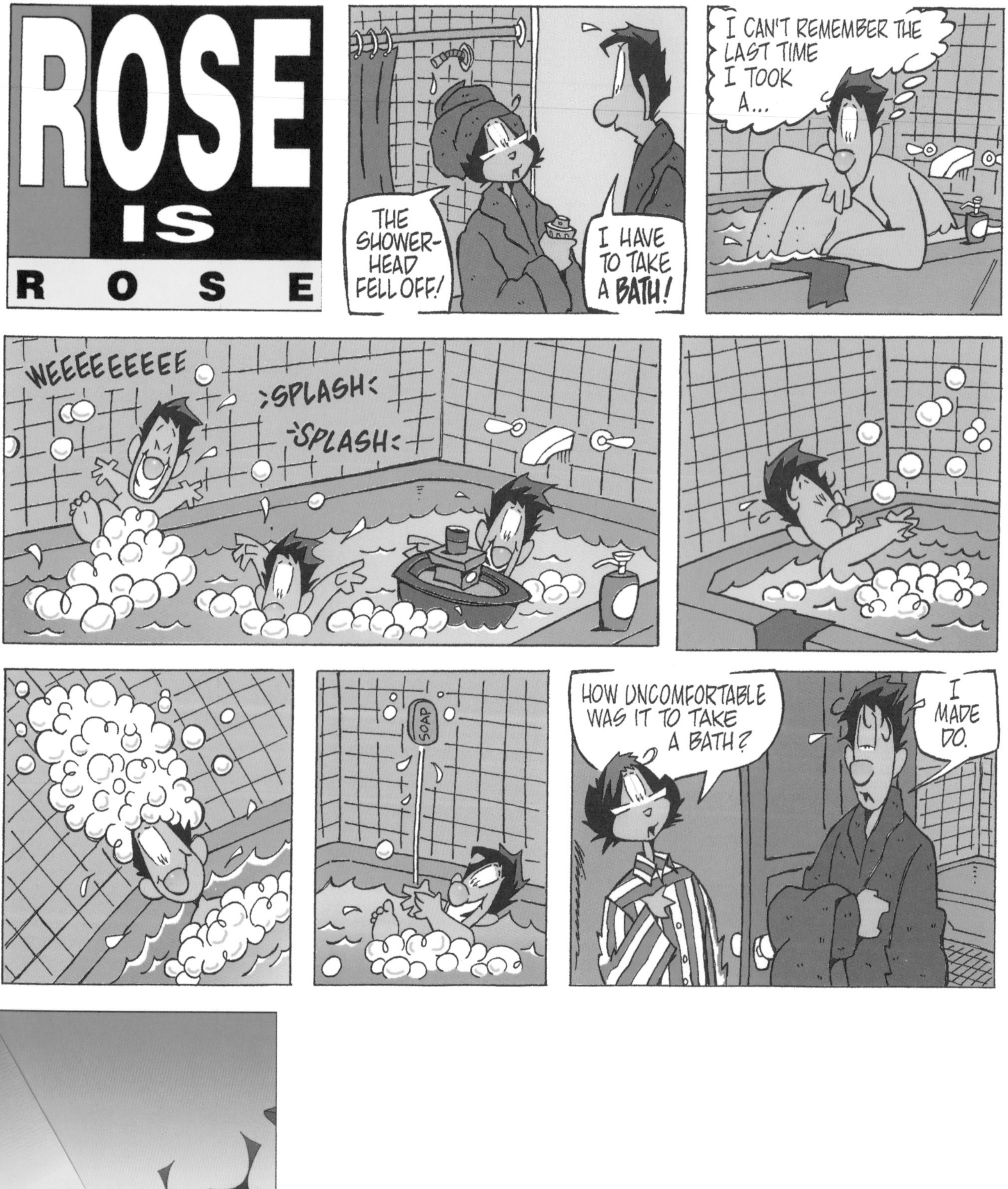
ROSE IS ROSE
THE SHOWER-HEAD FELL OFF!
I HAVE TO TAKE A BATH!
I CAN'T REMEMBER THE LAST TIME I TOOK A...
WEEEEEEEEE
>SPLASH<
>SPLASH<
SOAP
HOW UNCOMFORTABLE WAS IT TO TAKE A BATH?
I MADE DO.

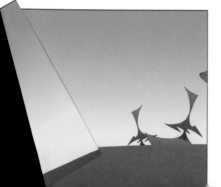

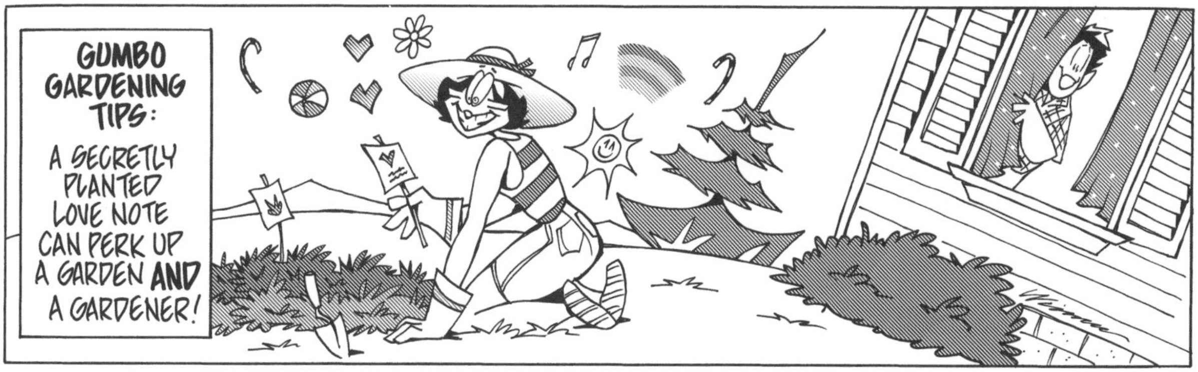
GUMBO GARDENING TIPS:
A SECRETLY PLANTED LOVE NOTE CAN PERK UP A GARDEN **AND** A GARDENER!

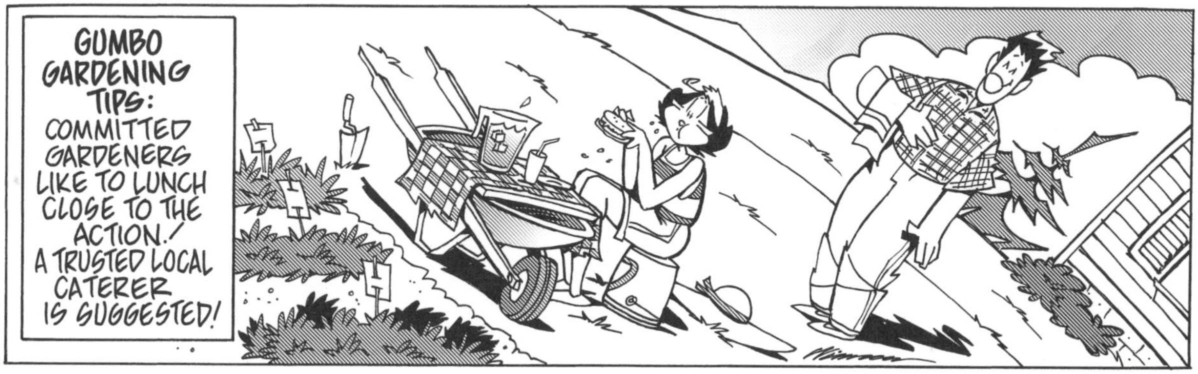
GUMBO GARDENING TIPS:
COMMITTED GARDENERS LIKE TO LUNCH CLOSE TO THE ACTION.! A TRUSTED LOCAL CATERER IS SUGGESTED!

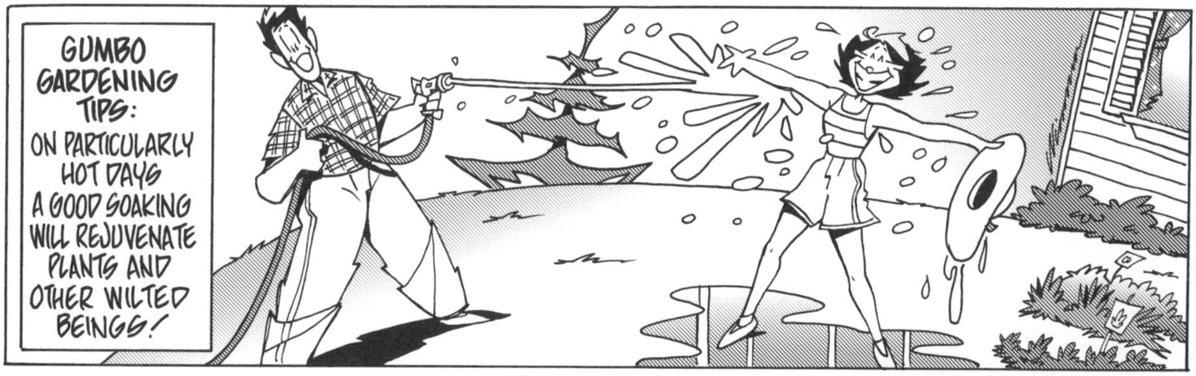
GUMBO GARDENING TIPS:
ON PARTICULARLY HOT DAYS A GOOD SOAKING WILL REJUVENATE PLANTS AND OTHER WILTED BEINGS!

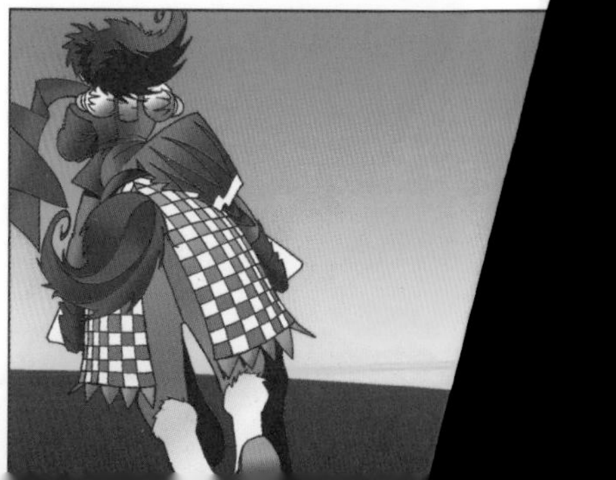

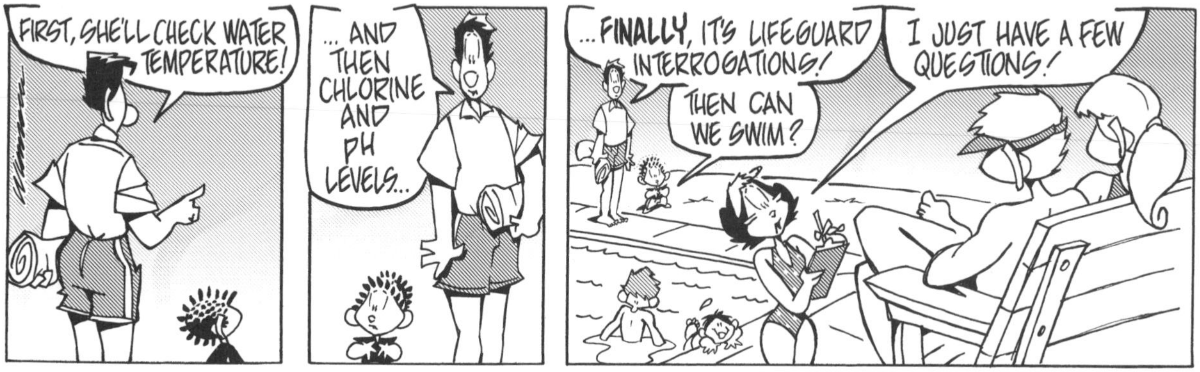
FIRST, SHE'LL CHECK WATER TEMPERATURE!
... AND THEN CHLORINE AND PH LEVELS...
... FINALLY, IT'S LIFEGUARD INTERROGATIONS!
THEN CAN WE SWIM?
I JUST HAVE A FEW QUESTIONS!

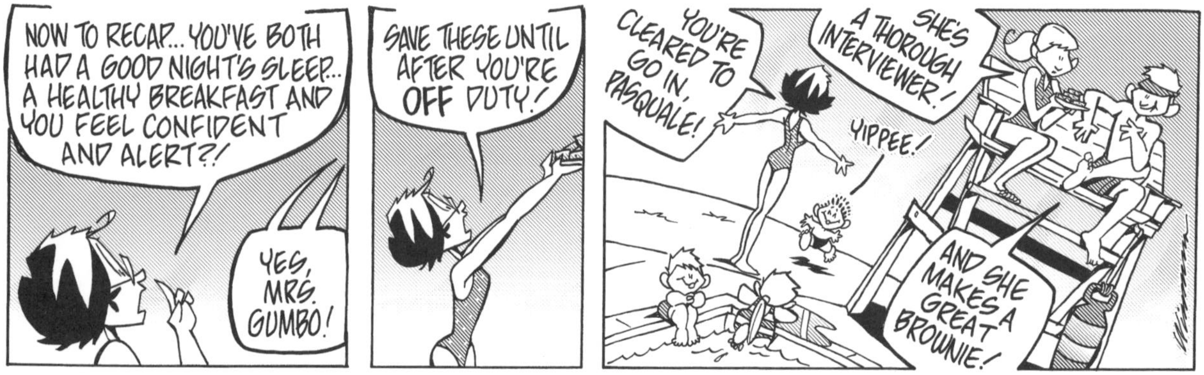
NOW TO RECAP... YOU'VE BOTH HAD A GOOD NIGHT'S SLEEP... A HEALTHY BREAKFAST AND YOU FEEL CONFIDENT AND ALERT?!
YES, MRS. GUMBO!
SAVE THESE UNTIL AFTER YOU'RE OFF DUTY!
YOU'RE CLEARED TO GO IN, PASQUALE!
SHE'S A THOROUGH INTERVIEWER!
YIPPEE!
AND SHE MAKES A GREAT BROWNIE!

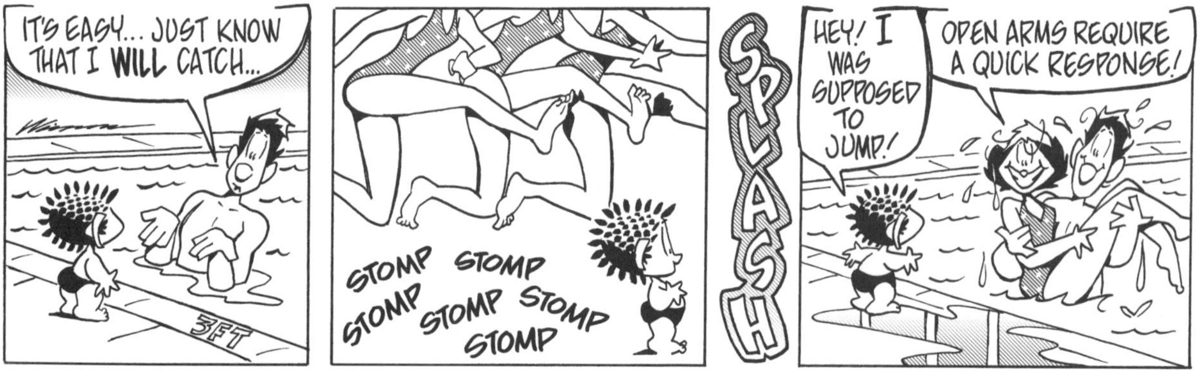
IT'S EASY... JUST KNOW THAT I WILL CATCH...
3FT
STOMP STOMP STOMP STOMP STOMP STOMP
SPLASH
HEY! I WAS SUPPOSED TO JUMP!
OPEN ARMS REQUIRE A QUICK RESPONSE!

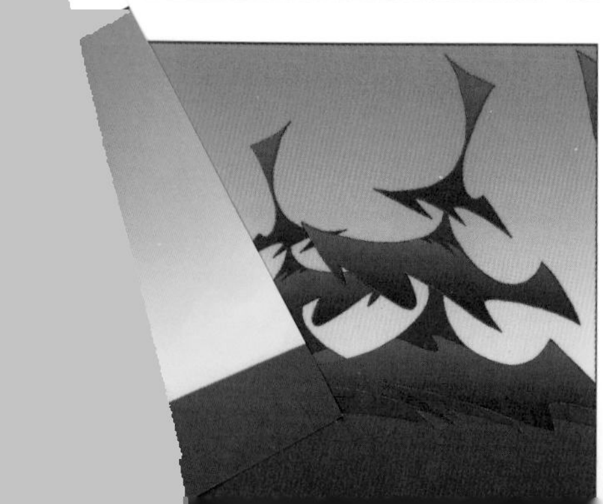

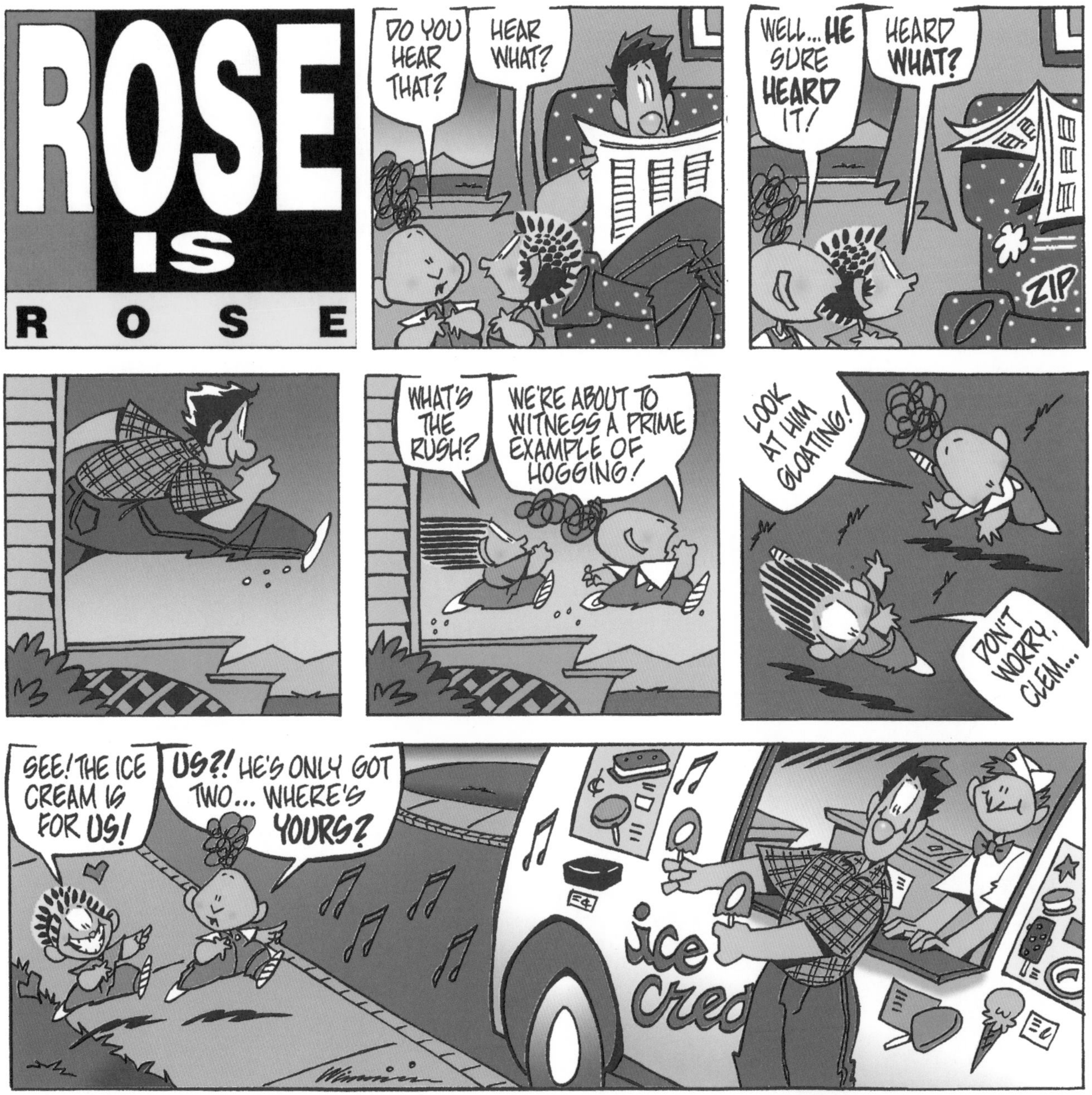
ROSE IS ROSE
DO YOU HEAR THAT?
HEAR WHAT?
WELL... HE SURE HEARD IT!
HEARD WHAT?
ZIP
WHAT'S THE RUSH?
WE'RE ABOUT TO WITNESS A PRIME EXAMPLE OF HOGGING!
LOOK AT HIM GLOATING!
DON'T WORRY, CLEM...
SEE! THE ICE CREAM IS FOR US!
US?! HE'S ONLY GOT TWO... WHERE'S YOURS?
ice crea

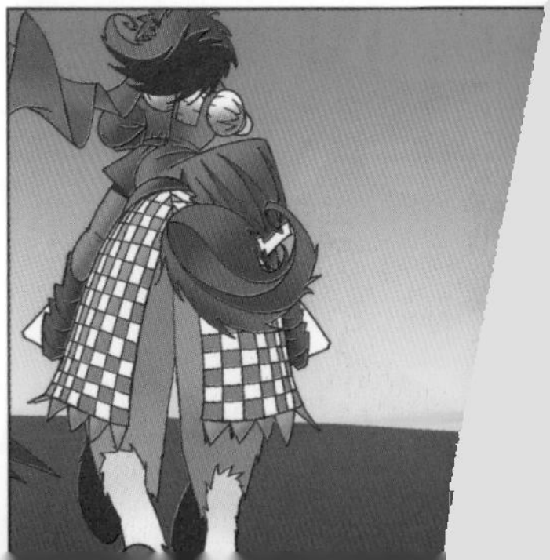

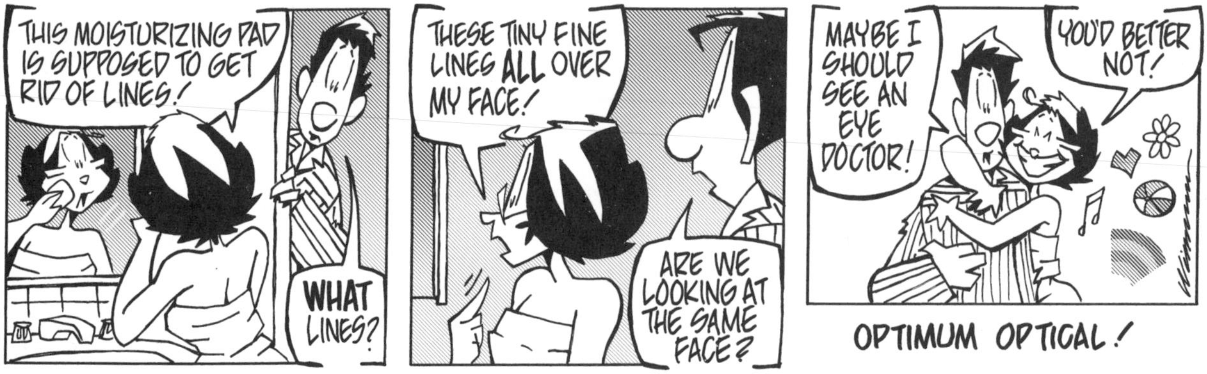
THIS MOISTURIZING PAD IS SUPPOSED TO GET RID OF LINES!
WHAT LINES?
THESE TINY FINE LINES **ALL** OVER MY FACE!
ARE WE LOOKING AT THE SAME FACE?
MAYBE I SHOULD SEE AN EYE DOCTOR!
YOU'D BETTER NOT!
OPTIMUM OPTICAL!

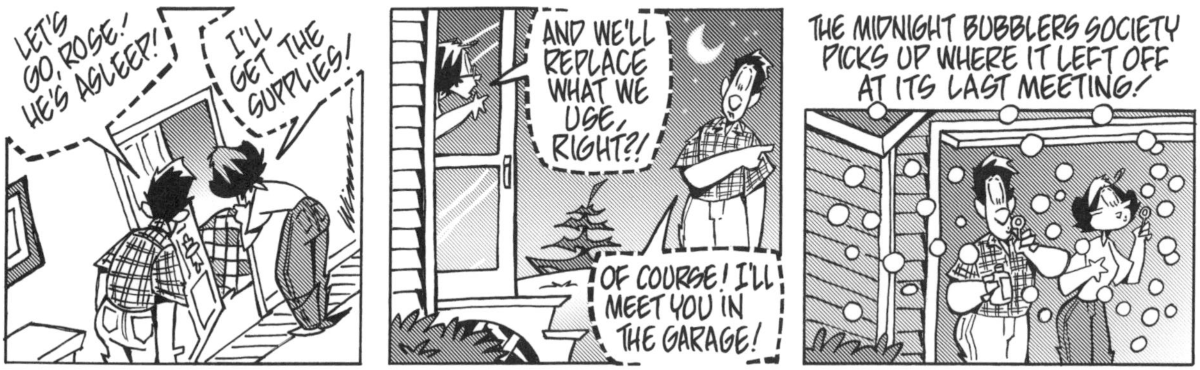
LET'S GO, ROSE! HE'S ASLEEP!
I'LL GET THE SUPPLIES!
AND WE'LL REPLACE WHAT WE USE, RIGHT?!
OF COURSE! I'LL MEET YOU IN THE GARAGE!
THE MIDNIGHT BUBBLERS SOCIETY PICKS UP WHERE IT LEFT OFF AT ITS LAST MEETING!

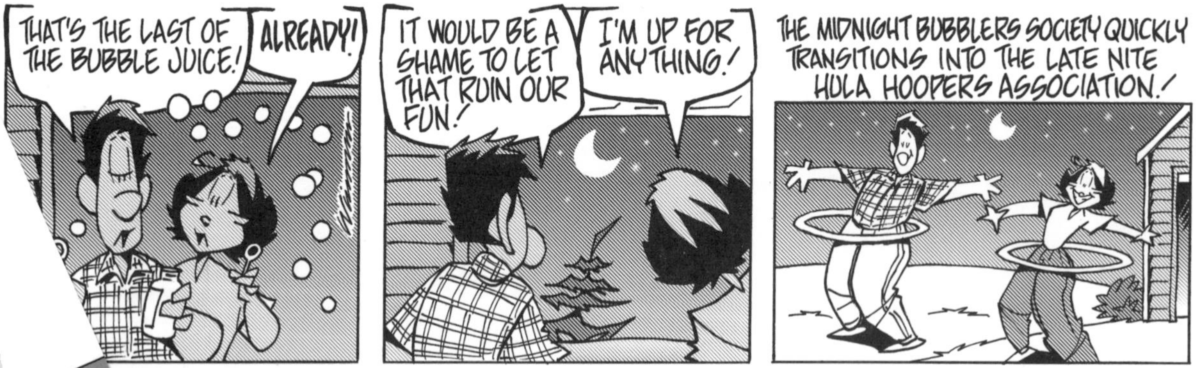
THAT'S THE LAST OF THE BUBBLE JUICE!
ALREADY!
IT WOULD BE A SHAME TO LET THAT RUIN OUR FUN!
I'M UP FOR ANYTHING!
THE MIDNIGHT BUBBLERS SOCIETY QUICKLY TRANSITIONS INTO THE LATE NITE HULA HOOPERS ASSOCIATION!

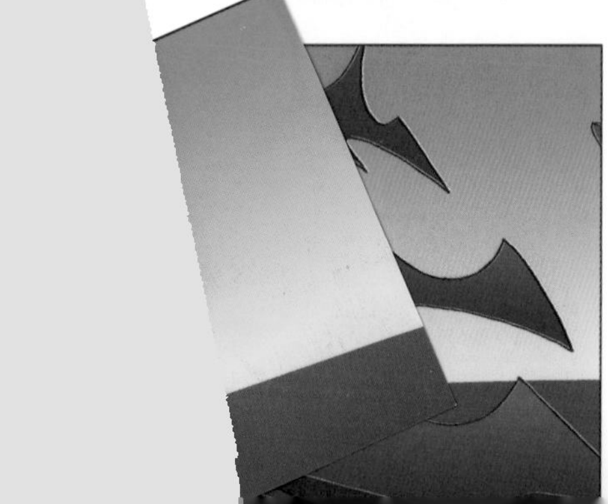

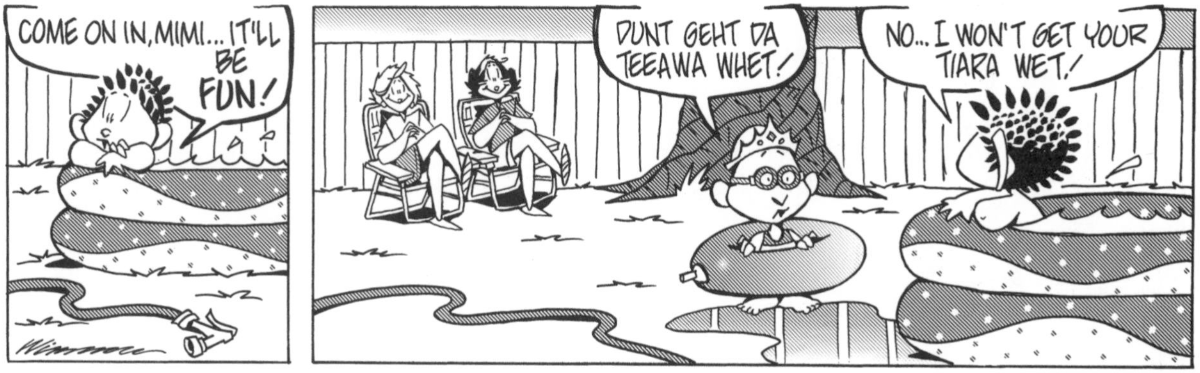
COME ON IN, MIMI... IT'LL BE FUN!
DUNT GEHT DA TEEAWA WHET!
NO... I WON'T GET YOUR TIARA WET!

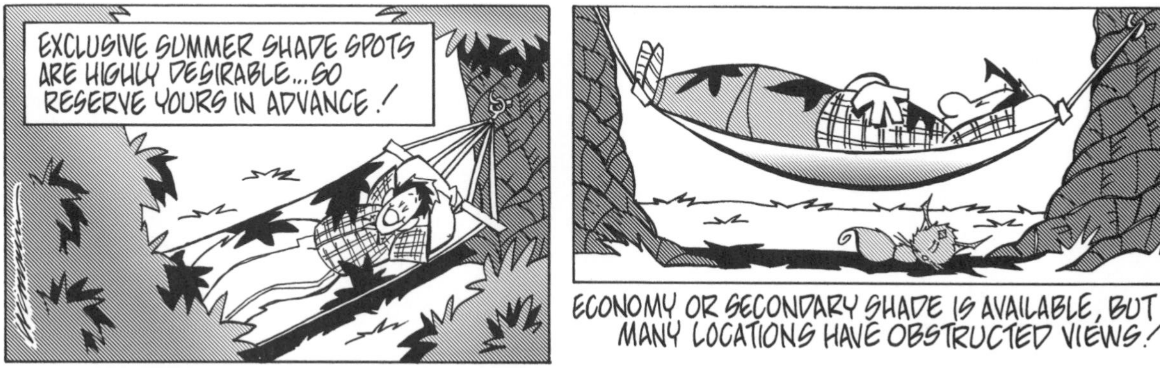
EXCLUSIVE SUMMER SHADE SPOTS ARE HIGHLY DESIRABLE... SO RESERVE YOURS IN ADVANCE!
ECONOMY OR SECONDARY SHADE IS AVAILABLE, BUT MANY LOCATIONS HAVE OBSTRUCTED VIEWS!

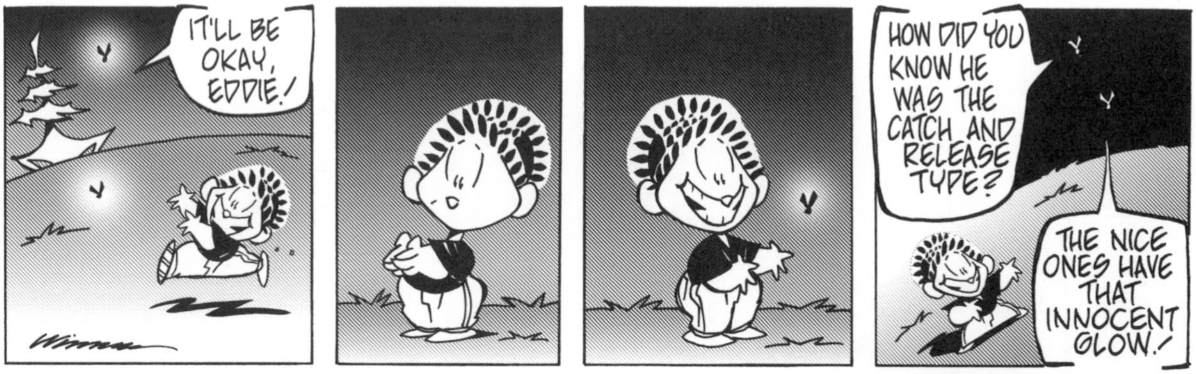
IT'LL BE OKAY, EDDIE!
HOW DID YOU KNOW HE WAS THE CATCH AND RELEASE TYPE?
THE NICE ONES HAVE THAT INNOCENT GLOW!

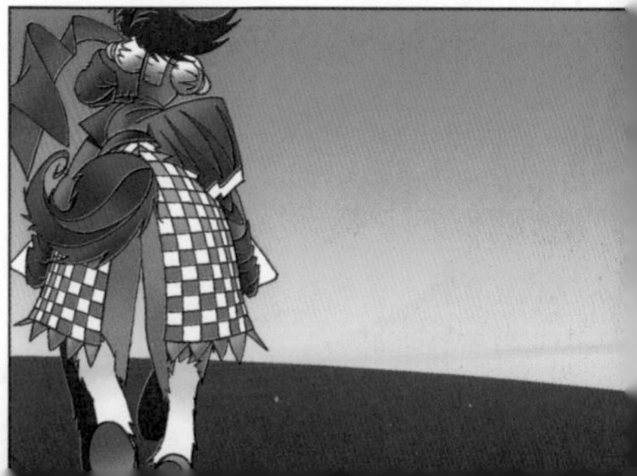

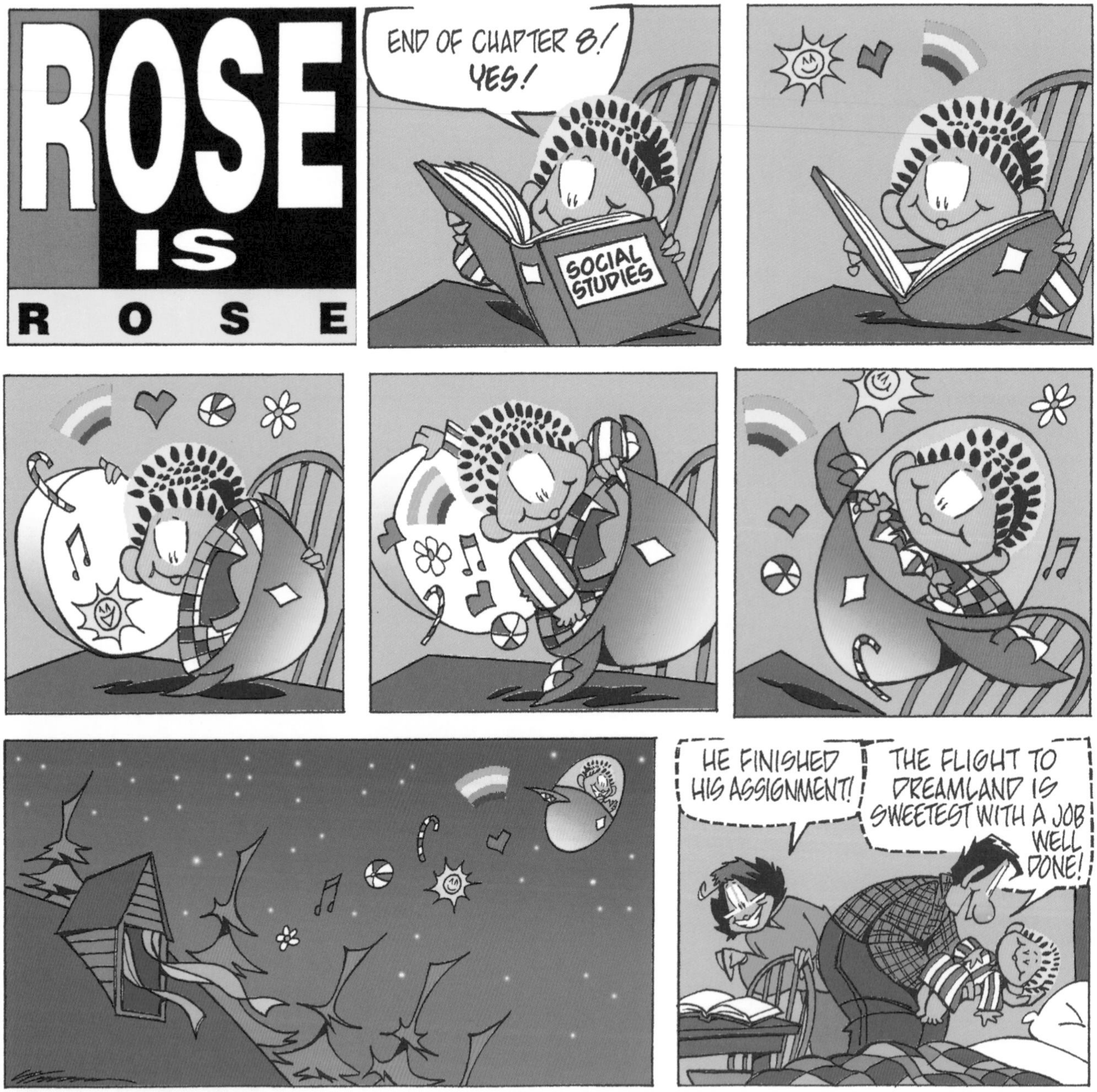
ROSE IS ROSE
END OF CHAPTER 8! YES!
SOCIAL STUDIES
HE FINISHED HIS ASSIGNMENT!
THE FLIGHT TO DREAMLAND IS SWEETEST WITH A JOB WELL DONE!

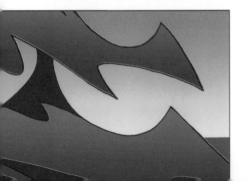

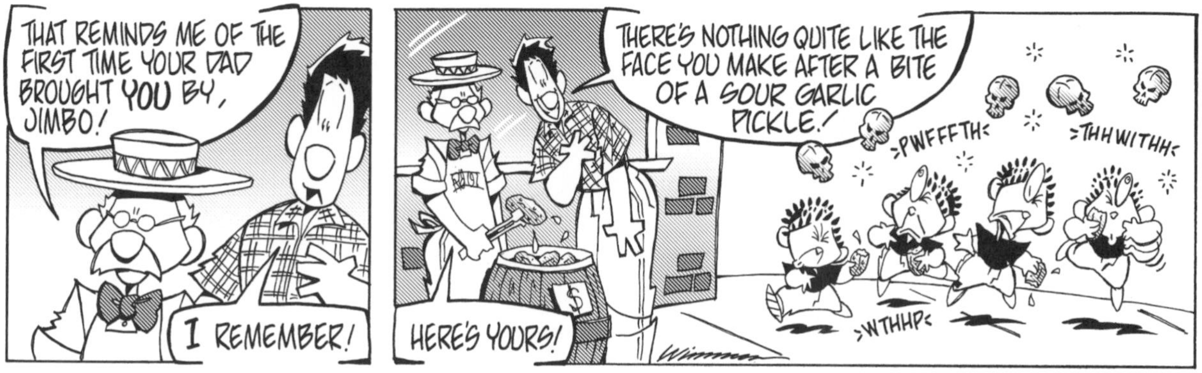
THAT REMINDS ME OF THE FIRST TIME YOUR DAD BROUGHT YOU BY, JIMBO!
I REMEMBER!
HERE'S YOURS!
THERE'S NOTHING QUITE LIKE THE FACE YOU MAKE AFTER A BITE OF A SOUR GARLIC PICKLE!
>PWFFFTH<
>THHWITHH<
>WTHHP<

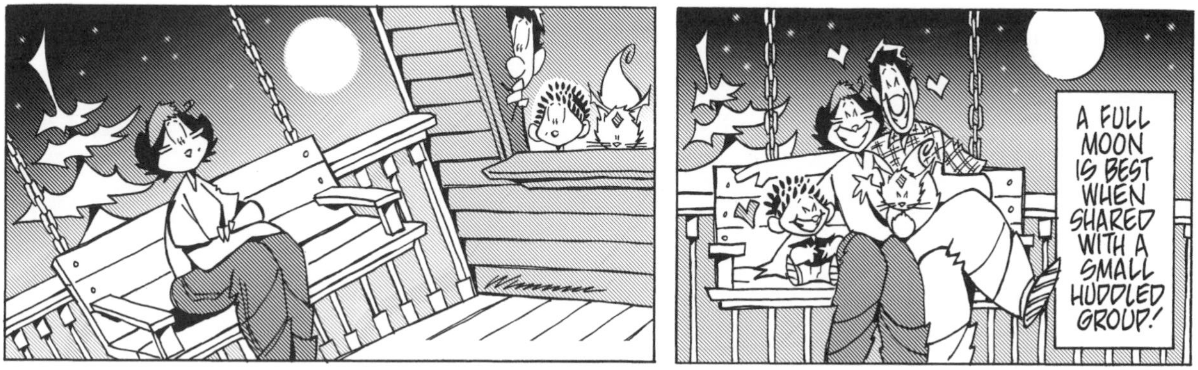
A FULL MOON IS BEST WHEN SHARED WITH A SMALL HUDDLED GROUP!

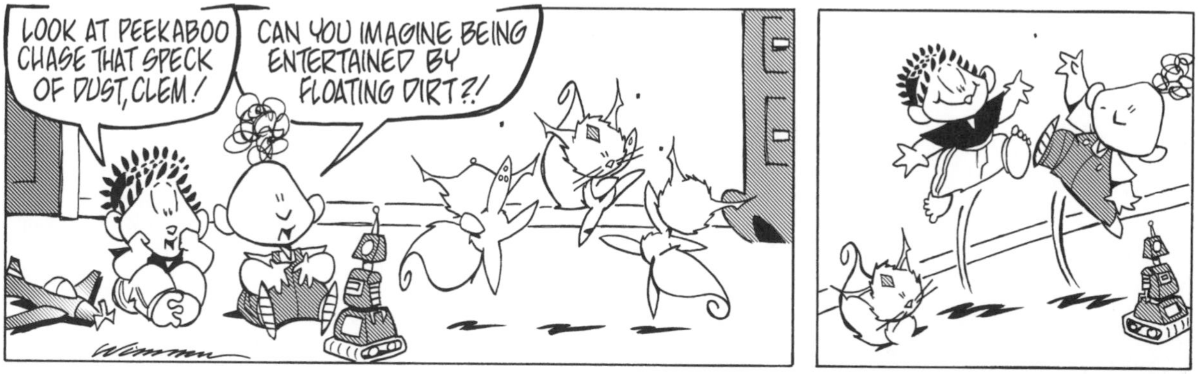
LOOK AT PEEKABOO CHASE THAT SPECK OF DUST, CLEM!
CAN YOU IMAGINE BEING ENTERTAINED BY FLOATING DIRT?!

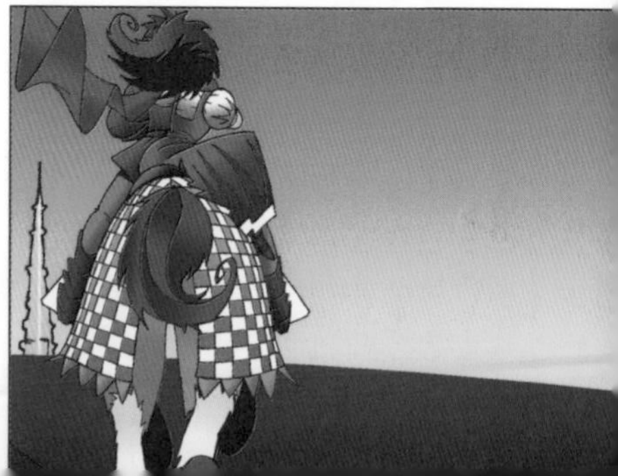

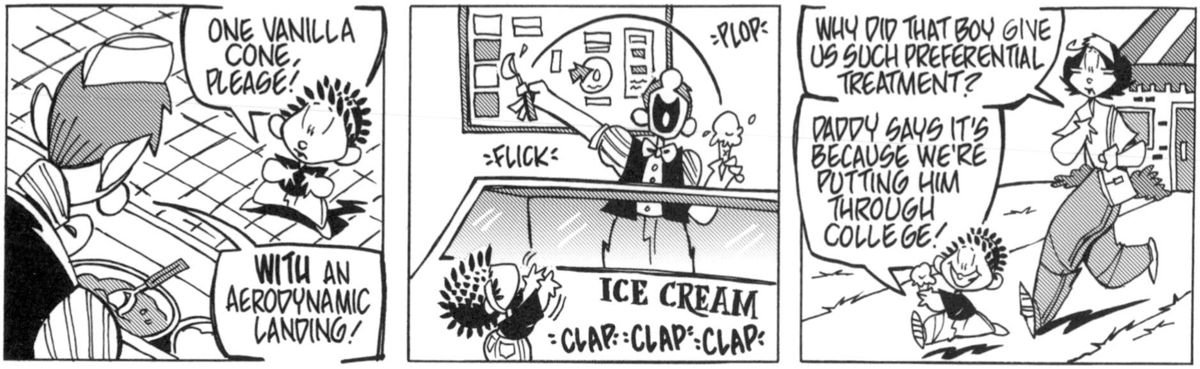
ONE VANILLA CONE, PLEASE!
WITH AN AERODYNAMIC LANDING!
FLICK
PLOP
ICE CREAM
CLAP CLAP CLAP
WHY DID THAT BOY GIVE US SUCH PREFERENTIAL TREATMENT?
DADDY SAYS IT'S BECAUSE WE'RE PUTTING HIM THROUGH COLLEGE!

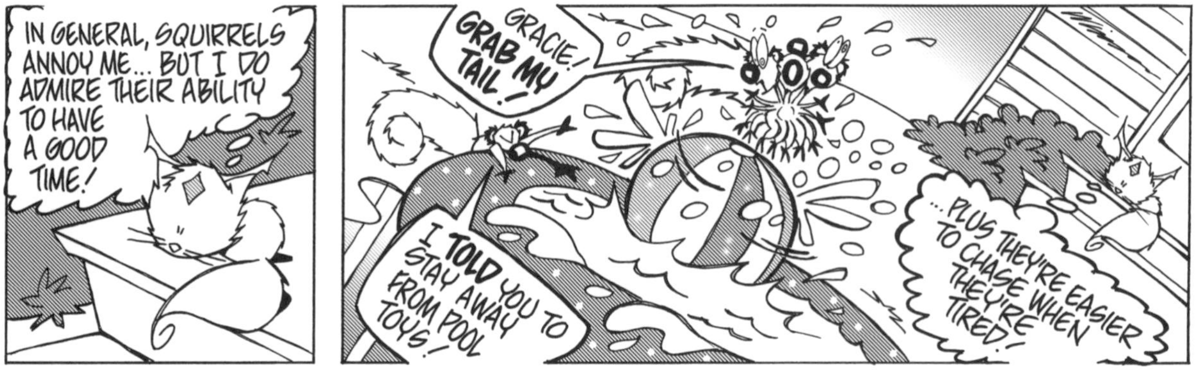
IN GENERAL, SQUIRRELS ANNOY ME... BUT I DO ADMIRE THEIR ABILITY TO HAVE A GOOD TIME!
GRACIE! GRAB MY TAIL!
I TOLD YOU TO STAY AWAY FROM POOL TOYS!
...PLUS THEY'RE EASIER TO CHASE WHEN THEY'RE TIRED!

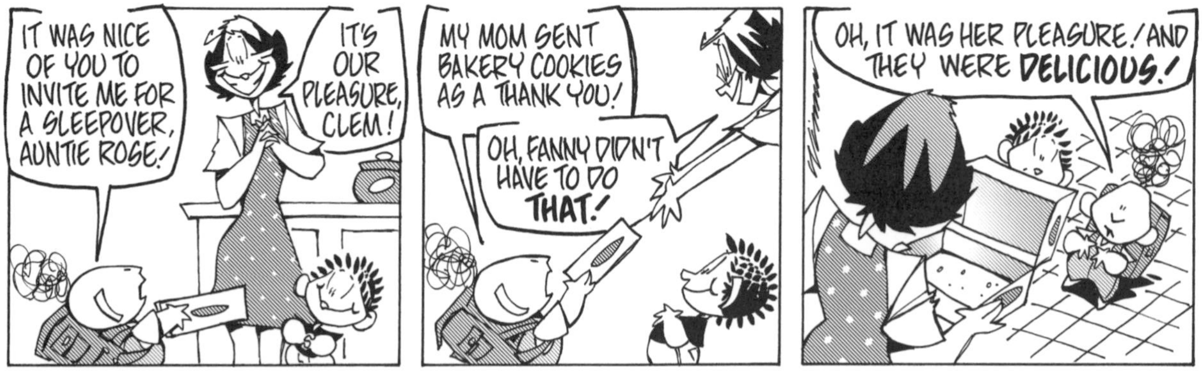
IT WAS NICE OF YOU TO INVITE ME FOR A SLEEPOVER, AUNTIE ROSE!
IT'S OUR PLEASURE, CLEM!
MY MOM SENT BAKERY COOKIES AS A THANK YOU!
OH, FANNY DIDN'T HAVE TO DO THAT!
OH, IT WAS HER PLEASURE! AND THEY WERE DELICIOUS!

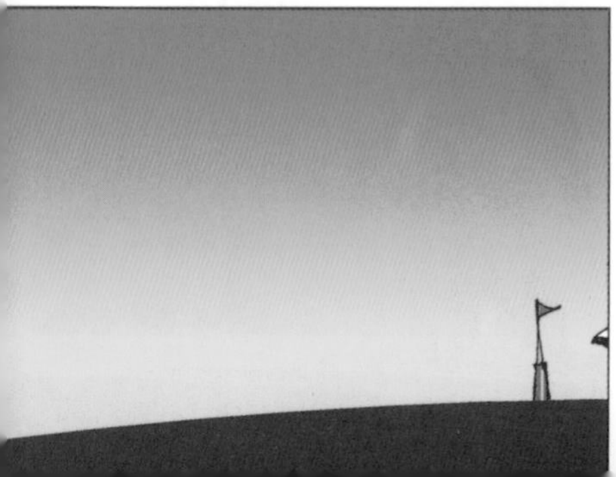

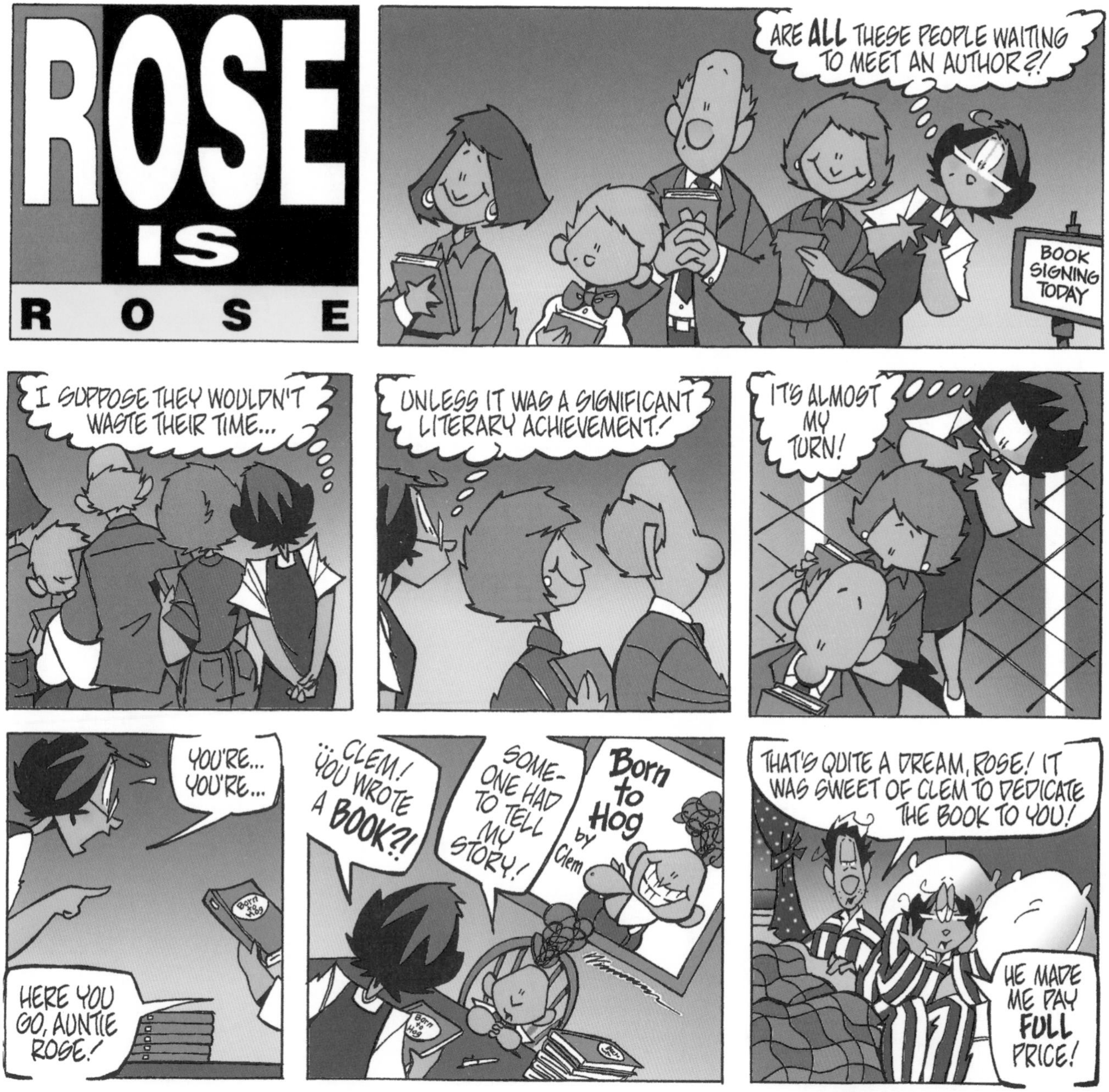
ROSE IS ROSE
ARE ALL THESE PEOPLE WAITING TO MEET AN AUTHOR?!
BOOK SIGNING TODAY
I SUPPOSE THEY WOULDN'T WASTE THEIR TIME...
UNLESS IT WAS A SIGNIFICANT LITERARY ACHIEVEMENT!
IT'S ALMOST MY TURN!
YOU'RE... YOU'RE...
HERE YOU GO, AUNTIE ROSE!
...CLEM! YOU WROTE A BOOK?!
SOME-ONE HAD TO TELL MY STORY!
Born to Hog by Clem
THAT'S QUITE A DREAM, ROSE! IT WAS SWEET OF CLEM TO DEDICATE THE BOOK TO YOU!
HE MADE ME PAY FULL PRICE!

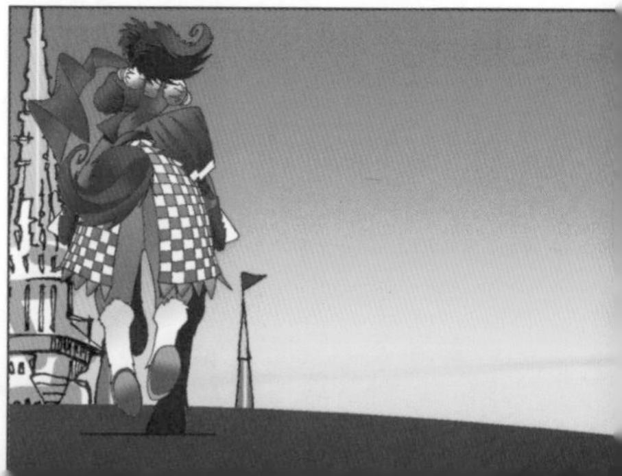

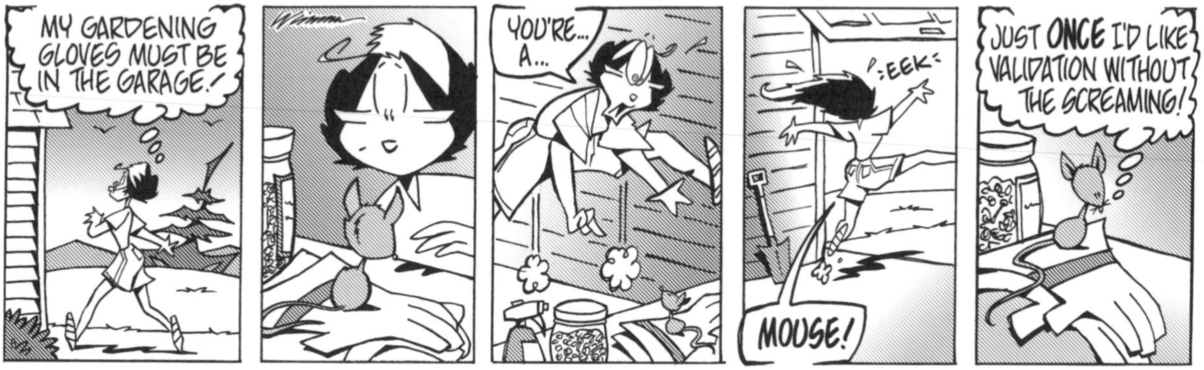
MY GARDENING GLOVES MUST BE IN THE GARAGE!
YOU'RE... A...
EEK
MOUSE!
JUST ONCE I'D LIKE VALIDATION WITHOUT THE SCREAMING!

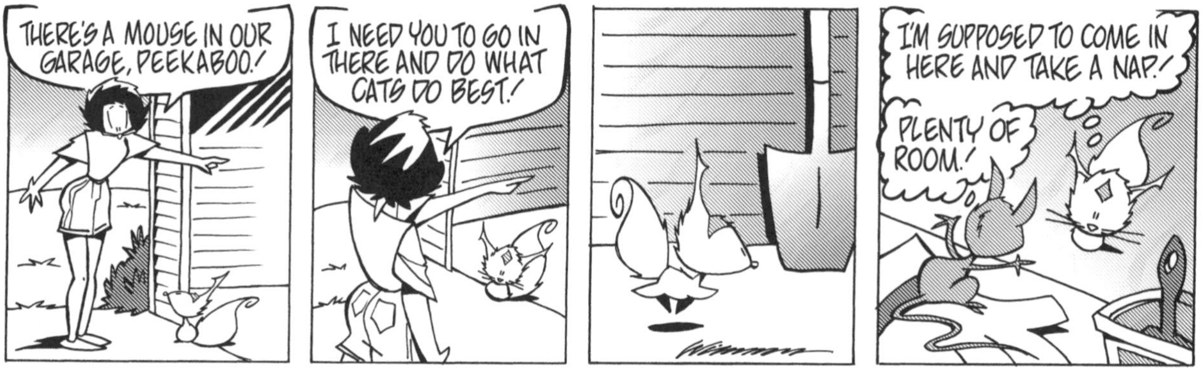
THERE'S A MOUSE IN OUR GARAGE, PEEKABOO!
I NEED YOU TO GO IN THERE AND DO WHAT CATS DO BEST!
I'M SUPPOSED TO COME IN HERE AND TAKE A NAP!
PLENTY OF ROOM!

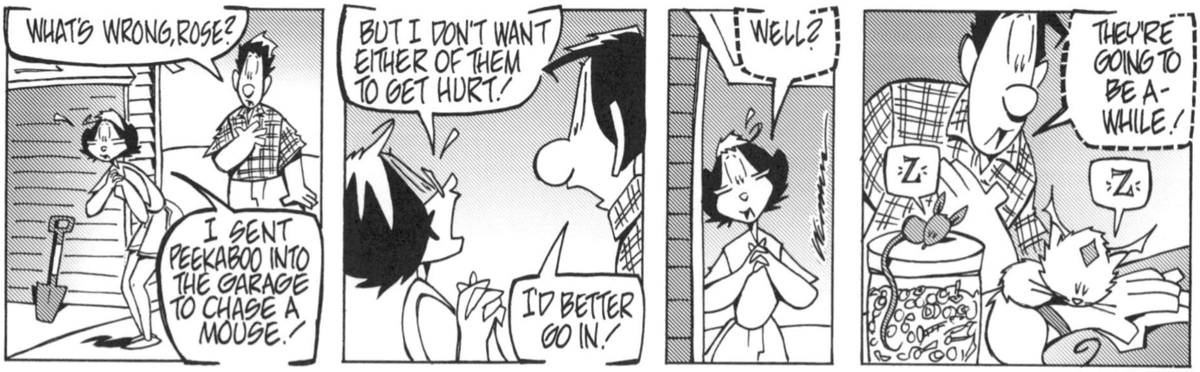
WHAT'S WRONG, ROSE?
I SENT PEEKABOO INTO THE GARAGE TO CHASE A MOUSE!
BUT I DON'T WANT EITHER OF THEM TO GET HURT!
I'D BETTER GO IN!
WELL?
THEY'RE GOING TO BE A WHILE!
Z
Z

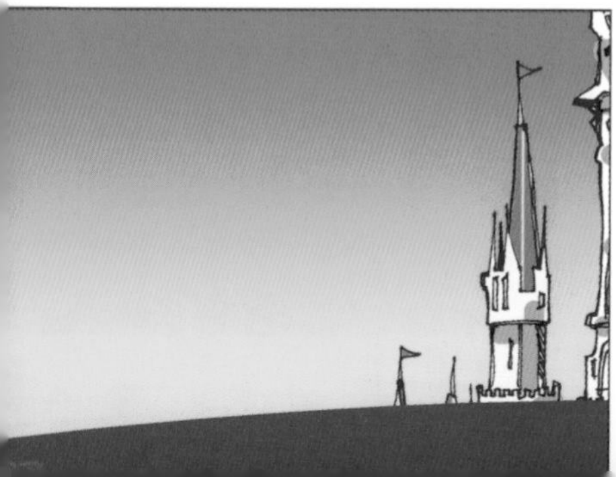

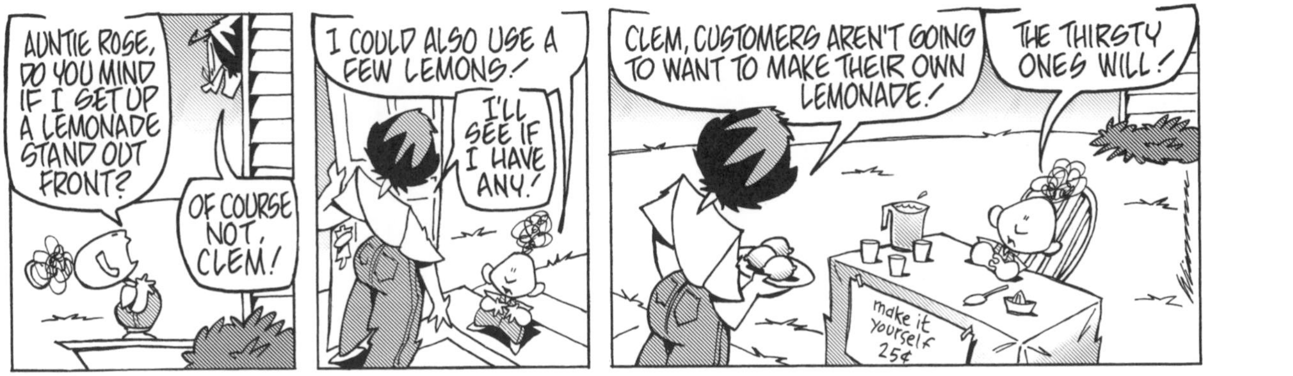
AUNTIE ROSE, DO YOU MIND IF I SET UP A LEMONADE STAND OUT FRONT?
OF COURSE NOT, CLEM!
I COULD ALSO USE A FEW LEMONS!
I'LL SEE IF I HAVE ANY!
CLEM, CUSTOMERS AREN'T GOING TO WANT TO MAKE THEIR OWN LEMONADE!
THE THIRSTY ONES WILL!
make it yourself 25¢

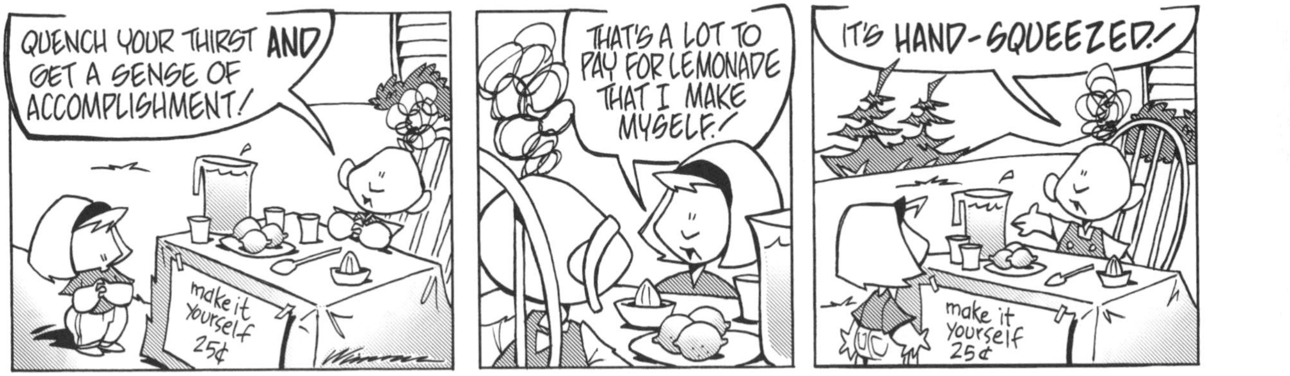
QUENCH YOUR THIRST AND GET A SENSE OF ACCOMPLISHMENT!
make it yourself 25¢
THAT'S A LOT TO PAY FOR LEMONADE THAT I MAKE MYSELF!
IT'S HAND-SQUEEZED!
make it yourself 25¢

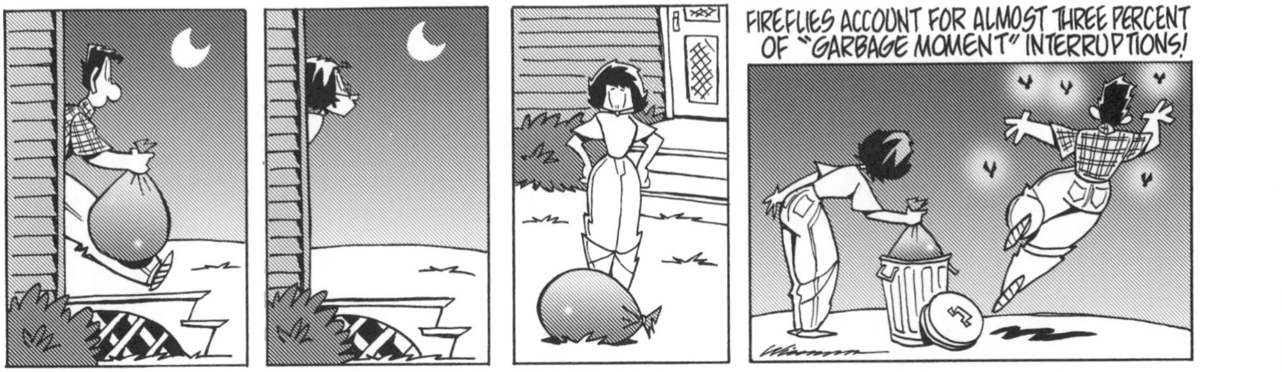
FIREFLIES ACCOUNT FOR ALMOST THREE PERCENT OF "GARBAGE MOMENT" INTERRUPTIONS!

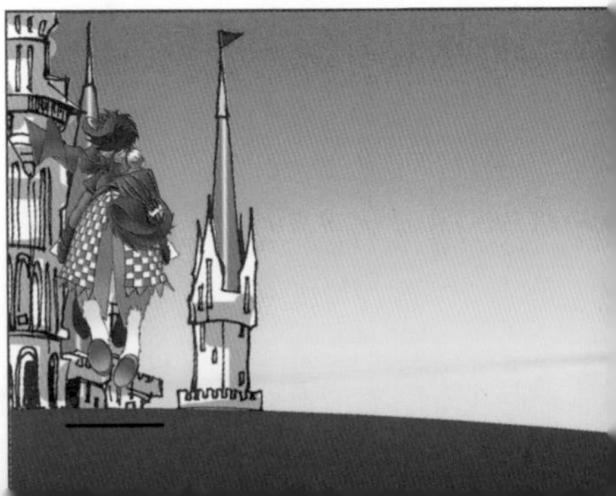

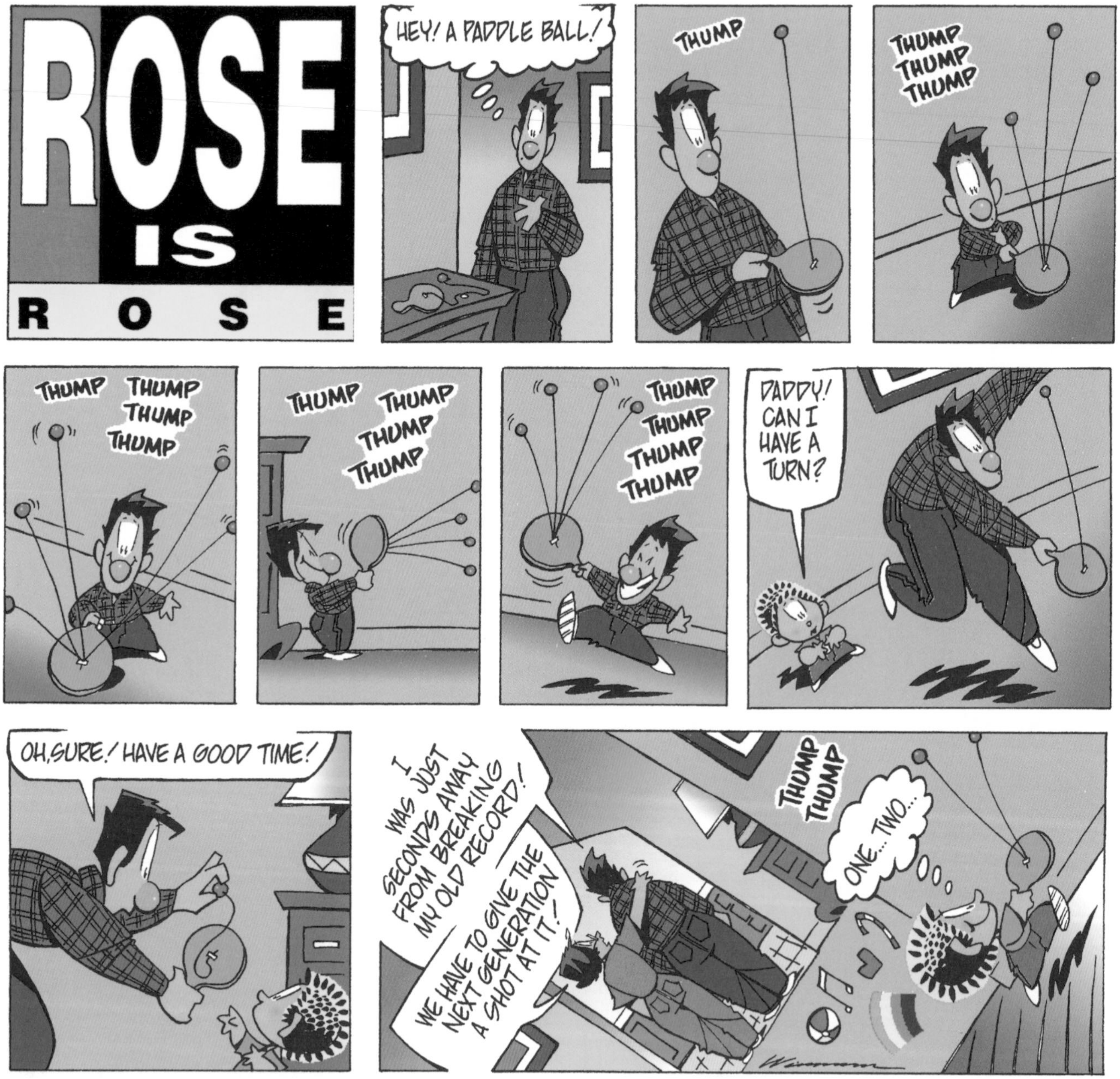
ROSE IS ROSE
HEY! A PADDLE BALL!
THUMP
THUMP THUMP THUMP
THUMP THUMP THUMP THUMP
THUMP THUMP THUMP THUMP
THUMP THUMP THUMP THUMP
DADDY! CAN I HAVE A TURN?
OH, SURE! HAVE A GOOD TIME!
I WAS JUST SECONDS AWAY FROM BREAKING MY OLD RECORD!
WE HAVE TO GIVE THE NEXT GENERATION A SHOT AT IT!
THUMP THUMP
ONE... TWO...

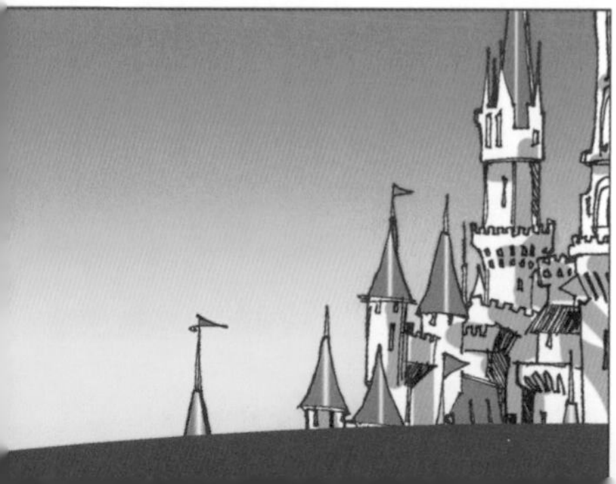

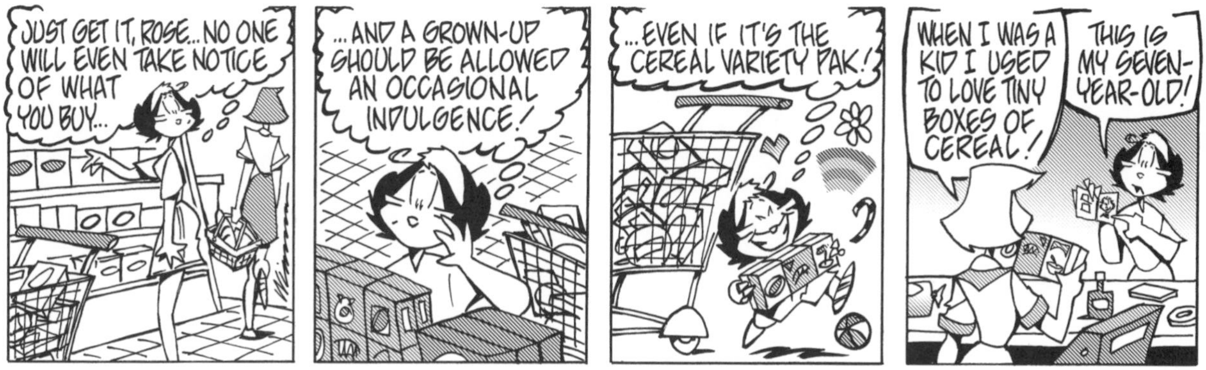
JUST GET IT, ROSE... NO ONE WILL EVEN TAKE NOTICE OF WHAT YOU BUY...
...AND A GROWN-UP SHOULD BE ALLOWED AN OCCASIONAL INDULGENCE!
...EVEN IF IT'S THE CEREAL VARIETY PAK!
WHEN I WAS A KID I USED TO LOVE TINY BOXES OF CEREAL!
THIS IS MY SEVEN-YEAR-OLD!

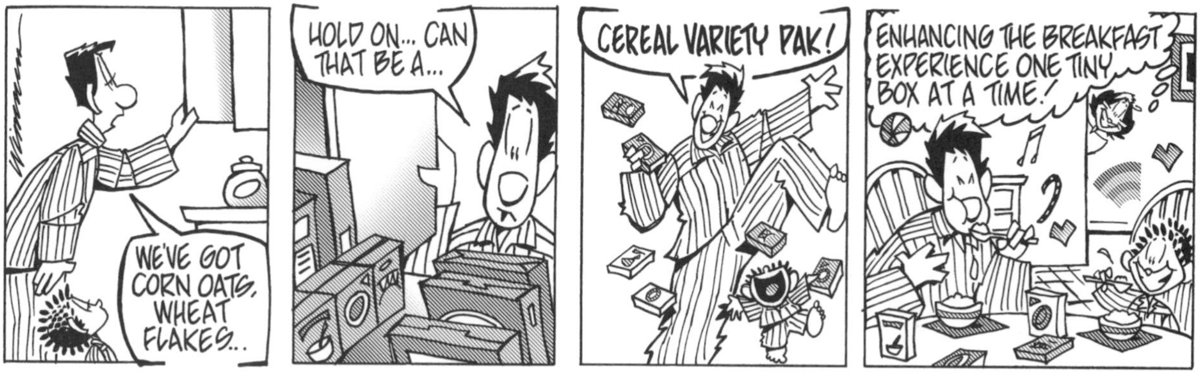
WE'VE GOT CORN OATS, WHEAT FLAKES...
HOLD ON... CAN THAT BE A...
CEREAL VARIETY PAK!
ENHANCING THE BREAKFAST EXPERIENCE ONE TINY BOX AT A TIME!

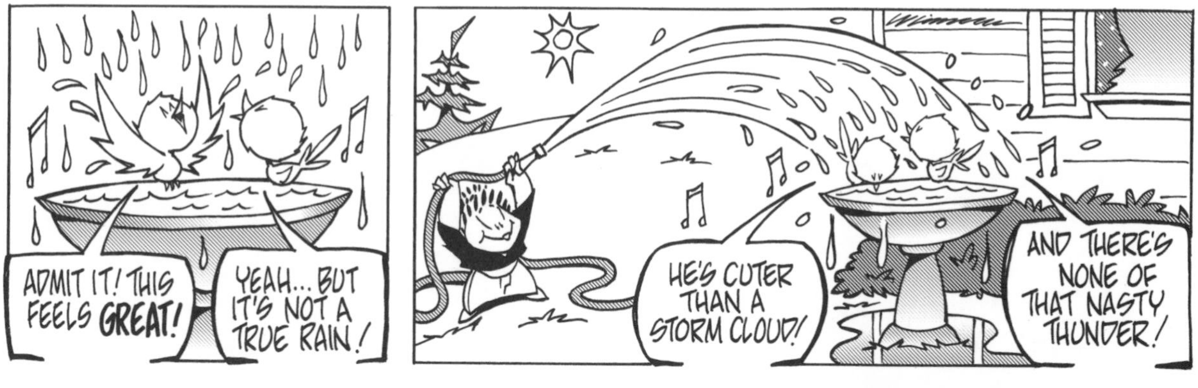
ADMIT IT! THIS FEELS **GREAT**!
YEAH... BUT IT'S NOT A TRUE RAIN!
HE'S CUTER THAN A STORM CLOUD!
AND THERE'S NONE OF THAT NASTY THUNDER!

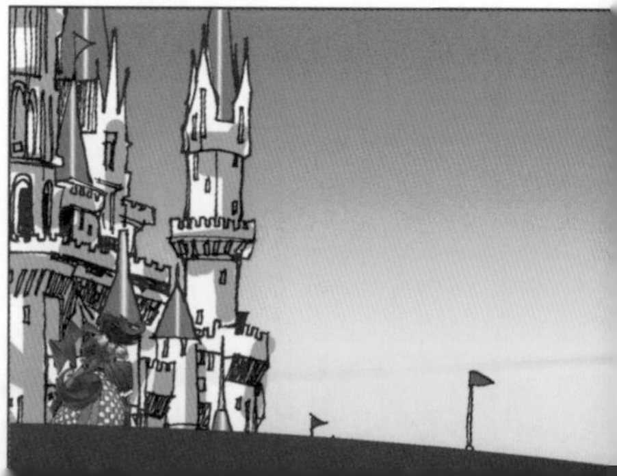

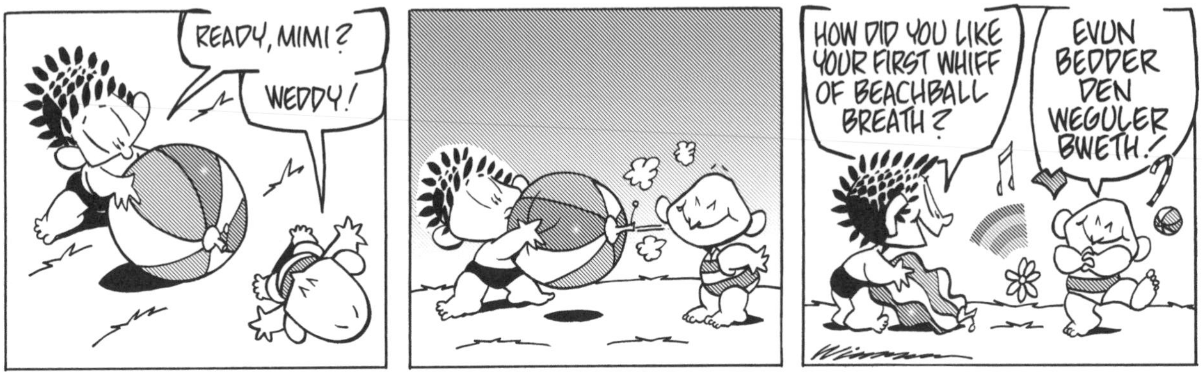
READY, MIMI?
WEDDY!
HOW DID YOU LIKE YOUR FIRST WHIFF OF BEACHBALL BREATH?
EVUN BEDDER DEN WEGULER BWETH!

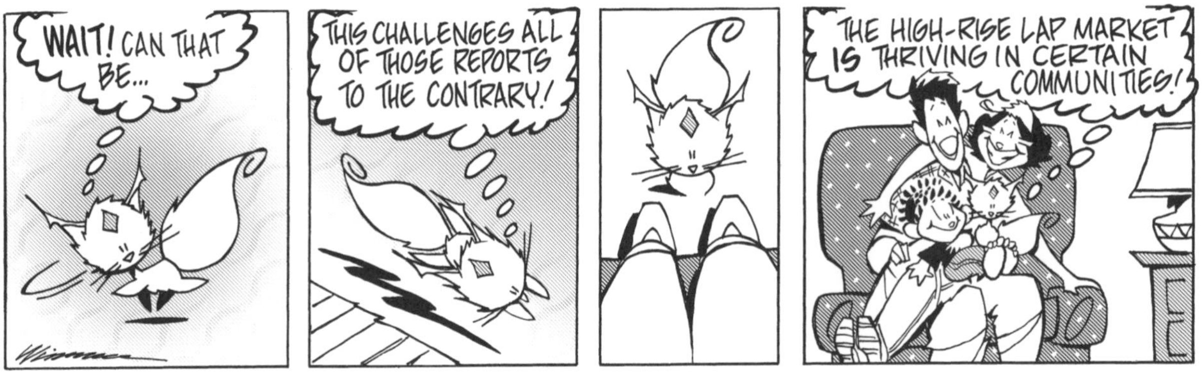
WAIT! CAN THAT BE...
THIS CHALLENGES ALL OF THOSE REPORTS TO THE CONTRARY!
THE HIGH-RISE LAP MARKET IS THRIVING IN CERTAIN COMMUNITIES!

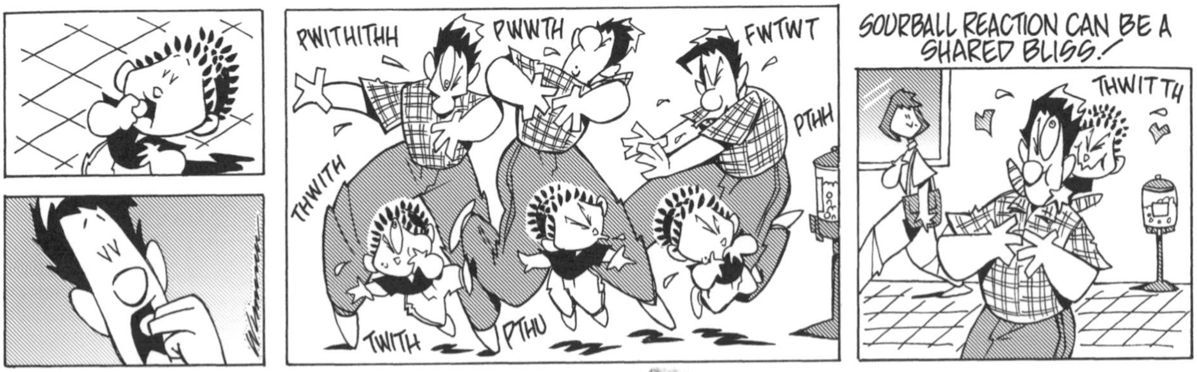
PWITHITHH
PWWTH
FWTWT
PTHH
THWITH
TWITH
PTHU
SOURBALL REACTION CAN BE A SHARED BLISS!
THWITTH

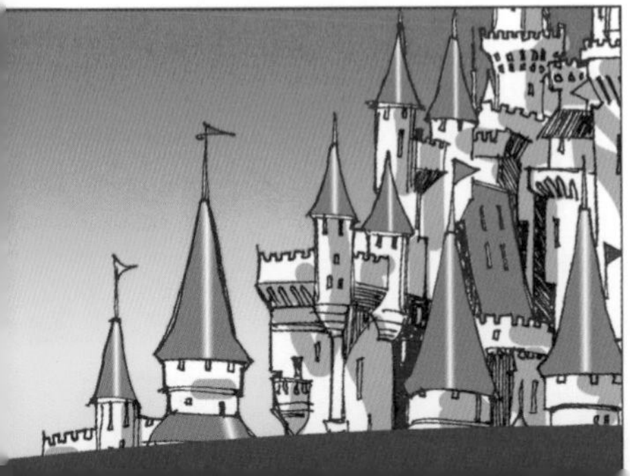

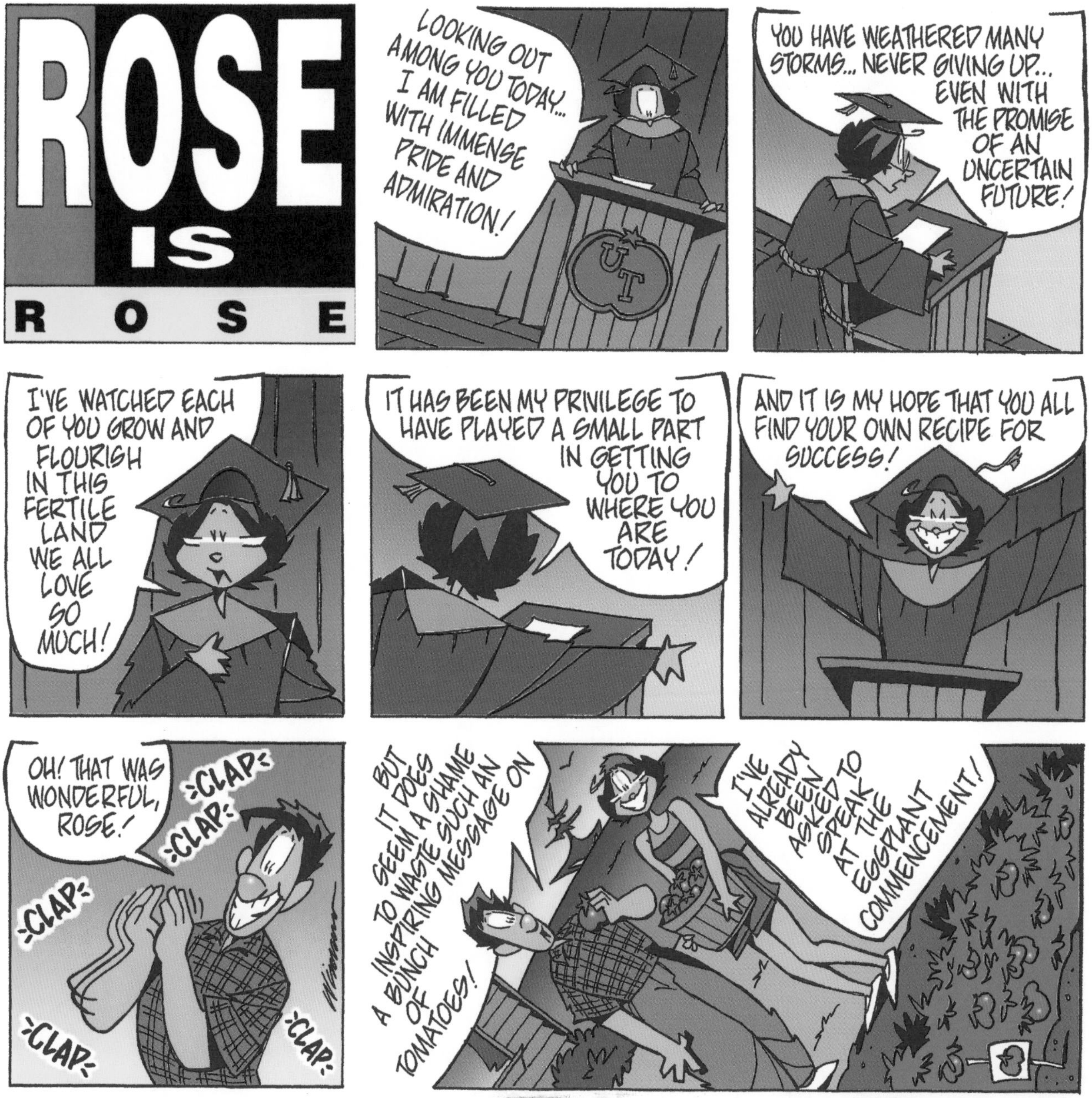
ROSE IS ROSE
LOOKING OUT AMONG YOU TODAY... I AM FILLED WITH IMMENSE PRIDE AND ADMIRATION!
UT
YOU HAVE WEATHERED MANY STORMS... NEVER GIVING UP... EVEN WITH THE PROMISE OF AN UNCERTAIN FUTURE!
I'VE WATCHED EACH OF YOU GROW AND FLOURISH IN THIS FERTILE LAND WE ALL LOVE SO MUCH!
IT HAS BEEN MY PRIVILEGE TO HAVE PLAYED A SMALL PART IN GETTING YOU TO WHERE YOU ARE TODAY!
AND IT IS MY HOPE THAT YOU ALL FIND YOUR OWN RECIPE FOR SUCCESS!
OH! THAT WAS WONDERFUL, ROSE!
CLAP CLAP CLAP CLAP CLAP
BUT IT DOES SEEM A SHAME TO WASTE SUCH AN INSPIRING MESSAGE ON A BUNCH OF TOMATOES!
I'VE ALREADY BEEN ASKED TO SPEAK AT THE EGGPLANT COMMENCEMENT!

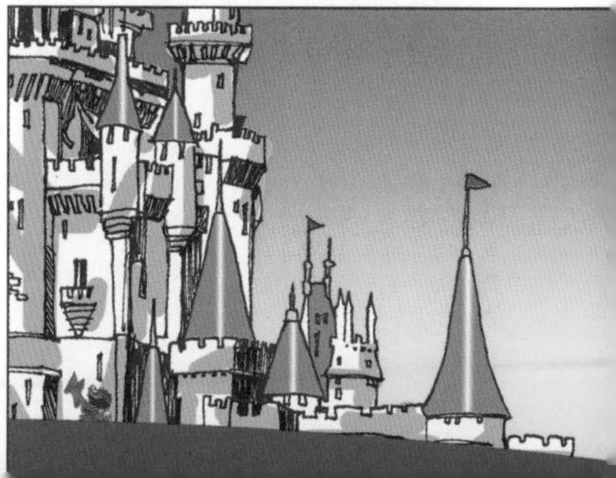

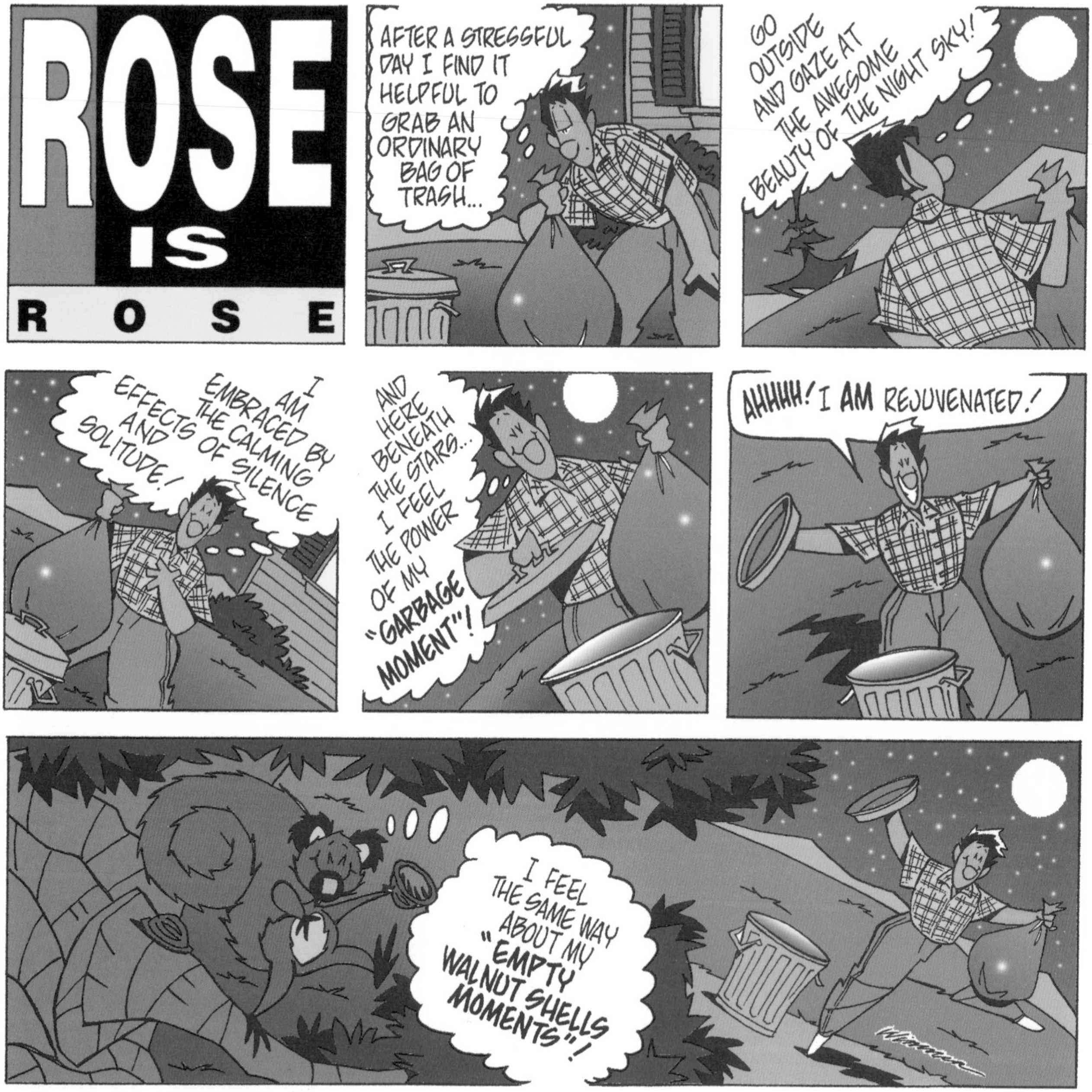
ROSE IS ROSE
AFTER A STRESSFUL DAY I FIND IT HELPFUL TO GRAB AN ORDINARY BAG OF TRASH...
GO OUTSIDE AND GAZE AT THE AWESOME BEAUTY OF THE NIGHT SKY!
I AM EMBRACED BY THE CALMING EFFECTS OF SILENCE AND SOLITUDE!
AND HERE BENEATH THE STARS... I FEEL THE POWER OF MY "GARBAGE MOMENT"!
AHHHH! I AM REJUVENATED!
I FEEL THE SAME WAY ABOUT MY "EMPTY WALNUT SHELLS MOMENTS"!

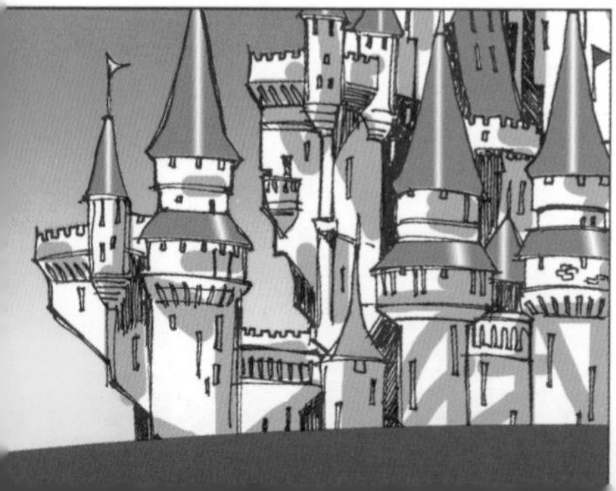

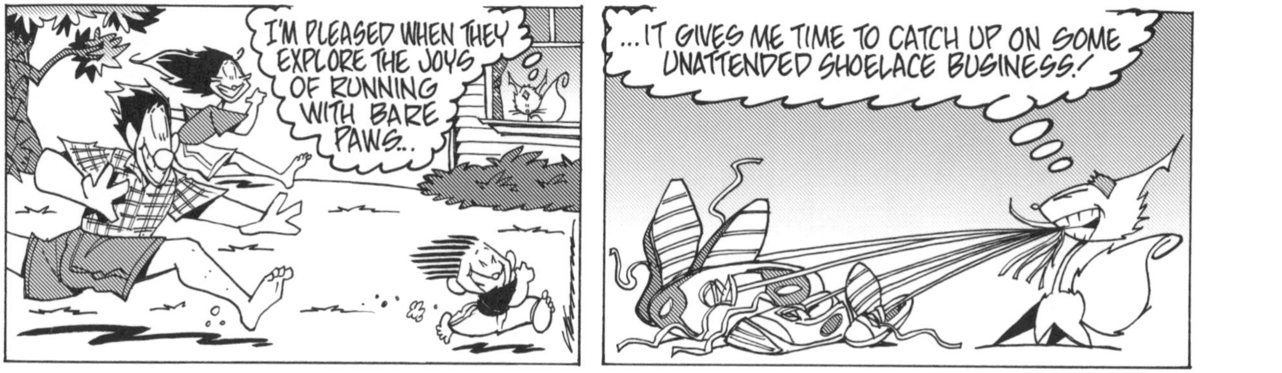
I'M PLEASED WHEN THEY EXPLORE THE JOYS OF RUNNING WITH BARE PAWS...
...IT GIVES ME TIME TO CATCH UP ON SOME UNATTENDED SHOELACE BUSINESS!

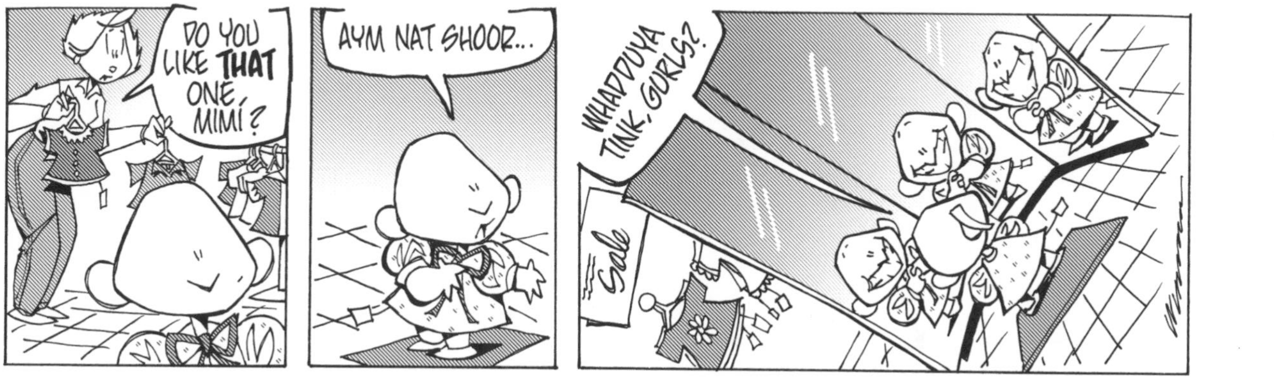
DO YOU LIKE **THAT** ONE, MIMI?
AYM NAT SHOOR...
WHADDUYA TINK, GURLS?
Sale

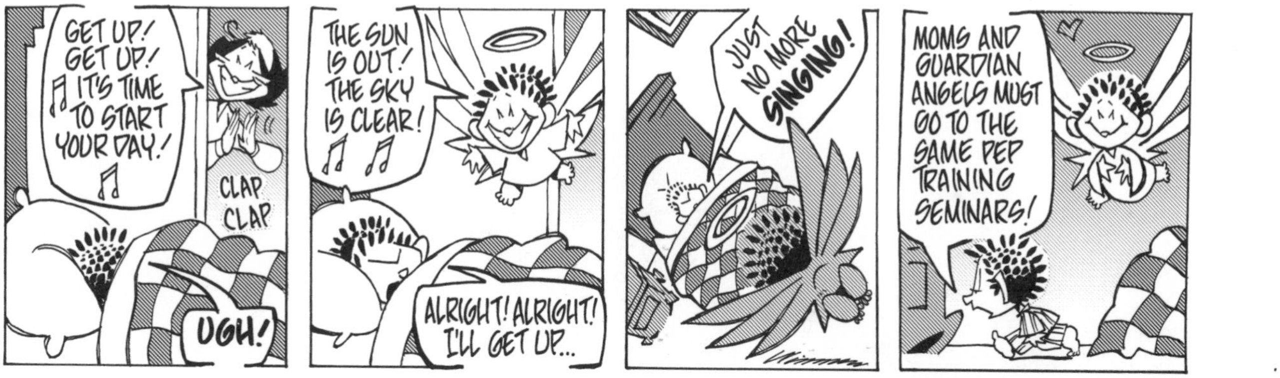
GET UP! GET UP! IT'S TIME TO START YOUR DAY!
CLAP CLAP
UGH!
THE SUN IS OUT! THE SKY IS CLEAR!
ALRIGHT! ALRIGHT! I'LL GET UP...
JUST NO MORE **SINGING!**
MOMS AND GUARDIAN ANGELS MUST GO TO THE SAME PEP TRAINING SEMINARS!

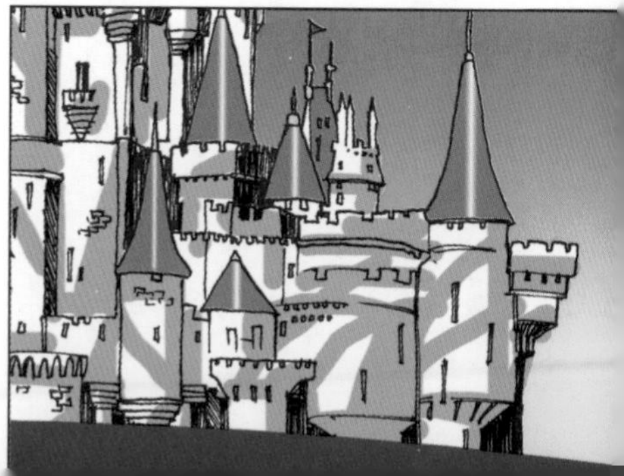

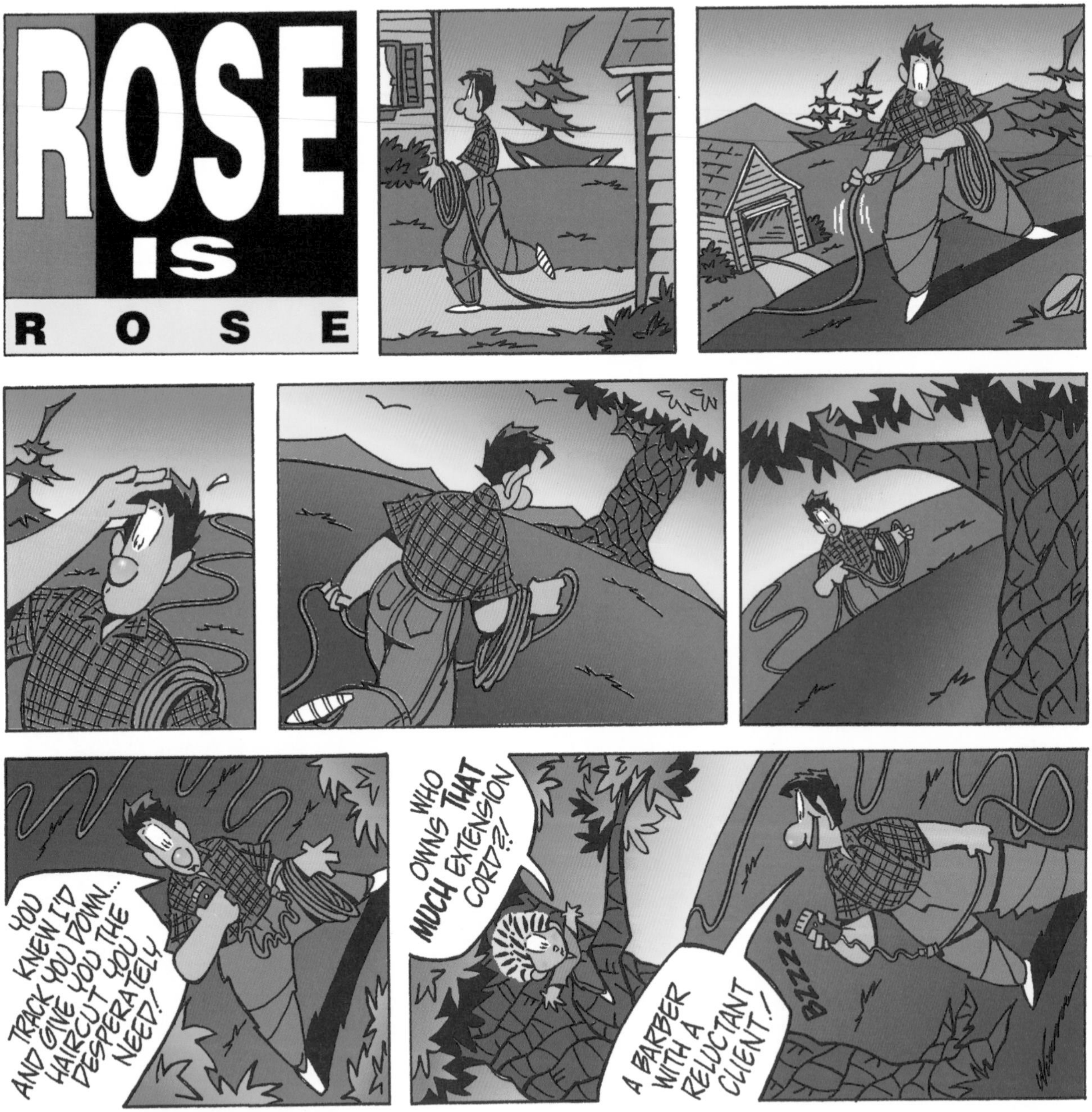
ROSE IS ROSE
YOU KNEW I'D TRACK YOU DOWN... AND GIVE YOU THE HAIRCUT YOU DESPERATELY NEED!
WHO OWNS THAT MUCH EXTENSION CORD?!
A BARBER WITH A RELUCTANT CLIENT!
BZZZZZZ

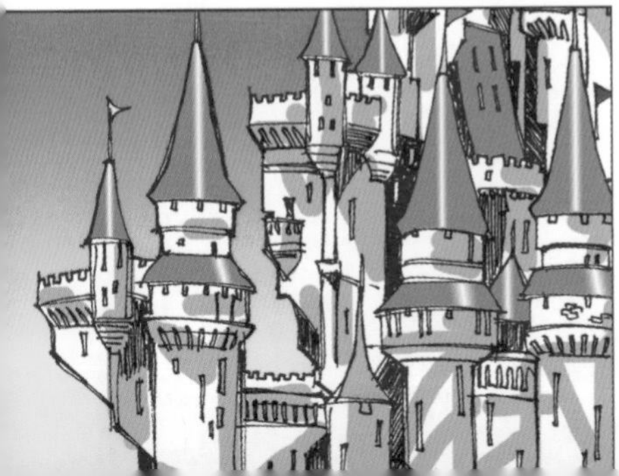

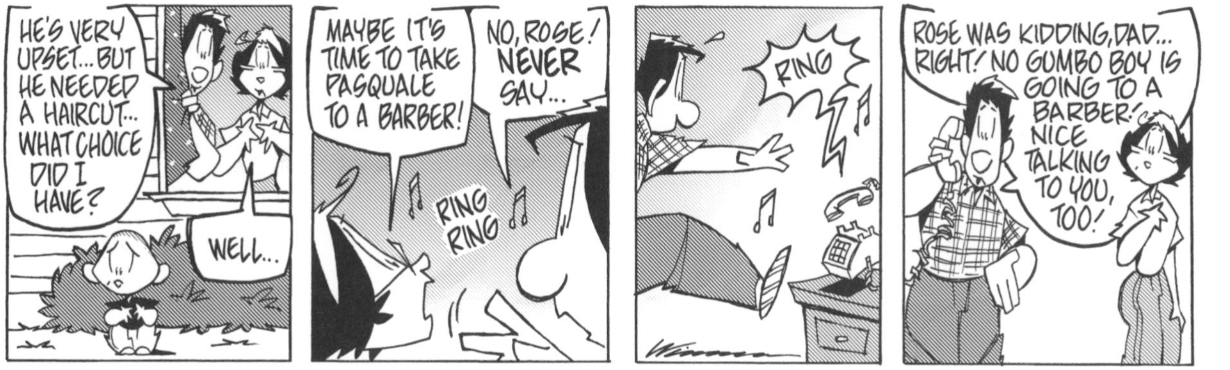

HE'S VERY UPSET... BUT HE NEEDED A HAIRCUT... WHAT CHOICE DID I HAVE?
WELL...
MAYBE IT'S TIME TO TAKE PASQUALE TO A BARBER!
NO, ROSE! NEVER SAY...
RING RING
RING
ROSE WAS KIDDING, DAD... RIGHT! NO GUMBO BOY IS GOING TO A BARBER! NICE TALKING TO YOU, TOO!

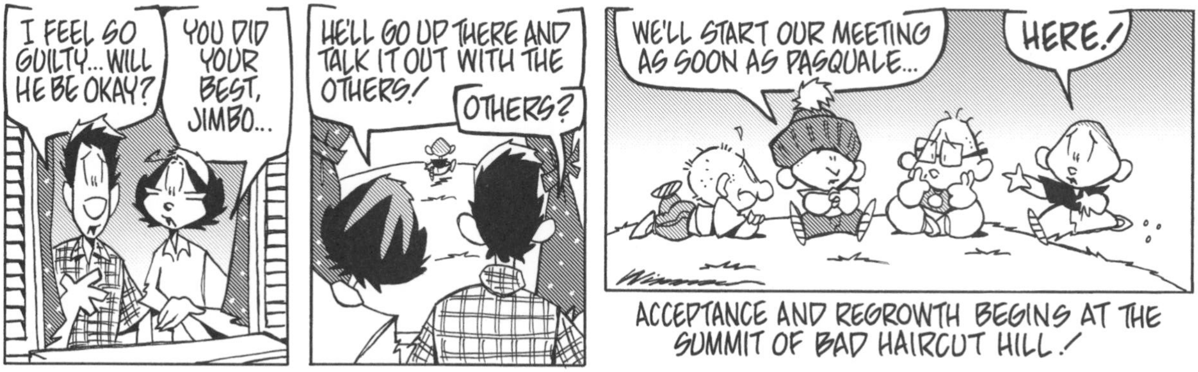

I FEEL SO GUILTY... WILL HE BE OKAY?
YOU DID YOUR BEST, JIMBO...
HE'LL GO UP THERE AND TALK IT OUT WITH THE OTHERS!
OTHERS?
WE'LL START OUR MEETING AS SOON AS PASQUALE...
HERE!
ACCEPTANCE AND REGROWTH BEGINS AT THE SUMMIT OF BAD HAIRCUT HILL!

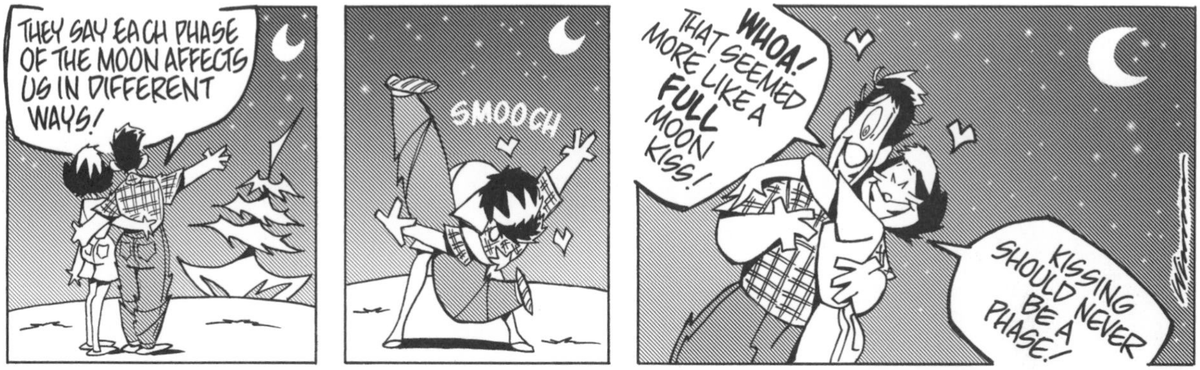

THEY SAY EACH PHASE OF THE MOON AFFECTS US IN DIFFERENT WAYS!
SMOOCH
WHOA! THAT SEEMED MORE LIKE A FULL MOON KISS!
KISSING SHOULD NEVER BE A PHASE!

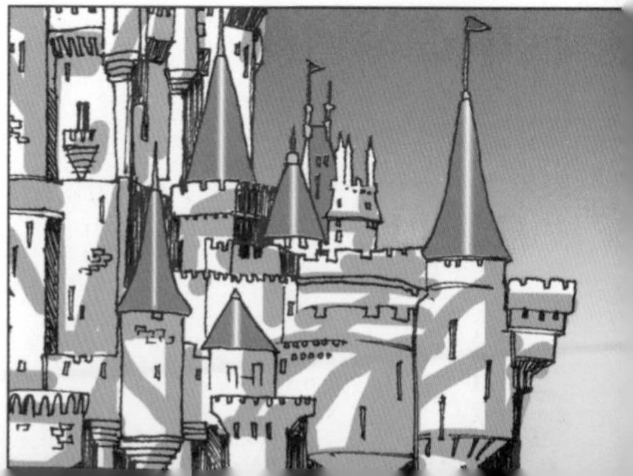

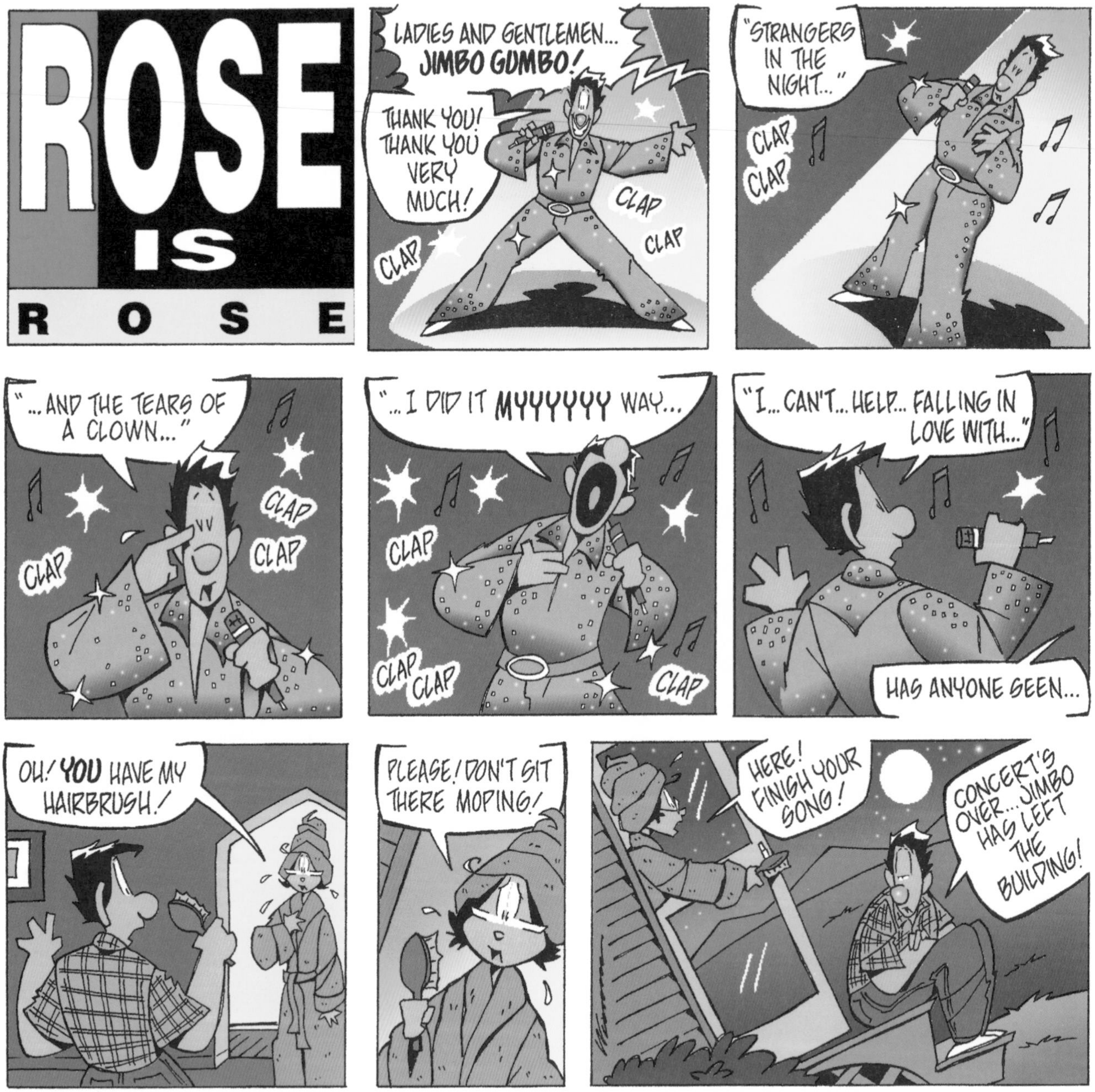
ROSE IS ROSE
LADIES AND GENTLEMEN... JIMBO GUMBO!
THANK YOU! THANK YOU VERY MUCH!
CLAP
CLAP
CLAP
"STRANGERS IN THE NIGHT..."
CLAP
CLAP
"...AND THE TEARS OF A CLOWN..."
CLAP
CLAP
CLAP
"...I DID IT MYYYYYY WAY...
CLAP
CLAP
CLAP
CLAP
"I... CAN'T... HELP... FALLING IN LOVE WITH..."
HAS ANYONE SEEN...
OH! YOU HAVE MY HAIRBRUSH!
PLEASE! DON'T SIT THERE MOPING!
HERE! FINISH YOUR SONG!
CONCERT'S OVER... JIMBO HAS LEFT THE BUILDING!

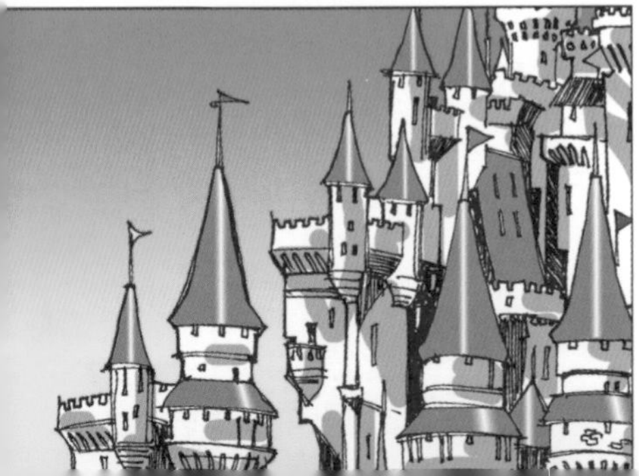

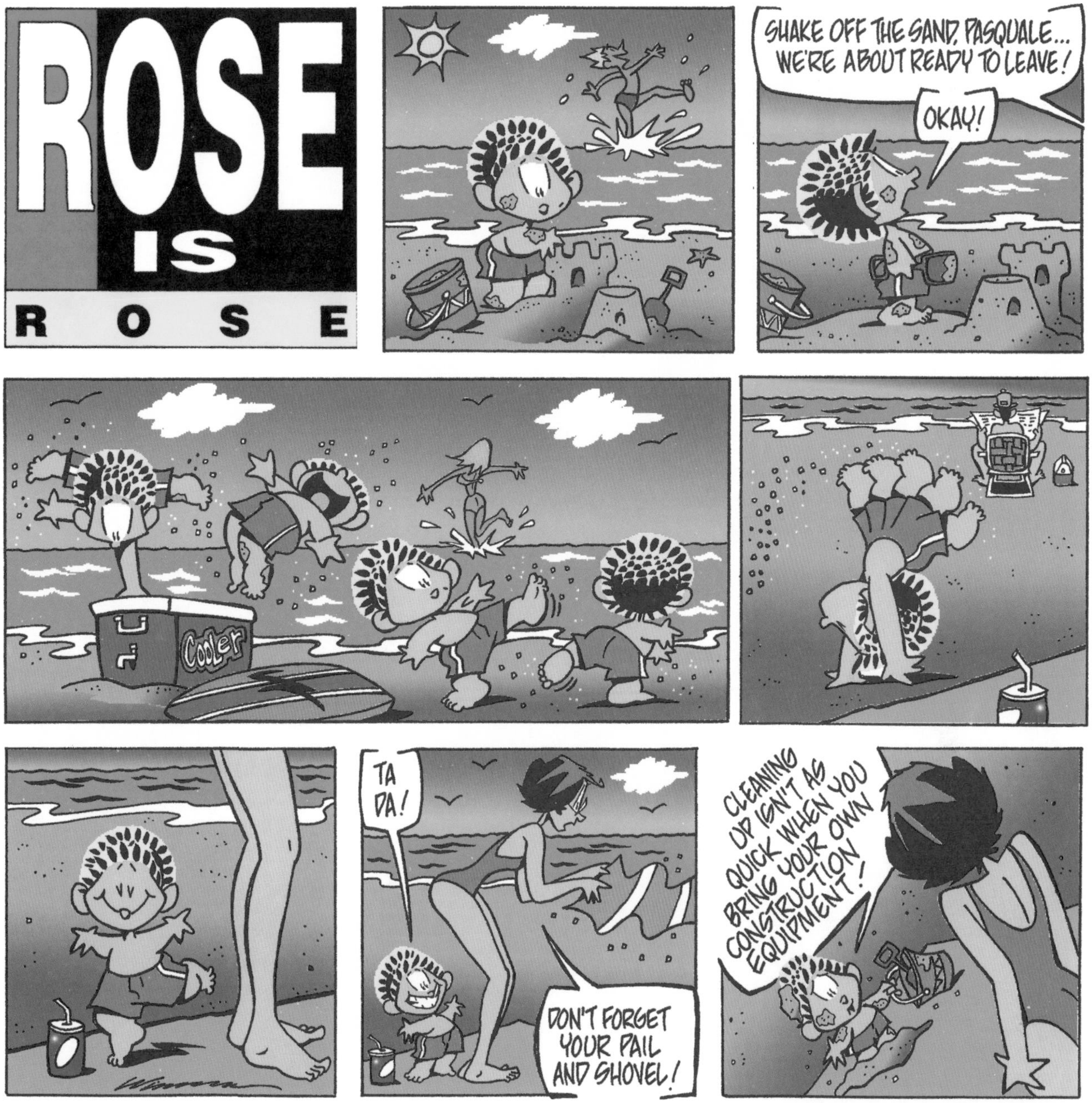
ROSE IS ROSE
SHAKE OFF THE SAND, PASQUALE... WE'RE ABOUT READY TO LEAVE!
OKAY!
Cooler
TA DA!
DON'T FORGET YOUR PAIL AND SHOVEL!
CLEANING UP ISN'T AS QUICK WHEN YOU BRING YOUR OWN CONSTRUCTION EQUIPMENT!

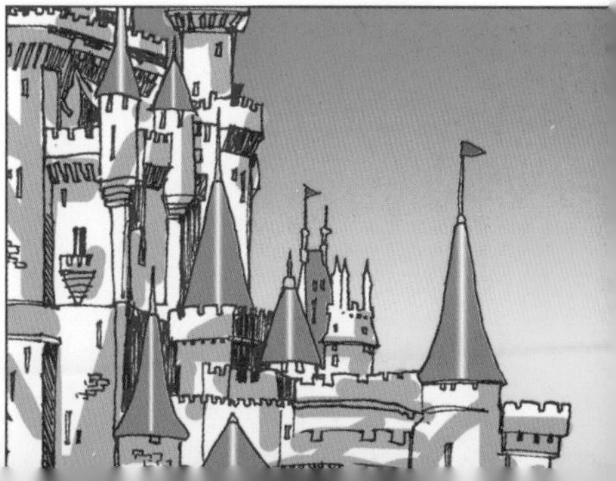

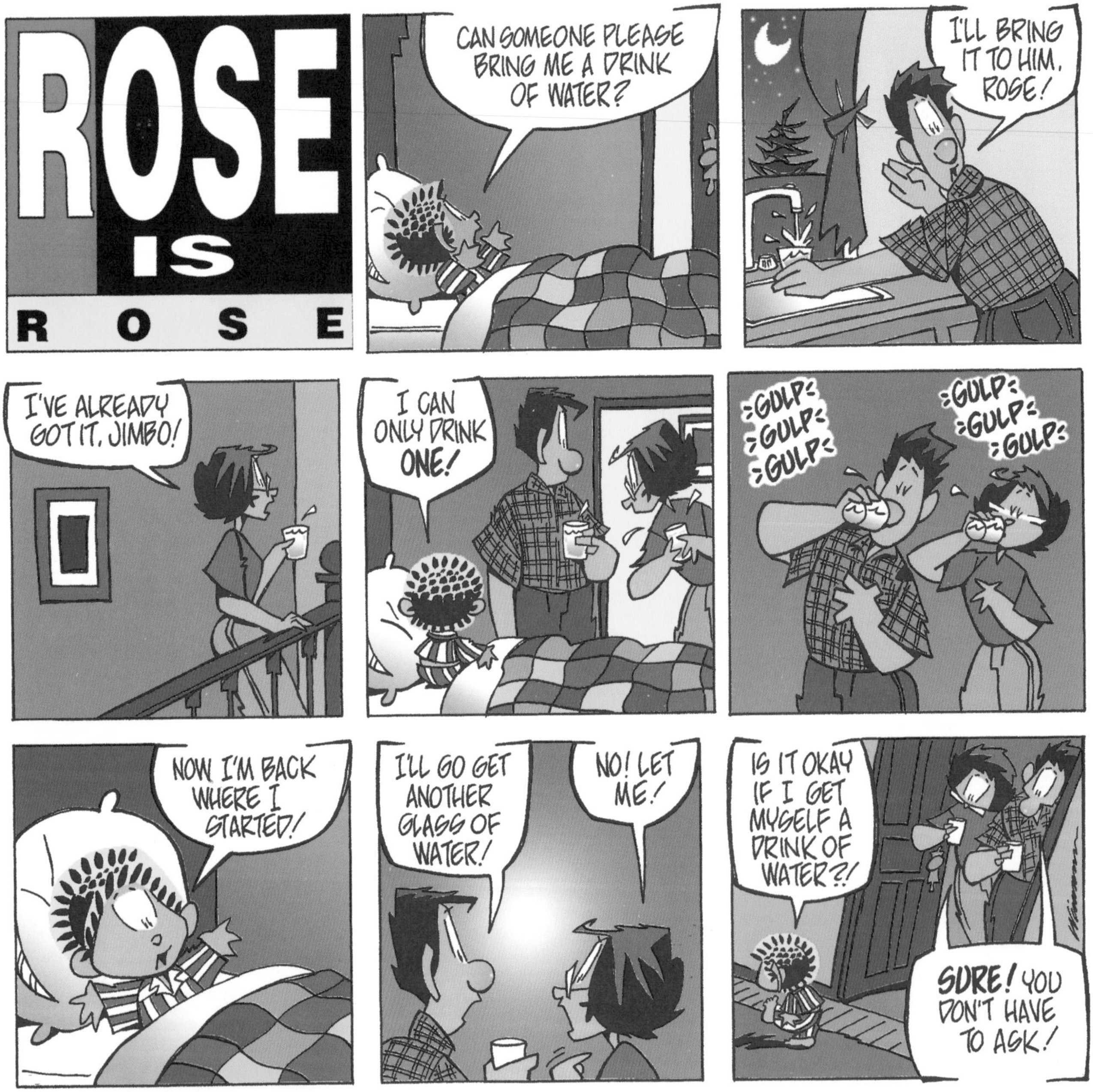
ROSE IS ROSE
CAN SOMEONE PLEASE BRING ME A DRINK OF WATER?
I'LL BRING IT TO HIM, ROSE!
I'VE ALREADY GOT IT, JIMBO!
I CAN ONLY DRINK **ONE**!
GULP GULP GULP
GULP GULP GULP
NOW I'M BACK WHERE I STARTED!
I'LL GO GET ANOTHER GLASS OF WATER!
NO! LET ME!
IS IT OKAY IF I GET MYSELF A DRINK OF WATER?!
SURE! YOU DON'T HAVE TO ASK!

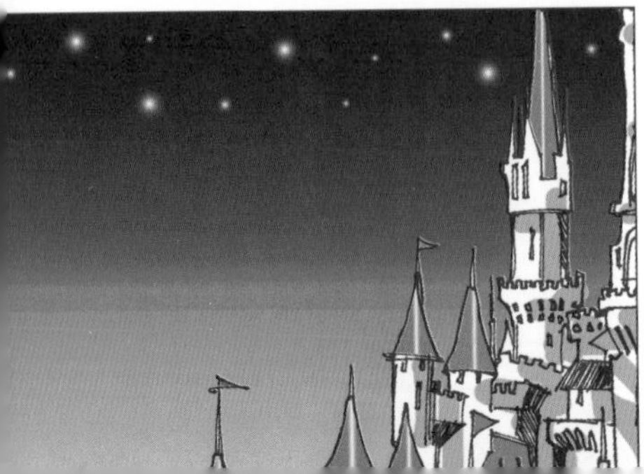

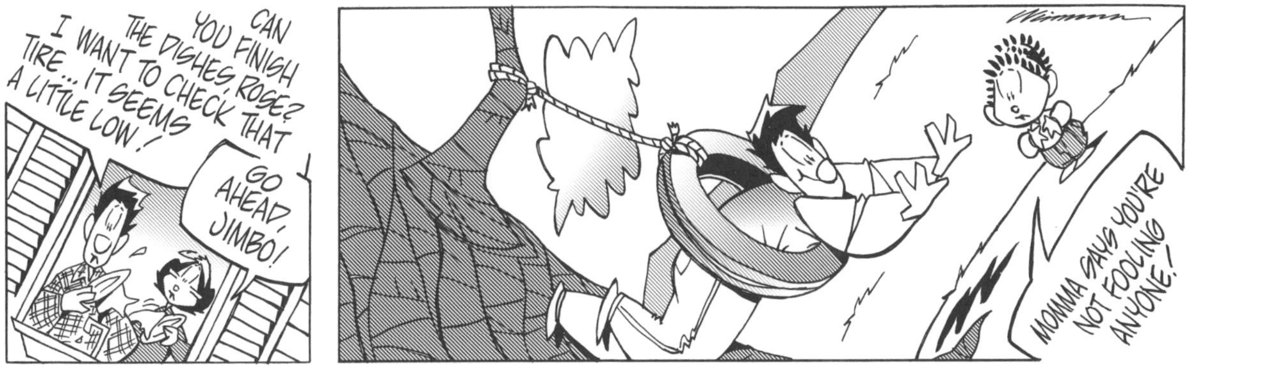
CAN YOU FINISH THE DISHES, ROSE? I WANT TO CHECK THAT TIRE... IT SEEMS A LITTLE LOW!
GO AHEAD, JIMBO!
MOMMA SAYS YOU'RE NOT FOOLING ANYONE!

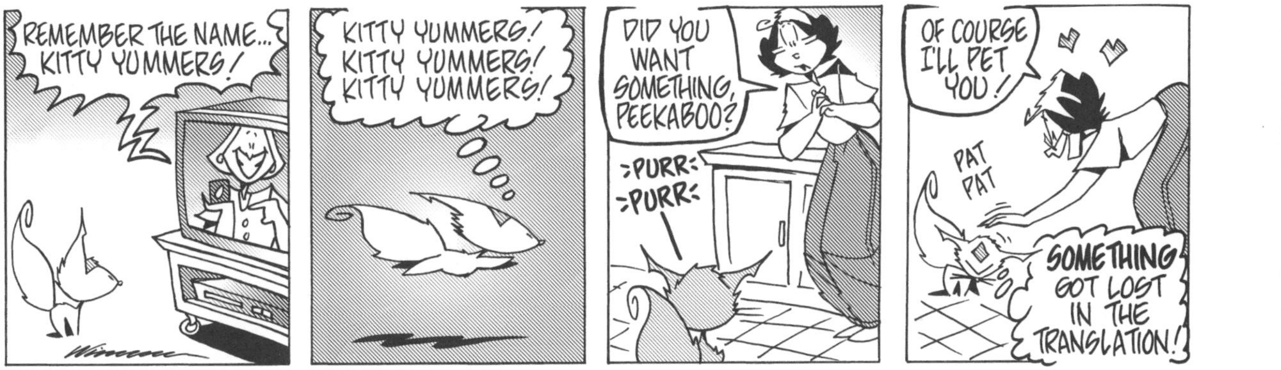
REMEMBER THE NAME... KITTY YUMMERS!
KITTY YUMMERS! KITTY YUMMERS! KITTY YUMMERS!
DID YOU WANT SOMETHING, PEEKABOO?
PURR
PURR
OF COURSE I'LL PET YOU!
PAT PAT
SOMETHING GOT LOST IN THE TRANSLATION!

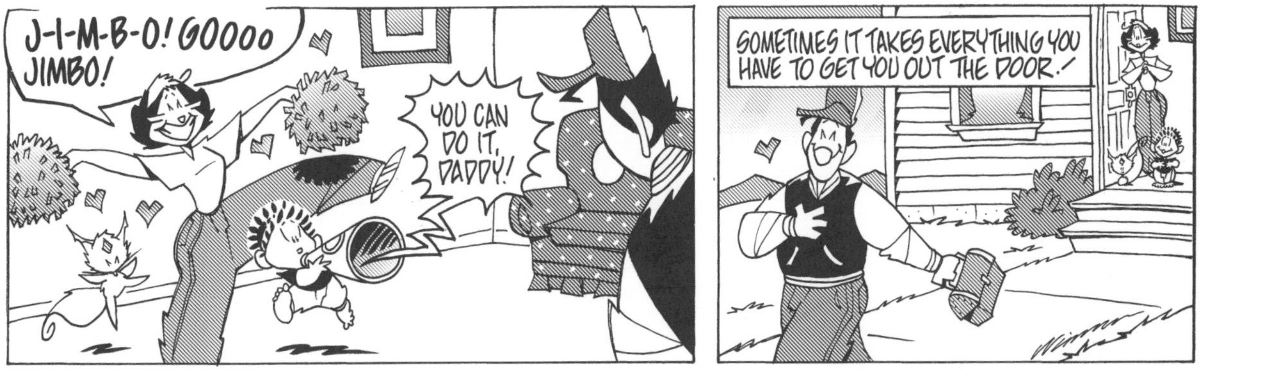
J-I-M-B-O! GOOOo JIMBO!
YOU CAN DO IT, DADDY!
SOMETIMES IT TAKES EVERYTHING YOU HAVE TO GET YOU OUT THE DOOR!

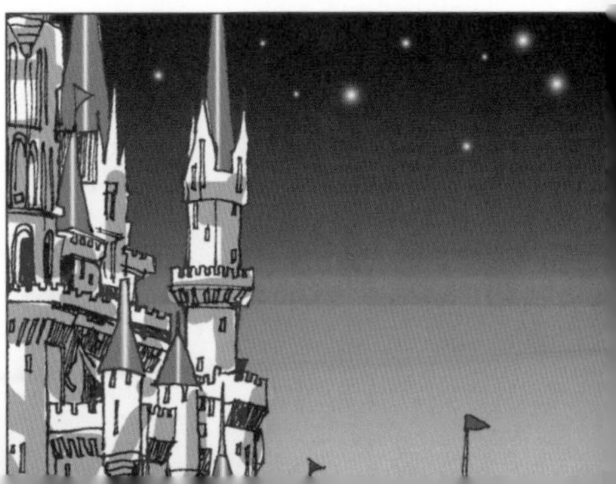

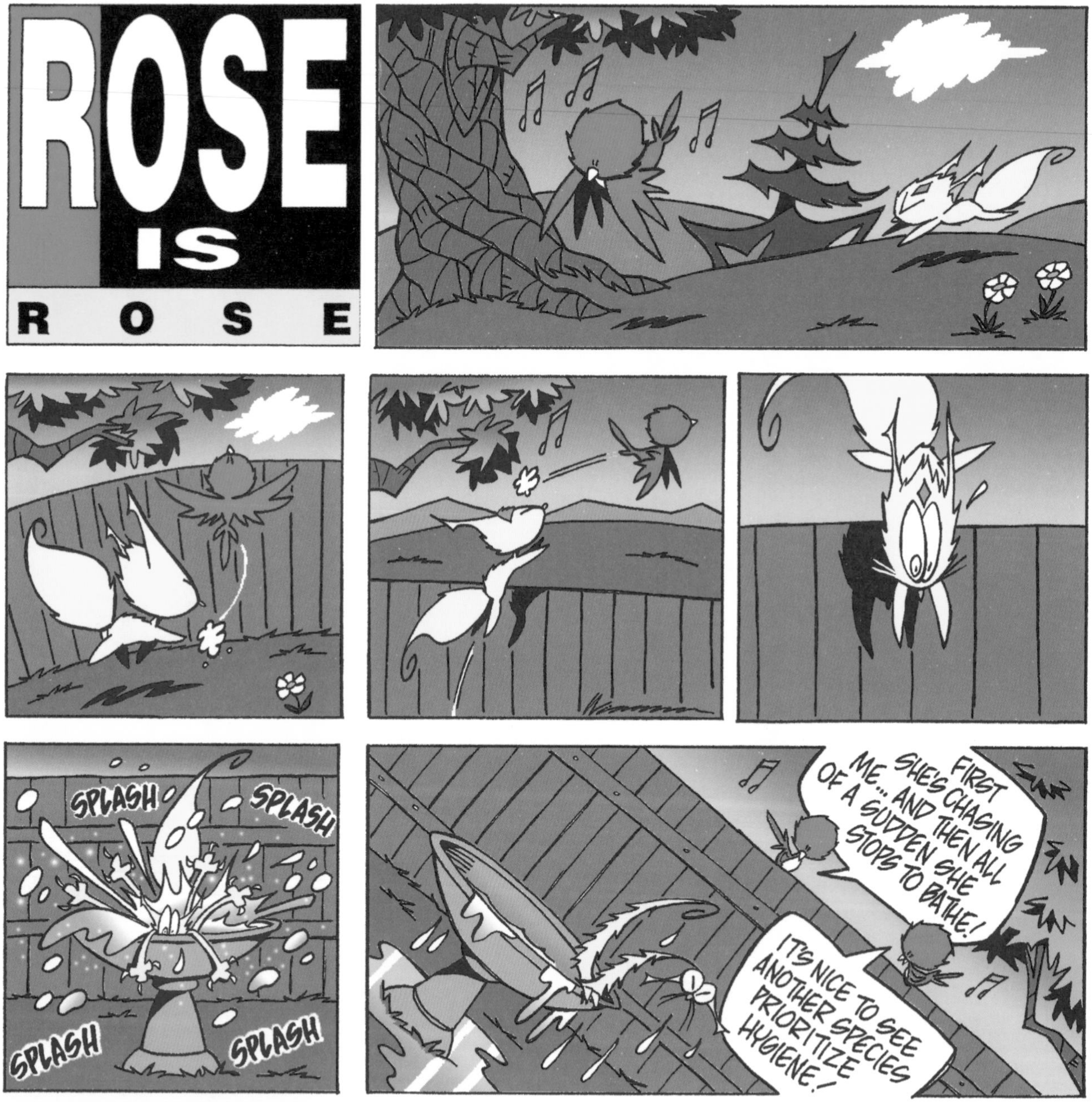
ROSE IS ROSE
SPLASH
SPLASH
SPLASH
SPLASH
FIRST SHE'S CHASING ME... AND THEN ALL OF A SUDDEN SHE STOPS TO BATHE!
IT'S NICE TO SEE ANOTHER SPECIES PRIORITIZE HYGIENE!

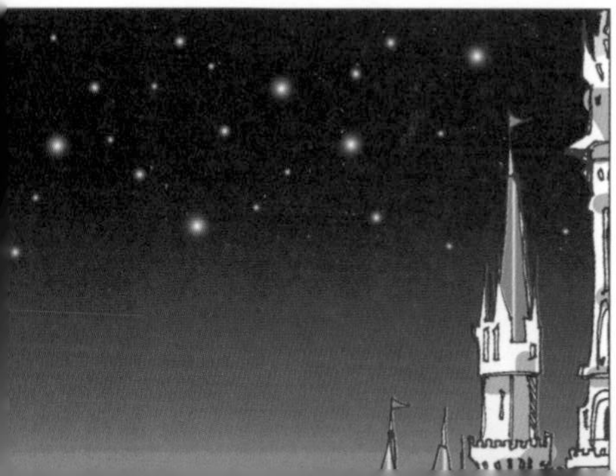

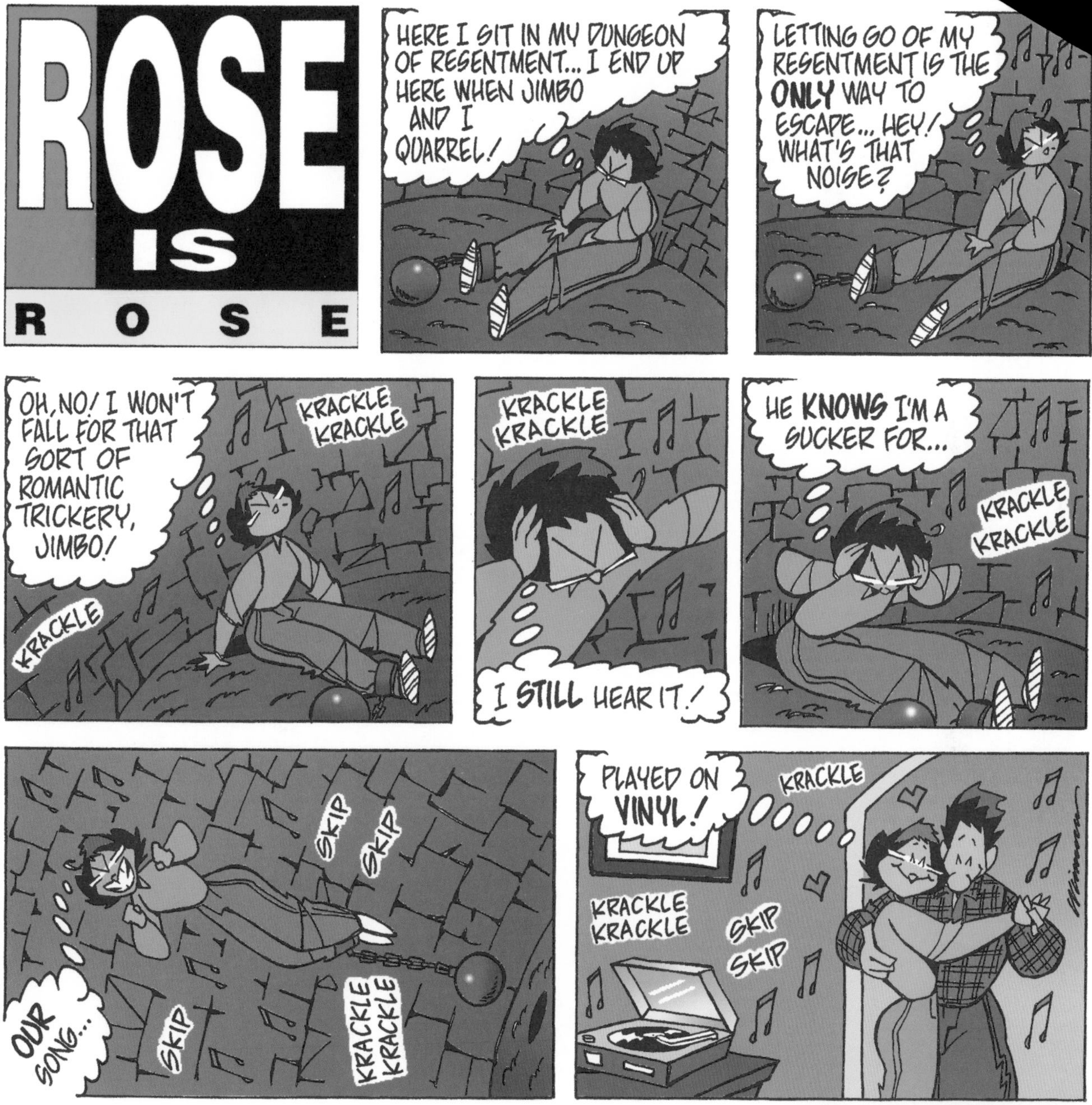
ROSE IS ROSE
HERE I SIT IN MY DUNGEON OF RESENTMENT... I END UP HERE WHEN JIMBO AND I QUARREL!
LETTING GO OF MY RESENTMENT IS THE ONLY WAY TO ESCAPE... HEY! WHAT'S THAT NOISE?
OH, NO! I WON'T FALL FOR THAT SORT OF ROMANTIC TRICKERY, JIMBO!
KRACKLE KRACKLE
KRACKLE
KRACKLE KRACKLE
I STILL HEAR IT!
HE KNOWS I'M A SUCKER FOR...
KRACKLE KRACKLE
SKIP
SKIP
OUR SONG...
SKIP
KRACKLE KRACKLE
PLAYED ON VINYL!
KRACKLE
KRACKLE KRACKLE
SKIP SKIP

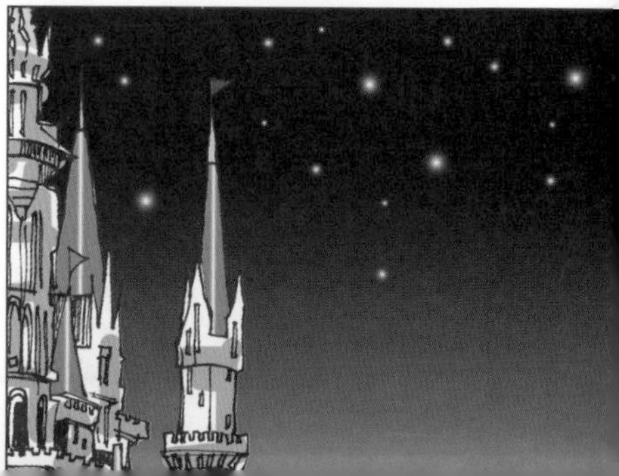

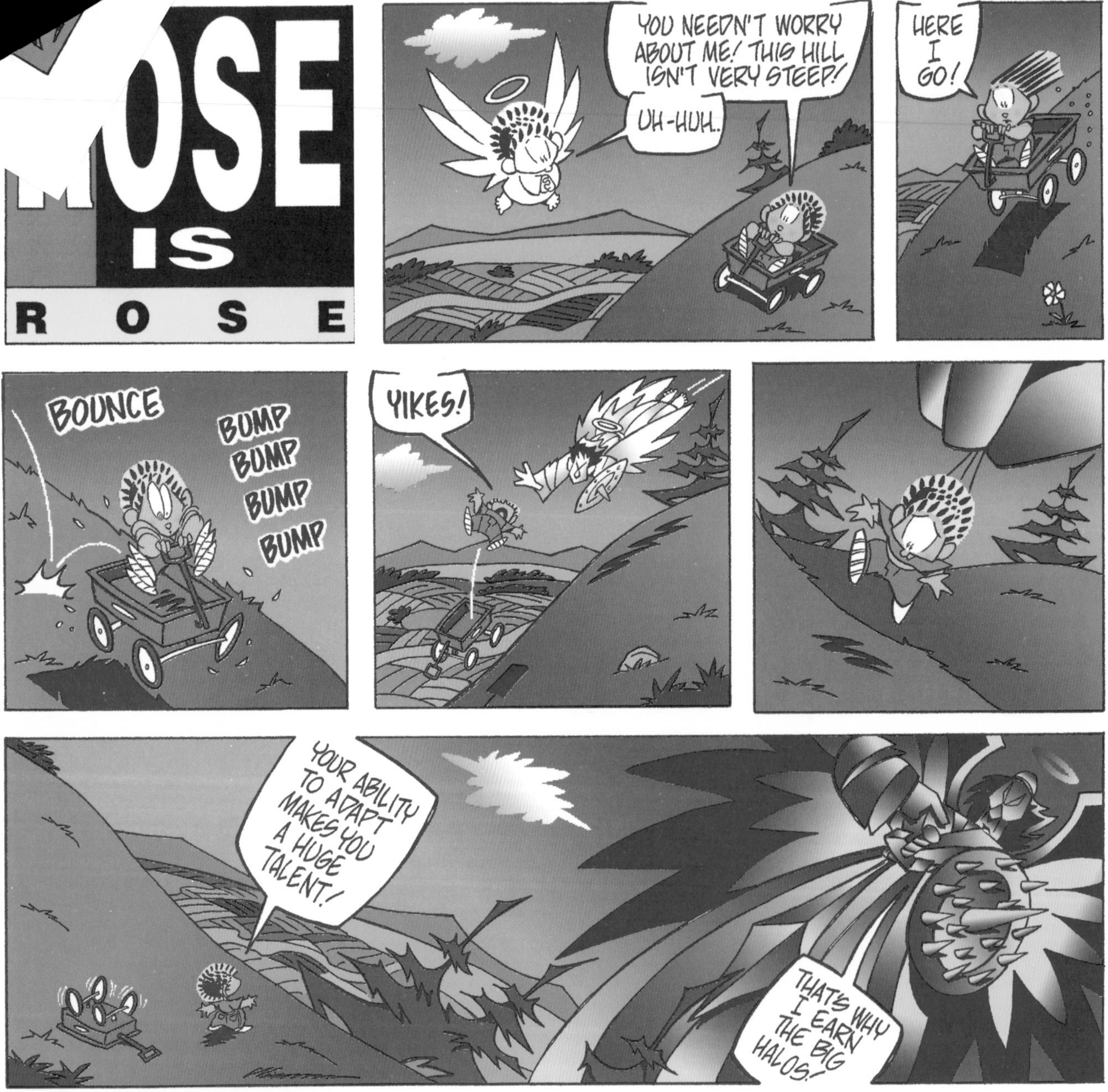
IS
R O S E
YOU NEEDN'T WORRY ABOUT ME! THIS HILL ISN'T VERY STEEP!
UH-HUH.
HERE I GO!
BOUNCE
BUMP
BUMP
BUMP
BUMP
YIKES!
YOUR ABILITY TO ADAPT MAKES YOU A HUGE TALENT!
THAT'S WHY I EARN THE BIG HALOS!

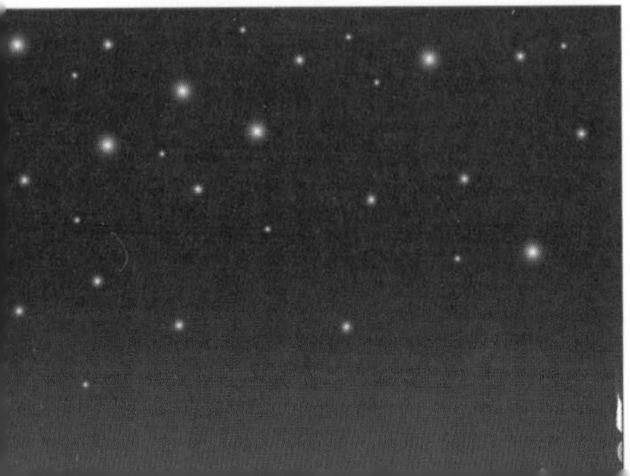

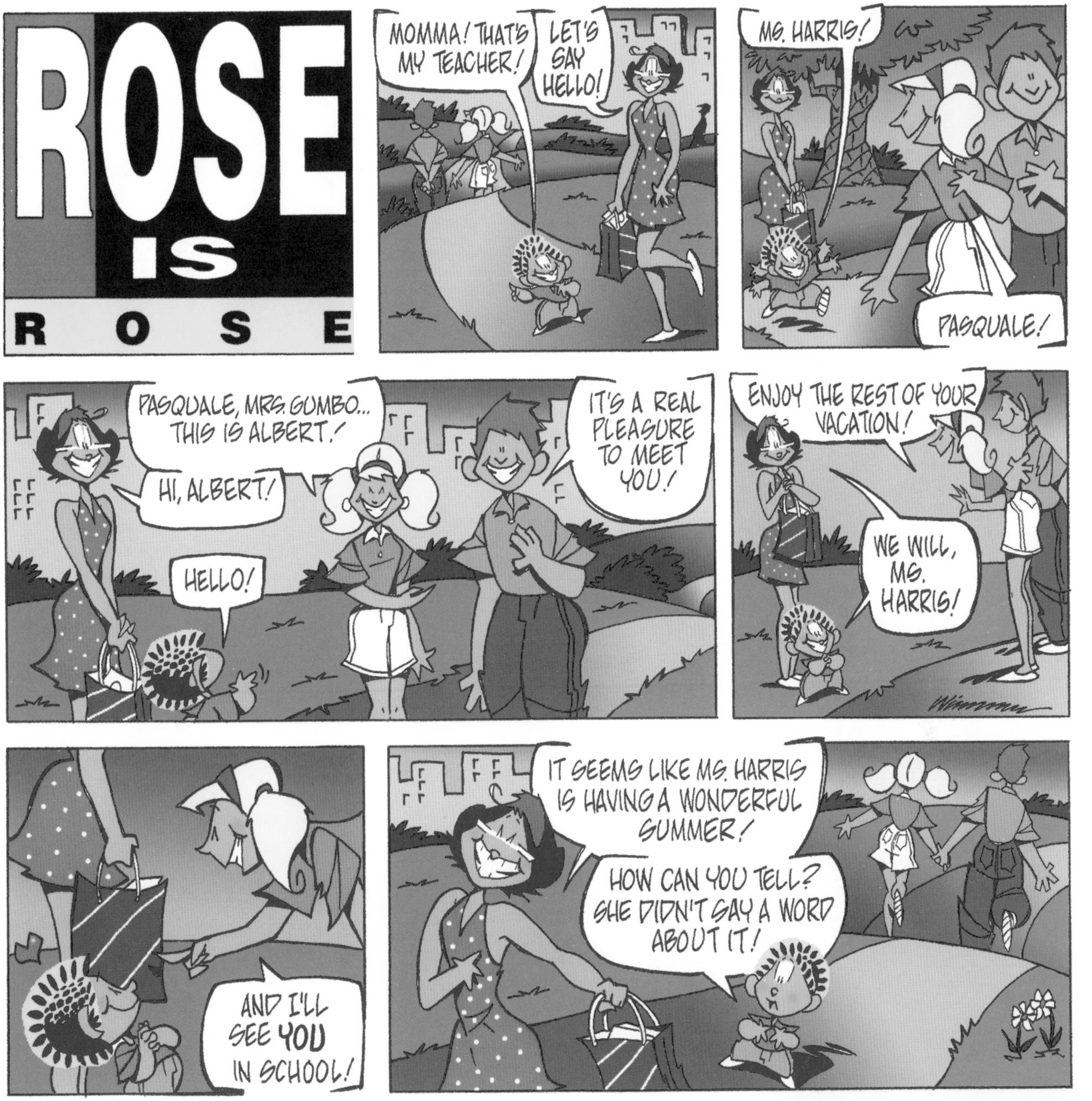
ROSE IS ROSE
MOMMA! THAT'S MY TEACHER!
LET'S SAY HELLO!
MS. HARRIS!
PASQUALE!
PASQUALE, MRS. GUMBO... THIS IS ALBERT!
HI, ALBERT!
HELLO!
IT'S A REAL PLEASURE TO MEET YOU!
ENJOY THE REST OF YOUR VACATION!
WE WILL, MS. HARRIS!
AND I'LL SEE YOU IN SCHOOL!
IT SEEMS LIKE MS. HARRIS IS HAVING A WONDERFUL SUMMER!
HOW CAN YOU TELL? SHE DIDN'T SAY A WORD ABOUT IT!

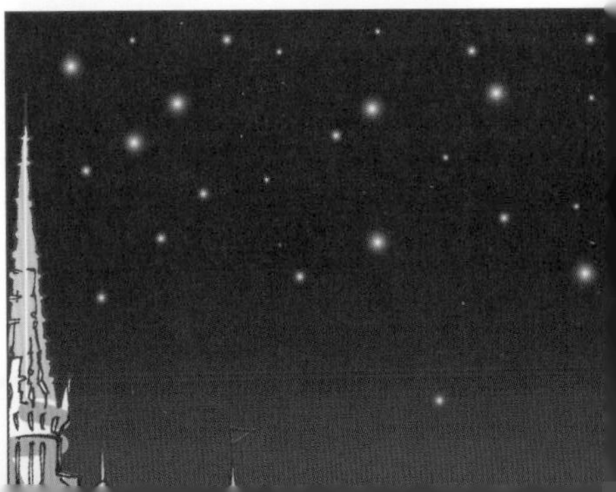

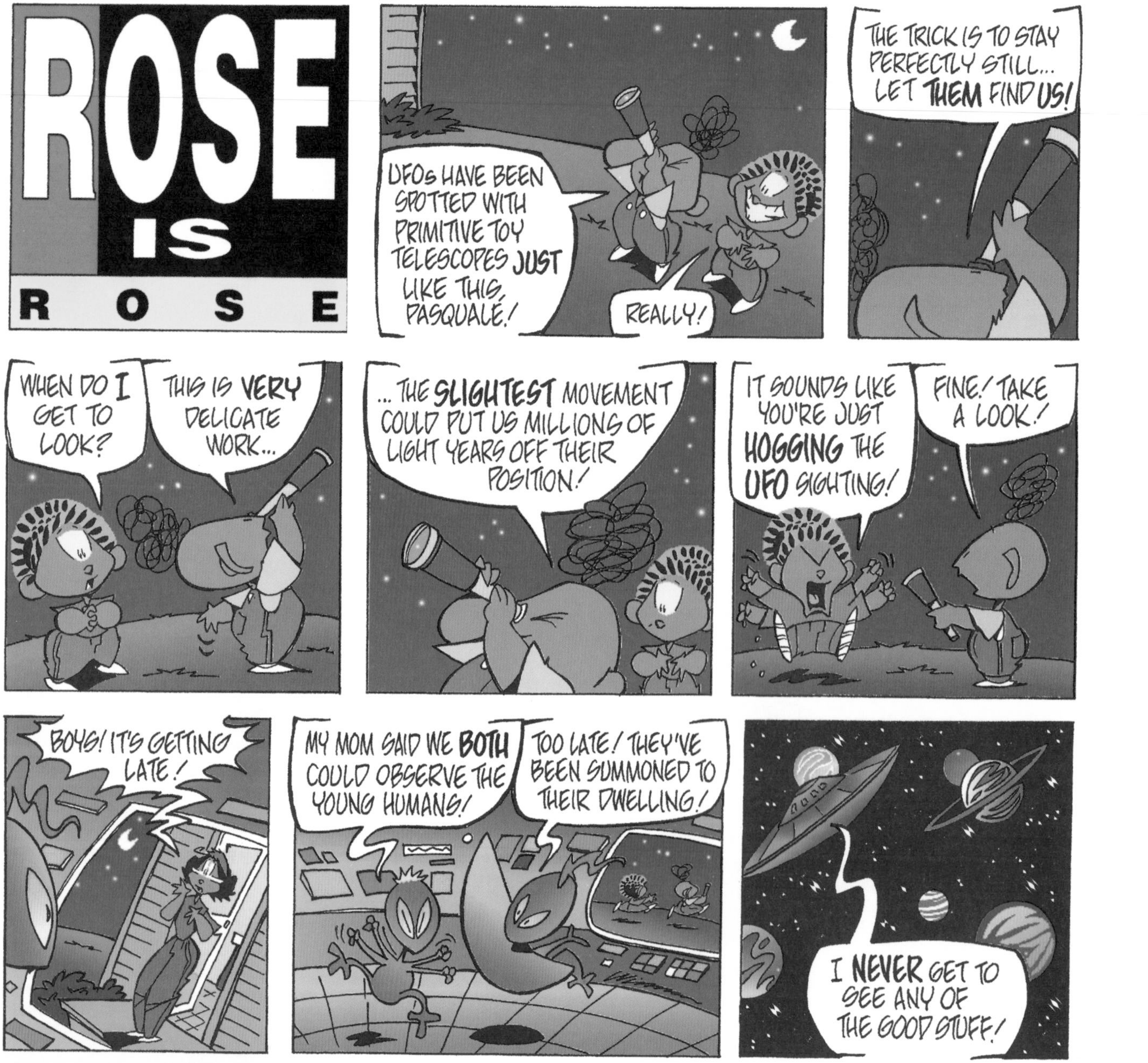
ROSE IS ROSE
UFOs HAVE BEEN SPOTTED WITH PRIMITIVE TOY TELESCOPES JUST LIKE THIS, PASQUALE!
REALLY!
THE TRICK IS TO STAY PERFECTLY STILL... LET THEM FIND US!
WHEN DO I GET TO LOOK?
THIS IS VERY DELICATE WORK...
... THE SLIGHTEST MOVEMENT COULD PUT US MILLIONS OF LIGHT YEARS OFF THEIR POSITION!
IT SOUNDS LIKE YOU'RE JUST HOGGING THE UFO SIGHTING!
FINE! TAKE A LOOK!
BOYS! IT'S GETTING LATE!
MY MOM SAID WE BOTH COULD OBSERVE THE YOUNG HUMANS!
TOO LATE! THEY'VE BEEN SUMMONED TO THEIR DWELLING!
I NEVER GET TO SEE ANY OF THE GOOD STUFF!

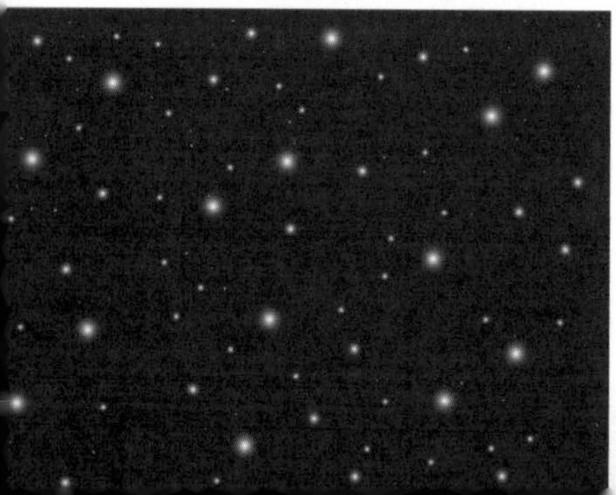

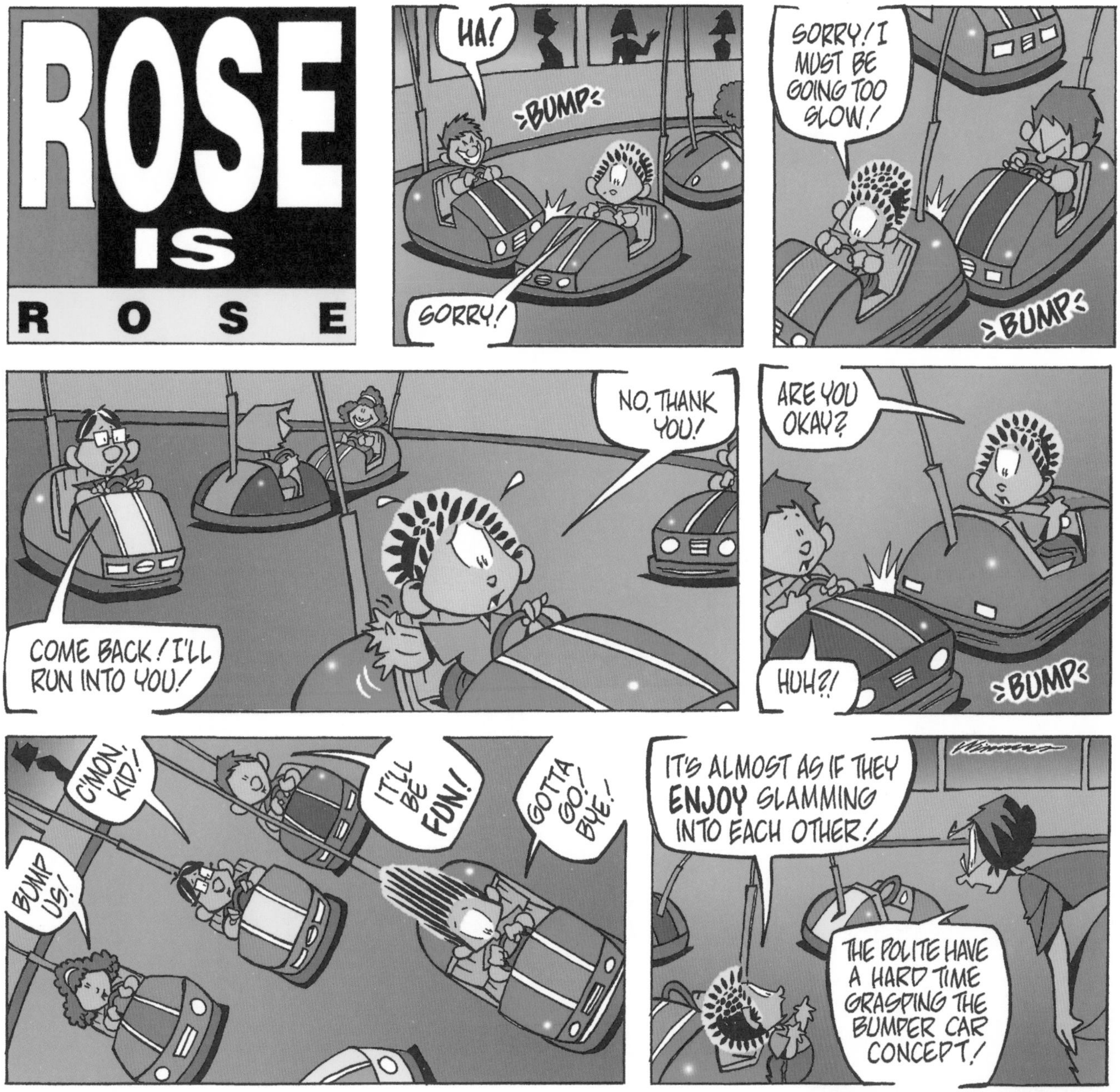
ROSE IS ROSE
HA!
BUMP
SORRY!
SORRY! I MUST BE GOING TOO SLOW!
BUMP
COME BACK! I'LL RUN INTO YOU!
NO, THANK YOU!
ARE YOU OKAY?
HUH?!
BUMP
C'MON, KID!
BUMP US!
IT'LL BE FUN!
GOTTA GO! BYE!
IT'S ALMOST AS IF THEY ENJOY SLAMMING INTO EACH OTHER!
THE POLITE HAVE A HARD TIME GRASPING THE BUMPER CAR CONCEPT!

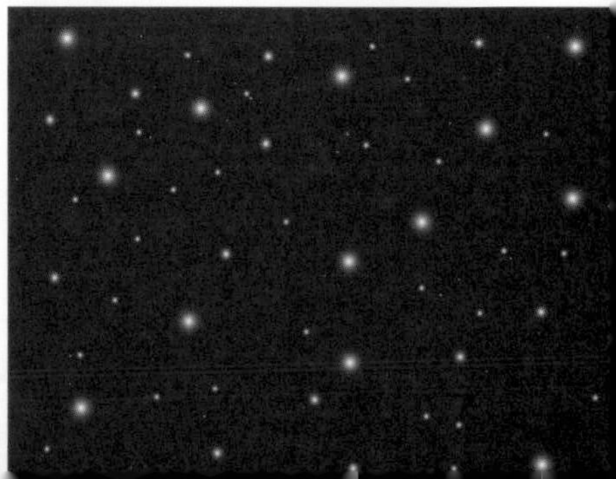

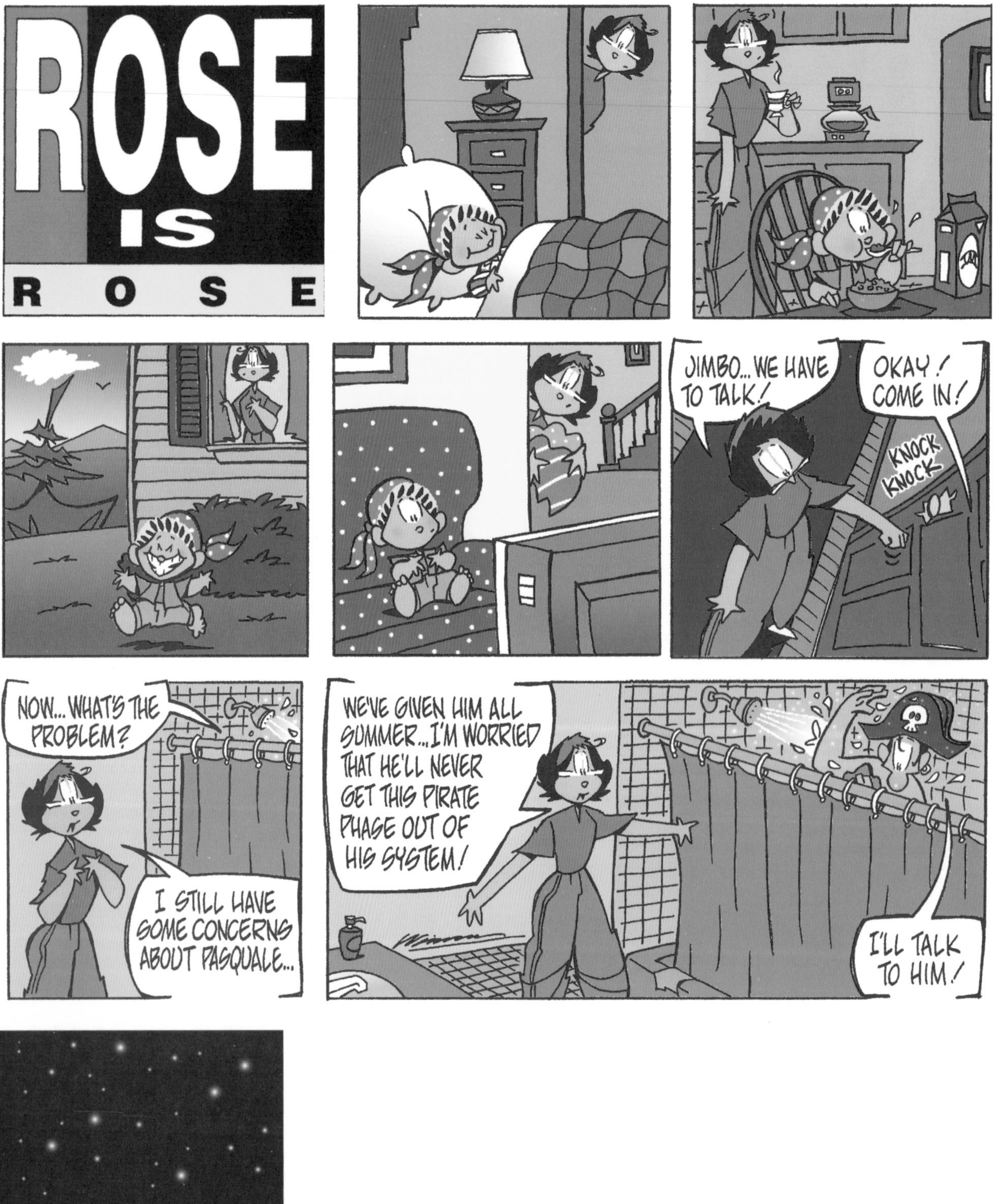
ROSE IS ROSE
JIMBO... WE HAVE TO TALK!
OKAY! COME IN!
KNOCK KNOCK
NOW... WHAT'S THE PROBLEM?
I STILL HAVE SOME CONCERNS ABOUT PASQUALE...
WE'VE GIVEN HIM ALL SUMMER... I'M WORRIED THAT HE'LL NEVER GET THIS PIRATE PHASE OUT OF HIS SYSTEM!
I'LL TALK TO HIM!

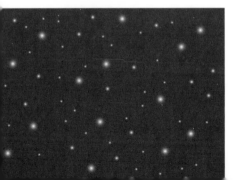

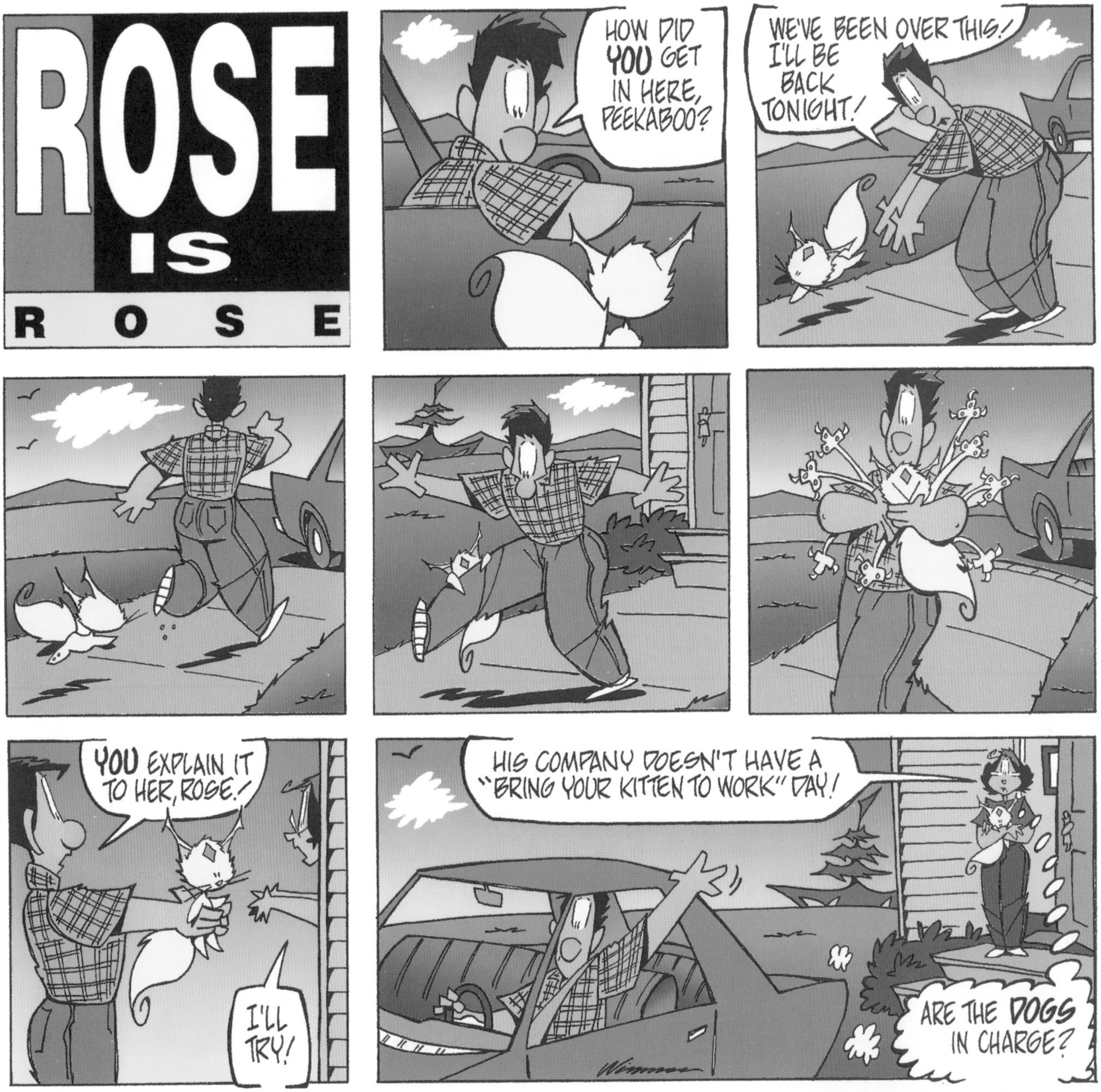
ROSE IS ROSE
HOW DID YOU GET IN HERE, PEEKABOO?
WE'VE BEEN OVER THIS! I'LL BE BACK TONIGHT!
YOU EXPLAIN IT TO HER, ROSE!
I'LL TRY!
HIS COMPANY DOESN'T HAVE A "BRING YOUR KITTEN TO WORK" DAY!
ARE THE DOGS IN CHARGE?

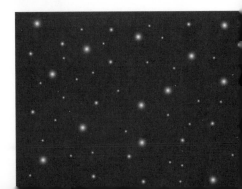

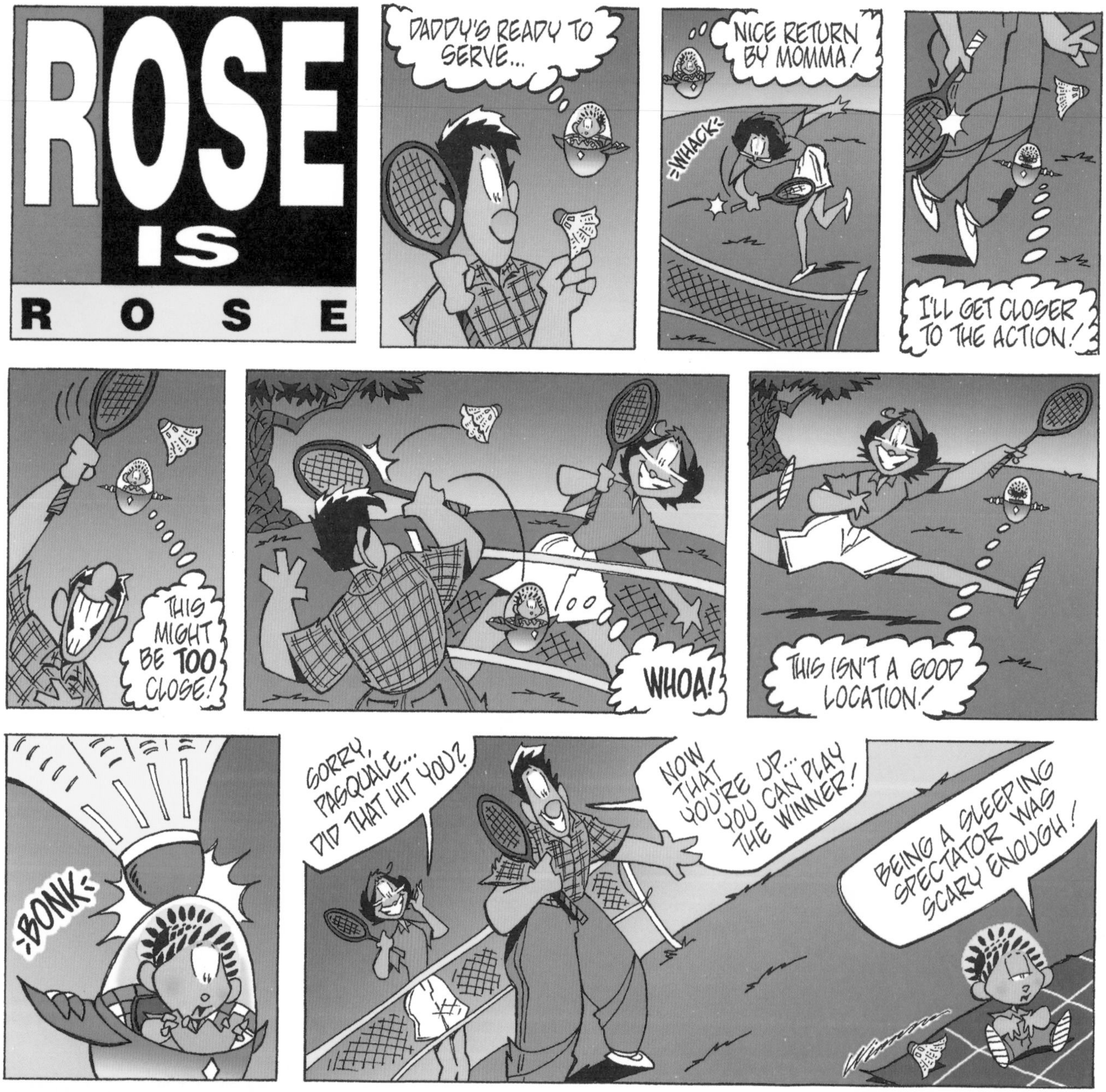
ROSE IS ROSE
DADDY'S READY TO SERVE...
NICE RETURN BY MOMMA!
WHACK
I'LL GET CLOSER TO THE ACTION!
THIS MIGHT BE TOO CLOSE!
WHOA!
THIS ISN'T A GOOD LOCATION!
BONK
SORRY, PASQUALE... DID THAT HIT YOU?
NOW THAT YOU'RE UP... YOU CAN PLAY THE WINNER!
BEING A SLEEPING SPECTATOR WAS SCARY ENOUGH!

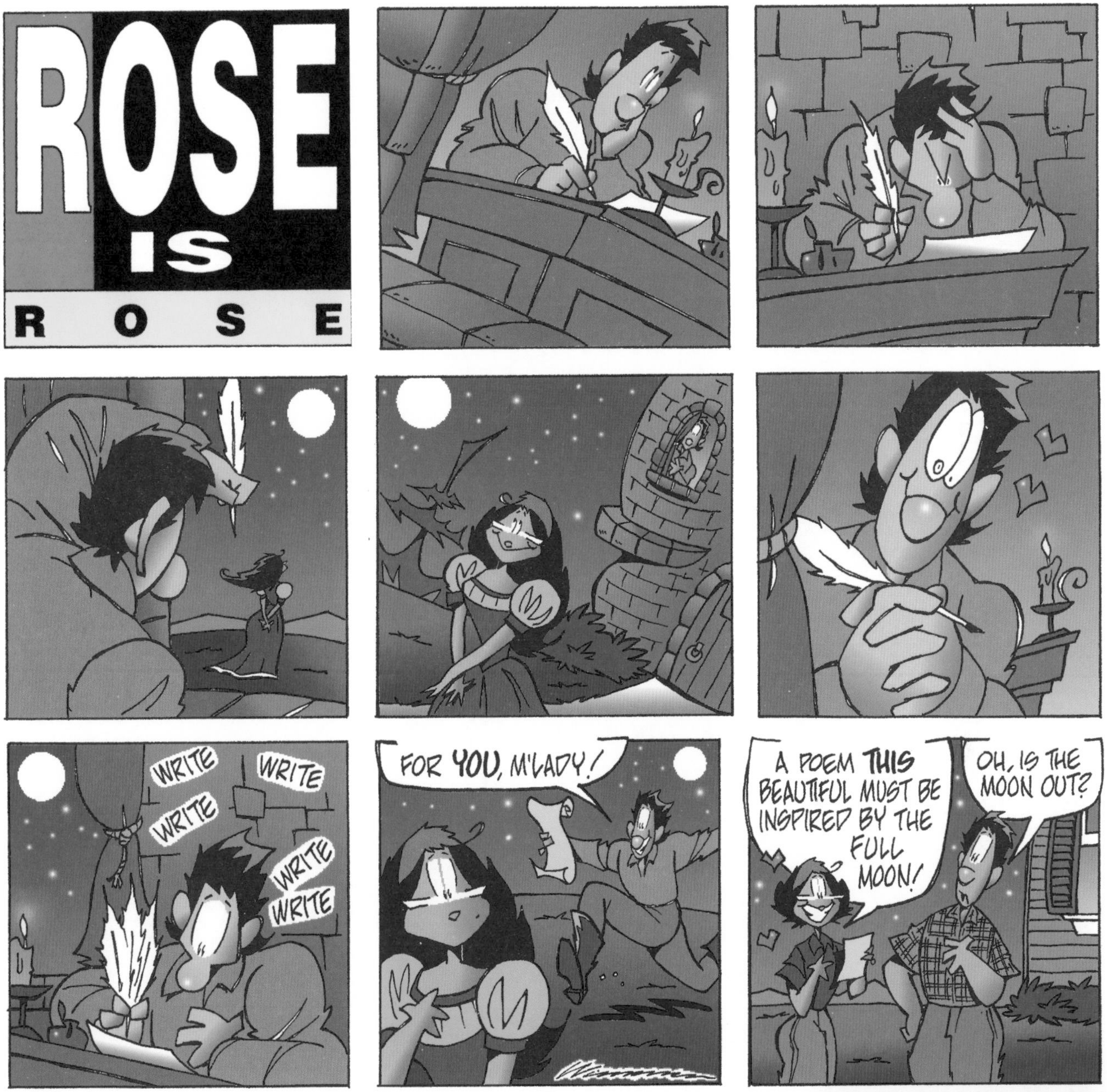
ROSE IS ROSE
WRITE WRITE WRITE WRITE WRITE
FOR YOU, M'LADY!
A POEM THIS BEAUTIFUL MUST BE INSPIRED BY THE FULL MOON!
OH, IS THE MOON OUT?

FLIP THE PAGE CORNERS FROM FRONT TO BACK AND WATCH BOTH SIDES TOGETHER!

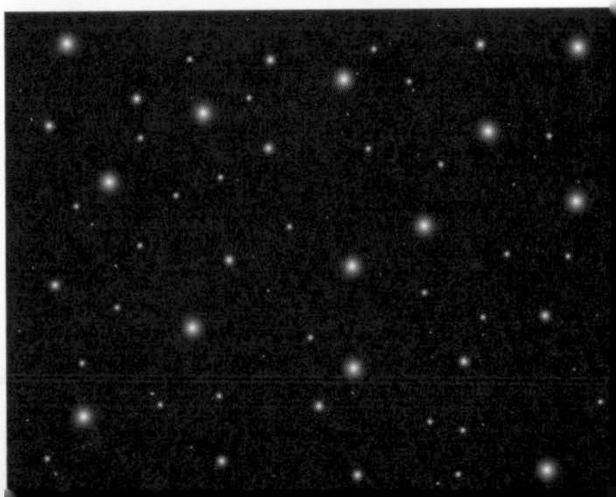

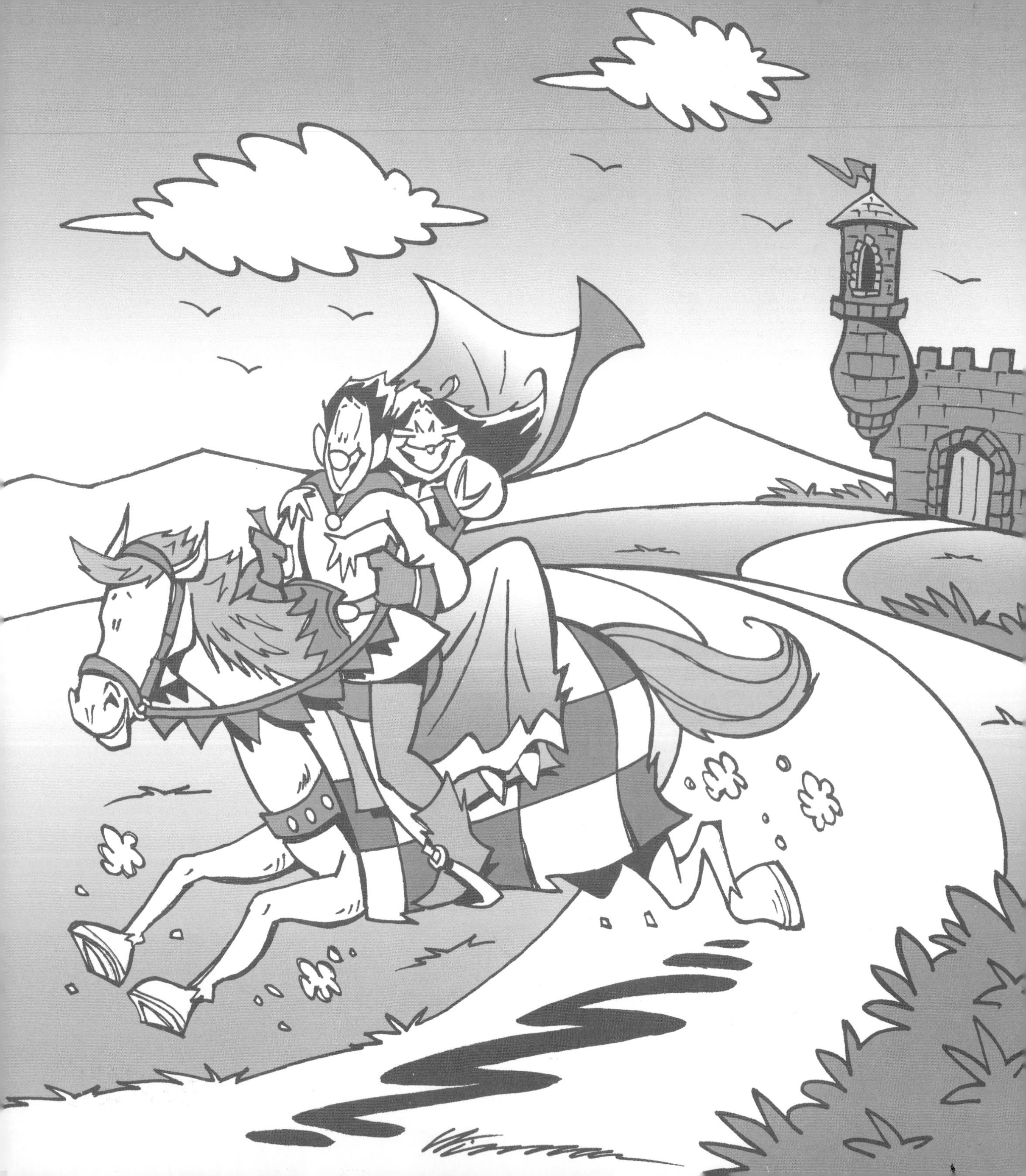